Divergent Memories

THE WALTER H. SHORENSTEIN
ASIA-PACIFIC RESEARCH CENTER

Studies of the Walter H. Shorenstein Asia-Pacific Research Center

Andrew G. Walder, General Editor

The Walter H. Shorenstein Asia-Pacific Research Center in the Freeman Spogli Institute for International Studies at Stanford University sponsors interdisciplinary research on the politics, economies, and societies of contemporary Asia. This monograph series features academic and policy-oriented research by Stanford faculty and other scholars associated with the Center.

# Divergent Memories

OPINION LEADERS AND THE ASIA-PACIFIC WAR

*Gi-Wook Shin and Daniel Sneider*

Stanford University Press
Stanford, California

Stanford University Press
Stanford, California

©2016 by the Board of Trustees of the Leland Stanford Junior University. All rights reserved.

No part of this book may be reproduced or transmitted in any form or by any means, electronic or mechanical, including photocopying and recording, or in any information storage or retrieval system without the prior written permission of Stanford University Press.

Printed in the United States of America on acid-free, archival-quality paper

Library of Congress Cataloging-in-Publication Data

Names: Shin, Gi-Wook, author. | Sneider, Daniel C., author.
Title: Divergent memories : opinion leaders and the Asia-Pacific War / Gi-Wook Shin and Daniel Sneider.
Other titles: Studies of the Walter H. Shorenstein Asia-Pacific Research Center.
Description: Stanford, California : Stanford University Press, 2016. | Series: Studies of the Walter H. Shorenstein Asia-Pacific Research Center | Includes bibliographical references and index.
Identifiers: LCCN 2015047456| ISBN 9780804798891 (cloth : alk. paper) | ISBN 9780804799706 (pbk : alk. paper)
Subjects: LCSH: World War, 1939–1945—East Asia—Historiography. | Sino-Japanese War, 1937–1945—Historiography. | Nationalism and collective memory—East Asia. | East Asia—History, Military—20th century.
Classification: LCC D767 .S5556 2016 | DDC 940.53/5—dc23
LC record available at http://lccn.loc.gov/2015047456

ISBN 9780804799720 (electronic)

Typeset by Newgen in 11/14 Garamond

# Contents

*Acknowledgments*   ix

### I. INTRODUCTION

1. Historical Memory, National Identity, and International Relations   3

### II. NATIONAL MEMORIES

2. Fashioning a Patriotic Narrative in Contemporary China   23
3. Confronting Collaboration in Korea   64
4. Multiple Memories of War in Postwar Japan   100
5. The Uncomfortable War: The Pacific War in American Memory   147

### III. DIVIDED MEMORIES: THE MAJOR CONTROVERSIES

6. Japanese Colonial Rule, Forced Labor, and Comfort Women   195
7. The Sino-Japanese War and Japanese War Crimes   214
8. The War in the Pacific   231
9. The Atomic Bombings of Japan   249
10. The United States and Postwar Settlements   266

## IV. CONCLUSION

11  Toward Historical Reconciliation in the Asia-Pacific                293

   *Appendix: Opinion Leaders Interviewed*                              311
   *Notes*                                                              315
   *Index*                                                              345

# Acknowledgments

This book is the final product of a multiyear project, Divided Memories and Reconciliation, undertaken by the Walter H. Shorenstein Asia-Pacific Research Center. Divided Memories and Reconciliation has already produced a volume on the comparative analysis of high-school textbooks in China, Japan, South Korea, Taiwan, and the United States; a second volume examining the impact of dramatic film and other forms of popular culture on the formation of wartime memory (2016, University of Hawaii Press); and a third volume comparing East Asia with Western Europe with respect to their conflicting memories of the wartime past. The project was made possible by generous support from the Northeast Asian History Foundation (NEAHF) of South Korea, the United States–Japan Foundation, and the Taiwan Democracy Foundation. We express our deep gratitude to these institutions. In particular, we acknowledge the individual support and assistance of Dr. Yeong Dok Kim, former president of the NEAHF, and David Janes, director of foundation grants of the U.S.-Japan Foundation. As always, we are grateful for the support of the Walter H. Shorenstein Asia-Pacific Research Center.

We also recognize the important contributions made by colleagues both within Stanford University and without and the Walter H. Shorenstein Asia-Pacific Research Center for its assistance in the conception and execution of this project at every stage. We thank the academic experts who helped us identify interviewees, connect with them, and carry out interviews in China, Japan, and Korea, as well as provided translations of these interviews when needed—Alisa Jones, Louisa Rubinfien, and Park Soon-Won. They all played a vital role in this project. We also express our appreciation to Joyce Lee and George Krompacky, who prepared the manuscript for publication, and those who provided sage advice along the way, especially Daniel Chirot and David Straub.

We extend our gratitude to our colleague Andrew Walder, editor of the Stanford University Press series Studies of the Walter H. Shorenstein Asia-Pacific Research Center, in which this book appears, as well as to our two anonymous reviewers. Their critical but sympathetic comments and suggestions considerably improved this book. Last but not least, we sincerely thank Jenny Gavacs at Stanford University Press, who has supported this book project throughout the process of review and publication; Rebecca Logan, who oversaw production of the book; and Jonelle Seitz, who was our copyeditor.

We have found it an invigorating experience to carry out this project and compare Asia's divergent colonial and wartime memories. Although many of the stories of our interviewees conflicted at times, we observed great efforts toward reconciliation taking place, albeit slowly, in all of the involved countries. We hope that this work will further inspire peaceful reconciliation in Northeast Asia and the Pacific in the near future.

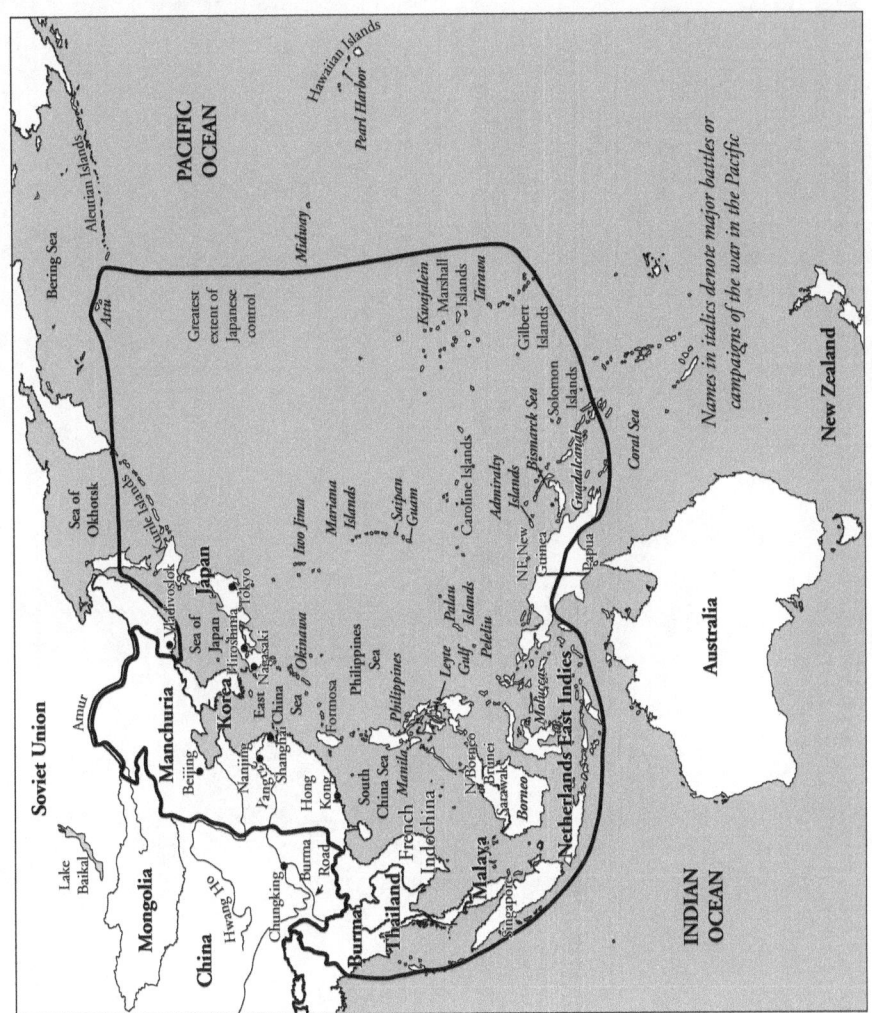

Asia during World War II

PART ONE

*Introduction*

ONE

# Historical Memory, National Identity, and International Relations

Lushun, a strategic seaport at the tip of the Liaodong Peninsula in northeastern China, sits at the crossroads of the turbulent history of colonialism and war that washed repeatedly over this corner of the earth in the century that stretched from the mid-1800s to the end of World War II and its immediate aftermath. For most of this time it was known as Port Arthur, named after the Royal Navy officer who surveyed the harbor from a British gunboat during the Second Opium War in 1860. Today, monuments to the ensuing battles for control of this coveted spot appear all across the city.

A somber memorial sits at the site where, in 1894, Japanese forces massacred thousands of Chinese inhabitants in their seizure of the city from the forces of the decaying Qing dynasty in the first Sino-Japanese War. Imperial Japan gained control of Taiwan in that war, but Russia, Germany, and France forced return of the seized peninsula, which was placed under tsarist Russian rule and built up as the terminus for the vital South Manchurian Railway. A decade later, the Japanese returned in a surprise attack that began the Russo-Japanese War. Imperial Japan marked its victory by erecting an imposing stone tower on a hilltop with sweeping views of the port, which is still maintained to remind the Chinese of the rapacious invaders. By 1905, Japan had occupied the peninsula and the whole of nearby Korea, creating the foundation of a colonial empire that waged a fifteen-year campaign to conquer China, ending only in Imperial Japan's defeat in 1945.

Visitors to the city are steered by the Chinese government to the site of a former Russian and Japanese prison, now restored as a museum detailing the depredations, from torture to forced labor, that the Japanese prison authorities inflicted on those who resisted their rule. Communist organizers are the most celebrated victims, but places of honor are also accorded to Korean independence activists. An engraved plaque marks the most famous prisoner, Ahn Jung-geun, who is celebrated by Koreans as a hero for assassinating the Japanese governor general of Korea, Ito Hirobumi, in 1909, but whom the Japanese still condemn today as a terrorist.

The historic tour ends at the Cemetery of Soviet Martyrs, a sprawling burial ground for both tsarist-era Russians and for the Soviet Red Army forces who "liberated" the area in 1945 from Imperial Japan and then stayed on for another decade. Rows of neatly maintained gravestones are still topped by red stars, some with carvings of jet fighters to memorialize Soviet pilots who died fighting in the Korean War in alliance with Communist Chinese forces.

The monuments that dot Port Arthur are a powerful statement that this wartime past is hardly forgotten. On the contrary, these memories of war and colonialism remain vivid and continue to affect the present and future of all the nations involved, shaping national identities and the relationships among the former combatants. The governments of these nations embrace the past as a tool to guide the political destinies of their peoples. The museums and monuments of Port Arthur, for example, constitute part of what the Chinese government calls "National Patriotism Education Demonstration Bases," many of which were built or refurbished beginning in the mid-1990s as part of a concerted effort to shift the national identity of the Chinese from the discredited pursuit of Communism to the cause of building a great and powerful China celebrated for its resistance to the marauding European and Japanese imperialists.

As historians know all too well, history is not simply about recording past events—it is more importantly about how one understands the past.[1] History writing inherently involves interpretation and even judgment, which, in turn, requires remembering certain things and forgetting others. In other words, collective memory becomes a crucial part of history, though history is not merely a matter of remembrance. Furthermore, historical memory is often contested, negotiated, and reshaped over time, as multiple actors, from the government to the media to ordinary people, become involved. Such contention and negotiation can occur between the state and civil society, between the left and right, and between neighboring countries, influencing domestic politics and international relations.

Indeed, contention over the wartime history of Northeast Asia remains surprisingly intense, with few signs of diminishing. Issues that arose out of the war brought relations between Japan and its neighbors in China and Korea to a near standstill in recent years, confounding those who hoped that the scars of war would fade with time. Korean leaders demanded that Japan offer fresh apologies and compensation to the handfuls of remaining Korean women, infamously known as "comfort women," who had been forcibly dragooned into wartime brothels to service Japanese troops before they could meet. American policy makers were so concerned by the inability of the leaders of Japan and South Korea, the two principal security allies of the United States in the region, to even sit down with each other that in March 2014, President Barack Obama organized a trilateral meeting in Europe, focused on the common security threat of nuclear-armed North Korea. But at a closing press conference, the two Asian leaders, seated on either side of the president, could barely glance at each other.

The next month the president visited both countries, urging reconciliation. At his first stop, in Tokyo, the President politely skirted the war issues, hoping to quietly urge steps toward reconciliation. But Obama was visibly pained when Japanese Prime Minister Shinzo Abe concluded a joint press conference with an unrepentant defense of his decision the previous December, against American advice, to pay a ceremonial visit to the Yasukuni Shrine. The memorial to Japan's war dead controversially honors the wartime leaders of Japan who were condemned, many of them executed, by the United States and its allies for war crimes.

At his next stop, in Seoul, President Obama pointedly took up the war history issues. "With respect to the historical tensions between South Korea and Japan," the president told a joint news conference, "I think that any of us who look back on the history of what happened to the comfort women here in South Korea, for example, have to recognize that this was a terrible, egregious violation of human rights. Those women were violated in ways that, even in the midst of war, was shocking. And they deserve to be heard; they deserve to be respected; and there should be an accurate and clear account of what happened."[2]

The president offered the conviction, though it was more likely the hope, that Prime Minister Abe and, more certainly, the Japanese people are ready to honestly face the past. And he urged both peoples to resolve their differences in favor of pursuing their shared interests. "It is in the interest of both

Japan and the Korean people to look forward as well as backwards and to find ways in which the heartache and the pain of the past can be resolved," he said, in almost plaintive terms, "because, as has been said before, the interests today of the Korean and Japanese people so clearly converge."[3] Though this appeal largely fell on deaf ears, the president can be partially credited for a limited agreement reached by South Korea and Japan in December 2015 offering apology and compensation for the surviving Korean comfort women.[4]

Why is reconciliation in Northeast Asia so difficult, particularly when compared with the ability of Europe to largely overcome its wartime divisions? This book is based on the premise that the greatest obstacle to reconciliation in Northeast Asia is the existence of divided, and often conflicting, historical memories.[5] From Japanese colonialism in Korea and atrocities in China to the American decision to drop atomic weapons on Japan, no nation is free from the charge that it has formed a less-than-complete view of the past. And all nations, even Japan, the architect of repeated aggression in this century, tend to blame others rather than fully confront the complexity of that past. Contention over history is so intense and emotionally engaging because it touches on the most sensitive issues of national identity.[6] Even the territorial disputes between Japan and China, or between Japan and Korea, are closely related to history and national identity. Despite globalization and the rise of vibrant civil society, nationalism remains strong, and the government continues to exert a strong influence on history writing and education in all of these countries.

Rather than ignoring others' views as "distorted" or trying to forge a common historical account of specific events, we believe that a more fruitful approach is to understand how historical memories have been formulated and contested in each country. By uncovering the existence of different historical memories both within and between societies—and by identifying key factors responsible for these differences—we hope to enable individuals to acquire more self-critical, self-reflective approaches to their histories and national identities and be more understanding of others.

To be sure, Northeast Asian nations have recently recognized the importance of coming to terms with their past and thus have pursued various means of reconciliation, ranging from apology to litigation to common history writing.[7] However, as noted elsewhere, all of these tactics have reached clear, perhaps insurmountable, limitations, as illustrated by Japan's "apology fatigue," the rejection of all legal claims of Korean and Chinese victims by Japanese and American courts, and repeated failures to produce a shared view of history. There appears to be little hope for significant progress in these areas in the near future. In addition, while these countries are actively engaged in promoting their own historical memories and identities, they have lagged behind in understanding the other side's story. There exists not only widespread disagreement in views of past events but also an imbalance in the importance each country gives to specific events and their relative importance in shaping their perception of the past. In this context, an important step toward historical reconciliation would be recognizing and understanding, rather than ignoring or overlooking, the nature and substance of the divided or contested historical memories that are present in the Asia-Pacific, even if one may not agree with the others' views.

To this end, we at the Shorenstein Asia-Pacific Research Center at Stanford University launched a multiyear project, Divided Memories and Reconciliation. The first phase of the project produced a comparative analysis of high-school textbooks of China, Japan, South Korea, Taiwan, and the United States.[8] The second phase examined the role of popular culture, and, in particular, dramatic film, in the formation of historical memory.[9] The third phase compared East Asia with Western Europe with respect to how each region constructed historical memories of wartime past while also examining how those legacies continue to shape current histories.[10] This book draws on these earlier phases of the project but goes beyond them to delve into the views of the elites that guide each nation and the roles that opinion leaders play in shaping memories of colonialism and war in Northeast Asia and the United States. We conducted detailed interviews with selected elite opinion leaders, from historians and journalists to government officials and civil-society activists, in China, Japan, South Korea, and the United States, who played a critical role in shaping wartime memory. We explored not only their personal histories but also their understanding of historical events, providing comparisons both within and between nations. These new materials and this novel approach offer a critical and fresh understanding of the nature of wartime memories in the Asia-Pacific region, providing sometimes startling comparisons of views of the same events through different sets of eyes.

## Colonial and Wartime Memories in Northeast Asia and the United States

Memories of wartime events among the Chinese, Koreans, the Japanese, and Americans are fractured and contested. One such example is the ways that people in these societies remember the U.S. atomic attacks on the Japanese cities of Hiroshima and Nagasaki. While some facts, such as the number of human casualties, are well established, memories of the events and their ramifications are diverse and frequently at odds among the nations involved. For Americans, the use of atomic weaponry was a necessary means to end a destructive war with fewer casualties than otherwise, but the fact that Japan was the first and only victim of atomic strikes left room for Japan's own victimhood. On the other hand, Koreans and the Chinese view Japan as an aggressor that was rightly retaliated against.

The contested nature of wartime memories surfaced again in August 2010, when U.S. Ambassador John Roos attended the annual ceremony at Hiroshima Memorial Park honoring those Japanese who had died in the bombings. While East Asian countries celebrated the sixty-fifth anniversary of the end of World War II, the commemoration took different forms in each nation. In Korea, groups of former "comfort women" and other victims of Japanese colonial rule rallied in front of the Japanese Embassy in Seoul, demanding compensation from the Japanese government. In China, hundreds gathered in the eastern Chinese city of Nanjing to commemorate the victims of the 1937 Nanjing Massacre. However, while the voices of these people were hardly acknowledged by the Japanese government, Japan held its annual ceremony to honor Japanese victims of the atomic bombings. President Obama's decision to send a U.S. representative to the Hiroshima commemoration in 2010 seemed to reflect his efforts to realize a world without nuclear weapons. However, Ambassador Roos's visit was perceived critically by China and Korea as an action that left the two "real" victim countries out of the equation.

While there was some hope among the Japanese after the ambassador's visit that President Obama might also attend Hiroshima or Nagasaki memorials in the near future, this same prospect caused concerns for Koreans and the Chinese. Because Hiroshima is the very site that gave the Japanese a justification for their underlying theme of victim identity, for instance, many Chinese and Koreans are worried that a presidential visit would further impede Japan's confrontation with authentic memory and history with its neighboring countries. For this reason, many opinion leaders in China argue that the Japanese prime minister should visit Nanjing to pay respects to the victims of Japanese aggression before the U.S. president makes his trip to Hiroshima or Nagasaki. Bu Ping, a well-known historian who headed the Chinese delegation to the China-Japan Joint History Research Committee, says that "it is fine for the U.S. president to go [to Hiroshima or Nagasaki], but I think it is inappropriate for him to go there and apologize until Japan thoroughly apologizes [to the Chinese] for its own actions."[11] Likewise, South Koreans feel that the United States should not apologize to Japan but that Japan should first offer apologies, backed by sincere action, to its former colonies. Ambassador Roos's visit to Hiroshima made it clear that Asian history disputes are not limited in their relevance to Asia alone and that the United States, too, must play a critical role in bringing about a solution, as it has been a part of the problem.

## Diversity in Historical Memory

The "history question" in Northeast Asia, from its colonial roots to the clashes on the battlefield, has been a source of tension in the region and with the United States for decades. In 1982, for instance, Japanese history textbooks changed the term describing the 1937 Japanese military aggression against China from "invasion" to "advance," which provoked fierce protests in China. This is considered the start of the so-called history question in Northeast Asia. A dominant view of Japanese colonialism in Korea stresses the exploitative and repressive nature of colonial rule, while the Japanese often point to some positive "economic" effects of their rule in Korea and Taiwan. Even Koreans and the Taiwanese disagree about the nature of Japanese colonialism and its legacy in their societies.[12] While most Americans accept the view that the atomic bombings of Hiroshima and Nagasaki were necessary to end the war with as few human casualties as possible, many Japanese question the motives underlying such an argument, and some even entertain the idea of racism. These are only a few examples of the differences and disputes that exist among Northeast Asian nations and the United States, which are well documented. They are actively presented, promoted, contested, and refuted through various means such as textbooks, films, museums, academic and popular writings, and the mass media.

However, what is often overlooked—but no less important—in discussing the divided nature of historical memories in the Asia-Pacific region is the difference in focus that shapes the formation of war memories in these countries. For the Chinese and Koreans, we all know, Japanese acts of aggression, like the Nanjing Massacre and forced labor and sexual slavery, are the most crucial in their memories of the war. On the other hand, actions related to the United States, such as the attack on Pearl Harbor and the U.S. bombings of Japanese cities (both atomic and firebombing), carry the most weight in shaping Japanese war memories. In particular, our Japanese interviewees unanimously demonstrated that the American firebombings of Japanese cities constitute a key element in their war memories. China and Korea play a role, but only a secondary one compared to that of the United States. Ironically, the atomic bombings of Japanese cities and their aftermath are omitted from South Korean history textbooks, and most Koreans do not know that many Koreans suffered in the bombings, too. In sum, China and Korea are not as significant to Japanese war memories as is the United States, while Japan figures prominently in the war memories of Koreans and the Chinese. Likewise, Japan, more so than China or Korea, is a central player in American memory formation of the Asia-Pacific War. This imbalance in focus helps to explain much of the complexity of the formation of historical memory and reconciliation in the Asia-Pacific region. For instance, the focus on the United States in Japanese war-memory formation both reflects and explains Japan's victim identity and reluctance to fully engage Asian neighbors regarding colonial aggression and issues of wartime atrocities. Unlike Germany, postwar Japan witnessed the development of a mythology of victimhood in which many innocent civilians were sacrificed as a result of the massive and destructive U.S. bombings of cities. The Japanese charge that the United States did not address its own "crimes against humanity." Historical memory based on victimhood served to pardon the Japanese of their guilt, foster an already ubiquitous sense of self-pity, and impede the search for historical truth. Subsequently, victim consciousness provided fertile soil for the growth of a postwar neonationalism that denied Japan's responsibility for wartime atrocities.

The notion of American guilt and Japanese victimhood, with much silence on the topic of Japanese aggression against its Asian neighbors, is a prevalent theme in the exhibits of the Yushukan museum that is part of the Yasukuni Shrine complex in Tokyo. Even historical museums memorializing nuclear victims present a view that questions America's justification for the bombings and deliberately avoids the question of Japan's responsibility for the war. It is in this context that Kiyoteru Tsutsui's content analysis of editorials published in three major Japanese newspapers from 1945 to 2000 found that "evasion" has been the most dominant approach in the Japanese media's discourse on the war.[13] The evasion frame partially accepts guilt but evades the trauma of perpetration by shifting focus to one's own victim consciousness. Within this frame, the Japanese underline the suffering of their own citizens during the Asia-Pacific War, while ignoring Asian victims of Japanese aggression.

In recent years, the Japanese have been calling for a U.S. presidential visit to the sites of the nuclear attacks in order to remove the "historical thorn" that exists between the two allies. The Japanese journalist Hisayoshi Ina goes so far as to suggest that "a visit to Hiroshima by the U.S. president, if realized, will be implanted deeper in history than Kennedy's Berlin speech."[14] However, the Japanese are reluctant to support a similar visit by the Japanese prime minister to Nanjing to pay tribute to the victims of the 1937 massacre. Most Japanese who support a U.S. presidential visit seem to see its merit mainly in terms of reconciling historical issues between the United States and Japan rather than as part of a broader effort toward regional reconciliation. Such an attitude once again reflects the nature of Japanese war memories formed primarily vis-à-vis the United States, not Asian neighbors. However, Koreans and the Chinese, who view the atomic strikes as having been a necessary means of ending the war, and who consider Japanese wartime atrocities to have been far worse, wonder why a U.S. president would make a symbolic visit to the bombing sites when Japanese leaders have not done their part.

This imbalance in memory formation creates perception gaps, hindering mutual understanding and historical reconciliation. Consequently, an important step toward reconciliation is to identify and understand the key factors that influence the formation of historical memory in each nation and to recognize the different weight of these factors. Koreans and the Chinese, for example, need to understand how and why the victim identity of conservative Japanese elites (unlike their German counterparts) came about and how it has posed a chief obstacle to Japan's reconciliation with its Asian neighbors. Likewise, Japan must become cognizant of just how central the historical legacy of its aggression has been in shaping the collective identities of Koreans and the Chinese. For instance, in Japanese history textbooks, only 4 percent of the coverage of Japan's modern history (1868 to 1945) is devoted to Korea; the United States is the main player. In contrast, in Korean history textbooks, Japan occupies almost one quarter of the coverage of modern history (late 1800s to 1945). In other words, Japan figures far more prominently in the historical memory and identity of Koreans and the Chinese than do Korea and China in those of Japan. Once again, this imbalance in focus accounts for much of the divided and fractured nature of wartime memories that exist in the Asia-Pacific region.

Historical memory is not a constant; it is subject to internal contention and outside influence. A superficial examination might give an impression that there is only a single historical memory for each country in Northeast Asia. To be sure, each country is obsessed with national history, has emphasized a single historical memory, and has produced powerful nationalist "master narratives." In addition, the governments have been deeply involved in fashioning collective memory and national identity through history education. In both Japan and South Korea, the ministries of education require all textbooks to undergo a strict screening process.[15] In China, the education ministry has a more direct role in textbook writing, as history textbooks must "accord with fundamental policies of the government."[16] Although there is more flexibility in the United States, most history textbooks aim to teach youth a specific accepted master narrative as part of defining the nation's collective identity, and thus history education plays a powerful role in shaping collective memory and national identity.

There are certainly issues or topics of (near) consensus on the national level. For instance, there is hardly any dissenting view of the Nanjing Massacre among the Chinese. Likewise, few Koreans would dispute the forced and inhumane nature of the sexual slavery of so-called comfort women. Many Japanese feel victimized by the American firebombings and atomic bombings, while most Americans see these bombings as having been necessary measures, if tragic in human terms. These widely held positions are well incorporated into the master narratives of wartime memories in these nations.

Nonetheless, there is internal diversity and contention regarding historical memory in each nation of the Asia-Pacific region. In both Japan and South Korea, there are intense debates over war memories between progressives and conservatives. In Japan, progressive scholars and intellectuals have embraced wartime responsibility as embodied in the International Military Tribunal for the Far East, commonly know as the Tokyo War Crimes Tribunal, while conservative counterparts have stressed Japanese victimhood. In Korea, too, some scholars and experts acknowledge the oppressive but modernizing effect of Japanese rule, while the prominent view still emphasizes the exploitative nature of colonialism.

Even in authoritarian China, diverging views exist on whether the Japanese invasion of China was initiated by a grand plan or by a series of random events, such as the Marco Polo Bridge Incident, or whether the number of Chinese killed in the Nanjing Massacre was actually three hundred thousand (the figure officially recognized by the Chinese government). Li Datong of *China Youth Daily* offers a dissenting view: he says that the number could not be three hundred thousand, since that was the total population of Nanjing at the time, and that a large number of casualties were Kuomintang (KMT) troops and not Nanjing residents.[17] In Japan, opinion leaders often disagree about whether the attack on Pearl Harbor was an act of aggression or an essentially defensive move, whereas in Korea, opinion leaders recall differently whether the mobilization of laborers and soldiers was done by force or by deception, with victims misled by promises of high income.

Not surprisingly, there exists greater diversity of historical views in democratic nations such as Japan than in authoritarian states like China. In a politically liberal environment, issues of historical injustice can no longer be monopolized or controlled by the government. Instead, civil society and transnational nongovernmental organizations (NGOs) become increasingly involved in the issues of historical injustice and reconciliation. Contrary to conventional wisdom, one finds a good deal of memory diversity among the Japanese, perhaps more so than in Korea or China. This diversity largely owes its existence to civic groups and liberal academics who dispute the master narratives of the conservative Liberal Democratic Party–led governments. In Korea, too, democratization since the late 1980s has led more people to come to the realization that Koreans were not merely victims but also, at times, perpetrators. Apart from their suppression of Korean civilians, Korean troops committed the same sorts of atrocities against innocent Vietnamese that Americans were accused of carrying out against Koreans during the Korean War. Even in China, where the authoritarian state holds the upper hand in the production of historical memory, "history activists" have been key players in dealing with the history question.[18]

In addition to democratization and other forms of political "opening," a growing global attention to ethnic or national identity, human rights, and historical injustice has broadened and diversified views of and approaches to the history question. In the past, for instance, Koreans regarded the issue of comfort women primarily from a strictly anti-Japanese nationalist standpoint. More recently, there has been an increased tendency to approach it from a broader feminist or human-rights-centered perspective. Similarly, heightened regional interactions have encouraged the exchange of ideas and collaboration among NGOs on contested historical issues. Increasing numbers of civic activist groups, especially in Japan and South Korea, have joined together in history-redress movements, including data and testimony collection, documentary filmmaking, and public history propaganda work. It seems that democratization, globalization, and regionalism will continue to contribute to an enhancement of diversity in historical memory beyond state-sanctioned master narratives, though nationalist sentiments remain strong in Northeast Asia.

## *Memory Formation and Transformation*

An important consequence of internal contention and outside influence is memory transformation. History memory is not fixed—it changes over time. It occurs not only in democratic countries such as the United States but also in authoritarian ones such as China. In addition, we observe memory transformation in aggressor nations (e.g., Japan) as well as victim nations (China and Korea).

Scholars of memory formation and transformation generally agree that national memory develops and takes shape over the course of several stages. In the case of China, Japan, and Korea, these stages have taken somewhat different paths but have led to common underlying themes. For almost four decades after the end of the war in Asia, the involved countries struggled to recover from the trauma and the aftermath of the war, both economically and psychologically. In Japan, early efforts to address war responsibility led by progressives gave way to conservative nationalist arguments that evaded Japanese guilt for aggression and instead stressed their victim consciousness. In China and Korea, remembering the war history was secondary to other urgent issues, such as the economy and politics, and was considered a "luxury." The South Korean academic-turned-cartoonist Yi Won Bok recalls the period: "During that time, the problem was all about survival. Nobody was interested in history."[19] This period of long silence was further reinforced by the Chinese and Korean governments, as they were eager to receive economic assistance from Japan in order to gain footholds for their national development. All in all, for each of the three countries, there existed an urge to forget the humiliating past and trauma and redefine what it meant to be Chinese, Korean, and Japanese. It was not until the early 1980s that historical disputes among the three countries surfaced.

Although the Japanese themselves had been debating the content of their textbooks since the immediate aftermath of the war, this did not become an international issue until the Japanese media reported, in 1982, the attempt to downplay the wording of textbook references to the start of the war with China. Matsuno Takayasu, the Japanese minister of national land, claimed, "There was no 'invasion' when the war started, so it is time to eliminate it from the textbooks." Such high officials' denial of Japan's wartime crimes immediately provoked Chinese resentment. The media began to focus on reporting witnesses' bitter personal memories of Japan's atrocities and appealed to the Chinese people to "never forget that the war caused tremendous disasters by Japanese aggressors." Meanwhile, historians and scholars in China held various symposiums to commemorate the thirty-seventh anniversary of the triumph of the Chinese people's resistance against Japan. Finally, in August 1982, a special exhibition titled *Historical Exhibits of the Nanjing Massacre Committed by Japanese Aggression* was opened in the Museum of Nanjing. This was the first public exhibit to show Japan's wartime crimes in that city.[20] The commemoration of the anniversary of the end of the war that year was bathed in nationalist rhetoric. In 1985, the Memorial Hall of the Nanjing Massacre and the Museum of Evidence of War Crimes by Japanese Army Unit 731 opened primarily to expose Japan's wartime crimes and brutality, rather than to honor victims.

In Korea, too, distorted descriptions of Japanese colonial rule and the repeated denial of wartime crimes by Japanese officials prompted strong reactions on the national level. The Korean government demanded the "correction" of nineteen items in Japanese history textbooks. In addition, Korean activists began criticizing the authoritarian Park Chung Hee regime that put aside history issues when Korea normalized relations with Japan in 1965 and protested Japanese history textbooks' descriptions of colonial rule in Korea. War victims, including former comfort women in Korea, started to speak out about their experiences, and some even filed belated lawsuits against the Japanese government. The tales of comfort women became powerful symbols of the inhumane aggression of Japan and Korean victimization. Disputes over history textbooks and over the sovereignty of a small group of islets—Dokdo to the Koreans and Takeshima to the Japanese—began to shape bilateral relations between two key allies of the United States.

In Japan, progressives were the most active in early attempts to promote a Japanese war memory that accepted wartime responsibility. However, as the Cold War progressed, their voices were drowned out by a more conservative perspective that advocated victim identity, leading to historical amnesia. Japanese conservatives advanced the view that their country had acted in self-defense against foreign aggressors and that Japan's creation of a "Greater East Asian Co-Prosperity Sphere" had been aimed at "liberating" Asia from white imperialists.[21] They focused on commemorating the atomic bombings of Hiroshima and Nagasaki, and their narrative of self-victimization further reinforced Japanese war amnesia. Japanese high officials began to deny past wrongdoings, even going so far as to remove descriptions of Japan's wartime crimes from national textbooks on the grounds that "otherwise our younger generations will not respect our ancestry, as they would think that they had done something really bad in history."[22] Even Minister of Justice Nagano Shigeto once proclaimed that Japan's aim in World War II was to "liberate East Asia."[23]

## *The United States and Northeast Asia*

The United States is integral to the history question in Northeast Asia. Besides fighting against Japan in World War II, the United States, the principal victor in the war, constructed the settlement that formed the foundation of the post-1945 regional order in East Asia. It also played a critical role in shaping the ways in which the Japanese would remember the war years and address reconciliation issues with their Asian neighbors. The United States made fateful decisions in the treatment of Japanese war crimes, from the decision to put the issue of the Emperor's responsibility aside to the rehabilitation of nationalist conservatives to counter Japan's leftward drift. The unresolved territorial issues that irritate Japan's relations with its neighbors are all the result of American decisions in postwar settlement. The normalization treaty between Japan and the Republic of Korea was brokered by

Washington, which pressed the Koreans to put aside compensation issues in response to Japanese resistance. In short, the United States is the single most important foreign actor in creating a postwar regional order and shaping Japanese war memories and approaches to historical reconciliation with the country's neighbors.

In the past, the United States has taken the position that historical disputes in Northeast Asia are matters to be settled among Asians and that, therefore, the United States should not be involved. Even when historical disputes reemerged at the turn of twenty-first century, President George W. Bush, referring to anti-Japanese protests in China and South Korea, urged Asian nations to put their past behind them "to overcome the tension standing in the way of . . . an optimistic future," suggesting that it is possible, though difficult, to forget the past.[24] However, as tensions intensified in recent years over historical and territorial disputes between key allies of the United States, American officials have expressed concerns. For example, Kurt Campbell, who served as assistant secretary of state for East Asian and Pacific affairs during President Obama's first term, proclaimed the tensions "as the biggest strategic challenge to American interests in Asia."[25]

Simply put, the United States is not an outsider or observer to the history question in Northeast Asia but an integral part of it. It can no longer ignore growing tensions over history in the region as matters that involve only Asians. Therefore, it is only fitting to include the United States as part of this project, and the chapters to follow in this book demonstrate the necessity of including the United States in the study of history wars in Northeast Asia.

## *Opinion Leaders and Historical Memory*

In this book, we focus on opinion leaders' views with regard to wartime memories in China, Japan, South Korea, and the United States. These men and women often play a critical role in shaping the formation of historical memory as historians and writers, filmmakers, or activists. But, often, little is known about how they formed their own memories of the wartime past and how they understand the series of events that led to war.

Individuals directly involved in the tragic events of colonialism and war have written memoirs, offering firsthand stories, but wartime memories are largely socially and collectively constructed.[26] As many experts point out, the politics of memory is a process of negotiation between interested parties, such as victims and their families, veterans' organizations, and NGOs, which is often brokered by the government.[27] Besides formal history education, war commemoration through popular media such as films and museums render vivid narratives widely available to those who did not experience wartime events themselves. What Alison Landsberg refers to as "prosthetic memories" are "privately felt public memories that develop after an encounter with a mass cultural representation of the past, when new images and ideas come into contact with a person's own archive of experience."[28] This way, she writes, "it becomes possible for a person to acquire memories that are not his or her 'natural' or biological inheritance."[29] Thus, memory formation is a complex process that involves multiple actors and institutions, and existing scholarship has sought to capture this process through the analysis of history textbooks, films, museums, novels, public opinion polls, and so on.[30]

However, few attempts have been made to examine the role of opinion leaders who were not directly involved in the war but whose thoughts and beliefs play a distinctive part in the formation of collective or social memories of the nation. As with education and popular culture, how elites in politics, media, academia, and business view the past is crucial to forming wartime memory in a nation. In addition, there are few works that take an explicitly comparative approach, especially one that includes the United States. What has been missing in studies of Asia-Pacific War memories is discussion of the role of the United States, doubtless a main player in the war and its aftermath, in the resolution of contested history issues.

To fill this research gap, our book examines the views of opinion leaders in each of these three Asian nations and the United States—including historians, public intellectuals, activists, former government officials, creators of television and film, media figures, and museum directors—who have influenced wartime memory. We compiled our list of interview subjects in collaboration with scholars of those countries, trying to assemble a diversity of voices with regard to age, social roles, and, where possible, gender. In our in-depth interviews, all interviewees were asked the same set of questions about their understanding of the wartime period from 1931 to 1951. Each talked at length about his or her personal history and how the direct experience of war and its aftermath, including postwar education and family considerations, shaped his or her wartime memories. The interviews have yielded a remarkable cross-national study of key issues in wartime memory formation in the Asia-Pacific, allowing us to compare how elites in China, Japan, Korea, and the United States view events such as the attack on Pearl Harbor, the Nanjing Massacre, the atomic bombings of Japan, and the experience of Japanese colonial rule in Asia.

While we cannot claim that our interviewees constitute a representative sample of opinion leaders in each country, what emerges from these interviews is a rich tapestry of the wartime past that offers deep insight into how elites understand that past and have acted to guide their nations' memories of those events. Often moving and deeply personal, tales of the interviewees provide a fascinating window into how the wartime period was experienced and has been remembered. Combined with research into existing work in all of the countries under study and visits to museums and other key sites that underpin the narrative of the wartime past, these interviews create a unique comparative understanding of the divided nature of wartime memories in the Asia-Pacific region.

It is our hope that greater mutual understanding will lead to reconciliation. One of our Chinese interviewees, Bu Ping, revealed during his interview that it was *possible* to change one's attitude toward, and prejudice against, the opposite side—in this case the Japanese. He acknowledges,

> After my first visit to Japan in 1986, I really disliked the Japanese. They were always saying they were the victims. They did not say anything about the victims of their weapons in China. . . . When I went to Japan for the second time in 1992, I had already got to know many Japanese scholars, mostly in China. I discovered that a lot of Japanese people were nothing like *the Japanese* we had always *imagined*. I also learned about things that Chinese people didn't know. For example, a great number of Japanese scholars were researching the issue of chemical weapons used during the war [with China], and they gave us a lot of materials. I was shocked when I learned that some Japanese people vehemently opposed war and that some soldiers had even established antiwar organizations after returning to Japan after the war.[31]

An introspective effort such as this one has the potential to lay the foundation for a greater mutual understanding of historical memory and eventual historical reconciliation in the region, and we hope that this book will contribute to the attainment of this goal.

## Structure of the Book

This book takes the reader first into how each nation constructs its national memory, using site visits to museums, textbooks, films, and other windows into an often-contested landscape of memory. Out of our interviews, we tell you the stories of five people in each country, selected for their importance in illustrating specific issues and for the often-compelling stories that these individuals tell about the colonial and wartime past and their relationships to those historical memories.

We then draw on our interviews and other research to compare across the four countries the historical memories of five key issues in the wartime period. We begin with the highly sensitive issue of Japanese colonial rule and the problem of forced labor, including that of the comfort women. We follow this, chronologically, with the Sino-Japanese War of the 1930s, including the issue of Japanese war crimes in China, and the war in the Pacific, from the events leading up to the Japanese attack on Pearl Harbor to the long struggle to Allied victory. We conclude with a comparative examination of the still highly sensitive issues surrounding the American decision to use atomic weapons against Japan and, finally, the postwar settlement, largely constructed by the United States, and whether justice was done.

The book concludes with what we hope is a fruitful discussion of the process of historical reconciliation. In that final chapter, we are most concerned with past efforts at reconciliation and what might be done, in very practical terms, to finally heal the wounds of war in Northeast Asia.

PART TWO

*National Memories*

TWO

# Fashioning a Patriotic Narrative in Contemporary China

In the southwest suburbs of Beijing, the granite Lugou Bridge stretches across the Yongding River, supported by hundreds of stone pillars, each of which is topped with a carved lion. Built originally in the twelfth century, the bridge was such a marvel that it drew the recorded admiration of the famous thirteenth-century Venetian traveler, Marco Polo, leading it to be known in the West as the Marco Polo Bridge.

The bridge acquired a much different significance in Chinese history on the night of July 7, 1937. Chinese and Japanese troops engaged in a brief exchange of fire at the western end of the bridge, leading to a skirmish known to Western historians as the Marco Polo Bridge Incident. This minor clash led to the eruption of full-scale war between imperial Japan and China later that month, a war that went on for more than eight years and resulted in the deaths of millions and the destruction of a nation.

The scale and brutal character of the war in China is largely invisible to Westerners who are otherwise steeped in the history of their own participation in the global conflict known as World War II. Japanese losses in the Sino-Japanese War period, from 1937 to 1941, are estimated at 410,000 deaths and some 920,000 people wounded. Figures for Chinese suffering are less reliable, but Western historians believe that as many as 10 million Chinese soldiers were killed in the fighting and that civilian casualties were at least as high and perhaps as large as twice that number. The battles that stretched from the north of China to the jungles of Burma made tens of millions of Chinese into refugees and shattered the economic and political structure of China, literally ripping the country apart.[1]

A ceremony marking the seventy-eighth anniversary of the Lugou Bridge Incident, in front of the Museum of the War of Chinese People's Resistance Against Japanese Aggression. Source: Kyodo.

To commemorate this war, the Chinese government erected a low-slung, stolid museum, a stone's throw from the end of the Lugou Bridge, which opened its doors in July of 1987. A bronze sculpture, *The Awakening Lion*, meant to echo those on the nearby bridge and embody a China arisen from its slumber, sits in the center of a large plaza outside the gates to the white marble building. The ponderous title of the museum, inscribed in large gold Chinese characters above the entry doors, leaves no doubt about what message is to be received within: Museum of the War of Chinese People's Resistance Against Japanese Aggression.

In the entry lobby, the visitor is greeted by a massive wall sculpture of Chinese soldiers and an array of grim citizens, united in their collective resistance to the Japanese invader. The museum tells a clear and simple story of a united people, led by the Communist Party of China, engaged in heroic struggle. The war is not so much a tale of suffering as a rallying of the Chinese people against imperialist aggression, the beginning of the reversal of centuries of decline.

On a recent spring morning, the museum was almost entirely filled with groups of Chinese schoolchildren, dressed in matching shirts and jackets and with the obligatory red scarves tied around their necks but also sporting backpacks decorated with Garfield and anime heroes. Their teachers lectured them as they passed by battle dioramas and a reproduction of a cave in Yan'an where the Communist leadership huddled to plot military strategy. Another room detailed Japanese atrocities—nine hundred cities bombed, civilians murdered, prisoners of war killed, slave labor, biological and chemical warfare, slave education, opium traffic, a plundered economy. The captions on the museum exhibits are only in Chinese—the audience for this history lesson is almost entirely internal, though museum officials say some two hundred thousand foreigners, most of them Japanese, have visited since it opened.

A little over a thousand kilometers to the south, in the old capital of Nationalist China, Nanjing, a modest museum commemorating the infamous Japanese atrocities committed in that city in 1937 opened its doors around the same time, in 1985. Beginning in the mid-1990s, however, the Nanjing memorial underwent major renovation and expansion, with the latest addition completed in 2007. The modernized museum conveys a narrative of Chinese victimization at the hands of a depraved Japanese army, suggesting China's history of humiliation at the hands of Western and Japanese imperialists. The museum graphically depicts the deliberate murder, sometimes by hand, of some three hundred thousand Chinese soldiers and civilians, including women and children, in the battle to conquer the old Chinese capital. The formal title of this public structure also bears a long, but clear, title: Memorial Hall of the Victims in Nanjing Massacre by Japanese Invaders.

In contrast to the Beijing museum, the Nanjing memorial is clearly aimed at a global audience as well as a Chinese one. Captions are translated into Japanese and English, and a gift shop offers an array of materials in foreign languages. The museum, which has no entrance fee, attracts more visitors than any other in China—some five and a half million per year. On a weekday, the visitors were a mix of adults and children, including groups of military recruits.

According to the museum director, Zhu Cheng Shan, the renovation was intended to emulate, in its design and content, the emotionally wrenching Holocaust Museum in Washington, DC, and similar memorials such as Yad Vashem in Jerusalem and Auschwitz in Poland, and even the Japanese museums in Hiroshima and Nagasaki that memorialize the victims of the atomic bombings.[2] The main hall is a modern structure, featuring a long swooping roofline, with a dizzying array of architectural elements outside and within, drawn from those and other museums around the world. On a long black marble wall in the entry plaza, the number 300,000 is emblazoned, along with the word "victims" in multiple languages, on what the museum calls the *Wall of Calamity*. Inside, visitors are guided through a sophisticated series of well-designed exhibits of artifacts of the slaughter, from photos to the preserved site of a mass grave discovered in the renovation process. The narrative skillfully weaves together the stories of not only Chinese victims but also the foreigners who played key roles in trying to protect them and in telling the story of the massacre to the world. A multistory wall of archival materials stores the recorded testimony of survivors.

The message of the Nanjing Massacre Memorial Hall is unrelentingly clear—this is China's own Holocaust. In a small corner of the courtyard in front of the museum offices stands a bronze statue of the Chinese American writer Iris Chang, the author of the 1997 book *The Rape of Nanking: The Forgotten Holocaust of World War II*. The book is widely credited with bringing global attention to these events, and the Chinese authorities have unreservedly embraced her ideas. They have been reinforced through a steady stream of films, books, and television productions, a wave of which marked the seventieth anniversary of the event.

Both the assertion of a united national resistance and the embrace of China's suffering at the hands of foreign invaders are relatively new in revolutionary China. In its first decades in power, Chinese Communist leadership had deliberately downplayed the anti-Japanese struggle in the early years of the People's Republic of China (PRC) in favor of a historical narrative that focused on the civil-war contest between the Communists and the Kuomintang (KMT; the Chinese Nationalists). The focus was mainly on the purported Communist role in leading that struggle and the Nationalist failure to fight the invader—indeed, the KMT's betrayal of the united front against the Japanese for the sake of its struggle against the Communists. During the Cultural Revolution, when formal education was virtually halted, the wartime era was mainly portrayed through propagandistic films. The so-called red classics, such as *Tunnel Warfare* and *Landmine Warfare*, depicted Communist guerrillas of the Eighth Route Army in the north and the New Fourth Army in the south successfully attacking the Japanese army.

The main battlefronts of the Sino-Japanese War, which were under the leadership of the KMT, were almost absent from this narrative of the war. This was a narrative shaped to serve the ongoing contest for legitimacy between the Chinese Communist Party (CCP) and the KMT. In the Cold War decades, when the PRC still counted itself as part of the Communist world, albeit in competition with the Soviet Union for leadership of that world, the Chinese Communists were also not eager to acknowledge a war of resistance in which China and the United States were allied.

Remembrance of the Nanjing Massacre posed particular challenges for Communist historical narratives about the war. The battle in Nanjing was entirely a KMT affair, without any Communist involvement, and it was hardly a heroic affair. The KMT government made initial efforts after the war to gather evidence of Japanese crimes to submit to the war crimes tribunals in Tokyo and those held in China, as well as to memorialize the event. But the civil war, and the Cold War that followed, cut off any further contacts with the wartime allies and even with Japanese historians seeking to illuminate the crimes of imperial Japan.

"It is a great shame that commemoration of the massacre was interrupted by domestic conflict and the international situation," says museum director Zhu. "Political contradictions prevented these kinds of issues from being addressed."[3] There was also a pragmatic reason for the Chinese government to downplay the war against Japan before the 1980s: Beijing was eager to normalize relations with Japan, which it did in 1972, and to open up the flow of Japanese economic aid that followed that decision. Japanese assistance was crucial to the early stages of Chinese economic recovery and growth following the disastrous years of the Cultural Revolution. The decision to erect these two museums in the mid-1980s marked the first steps toward a changed policy on the construction of historical memory about the wartime period in Communist China. Over a period of two decades, from the early 1980s onward, the CCP began to downplay the civil war in favor of a national war against Japan. Faced with the shocking challenge to its leadership from Chinese youth in the Tiananmen revolt of 1989, the Communist regime accelerated this shift in historical narrative with the launching of the Patriotic Education Campaign. Begun in 1991, the campaign was designed to provide Chinese youth with a version of history that de-emphasized the Maoist-era narrative of class struggle within China in favor of the depiction of China as a victim of humiliation and brutality at the hands of foreign powers, going back to the days of the Opium Wars.[4]

External factors certainly had some impact on this shift. Nanjing memorial director Zhu claims that the idea for the construction of his museum was prompted by the dispute that erupted with Japan in 1982 over the revision of Japanese history textbooks to remove language describing the war as an "invasion" and an act of aggression.[5] The dispute and the apparent lack of recognition of the Nanjing events in Japanese textbooks encouraged some in China who argued that there was a need to commemorate and document the Nanjing Massacre.

Chinese commentators also attribute this shift to the impact of the process of reform and opening after 1979, which brought with it a greater flow of information, including access to the translations of Western historians. The CCP began revising its own history to some extent in the mid-1980s, admitting the Nationalist role in the war against Japan, says Li Datong, who led an effort at the party youth newspaper, *China Youth Daily*, to challenge the orthodox version of wartime history.[6]

In public, however, the wartime historical narrative changed much more slowly. The war resistance museum acknowledges the contribution of the KMT in the war, but it still is careful to claim the CCP's leadership of that effort. The museum's exhibits devote considerable space to the Communist war effort, with photos of Mao, Zhou Enlai, and others plotting strategy in the caves of Yan'an. But the account now gives a nod to the KMT's role in fighting the Japanese, as the illustrated history of the war distributed at the museum summarizes:

> China's War of Resistance Against Japan was a nationwide war against aggression. The troops of the Kuomintang and the Communist Party fought against Japanese invaders sometimes each on their own, while at other times in coordination. Both battlefields were important components of the Chinese people's War of Resistance. However, taking a panoramic view of the eight-year history of the War of Resistance, we must point out that the Chinese Communist Party and the people's armed forces under its leadership played the role of mainstay in the war. . . . The political influence and leading role of the Communists cannot be measured by gains from a few military campaigns.[7]

This backhanded acknowledgment of the KMT's role is used to build another, broader and more important assertion about the war—that Chinese resistance, overcoming more than a century of humiliation, was decisive in defeating Japan as part of the global antifascist war. China is depicted as the "first country to fight the fascist aggressor," its contribution decisive in the outcome of the global conflict, pinning down millions of Japanese troops, allowing the West and the Soviet Union to concentrate their forces on Nazi Germany, and defeating Japanese forces in the battlefield. According to this revised historical narrative, Soviet entry into the war, once celebrated according to Marxist orthodoxy, and the American battle in the Pacific, including the use of atomic weapons, did not decide the outcome. Those two events "hastened the surrender," war resistance museum director Li Zongyuan says, "but they didn't play a decisive role."[8]

This assertion of Chinese primacy in the outcome of World War II proved to be an even more contentious issue than that of Japanese war crimes when a Harvard-organized conference of Western, Japanese, and Chinese scholars gathered in 2004 to discuss the military history of the Sino-Japanese War. "The China theater was not merely important, it was *the* critical theater in World War II," Chinese participants argued.[9] The Western scholars who edited the volume that emerged from the conference begged to differ: "The fact of the matter is that China was indeed a tertiary theater in World War II."[10]

The debate over the cause of Japan's defeat was also contentious. Western and Japanese scholars point to the American naval war as the key to Japan's downfall. "Japan, including its forces in China, was brought to its knees not by Chinese armies but through the destruction of the Japanese homeland by aerial bombs, submarine torpedoes, and nuclear weapons," the war scholars concluded.[11]

Such judgments are not found in Chinese histories and certainly not in the textbooks and other materials that are used to shape the historical memory of Chinese youth. China's secondary-school history textbooks provide a window into both the shifting nature of the historical narrative offered within China and the rather dramatic embrace of this newer, patriotic version of the past.

The standard textbook on Chinese contemporary and modern history, published by the state's Peoples Education Publishing House, was in circulation from the 1980s through the middle of the first decade of this century. Beginning in 2004, it was gradually replaced throughout the country by a new, completely revised textbook, *Chinese History*, which offered a significantly altered version of the wartime period, one more in tune with the Patriotic Education Campaign begun in the 1990s.[12]

The older volume, which features Mao standing before a microphone to announce the formation of the People's Republic, reflects the more traditional Communist narrative about this period, though with some sense of the shift already taking place in the 1980s. It divides the wartime era into two chapters. The first, titled "The Ten-Year Confrontation Between the CCP and KMT (1927–1937)," is twenty-seven pages. The second, titled "The Anti-Japanese War of the Chinese Nation (1937–1945)," is shorter, some twenty pages.

The first chapter offers a classical account of the confrontation between the CCP and the KMT, describing the latter as increasingly becoming an accommodator of Japanese imperialists and an instrument of British and American pursuit of their own interests in China. It condemns KMT leader Chiang Kai-shek's policy of "no resistance" to Japan's takeover of Manchuria in 1931 and its advance into northeast China. The second chapter offers a more redemptive tale of the formation of a united front, at the urging of the CCP, to resist Japan's expansion into full-scale war in 1937. Nationalist troops are credited with waging many battles against the Japanese invaders, from Shanghai to the south. The Nanjing Massacre is asserted as fact but given relatively short shrift—it occupies only two paragraphs, with only one photo of bodies being buried by Japanese soldiers. It is Mao's strategy of "protracted war" that is credited with drawing Japan into a quagmire of extended conflict. Students are asked to answer the question "After the Marco Polo Bridge Incident, what were the differences and similarities between the attitudes of the CCP and the KMT in confronting the invasion by Japanese imperialism?" As the narrative moves on, the textbook describes how KMT policy "turns reactionary," sabotaging the united effort by turning its fire more toward the Communist foe. The CCP, in contrast, is depicted as the true nationalist, rallying the populace against Japan.

The end of the war is given in a brief summary: The war concludes in Europe in May 1945. The Soviet Union declares war on Japan and destroys the elite Japanese Kwantung Army in the northeast. Communist forces launch a nationwide counterattack. And, on August 15, the Japanese surrender (no mention of the atomic bombing appears in this account). "Thus the Chinese People's Anti-Japanese War ultimately achieved its final victory," concludes the textbook chapter.

The revised Chinese history textbook offers some continuity with this historical narrative but also some stunning revision. The events of the civil war are dealt with separately from those of the anti-Japanese war, as part of a section on "democratic revolutions in modern China" from the Taiping Rebellion to the establishment of the PRC. The war with Japan is the second lesson: a chapter titled "World Powers' Military Aggression and Chinese Peoples' Resistance (1840–1945)" tells a narrative of foreign intervention and resistance from the Opium Wars to World War II.

The lesson on the anti-Japanese war is now brief—a mere three pages is devoted to the subject—and deeply imbued with the didactic themes of the patriotic education campaign. The chapter begins with Japan's surrender, described as a moment of "victory after the brave eight-year fight." The war is set in the context of a Japanese imperial design to conquer China, going back to the Sino-Japanese War of 1894–1895 and proceeding through the Manchurian Incident of 1931, growing tensions in Shanghai and northern China, and leading to the opening of full-scale war in 1937. "Facing the threat of Japan's invasion," the textbook tells students, "the KMT and CCP stopped their civil war and built an anti-Japanese national united front." Nothing is said about later KMT betrayal, though the CCP is given credit for leading the battle after 1941.

This new patriotic version devotes far more space to a detailed description of the Nanjing Massacre, including graphic accounts of atrocities there and elsewhere in China. It poses a discussion subject for students: "Japanese rightwing forces vigorously deny that the Japanese military committed the Nanjing massacre—the ultimate act of human cruelty—during its invasion of China. They consider it a type of wartime behavior. What do you think of the issue?"

Finally, while the textbook links the surrender of the Japanese to the success of "world anti-Fascist forces," it places this "victory" in a clearly nationalist framework:

> The victory in the Anti-Japanese War was at the time the first complete success that the Chinese people had achieved in fighting against foreign invaders in more than 100 years. It greatly strengthened Chinese national pride and the confidence of people throughout the nation and established a firm foundation for the victory of the democratic revolution in the whole country. China's Anti-Japanese War was an important part of the world Anti-Fascist War. The Chinese peoples' resistance against the Japanese made a great contribution to the victory of the world Anti-Fascist War. The international status of China was raised.

This textbook reflects the rise of Sino-Japanese tensions at the time, triggered in part by the decision of Prime Minister Koizumi Junichiro to conduct annual visits to the Yasukuni Shrine to Japan's war dead, beginning in 2001. Those tensions were fed by the approval in 2001 of a Japanese history textbook authored by right-wing scholars, *New History Textbook*, which offers a more unrepentant account of Japan's aggression in Asia. In the spring of 2005, the Chinese government backed a massive Internet campaign to collect signatures opposing Japan's bid for permanent membership in the United Nations Security Council. A central theme of this campaign was that Japan was unsuited for membership because of its failure to face up to its wartime past. A Japanese government decision to authorize a second edition of the right-wing textbook in April of 2005 triggered a wave of protest across China.[13]

In September 2005, Chinese leader Hu Jintao gave this new version of wartime history an official imprimatur in a speech marking the sixtieth anniversary of the end of the war. Significantly, Hu acknowledged the contributions of the KMT in fighting the Japanese, while at the same time continuing to assert Communist leadership. The speech was aimed in part at Taiwan, pairing a warning against pro-independence forces then in power with an offering of an olive branch to the KMT, which the Chinese government saw now as a force against secession on the island. Hu had invited the Nationalist leader to visit the mainland that spring, the first such visit since 1949.

One motivation for the revision of history was the situation in Taiwan and the attempted rapprochement with the KMT, says *China Youth Daily* editor Li. "The KMT's first condition is that they want an acknowledgment of their contribution to resisting the Japanese. They have got this now."[14]

This gesture has limits, which Li found out when he lost his job after publishing a lengthy article questioning the Communist claim to have led the forces that fought an early and famous battle against the invading Japanese at Pingxingguan in mid-September 1937. The article was criticized at a high level by the CCP, which still maintains strict control over the approved military history of this period.

While behind closed doors, tensions remain over the rendering of historical truth about the wartime period, the patriotic campaign can claim success in implanting its message, particularly among China's younger generation. Polls conducted over the last decade exploring Chinese attitudes toward Japan indicate a strong association with wartime memories, showing that they are relatively undiminished even when relations have markedly improved.

Since 2005, the Japanese think tank Genron NPO and *China Daily* have conducted a joint opinion poll in both countries, which has explored mutual perceptions. Asked what comes to mind when they think of Japan, Chinese respondents have consistently put the Nanjing Massacre and Japanese electronic goods at the top of the list.[15] The history issue is named by the vast majority of Chinese respondents as the main obstacle to development of better relations. Even in a recent poll, released in September 2014, almost 60 percent of Chinese respondents attribute their negative perceptions of Japan (which remain held by an overwhelming majority) to the wartime past and "Japan's lack of a proper apology and remorse over the history of invasion of China."[16]

At various moments, the Chinese state has unleashed this new patriotism for its own policy ends. But often it finds itself having to pull back on the reins for fear that antiforeign feelings can turn inward. Indeed, in the relatively less-controlled world of the Chinese Internet, "netizens" engage in often vitriolic assaults on those who are considered less than patriotic. Chinese filmmaker Lu Chuan found this out after the 2009 release of his powerful film on the Nanjing Massacre, *City of Life and Death*.

Lu Chuan is considered one of China's rising cinematic stars, and he embarked on the project to make a film about Nanjing with the full backing of not only his financiers but the Chinese state. Lu had spent four years in Nanjing being trained as an English interpreter at the People's Liberation Army's International Relations Academy. Aside from an immersion in American films, which set him on a path to his directing career, Lu and his classmates were taken for multiple visits to the Nanjing memorial museum. "Each time, we were totally shocked," Lu recalls.[17]

Some years later, Lu decided to make a film about the Nanjing events. He started out animated, in his own words, by a "strong hatred of Japan," determined to expose a "truth" that the Japanese were denying about the massacre. But in the course of his research for the film, Lu came upon the diary of a Japanese soldier that had been translated and published in China. It led him to write a script in which a part of the story is told through the eyes of a single Japanese soldier, one who is conflicted about what he sees and the acts of cruelty he himself carries out. It is hardly a sympathetic portrait of Japan, but it offers an attempt to present a more universal message—as Lu put it, "that people who we always think are monsters or beasts are still human beings, even on the battlefield."[18]

The film script passed through the Communist Party censors without serious change—except for the removal of some scenes of violence that were considered too shocking, even for this purpose. But when the film hit the screen in China, the Internet commentary exploded with attacks for the portrayal of a Japanese soldier as an even remotely empathetic character. "People began to call me a traitor," Lu says, still shaken. "I found death-threat letters in my mailbox."[19] He was ordered to keep quiet and not to respond to these attacks.

The construction of wartime memory in China thus remains an ongoing process, entangled in the complex needs of the Chinese state and Communist Party to retain legitimacy in a rapidly changing China. Because of the country's need to offer a new, patriotic narrative to replace the Marxian ideology of the past, it has opened the door to both a potentially uncontrolled nationalism and a questioning of its legitimacy. Despite the power of the state and party to enforce orthodoxy, there now exists a real and growing debate about the past in China. As the profiles of some of the actors in this debate may illuminate, there is a much richer dialogue going on behind the formal unity of the accepted wartime memory than most outsiders understand.

## Bu Ping

In April of 2005, a wave of anti-Japanese protests swept across China, starting in the capital of Beijing and spreading to cities across the country, the largest gathering of public protest since the antigovernment demonstrations that filled Tiananmen Square in 1989. Crowds of young people, mostly college students, gathered around the Japanese embassy and consulates, at the offices of Japanese companies, and even at Japanese restaurants, chanting slogans and throwing rocks and bottles. "Japanese pigs get out," some screamed, while others carried banners calling for the boycott of Japanese products. Outside the embassy, tens of thousands converged, shouting, "Be ashamed of distorting history!"

Tensions between Japan and China had been building for years, fed by the Japanese government's approval of textbooks submitted by a right-wing

Bu Ping

group. The Japanese Society for History Textbook Reform, known by its shortened Japanese name, Tsukurukai, had been formed in the mid-1990s to offer a less repentant view of Japan's wartime past, arguing that Japanese textbooks offered a one-sided and "masochistic" version of the past. "The people that does not have a history to be proud of cannot constitute itself as a nation," the organization's founder writes.[20]

The ascension to power in Tokyo of Liberal Democratic Party Prime Minister Koizumi Junichiro in 2001, and his decision to officially visit the Yasukuni Shrine to Japan's war dead, sent Sino-Japanese relations into the deep freeze. The upsurge in protests in 2005 were in part an orchestrated Chinese campaign against Japan's bid for permanent membership in the United Nations Security Council, which Chinese officials and scholars opposed on the grounds that a Japan unwilling to face its wartime past was unfit to join the five permanent members, the victorious powers in World War II. The immediate catalyst for the violent April protests, however, was the announcement, on April 6, of the authorization of a new set of middle-school history textbooks authored by the right-wing reform group. The books pointedly obscured or removed references to Japanese war crimes, from the mass murders in Nanjing and the forced recruitment of women for wartime brothels to the actions of a notorious biological and chemical weapons research unit that used the Chinese as test subjects.

The protests and their aftermath prompted a prolonged effort to repair relations, culminating in the October 2006 visit of newly installed Liberal Democratic Party Premier Abe Shinzo, who in his first week in office headed off to Beijing and Seoul to try to restore normal ties. One outcome of his visit was the formation of a joint history research project that would bring Chinese and Japanese academics together to try to come to a common understanding of their shared history. The project, modeled on a similar joint committee formed between Japan and South Korea earlier in the decade, began its work in December of that year in Beijing.

The Chinese academic chosen to lead his country's representatives in this highly charged and politically risky venture was a bespectacled historian with a long record of engaging the prickly issues of the war—Bu Ping, the director of the Institute of Modern History at the Chinese Academy of Social Sciences (CASS), the premier Chinese academic institution. Bu was born in Beijing a few years after the end of the war, in 1948, the son of a Chinese bank worker who told tales of dodging air raids in the wartime capital of Chongqing, where he had fled the Japanese invasion. Bu began his career in the late 1970s as a historian in the Heilongjiang Academy of Social Sciences in the northeastern center of Harbin, where he had gone to university after being sent to the region as a laborer during the Cultural Revolution.

"I remember very clearly something that happened after I went to Heilongjiang," Bu recounts. "We were undergoing some kind of class reeducation and were visiting a coal mine. The mine had a huge mass grave. In it were buried laborers who had worked at the mine. It had been run by the Japanese, and the conditions were extremely harsh, so lots of people had died there, and their bodies had been thrown into a big pit. When we went, we saw a huge sea of bones."[21]

Initially, Bu researched relations with Russia, which shares a border with Heilongjiang province. As the head of the Institute of Historical Research, Bu was dragged into the anti-Japanese history campaign that took off in the mid-1980s. "Everyone was focused on and criticizing Japan, so in the Northeast we thought we ought to research Japan's invasion of our region," he recounts, and he organized a project to cover the fourteen years from 1931 to 1945. Along with a group of young researchers, Bu set off to the Sino-Soviet border area, where there were remains of Japanese military fortifications. Local guides told them of Japanese shells filled with poison gas buried in the mountainside, still sometimes causing serious injuries among the farmers who dug them up for scrap metal. Bu and his group began conducting surveys about this problem and the work of the infamous Unit 731, a secret Japanese wartime program to develop chemical and biological weapons that conducted horrendous experiments on Chinese prisoners.

In 1991, a Japanese journalist came to interview Bu. He told the Chinese historian about the case of a Japanese island where a poison gas factory had been located during the war and the suit brought by Japanese workers who suffered health problems and demanded compensation. The following year, Bu visited Japan, meeting the director of an island museum who had gathered historical archives on the gas program (it was Bu's second visit to Japan) and developing contacts with Japanese scholars and activists who had worked to uncover secrets about the use of chemical weapons during the war. "I had no idea that Japanese scholars were researching this issue before then," Bu says. "When we met these scholars, they gave us lots of materials. I also met some Japanese soldiers who had fought in the war. These soldiers had reflected deeply on the Japanese military and, after their return to Japan, had established some antiwar organizations. Since then, I have been to Japan almost every year to meet with these people."

Based on that experience, Bu, with Japanese and Korean historians, organized a trilateral, nongovernmental joint history research effort, designed to counter the new right-wing textbooks in Japan. The effort yielded a common book on the history of the region that was published in all three countries. So it was logical that when the official committee was formed in 2006, the Chinese Foreign Ministry came to Bu, who had moved to Beijing two years earlier. But it was not without trepidation that he took on the task. "I was definitely worried," Bu recalls. "When this project was announced, there were very high expectations on both sides among the public. Everyone was watching to see what we would produce." Emotions had been running high, and the support for actual joint understanding and reconciliation was, in Bu's careful words, "very shallow."

Bu was barraged with letters from the Chinese, the Taiwanese, and even from the Chinese overseas in the United States. Some of them opposed the very idea of discussion with Japan. "They didn't think there were any questions about history to discuss: 'The Japanese were the invaders, so if you sit down and talk to them, you have already lost,' they wrote." For the Chinese, this was a matter of once again defeating Japan. "So there was tremendous pressure. There were a few who supported reconciliation but not many."

The joint project covered the entire two-thousand-year span of history of contact and exchange between China and Japan, in part because of Japanese insistence that it not focus solely on the wartime period. But from its opening meeting in late December of 2006, it was clear that the war would preoccupy the group of twenty-two scholars—divided equally between the two countries. Bu, addressing the inaugural meeting, pointed a finger at those in Japan who refused to "accept responsibility for the war" and who "deny even the historical facts of its aggressive war. It offends the victim country and is the reason why the historical issue has not yet been resolved." The committee was tasked, in his view, with the goal of creating a "common historical perception" built on "the joint confirmation of historical facts." The model for this view was the joint commission formed by France and Germany after World War II, which yielded a common textbook.

The Japanese committee chairman, political scientist Kitaoka Shinichi, who had served in the Japan-Korea committee, had a much more modest goal of narrowing the gap of historical understanding between the two countries. By the second meeting, in March 2007 in Tokyo, the committee had indeed abandoned the idea of creating a joint textbook or even agreeing on a single rendition of events. Instead, they opted for the formula that was adopted in the Korean committee—writing two parallel histories that allowed them to identify areas where they agreed, and disagreed, about the past. Problems arose in dealing with not only wartime issues such as the Tokyo War Crimes Tribunal but also postwar events such as the Cultural Revolution, which is still a matter of great sensitivity in China. When the final report was issued in 2010, the section on the postwar period was kept confidential at the request of the Chinese, and other parts were published without a summary of their discussion. "The postwar period is precisely one of those areas in which politics and academia intersect," Bu acknowledges. "We can't separate them." This is perhaps more pronounced in China. Still, both sides give credit to a process of largely dispassionate discussion among academics, one that created networks of contact and narrowed areas of disagreement. Both sides characterized the 1937–1945 Sino-Japanese War as a "war of aggression" waged by Japan, an admission that brought criticism from the Japanese right wing. "I think it's a foundation," Bu says, reflecting on the outcome. "During this process, we ran into some obstacles that led to heated debate. But, slowly, we resolved them on an academic level. Of course, when we made our findings public, there was plenty of criticism for each side."

When it came to controversies such as the Nanjing killings, both sides agreed that atrocities took place, but they disagreed over the scale of the deaths, with the Chinese sticking to the official figure of three hundred thousand victims. The Japanese insisted on a scale of estimates, beginning at the low end with twenty to forty thousand. Even that was a target of attack for Japanese conservatives. "I don't think the numbers are important at all," Bu says, a view that is hardly accepted in Chinese official narratives. "The events of the Nanjing Massacre speak for themselves, and given the chaos of the situation [in Nanjing] at the time, it is impossible to arrive at an accurate figure. Both sides reached agreement on the understanding of this issue."

Bu's own views on the history of the war in Asia reflect moderation and willingness to forge an understanding with non-Chinese historians. He dismisses the propaganda claim that Japan's defeat can be claimed as a Chinese military victory. "China played a partial role, but there are many factors that led to Japan's surrender," he says. "Of course, China kept Japanese military and financial resources tied down in this theater, but I don't think China's efforts alone caused Japan to surrender." Bu credits the U.S. war effort, and, at the end, the Soviet entry into the war, with forcing Japan to surrender.

The decision to drop the atomic bombs on Japan "was extremely immoral," Bu says, but "it was reasonable. The U.S. used the atomic bombs to defeat Japan more quickly. Had they not done so, Japan would have continued fighting, and perhaps the result would have been even worse; perhaps there would have been even more terrible sacrifices. As a weapon, the atomic bomb was a double-edged sword. On one hand, it could kill and injure a great many of the other side's soldiers and weaken their military capabilities. But on the other hand, ordinary people would also suffer. Most of the victims were not soldiers but civilians. From this perspective, it is problematic."

Bu places equal responsibility for Japan's decision to go to war on the emperor, the military, and the political leadership of the country. He also rejects the view that it may have been possible to negotiate a peace deal with Japan in the final months leading up to the attack on Pearl Harbor. "I think there was no chance [to negotiate peace]," he opines. "In Chinese there is a saying: 'It's difficult to get off when you are riding a tiger.' If you are riding a tiger, you don't dare dismount. If you do, the tiger will eat you, so you have to stay on it. At that time, Japan was precisely in this position. It had no choice but to keep on going. It was impossible for Japan to leave China, and in order to keep fighting in China, it needed oil and rubber from Southeast Asia; otherwise, it would have to go north and fight the Soviet Union. Japan had already prepared to fight the USSR, but its plans were not yet mature, so it preferred to go south and fight the U.S."

When it comes to the postwar settlement, Bu joins the chorus of Chinese scholars and others who believe that Japan failed to adequately compensate the war's victims or to offer consistently sincere apologies for its wartime acts. He traces this back in part to the Cold War–driven decision not to hold the emperor and others responsible for the war or deal with crimes such as the use of chemical and biological weapons and use of forced laborers.

For Bu Ping, the road to reconciliation remains open, but the journey is far from finished.

## *Li Datong*

Li Datong was born into China's Communist elite. He is the son of a veteran of the Communist revolutionary struggle who, as a young man, joined the forces in the mythic stronghold of Yan'an in 1937. His father became a leader of the Communist 8th Route Army that fought in northern China against the Japanese invaders, was wounded in battle, and rose to become a senior official of the Communist Party in Beijing. But like many of the old generation of Communist revolutionaries, Li's father ran afoul of the political gyrations of the Cultural Revolution. He was denounced in 1966 as a "capitalist roader" and sent off for what became twelve years of de facto imprisonment in the countryside. Li followed him into internal exile a year later, at the age of sixteen, into the windswept and empty plains of Inner Mongolia, where Li remained for eleven years, until 1979, liberated only after his father had been freed from his long political exile. Since his return to the mainstream of Chinese society, Li has worked as a Communist

Li Datong

journalist, undergoing his own ideological journey from power to dismissal and condemnation. Li's crimes in the eyes of the Communist authorities, however, center on his attempt to unveil what he views as inconvenient truths of Chinese history, particularly those of the wartime past in which his father became a hero.

Li grew up with the images and stories of his father's wartime exploits. As a young man, he and his siblings would ask their father, "How many Japanese devils did you kill?"[22] They would take feather dusters and pretend they were swords, play-fighting their father as the "Japanese devil." Later, when Li was allowed to visit his father in his political exile in Liaoning, he listened to stories of guerrilla war against Japan, the only subject that was politically safe to discuss.

Li's father was the leader of a guerrilla unit in western Inner Mongolia, between Hohhot and Baotou. Late in the war, in 1944, Li was attending a meeting of about one hundred other senior commanders from the Eighth Route Army whose location was betrayed to the Japanese. Everyone was killed except Li's father and a young soldier. Li's father told the young comrade to take off his uniform and flee and proceeded to destroy the remaining weapons and jumped off a cliff. "He preferred to die than be captured," Li recounts, "but he didn't die." His father survived the jump but was severely injured—both legs were shattered, resulting in disability for the rest of his life.

Years later, after returning from exile after the end of the Cultural Revolution and being rehabilitated by the Communist Party, Li's father's faith in the cause of his lifetime had worn thin. But what was left intact was his wartime experience. "On my father's seventieth birthday, the whole family was celebrating," Li recalls. "On that day, I asked him, 'What part of your life has had the most value?' He was silent for a moment; then he said, 'The War of Resistance against Japan.'" The feelings generated in that struggle remain. "My father still hates Japan deep in his bones," says Li. "When I went to Japan for a trip the first time, he was furious and yelled, 'How can you go to Japan? You can't go to that place.' His generation really has a lot of animosity toward Japan."

Li himself joined the Communist Party while in Inner Mongolia, though he was prevented from attending university because of his father's classification as a "capitalist roader." After his release from internal exile, Li chose to stay in Inner Mongolia as a reporter for the party's youth paper, *China Youth Daily*, based on the strength of his command of Mongolian. It was the beginning of more than three decades of service for one of the more widely read Communist journals in China. Two years later, in 1979, he was transferred to Beijing to be an editor.

Li's doubts about the history of the war in which his father became a Communist hero began to creep in as he was exposed to new sources of information. "I think it must have been after 1979, after reform and opening, when China began to open up to the outside world and new things started coming in, [that] a lot of information and Western writings started being translated." The Communist Party, compelled to deal with massive mistakes of the Maoist era, also began to reexamine its own history. Li recalls a moment in 1985, when the *China Youth Daily* editors received a stunning document from the party leadership. "We received a memo from above telling us that more than three million Kuomintang troops had been killed in the War of Resistance against Japan. We were stunned. If three million KMT troops had lost their lives, how could they have not been resisting the Japanese? In our textbooks, it was written that as soon as the KMT saw the Japanese troops, they would run, that only the Eighth Route Army was fighting the Japanese. But in that moment, when we received this internal memo and learned that the KMT had lost three million troops and that over two hundred generals and other senior officers had died on the battlefield, we saw that this far exceeded CCP losses." Li did his own calculations. The CCP-led forces had grown in strength more than tenfold during the course of the war, while the KMT army was decimated. "The CCP had so many troops, occupied so much territory, and had suffered minimal losses—they had not fought at all," Li concludes. "When [the CCP forces] saw the Japanese army, *they* fled," he says harshly. "The so-called guerrilla troops saw the Japanese devil and ran away."

Such heretical thoughts almost brought Li's journalism career to an abrupt end in 1989, when he joined forces with the pro-democracy demonstrators gathered in Tiananmen Square. He was banned from work for five years, only to be reinstated in the mid-1990s, when China took a liberalizing turn. He launched the pioneering *Bingdian* (Freezing Point), a weekly supplement to the *Youth Daily*. The paper became a voice for reform and one of the most popular publications in China.

In his own writing, and as an editor, Li continued to delve into the past and to pick away at the myths of Communist historiography, particularly about wartime and the Civil War era. In 2005, he came across research work by a historian of one of the most storied battles of the war against Japan: the Battle of Pingxingguan Pass in September 1937, in the early days of the conflict. In the CCP account, this was a stunning victory for some six thousand men of the 115th regiment of the Communist forces, led by the young Lin Biao, later one of the leaders of revolutionary China. They carried out a surprise attack, according to the CCP account, killing three thousand Japanese and dealing the first major blow of the war.

But Li devoted a whole issue of his publication to a very different version of this event. The paper revealed that the main brunt of the fighting was actually carried out by troops of the Chinese central army, under KMT leadership, who suffered huge losses (his researcher claimed some fifty thousand men died) and dealing the Japanese losses of some two hundred men. Li says,

> The KMT fought the main battle. Lin Biao's 115th regiment was just on the flanks and joined in for a little while, losing about the same number of troops as

the Japanese. Until then, I, too, had believed that the Victory of Pingxingguan had been won by the CCP, so I was shocked when I learned that the battle had been fought principally by the KMT with just a little help from the CCP. The whole nation had been lied to for decades! Not one word had ever been said about the sacrifices of the KMT—just that the CCP had won the victory with a little help on the side from the KMT, which was completely false. We published the truth about the battle, including listing all the regiment numbers of the KMT troops and names of their commanding officers, including photographs. It was a very solid report.

The Communist Party responded quickly, vehemently, and at the highest level. A senior member of the party Politburo sharply criticized the report. The paper was ordered to print another article stating that the victory was won by the Communists. But even the author of the second article felt compelled to acknowledge that the KMT had borne the brunt of the fighting, despite claiming that Lin Biao's unit had been at the center of the fight. "The CCP wants to monopolize historical interpretation," Li says. "Whatever history they provide is the history you are required to believe."

When it comes to his own view of the wartime period, there is little question that Li has forged a view of the past that is distinct from that held by most Chinese historians and opinion makers. Japan's advance into China was not driven by a grand plan, he says. "It just happened step by step. The primary goal was to control the Northeast." The massacres in Nanjing in 1937 certainly took place, he says, but they were the product of loss of control by Japanese commanders over their men, not a systematic policy of the occupiers. Asked if China defeated Japan in the War of Resistance, a standard contention of Chinese Communist historians, Li is dismissive of the conventional narrative:

> China certainly did not defeat Japan. From the beginning to the end of the war, China was on the defensive, retreating. At no point did it have the upper hand, not even at the end of the war. The victory was achieved by the Allies. The U.S. was already threatening the Japanese mainland; then it dropped the atomic bombs. The Soviet army was driving the Japanese out of the Northeast. At the time, the Kwantung Army still had a million troops in the Northeast, but the Soviets drove them out as if it were a game; it was nothing for them. But the Chinese army had been fighting for eight years and hadn't even made a dent in the Kwantung Army. So, no, China didn't defeat Japan. The Allies defeated Japan and brought the Chinese along to the victory. But the Chinese people and

the Chinese army played a very important role in keeping the Japanese army bogged down so they couldn't leave [to fight elsewhere]. At the outset of the war, both Chiang Kai-shek and Mao Zedong believed that China could not defeat Japan alone. They were very clear about this. But Japan would inevitably lose, as it would not be able to resist an international alliance of forces, especially if the U.S. joined the war. [In the meantime, however,] China had to hold out for a very long time. They would exchange space for time, giving up territory to Japan to gain time, and eventually they would be victorious. But, of course, we didn't achieve the victory; it was the international alliance that won it.

While Li accepts the necessity of the American decision to drop atomic weapons on Japan to defeat Japan, he questions its fundamental morality, a view not shared by many Chinese. "Looking at it from today's perspective, it wouldn't be allowed. But it was in keeping with the rules of war at the time. The atomic bombs didn't kill any more people than carpet-bombing. In just one firebombing of Tokyo more than one hundred thousand people were killed. One hundred thousand—it's unbelievable! The Allies razed Dresden—weren't those civilians too? Both sides did this. The Germans bombed London. They didn't care whether it was a military or a civilian target; they just attacked. During World War II, everything was permissible under the rules of war as they were understood then."

Li breaks ranks as well in backing the American decision to not try the emperor in the postwar tribunals. To do so would have lead inevitably to a death penalty, leaving the United States to confront an uncontrollable situation in the occupation of Japan. Perhaps most provocatively, Li has little interest in the demands for further Japanese apology and atonement for the past. Japan's apologies and reparations have been sufficient, he argues.

> Of course, there weren't any [formal] reparations. China renounced claims to reparations, but can we say they haven't received anything at all? In fact, although reparations claims were abandoned, quite a lot has been received—long-term low-interest or even interest-free loans, et cetera. Every year, China has received billions of dollars of support for economic development. This has been a kind of atonement. In addition, Japanese prime ministers have expressed [remorse] many times. In my opinion, it's enough. For China and Japan still to be enmeshed in a past war is boring, meaningless, and unnecessary. When you go to Japan today, you can see how democratic it is, what a likeable country it is. I went to the Yasukuni Shrine. I read the messages people had pinned on the trees—they were all notes for their relatives, wishing them well: "I hope you find

a good job," "I wish you good health," nothing to do with the war at all. It is a completely peaceful memorial.

Li Datong revels in the deliberately provocative nature of his rendition of wartime history. He knows that his own father could not swallow such views. But Li shrugs his shoulders. "There is a big gulf between the views of my generation and those of his generation when it comes to the war," Li proclaims. "So our views are going to clash with one another."

## *Song Qiang*

China's embrace of market reform and its opening to the outside world, launched by Deng Xiaoping in the late 1970s, is widely praised for having remade China into a global power. But it is not without its critics within China, from leftists nostalgic for the ideological purity of the Maoist era to advocates of Western-style democracy and political freedom. The most popular camp of critics lies, however, neither in the left nor among the pro-Western liberals—it is China's populist nationalists, what one American scholar terms "nativists."[23]

Song Qiang

The nationalists burst into the popular imagination in China in 1996 with the publication of a mass-circulation collection of essays titled *The China That Can Say No*. It was a title, and a concept, ironically copied from a popular Japanese book written in the late 1980s by a prominent Japanese right-wing nationalist and the then-chairman of Sony Corporation. In the midst of Japan's trade and economic wars with the United States, the Japanese authors called on Japan to say no to their American ally and overlord, not least to say no to the American model of capitalism in favor of Japan's state-guided capitalist system, which many thought to be superior to the predatory nature of the American marketplace.

The Chinese version of this call to arms was similarly anti-Western and anti–United States in its broad theme but with a heavy dose of anti-Japanese sentiment mixed in. In the book, and in a subsequent volume published in 1996 titled *China Can Still Say No*, Song Qiang and his coauthors accuse Japan of being in some ways even more distasteful than America. Reflecting on the flare-up over the territorial dispute in the Senkaku/Diaoyu Islands in the East China Sea that year, Song and his comrades write, "Sun Yat-sen [the founder of the Chinese republic, once an admirer of Japan] said that 'China and Japan are brothers—China is the older brother and Japan is the younger brother.' Unfortunately this 'younger brother'. . . does not treat his older brother like a human." Japan, the nationalists tell their readers, has become an immoral nation, which must be confronted by a rising China. "To the majority of contemporary Chinese, the mission of containing Japan has already begun; the final battle of the Western Pacific—protecting Diaoyu—has already become imminent."[24]

More than a decade later, however, Song's focus has shifted more to the West and America, in part because Japan was no longer worthy of being a primary target of Chinese nationalism. Song was one of five authors of another populist publishing triumph, *China Is Unhappy*, which became a best seller in China in 2009. The book calls for a break with the West and its model of capitalism and liberalism. Ironically, its principal author argues that Japan's state-directed form of capitalism, and protection of domestic industries against foreign competition, should be the model for China today.

"We should learn from Japan," proclaims Wang Xiaodong, a mathematician and economic management expert trained in part in Japan, who coauthored the book with Song. "Japan used state power to accelerate the development of high-tech industry. Had it operated entirely according to free-market principles, Japan would not have such advanced science and technology. In China, everyone was saying liberal economics was correct, but my teacher in Japan told me it's wrong. That was the first time I had ever heard someone say that Western economics was not right."[25]

Wang's advocacy of a strong China does not lead, however, to an embrace of Japan today. He is not interested in revisiting Japan's wartime crimes, but he is eager to take on Japan over oil and gas rights in the East China Sea and territorial issues, symbols of China's assertion of its interests. "Second, and more important, Japan is a U.S. ally and part of the military architecture that contains China. I think this is something we should think about more."[26]

Song, who was born in 1964 in the northeastern city of Dalian, once a center of Japanese influence, represents a Chinese generation that is postwar and post–early revolutionary. His parents, born in 1931 and 1938, reared him on tales of Japanese occupation and Chinese resistance. His father attended school in the Japanese puppet state of Manchukuo, where he was educated in Japanese (he taught Song some words of Japanese as a child). His mother recalled the occupation of her village on the Shandong Peninsula by Japanese troops. "One time the Japanese were burning down houses in the village," Song recounts his mother's story. "There was a retarded man there who didn't run away, so the Japanese took their bayonets and tried to push him into a burning house. But he clutched onto the bayonet, terrified, and refused to budge. Actually he survived the ordeal, and afterwards the villagers would tell it as a funny story."[27] His father described the Japanese as harsh but often as much toward their own troops as toward the Chinese. But the Koreans who served in the ranks of the Japanese army were the "worst," his father told Song. "They called these assimilated Koreans 'number two devils.'"

Song finished university in 1987 at a provincial Chinese school where he dreamed of becoming a writer. He neglected his classes in favor of a student poetry organization, the Summer Rain Poetry Society, many of whose leaders were later arrested and imprisoned as dissidents. Song was punished by being sent to work sites in the interior of China, eventually landing in the city of Chongqing, where he still lives, to work as a middle-school teacher. He quit, an act of rebellion even today, and made his living in a variety of jobs in advertising and as a journalist at a local television station, all while pursuing his literary dreams. His splash debut in the mid-1990s as a populist rabble-rouser fed his career as the author of increasingly popular television documentary programs, including a twenty-episode look at memories of Beijing.

Song embraces the style and language of an artist more than a nationalist agitator, dressing in jeans and a windbreaker, without the cool of Beijing's intelligentsia. For Song, the formation of memory is at the crux of his writing. "We were so closed off from the world for so long, then suddenly embraced it. We were so passionate about it, indiscriminately praising other countries, similarly indiscriminately berating ourselves, our culture, and our forefathers. So by the 1990s, we needed to take a step back, get back to our roots on an emotional level. I think that is primarily what I was trying to express."

Turning to Japan, Song also has evolved in his thinking from the mid-1990s, when he eagerly embraced the anti-Japanese nationalism of the day. Today, he says, "from the perspective of competing national interests, Japan is relatively harmless." He worries that pro-American Chinese intellectuals are too eager to encourage anti-Japan sentiments to confuse the younger generation. "The Chinese could learn a thing or two from the Japanese work ethic and their self-respect—cultural self-respect. The enmity between China and Japan at the popular level, judging from the Internet, has already reached a dangerous level that will be hard to rein in. Cynical youths can all use anti-Japan as a label. It is not serious."

It would be a mistake, however, to see Song's dismissal of such current anti-Japan sentiments as a retreat from a harsh judgment on imperial Japan's wartime role. In his view, the war began in 1931 with the Japanese occupation of Manchuria and the creation of the Manchukuo administration, which he regards as "a false state, an illegal state." Various parts of the Japanese state, led by the military but including others (though he regards the emperor as a figurehead in this process), made this move as a part of a larger aim. "Japan obviously wanted to annex China—that was the goal. This is not a matter of historical memory. Perhaps they had different methods for annexing China: one kind was what they did in Manchuria and the Mongolian border area, setting up false states as vassals of Japan; the other was direct colonial rule, as in Korea. . . . From the history I've learned, I truly believe that completely carving up China is what Japan was trying to accomplish."

Japanese criminality, as took place in Nanjing in 1937, is equally unambiguous to Song:

> The Japanese despised the Chinese in depths of their souls, and perhaps it was because they despised the Chinese that they were able to do such heinous things. So the wickedness of the Japanese and the atrocities they committed are embedded in the memories of several generations of Chinese, even if [for people who did not experience the events personally] these memories come from film, TV, or memoirs. I know that there were many massacres in the Northeast and, from recent revelations, massacres even as far south as Hubei. I think that the Nanjing Massacre was extreme, but it was part of the pattern of Japanese occupation of China. It was a method designed to wipe out any drop of courage among the Chinese. It was the same as the occupation strategy used by the Mongols. The Japanese were extremely evil—their rule of China was cruel. Even those who surrendered and the ordinary people were not safe. This has rarely happened in the history of the world. . . . China and Japan are always in dispute about the numbers of those killed in Nanjing. It's hard to say who is right and who is wrong about the particulars. Wouldn't it be best if both countries mobilized their human and material forces to clarify once and for all what really happened? Otherwise, this will be an endless headache. Japan should acknowledge its guilt—it has never really done so. As far as their leaders are concerned, yes, I know, the Socialist prime minister [Murayama] apologized, but I think that was just posturing. What I believe is that [the Nanjing Massacre] was a large-scale, planned killing.

Song does not hesitate to support the American decision to drop the atomic bombs on Japan. "If the war had continued much longer, Japan would really have fought to the bitter end," a judgment shared by many American observers. "Second, we in the East talk about cause and effect—karma. Throughout East Asia and China, Japan had carried out massacres. From the perspective of historical karma, the Japanese also had to suffer some consequences. I agree with what some Chinese scholars say about this—that the Japanese people were also guilty because they were the foundation on which militarism was built."

Song credits the United States and the Soviet Union equally with playing pivotal roles in the defeat of Japan, though he honors the Chinese for their prolonged resistance. The postwar tribunals were, if anything, too lenient in their judgment of Japanese criminality and too willing to let Japanese leaders live and soldiers to return home to espouse the views they had during the war. If this Chinese nationalist writer is willing to let Japan off the historical hook for the war, it is only to condemn the more immediate enemy today—the United States:

I think the U.S. forced Japan to declare war first, but the idea that Pearl Harbor was a [U.S.] conspiracy is going too far. Some people are saying that—that the U.S. deliberately allowed it to happen. But from the broader perspective, I do think the U.S. goaded Japan into it. This does seem quite likely, and the more I think about it, the more likely it seems. It is in keeping with the character of the U.S. I'm being very subjective, of course, but I do find this view very interesting.

## *Tong Zeng*

In a low-rise Beijing office building, down a bare corridor lit by fluorescent lights, the sign on a door proclaims the location of the China Fortune Investment Company. The spare furnishings of the offices behind the door provide no visible evidence of fortunes being earned. In the grandly labeled "Palaver Room," Tong Zeng, a slight, bespectacled man who describes himself as the company chairman, sits at a conference table.

As a Chinese businessman, Tong may not be a very imposing figure. But this is only one of his many identities. He is also the president of the China Federation for Defending the Diaoyu Islands, as well as the head of

Tong Zeng

the Chinese Association for Claiming Compensation from Japan. In those roles, Tong is a rare creature in the Chinese system—a citizen activist who almost single-handedly revived painful issues arising out of Japan's wartime role in China, including the forced recruitment of Chinese women into the brothels organized by the Imperial Army, the use of forced laborers by Japanese firms, and disputes over territory. Since the early 1990s, Tong led campaigns to bring these disputes to light, initially without the backing of the Chinese government and sometimes against its wishes, though at times with the encouragement, by his own account, of powerful forces within the Chinese Communist regime. His tale offers insights into not only the rise of popular Chinese nationalism but also the complicated relationship between China's citizens and its powerful state.

Tong's path to activism about the wartime period was far from predictable. He was born in 1956 in the former Nationalist wartime capital of Chongqing, the son of a KMT official-turned–factory engineer. His grandfather had also served as a senior official of the KMT. The family chose to shift their loyalties to the Communists, who took power in 1949. Tong grew up hearing almost nothing about the war, at home or in school. Like all Chinese children of his generation, his images of the war came solely from war movies such as *Tunnel Warfare* and *Landmine Warfare*, staples of Cultural Revolution–era propaganda about the feats of Communist guerrillas fighting the "Japanese devils." After being sent to the countryside during the final years of the Cultural Revolution, Tong gained entry into Sichuan University. There, he says, "I first had any real encounter with history books."[28]

At university, while studying economics and law, Tong came across the issue of reparations from Japan for the damage done during the war. In 1972, when China and Japan finally normalized diplomatic relations after decades of the Cold War, the Communist government decided to renounce any further claims for such reparations in exchange for massive Japanese loans, grants, and investment. With Soviet aid disappearing after the clashes of the Sino-Soviet split, Japan's assistance was vital to China's growth.

Tong went on to Peking University Law School in 1986 and then was assigned as an economics teacher at a chemical-industry management school. But the idea that China should not have renounced its claims to compensation stuck in his mind. Researching the case of reparations claims to a unified Germany by Eastern European countries, Tong concluded that even if the Chinese state renounced its claims, individuals should still be able to seek compensation. He authored a paper making this argument, but no one would publish it because it challenged the decisions of the Chinese government. Undaunted, Tong took his work in 1991 to delegates to the National People's Congress (NPC), the nominal parliament, in the form of a petition urging the NPC to authorize relevant departments to seek compensation from Japan for sufferings endured during the war. He found a handful of delegates who supported his cause, and, more importantly, his petition got coverage in foreign media as well as in Chinese media like the mainland-linked *Ming Pao*, a daily out of Hong Kong.

The petition, bearing the title "China's Demand for War Compensation Allows for No Further Delay," sought war-damage claims for Chinese people and property to the grandiose sum of $180 billion. "Japanese aggression from 1931 to 1945 inflicted untold sufferings on China," the document declared. "Millions of sons and daughters of China generously sacrificed their lives; 20 million more compatriots were either killed or wounded, while hundreds of millions of dollars [*sic*] worth of property went up in smoke. Whenever the Chinese people turn to this unparalleled page in history, they are overtaken by enormous grief and pain."[29]

The petition called on the NPC to create an association of Chinese war victims to investigate these crimes and register the claimants. It argued that this would be in compliance with international law, citing German compensation to Jews and Poles. The petition was blocked but the publicity led to the publication of Tong's article. By that time, he was working in a center for research on the elderly, where he encountered increasing numbers of victims of the Japanese wartime period seeking restitution. Some came in groups to find him at his workplace. Others sent letters, sometimes addressed to his name without an address. Many never reached him, but the ones that did were enough to begin to get the attention of the Chinese regime. "They were afraid of the masses getting riled up," Tong recounts. "China had already abandoned the pursuit of reparations, so they didn't want it raised again by us. Nevertheless, although there were restrictions, ordinary people continued to seek me out. Once they had found me, I would usually send [them] to the Japanese embassy."

The tales told by these Chinese covered a gamut of experiences. There were the Chinese who were taken to Japan to work in war factories, one of whom was in Hiroshima when the atomic bomb was dropped and survived. And there were "comfort women," who were taken to work in Japanese military-run brothels. Stories of Korean comfort women had begun to emerge in 1991, but the existence of large numbers of Chinese women forcibly recruited was not widely known.

Shanghai Normal University historian Su Zhiliang began to do research on this issue after coming to Tokyo University on a fellowship in 1991. A Japanese historian told him that the first "comfort station" had been established in Shanghai. The investigations Su began back in Shanghai in 1993 turned into two decades of work, led to four books on the subject, based on interviews with more than a hundred surviving women, and the creation of an archive of information on Chinese comfort women. Su, who has authored Chinese school textbooks used widely in Shanghai, believes that there could have been as many as two hundred thousand Chinese comfort women—a number that is close to previous estimates for the total numbers of women gathered for this purpose. "This is because the war was primarily fought in China," the historian argues. "The ubiquity and secrecy of this system far exceeded what we had originally imagined." His research found evidence of more than 140 comfort stations in Shanghai alone. Su, who was in close contact later with Tong, headed the Chinese delegation to various meetings with international activists, including the Japanese, and meetings such as the International Women's War Crimes Tribunal on Japan's Military Sexual Slavery, held in Tokyo in 2000.[30]

Those protest activities are viewed more favorably today, but, initially, Tong faced opposition from both the Japanese and Chinese governments. Japanese journalists and diplomats thought they saw the hand of the regime behind the demand for reparations. "Japanese journalists asked me whether the Chinese government was behind this," Tong says. "The Japanese ambassador also sought me out. He also asked me to tell him whether the Chinese government was backing me in this. But the Chinese government had renounced reparations claims to maintain good relations with Japan, so they pressured me." Tong was invited by Japanese activists to come and give lectures, but the Chinese government barred his exit. Tong had backers within the Communist regime:

> There were so many victims. More of them were coming out of the woodwork every day. There were too many to be suppressed. And there were people in the government who supported us. Backers would come and tell me they thought I was doing a good thing. . . . They told me that they also had victims

in their families, such as conscripted laborers.... No one would openly say they thought what I was doing was bad, of course. Had they done so, the ordinary people would have said they were selling out the country, that they were traitors.

But as Tong's efforts to organize victims became more public—often generating foreign press coverage—the Chinese security apparatus began to step in. Demonstrations of victims were suppressed. Whenever senior Japanese officials visited—as happened when the Japanese emperor and prime minister visited in 1992—Tong was quietly sent away to various tourist destinations on "business." In 1995, Tong planned to attend the United Nations World Conference on Women as a nongovernmental organization (NGO) delegate, where he planned to raise the issue of comfort women, but again, he was forced to leave Beijing until the meeting was over.

The winds began to shift from 1995 onward, as the Chinese regime began to quietly allow the anti-Japanese activists to surface, if not to encourage them when it suited its ends. "Things began to be a bit more liberal in China, and we were no longer seen as being antigovernment," Tong recounts. He worked with Japanese lawyers to file suit on behalf of Chinese laborers in Japanese courts in 1995—final verdicts came in the higher courts in 2007, turning down their claims. A legal Chinese NGO to pursue reparations from Japan was approved by the government. In 2001, Tong was allowed to go to Japan to attend a court hearing. Even so, he was fired from his job at the state research institute in 1998.

Tong's pursuit of compensation flows from his view of history and Japan's conduct of the war in Asia. For this Chinese activist, Japan's war crimes, from the massacre of civilians in Nanjing to the use of forced labor, are comparable to those of Nazi Germany, crimes for which Japan has failed to sufficiently atone. "Japan bears the responsibility for the war," Tong says. "In order to avoid repetition of the tragic wars of the past and prevent massacres from happening again, Japan should apologize, as Germany has done for all the Jews killed by Hitler. Only in this way can the Japanese people demonstrate that they will not commit war crimes again." Events such as those that took place in Nanjing may have been extreme, but the brutality displayed there was, in his view, "part of the Japanese national character." While today's Japanese and Germans may find this kind of behavior unimaginable, Tong says, this mind-set can reemerge under conditions of wartime expansion.

Tong places responsibility for the war not only on the Japanese military but also on the emperor and, indeed, on the entire society:

> I believe that all the people, including the ordinary people, caused the war. They supported the military—the military was just one institution that represented the people. The people served as soldiers; the army was made up of ordinary people. So the entire Japanese people are responsible—that includes the emperor, the military, ordinary people. They are all guilty.

The arc of the war, as Tong understands it, is one of steady Japanese colonial expansion guided by a long-term plan, beginning in 1931 with the seizure of Manchuria. He links the territorial disputes with Japan today with that history: "Expanding overseas is a Japanese tradition that has continued until today."

Tong took up the issue of the disputed islands—the Diaoyu Islands to the Chinese and the Senkaku Islands to the Japanese—in the mid-1990s, taking a lead from activists in Hong Kong. Initially his efforts were discouraged, but within a few years, as the Chinese Communists embraced the role of "patriotism," the movement to reclaim these islands from Japan gained steam, spurred in part by the growth of Internet-based nationalism. Tong and his followers organized a series of attempts to draw attention to this issue by landing activists on the islands, first in 2003 and more successfully in 2004, when a flotilla of fishing boats landed seven activists on the islands. They were arrested and deported by the Japanese authorities but returned home as heroes, celebrated not only by the nonofficial media but also by the Chinese Communist controlled outlets. At a time of growing tensions between China and Japan, propelled by the decision of the Japanese Prime Minister to officially visit Yasukuni, the Shinto shrine to Japan's war dead, Tong and his followers were now much more useful to the state. In the anti-Japanese demonstrations that swept across China in 2005, with the evident endorsement of the Chinese state through official media, Tong and his followers played a prominent role.

Now Tong's efforts to pursue compensation for Chinese laborers receive extensive coverage and support in the Chinese official media. His investment company was allowed to submit an application to China's State Oceanic Administration to develop the disputed islands for tourism in 2012, a move intended to counter the efforts of Japanese rightists to purchase the islands for allegedly similar goals. "I don't oppose the government, and

I speak for the Chinese government, so at the moment there are no restrictions on me," Tong says. In subsequent years, Tong remained free to operate, facing none of the political repression imposed on dissidents in China. But he offers the perhaps self-serving view that the activists force the hand of the government, which fears movements they cannot fully control. "They are passive," Tong says with evident disdain. "The government officials, mainly from the foreign ministry, think these issues are their province alone. They don't have the smarts to manipulate popular movements. What we do is all self-initiated, and they have no control over it. . . . If they really were able to use us to put pressure on Japan, Chinese society would certainly move forward."

The truth about the balance of initiative between Tong and his fellow nationalist activists and the role of the Communist Party and its state is hard to know. Undoubtedly, Tong's account is self-serving. But there is enough evidence to suggest that China has become a country where public opinion and civil movements are now actors in the formation of foreign policy.

### Zhang Zhenkun

Zhang Zhenkun was born on May 8, 1926, in a small village outside of the county seat of Shijiazhuang, in Hebei province, about one hundred miles southwest of Beijing. The son of a doctor, Zhang was sent to school from an early age, until his school life was interrupted by the outbreak of the Sino-Japanese War. The fighting, which had begun on the night of July 7, 1937, in Beijing, came quickly to his doorstep as advancing Japanese troops occupied the village.

Decades later, after a long career as an eminent historian and author of the most detailed and authoritative account of the Sino-Japanese War published in modern China, Zhang recounts his wartime memories with an alacrity and detail that testifies to the searing nature of the experience. It began with the arrival of a senior Japanese cavalry officer and his troops to their sprawling home, seized temporarily as their headquarters to prepare the attack on nearby Shijiazhuang.

> When the Japanese came to our house, we hid, of course. We had a big family—there were more than twenty of us—and we lived in a very large house with three courtyards. We ran to the rearmost room, which was my grandparents'

Zhang Zhenkun

room. My grandparents went outside to deal with the Japanese, and we waited. We soon heard the sound of their boots as they came into the courtyard. We crouched down next to the *kang* [a heated sleeping platform] so we couldn't be seen by the Japanese. The door was locked. Then they knocked on the door of the room. It was a moment of terror. My grandfather had accompanied them into the courtyard. He told them there was no one in the room, but they weren't deceived. They kept banging on the door very hard, so my grandfather finally called on us to come out. We were terrified.[31]

Out in the courtyard, a Japanese officer handed Zhang's grandfather an official document—a declaration from Japanese Imperial Army Command that they were seizing their house. The discovery of a letter from his father, sent from Japanese-occupied Dalian where he was working as a doctor, seemed to harden the attitude of the Japanese officers. The family was sent to the one-room home of a neighbor. Japanese soldiers kept coming by, opening the door, looking in menacingly, and then leaving. "They certainly didn't have good intentions," Zhang recalls.

Zhang's grandfather moved the family back to live in a tiny, dilapidated space next to the main building of their home compound. They spread straw on the ground and slept there, next to an open space now filled with Japanese soldiers and their horses. "It was at this time that we discovered there were Chinese and Koreans among the Japanese troops," serving mostly as translators. "Actually we hardly slept as there were a lot of shells exploding. This was the Japanese attacking Shijiazhuang. There were dazzling flashes as the shells went off close to our village. The Japanese soldiers kept coming over to monitor us. My grandfather was very worried and, on the second or third day, decided it was unsafe," says Zhang.

The family members crept out at dawn and made their way to Zhang's mother's home village, still unoccupied by the Japanese, about four miles to the north. They stayed there for more than a month, returning only after the Japanese troops had departed. His grandfather had narrowly escaped death at the hands of the Japanese, a bullet barely missing him when the officer's horse reared up, startled by the gunfire. Their home was a mess, ripped apart by the occupiers. "Someone had even defecated on the *kang*. This made a deep impression on me."

The following year, Zhang joined a propaganda team of the Communist Party's Eighth Route Army guerrilla forces who arrived near the village. "All of us, we school pupils, were very patriotic. We hated the Japanese very deeply. So when the propaganda team came to village, I voluntarily joined the team." But when the Japanese army returned to clear out the Communist-led guerillas, the team leader sent him home, deciding he was too young to flee with them. After a few months, his mother and grandfather sent him to a Catholic school—the only one still functioning after the Japanese shut down the other schools. In 1939, Zhang was sent to a Catholic middle school in Beijing, run by Germans who effectively protected them from the Japanese. But there was an American superintendent, Father Rosslyn, who was taken prisoner after the attack on Pearl Harbor, when the school was briefly shut down.

"Father Rosslyn taught us to be patriotic. He often told us, 'Your country is now occupied by the Japanese. You have to study hard so that when you grow up, you may serve your own country.'" Several teachers at the school were involved with the underground resistance movement run by the Kuomintang (KMT), the Nationalist government. More than seventy students and teachers from Fu Jen University, to which the school was attached, were arrested in a Japanese sweep in 1944, which stunned Zhang. Along with others, he made his way to the Nationalist wartime capital of Chongqing, where he entered university, finishing his degree in Nanjing in 1949, just as the Communists came to power.

Zhang's wartime experiences set the stage for a career as a historian, a dedication that survived the vicissitudes of Communist rule. His graduate training at Peking University ended in 1951 when Zhang, along with all the professors and students, were dispatched to Guangxi Province to participate in Communist land-reform campaigns. After graduation, he was about to be sent to carry out literacy campaigns in northern China, when the great post-1949 Chinese historian Fan Wenlan rescued him and brought him to the newly established Institute of Modern History in the Chinese Academy of Sciences. Zhang, who never joined the Communist Party, was assigned to a group researching the modern history of Sino-foreign relations, tasked with writing a book titled *The History of the Imperialist Invasion of China*, the first of a four-volume work intended to cover the period from the Opium Wars, beginning in 1840, to the establishment of the People's Republic of China in 1949.

The first volume was completed in 1957 and published the following year, just in time to be met with one of the major turns in Communist China—the antirightist movement. The book was vehemently attacked as a rightist work—the second volume would not appear until after the end of the Cultural Revolution, two decades later, when the Chinese Academy of Social Sciences (CASS) was established. During that time, Zhang helped write a three-volume history of modern China, which, too, was published only later. Like many others, he was sent off to the countryside to labor, participating in one mass mobilization campaign after another. "We didn't finish any of our work. We didn't have much time to write, and the manuscripts we did write were not published. Moreover, our institute did not want us to work individually—writing was to be done collectively."

Zhang, in his fifties, embarked finally on the most important work of his life, reaching back to the formative experience of his childhood to become the foremost historian of China's conflict with Japan. In 1982, the problem of wartime history erupted as an issue between China and Japan after the infamous decision by Japanese educational authorities to instruct textbook writers to remove references to Japan's "invasion" of China and replace it with more innocuous language about Japan's "advance" into the continent.

Word came down to Zhang from the Chinese authorities. "They demanded that we write some articles criticizing Japan, the Japanese invaders, [and] the Japanese senior government officials for distorting the history of the War of Resistance against Japan," he recalls. "We had to write articles criticizing them. We ourselves came to the conclusion that it would be better to write a book than a few articles." Zhang became the chief editor among the group of historians who proceeded to write what is still regarded as the most detailed Chinese account of Japan's imperialist expansion onto the Chinese mainland. *The 70 Year History of Japanese Aggression Against China*, a title that leaves little doubt as to the tilt of the volume, was finished in 1987 but not published until 1992. A second book, containing an even more detailed history of the eight-year Sino-Japanese War (1937–1945) was published in 1997. *The History of the War of Resistance Against Japan*, as it was titled, was translated into Japanese, the only time this was done. The books carefully kept to the orthodoxies of the Chinese Communist historiography, particularly the downplaying of the role of the KMT in the war against Japan. "Everyone wrote in accordance with the CCP's view," Zhang says. "The party didn't need to interfere."

Zhang's view of the wartime period remains shaped not only by his personal experience but also by a clearly patriotic understanding of history. He is not, however, a dogmatist—a trait he shared with his mentor, the historian Fan Wenlan. On key issues about the Sino-Japanese War, he is not afraid to express his own views, gesturing expressively with his hands as he talks in a meeting room of the academy, whose offices occupy old low buildings down a quiet, central Beijing side street.

Zhang shares the classical, Marxist historical view that downplays the role of individual Japanese leaders, such as Tojo Hideki, in the decision to go to war against China. "Japan as a whole wanted to invade and occupy China, to rule China," he says. "When we speak of Japan's invasion of China, we usually blame Tojo because he expanded the war, but I think Japan's entire militaristic system was at work." While Zhang pays slight homage to the view that Japan was pursuing a rivalry with other imperialist powers, such as Britain, to secure its control of China, for the most part, he places Japan in a separate category, noting that Britain and the United States "were on our side." While Western powers initially used force when they came to China, their pursuit of economic gain was "more peaceable than [that of] the Japanese," he argues. "Japanese colonialism affected everything—it was more severe."

When it comes to key moments in the war that remain a subject of intense controversy, particularly between Japanese and Chinese historians, Zhang has little patience for dispute. The Marco Polo Bridge Incident, the exchange of fire on the night of July 7, 1937, that triggered the wider war, "was not planned," says Zhang. The incident "was largely by chance," he says, a view that used to be beyond the pale in China. "But Japan had long before that thought about invading China from the north. That was a plan, especially after 1935 to 1936, when Japan began to consolidate its control in northern China. So, by the time 1937 arrived, such an incident was inevitable. Some Japanese scholars emphasize the question of who fired first. This is meaningless. Even if a Chinese had fired first, it is still meaningless because they were on Chinese soil, occupying Chinese territory."

Zhang has even less use for those who deny the mass killings in the seizure of the Chinese capital of Nanjing in 1937, though he does not swear by the Chinese official claims of some three hundred thousand victims. The number may not be certain, the historian says. "Massacre is certainly the right term to describe what happened, though I don't emphasize the number of people killed."

The historian takes a carefully balanced view on the question of whether China can claim responsibility for the defeat of Japan—a contention that long formed a central part of Communist accounts of the war:

> It is widely believed among the Japanese that Japan was defeated by the U.S.—that they lost to the U.S. and not to China. Conversely, in China, we say that China defeated Japan. In my opinion, Japan surrendered because they could not withstand the U.S. attack, not because they could not withstand the Chinese attack. Nevertheless, China still played a major role in defeating Japan that must be acknowledged. I've heard Western writings generally do not say much about China's role in resisting Japan during World War II and sometimes omit it altogether. I think that is not right.

Chinese troops tied down the bulk of Japan's army, making it impossible to redeploy it elsewhere, Zhang says. While China suffered huge casualties, it also inflicted great losses on the Japanese during the long war—a war that Japanese leaders never anticipated when they invaded in 1937.

Zhang also offers his own take on the issue of responsibility for the war in Japan. The orthodox view, offered first by Mao Zedong, placed responsibility solely on Japan's military leadership, removing the burden from the shoulders of the population itself. Zhang argues differently:

Japan had a global strategy in which the military, the government, and the cultural sphere were all complicit. The emperor was also responsible. All policies required his approval. Whether the emperor simply allowed them to make such schemes is hard to say, but he certainly bears some responsibility. In China, we always say the war was initiated by the rulers or a minority—that ordinary people were not responsible, that the war brought terrible suffering to the Chinese people but that the Japanese people also suffered. For propaganda purposes, it is fine, but, in fact, based on what I have read, I think the Japanese people are also responsible. They were not the instigators, but they were supporters. The vast majority of Japanese people supported the invasion of China. There is no question about this. After Nanjing fell, Tokyo held a celebration that many people attended. Very few opposed the war.

The American decision to drop the atomic bombs on Japan may not have been morally justified, Zhang opines, "but in terms of justice, I think it was completely justified." It hastened Japan's surrender—ordinary Japanese suffered, he acknowledges, but "from a harsher perspective, we can say that this was the price they paid for supporting the war."

Zhang gives a nod to the view, still embodied in Chinese textbooks, that Soviet entry into the war in its final days also hastened Japan's surrender. But with a wave of his hands, Zhang dismisses the Soviet decision as "opportunistic," grabbing a share of a victory that would have been won without them. Stalin was out to regain a foothold in northeast China to pursue Soviet interests.

When it comes to Japan's readiness to deal with its wartime past, Zhang is equally harsh in his assessment. "Japan has never properly apologized," he says, and he condemns the failure to offer compensation to war victims as taking advantage of the Cold War realities after the war.

As China's eminent historian of the Sino-Japanese War, Zhang is not concerned much with his audience outside of China. He has never exchanged views with Western historians, and he has limited contact with his Japanese counterparts. For Zhang, it is enough to stay true to recounting a history that began, for him, in a small village in northern China, with the arrival of the Japanese cavalry.

THREE

# Confronting Collaboration in Korea

Seoul's Dongnimmun, or Independence Gate, a stone archway modeled on the Arc de Triomphe in Paris, was erected in 1897 to mark Korea's bid to gain full independence from its status as a protectorate of imperial China. A short walk away stands Seodaemun Prison, a monument to Korea's loss of that independence to the rising imperial power in East Asia, Japan.

Seodaemun Prison is a dreary complex of red brick buildings, built by the Japanese in 1908, shortly after their forces came to occupy Korea. During the almost four decades of Japanese rule, tens of thousands of political prisoners passed through the prison. It was infamous in the lore of Korean resistance to Japanese colonialism. Beginning in the late 1980s, the prison was gradually converted into a public memorial and finally into a museum that opened its doors in 1998. Hordes of schoolchildren now visit the prison museum, trooping dutifully past carefully recreated prison cells where wax figures of Korean prisoners and their Japanese guards are depicted. Scenes of torture are graphically presented, along with information on the famous prisoners who died there from torture and malnutrition. "Korean Patriots who were confined at Seodaemun Prison had to groan under brutal torture by the Japanese authorities. The Japanese carried out inhumane torture on the prisoners, many of whom died or became disabled in the prison as a result of the torture itself and the aftereffect," reads one plaque, accompanied by images of prisoners. One of the most well known of these prisoners whose images are displayed in the Hall of National Resistance is the patriotic martyr Ryu Kwansun, whom Korean schoolchildren call "Sister Ryu

An exhibit at the Seodaemun Prison Museum showing a Japanese soldier with a bound Korean prisoner. Source: © Bryan Dorrough (via Flickr).

Kwansun." Ryu was a core organizer of the March 1st Movement of 1919. She was eventually arrested and sentenced to three years of imprisonment at Seodaemun Prison; however, she died in prison a year later, at the age of eighteen, as a result of regular beatings and extremely severe forms of torture. Reportedly, her final words were "Even if my fingernails are torn out, my nose and ears are ripped apart, and my legs and arms are crushed, this physical pain does not compare to the pain of losing my nation. My only remorse is not being able to do more than dedicating my life to my country."[1]

The Seodaemun Prison museum is a powerful depiction of the central narrative of modern Korean national identity: a tale of foreign invasion and the struggle for independence, and a self-image of victimization at the hands of cruel invaders and of heroic resistance. That narrative encapsulates Korea's historical role as the smaller power of Northeast Asia, trapped between two giants—China and Japan—and often trampled as a battleground for competing great powers, including nearby Russia and distant America. From the late nineteenth century to the mid-twentieth century, Korea was engaged in three major wars between foreign powers—namely, the Sino-Japanese War (1894–1895), the Russo-Japanese War (1904–1905), and the Korean War (1950–1953), which expanded to engage China, Russia, and the United States. This experience of being pushed over by greater powers created the mentality that Korea is a "shrimp among the whales." For Koreans, the drive to escape from this fate and to assert their own claim to great power status in the region is an enduring feature of not only public policy but also popular culture.

The desire to assert Korean national independence has, at times, an almost desperate quality, evoking wrought emotions that are easily tapped. In that emotional landscape, anti-Japanese feelings are the most deeply entrenched. Even decades after the end of Japanese rule, the imagery and events of the colonial and wartime era are remarkably fresh. Emblematic acts, such as the Japanese decision to force their Korean subjects to adopt Japanese names, remain powerful symbols of the loss of identity. The forced mobilization of Koreans to labor in Japanese mines and factories, or elsewhere in the Japanese wartime empire, has left a legacy of unresolved feelings and issues, including suits filed in Japanese courts seeking compensation for forced labor (see chapter 6).

The two countries did not normalize their diplomatic relations until 1965, some twenty years after the end of the war, despite the fact that both countries were allied to the United States. The normalization came primarily on a geopolitical basis, and historical reconciliation was put aside for the sake of peaceful cooperation on other, seemingly more important issues of that time. Relations between Japan and Korea greatly improved thereafter but still are subject to rapid swings toward tension, even more so in recent years, often provoked by what appear to be minor incidents.

The most emotionally wrenching aspect of that legacy resurfaced in the early 1990s, ironically because of the efforts of Japanese scholars, who unearthed evidence in Japan's archives of the forced recruitment of tens of thousands of Korean women (and other Asian women—even Japanese women) into sexual slavery in brothels organized by the Japanese Imperial Army to service soldiers across the vast Pacific battlefield. The tale of these "comfort women" has become a powerful symbol of Korean victimization. The aging victims of that system still gather to protest the failure, in their eyes, of the Japanese government to adequately recognize and compensate them for their forced prostitution. On March 1, 2015, President Park Geun-hye, in a speech marking the ninety-sixth commemoration ceremony of the

March 1st Movement, urged Japanese leaders to offer an apology and called Tokyo to use all means to resolve the issue, as the number of survivors rapidly dwindles. "We now have only 53 survivors, aged nearly 90 on average. Time is running out to restore their honor," said Park.[2]

The wartime past echoes in other ways in Korea. The ongoing territorial dispute between Japan and South Korea over the control of a small group of islets—Dokdo to the Koreans and Takeshima to the Japanese—located between the two countries is a direct consequence of the postwar settlement orchestrated by the United States. The territorial issue, often fed by disputes over the content of Japanese history textbooks, is almost a constant in the relationship, a steady reminder of the tortured past. The Korean government, starting in the early 1990s, has taken extensive efforts to "destroy bad legacies of Japan" in various ways, including demolishing buildings dating from the colonial period and changing Korean words that have a Japanese origin. For example, the general government building of colonial Korea, which had served as Seoul's major landmark since 1916, was taken down in 1995 because it reminded Korean people of the unfortunate era of colonial rule, and the Korean word for elementary school (*gungmin hakgyo*), which has roots in Japanese, was changed to *chodenng hakgyo* in 1994.

At the same time, however, the construction of historical memory remains an ongoing enterprise in Korea, one that is in some significant ways still a subject of controversy within the country. Less than an hour's train ride from the South Korean capital, outside of the city of Cheonan, the South Korean government constructed a national museum dedicated to the struggle against Japanese colonial rule. The Independence Hall of Korea is a sprawling complex of stone pavilions and modern exhibition halls set against a backdrop of forested hills. On a recent snowy weekday in December, the only visitors were small groups of schoolchildren and new recruits to the armed forces, marching through the exhibitions for the purposes of patriotic education.

The entrance hall offers an overview of some five thousand years of Korean history, from the prehistoric period to the modern era. From there, however, the exhibit offers an excruciatingly detailed rendition of the advance of Japanese imperialism into the Korean peninsula, the reaction of Koreans to the loss of their independence, and the ongoing struggle against "attempts to distort the country's national history" by Japan and others. *Torture Done by Japan,* a life-size display featuring some unfortunate mannequins, is one of the most popular exhibits. Like the Seodaemun Prison Museum, the hall recreates scenes of Japanese brutality, with torture implements on display, bloodstained walls, loudspeakers playing victims' screams, and mannequins of Japanese assailants and Korean victims. The hall also presents a classic tale of colonialism and resistance, with scant reference to those Koreans who supported Japan, benefited from its rule, and actively collaborated as members of the Japanese Imperial Army, as police officers, or even as guards in the prisoner-of-war camps in Southeast Asia.

The museum brushes aside the debate, now more vibrant in Korea, about the modernizing impact of colonial rule. "Japan looted Korea economically," the museum exhibit explains. "Korea was turned into a base for the supply of raw materials and cheap labor to Japan." The plundering of Korea is later linked broadly to Japan's "aggressive war," but otherwise the museum does not mention the Japanese invasion of China or the broader context of Japanese colonial policy, including the forced mobilization of labor that was prompted by the morass in China and the tide of defeat in the Pacific.

Most of the exhibit space is devoted to a detailed rendition, often accompanied by life-size dioramas, of every aspect of Korean resistance, from the student movements and exiled political groups to armed guerrilla movements (though without a nod to the Communist role in those movements). Dioramas show the Japanese torturing Korean prisoners, beating them to gain information. Others display the fate of the comfort women, the Korean women dragooned into brothels organized by the Japanese military to service its soldiers. The war's end is portrayed as the victory of Korean dedication to independence—there is barely any mention of the U.S. war in the Pacific.

This rendition of the wartime and colonial period is closely mirrored in Korean high-school history textbooks, which offer extended accounts of the colonial period, Japanese brutality and repression, exploitation of Korea, and Korean resistance. But they provide almost no context for these acts. There is very little teaching about the war that shaped the intensification of Japanese brutality and forced labor—indeed, Korean students are taught almost nothing about the Japanese invasion of China or the circumstances that led to Japan's surrender. The atomic bombing of Japan, in which tens of thousands of Koreans were also killed, is not even included in the ministry of education's history textbook, the main textbook in use in Korean schools.[3]

The question of collaboration is perhaps the thorniest one, and its avoidance in the museum is not surprising. The museum was built in the 1980s under the Chun Doo-hwan regime, at a time when it was facing growing resistance from within the country by students, human-rights activists, and others. The museum clearly reflects the desire to wrap authoritarian rule in the mantle of nationalism. Ironically, the museum opened its doors on the anniversary of liberation, August 15, 1987, less than two months after popular revolt forced the Chun regime to agree to free elections.

Korean democratization brought with it an effort to reopen the unhealed wounds of the Korean colonial experience. During democratic struggles, activists challenged not only the authoritarian regime but also its officially sanctioned view of colonial history. The new interpretation questioned elite-based views of history and sought to reexamine the people's struggles against foreign powers throughout Korean history. One radical reading circle studying "national liberation movements" explained the necessity for rethinking the colonial period's popular movements as follows: "The colonial period is not simply an era of the past but constitutes a critical part of the present. A proper understanding of the colonial period's struggles against foreign powers is essential to analyzing the nature and historical implications of transformative movements since 1945."[4] What was at stake, as Lee Namhee indicates, was the power to "reinterpret historical events hidden from the knowledge of the people and long co-opted and distorted by the power-that-be."[5] In this process of reexamining colonial history, Korean collaboration became an important and contentious issue as the initiative to prosecute collaborators and "set history right" increasingly gained public support. At the same time, many prominent Korean leaders, including former president Park Chung-hee, were found to have collaborated with the colonial authorities during the war years. As Mark Caprio points out, motivations for Korean collaboration may have been diverse, from sheer survival to capitalist interests; nevertheless, Korean collaboration could no longer be concealed in the history of modern Korea.[6]

The election of two successive progressive governments, beginning in 1997 with the victory of longtime opposition leader Kim Dae-jung, led to organized efforts to delve into previously hidden sore spots, among them the role of collaborators, the massacres of Korean leftists in the South during the early years after liberation, and American killings of civilians during the Korean War. Following passage of an act titled Clearing Up Past

Incidents for Truth and Reconciliation, a commission was formed in 2005 to investigate abuses under Japanese rule and the period of authoritarian government in South Korea.

In its official history, published after the Truth and Reconciliation Commission finished its work in 2010, the commission bemoaned the failure to "purge the legacy of the colonial rule" in the immediate aftermath of the war.[7] In 1948, under the newly established Rhee Syngman government, a Special Investigation Committee on Pro-Japanese and Anti-national Activities (*banmin teugwi*) was formed to address the question of Korean collaboration with Japanese rule. The committee handled 682 cases, 559 of which were handed over to a special prosecutor's office, which then handed down indictments in 221 cases. A special tribunal tried 38 cases and sentenced guilty verdicts and punishments in 12 cases, including one death sentence. Civil rights were suspended in 18 others, 6 were declared innocent, and the remaining 2 were found guilty but were exempted from punishment. The committee was under increasing political pressure to dissolve and did not survive even for a year.

The Truth and Reconciliation Commission puts the blame for the unsuccessful purge of traitors and dissolution of the special committee initially on the Americans, who established a temporary military occupation of the southern half of the peninsula—the Soviet Union was given the north as its occupation area—which lasted until 1948. "Despite widespread public support, however, the purge of collaborators was not easy under the American military occupation," states the commission report. "Out of convenience and necessity, the U.S. occupation government called back into service many of the government officials and police and military officers who had worked for the Japanese colonial government."[8] In the emergent ideological divisions of a divided Korea, the newly formed South Korean government led by Rhee Syngman in 1948 also protected some of these collaborators who were "his men" and loyal servants to his government. Right-wing political leaders such as Rhee and Kim Gu held that the establishment of a strong independent Korean government should take precedent over the punishment of collaborators, while left-wing political leaders felt that collaborators should be excluded entirely from participation in the formation of an independent Korean government. This ideological conflict between the left and right of the political leadership of liberated Korea complicated the issue of punishing the collaborators, and, as the matter had not been resolved, the purge of the pro-Japan collaborators remained an issue dormant but ready to explode, the commission report concluded.

Alongside the commission, private groups also formed to investigate the role of "pro-Japanese collaborators." In 2009, a three-thousand-page "dictionary" of collaborators was published by the Institute for Research in Collaborationist Activities. Altogether, 4,389 people were named in the reference work, among them former president Park Chung-hee. The publication intervened in a struggle over Korean history that had been broadly suppressed during the decades of authoritarian rule.

"The dictionary is significant as a record of the history of the collaborators," says progressive novelist Cho Jeong Rae, a board member of the institute, in an interview with us.

> It is a disgrace and misfortune of our nation that we could not resolve this issue just after liberation. We lost our national dignity and social order as a result of that failure. The policy agenda just after 1945, in both Koreas, was two things: to purge the pro-Japanese collaborators and the unconditional confiscation of their land and its redistribution for free. Unfortunately, we lost that opportunity and went for sixty-four years—longer than the colonial period—without any legislative action or resolution. Almost 99 percent of the collaborators have passed away in the meantime. But this doesn't mean we should discard the issue now. . . . How can we demand apology from Japan when we ourselves cannot resolve the domestic collaborator issue?[9]

The view of the past from Korean conservatives is, as one might expect, diametrically opposed. The dictionary "was compiled by a pro-North, leftist group," asserts Cho Gap Je, a journalist and the author of numerous books on Korean contemporary history, including a twelve-volume biography of Park. "Their acts are all based on ideology and propagandistic intention. The production of the dictionary is intended to attack the people who contributed to the building of South Korea. It sensationalizes the history of pro-Japanese activities," says Cho.[10] (The ideological battle led the conservative government of Lee Myung-bak to publish in return a list of one hundred pro–North Korea, antinational activists in 2010 under the Committee for Restoration of National Normalcy.)

Cho himself was born just after the end of the war in Japan, where his father had worked in the construction business since 1938, returning home only in 1946. Cho's family history illustrates the complexity of those who can be labeled "pro-Japanese." The term was originally limited to Koreans who had served in the Japanese police forces, which were notorious for their role in suppressing Korean resistance. "But I cannot agree to the broader definition used for the dictionary," Cho says, which includes people like Park.

This conflict has made its way into popular culture. The 2005 film *Blue Swallow* offered a somewhat heroic portrait of Park Kyung-won, an early Korean female pilot who was trained by the Japanese. Park took part in a "friendship" flight to Japanese-occupied Manchuria, earning her the label of pro-Japanese collaborator. The film proved to be highly controversial in Korea.

For some Korean historians, both the dictionary and the commission are problematic efforts to deal with a complex past. "I still have a picture of my father in a Japanese colonial uniform," says historian Kim Yeong Dok, who was tabbed to head the Northeast Asia History Foundation, a government effort to deal with international conflicts over the wartime past. "You need to try to find willing supporters with the intention of being harmful to Korea."[11]

Among Korean historians, an increasingly fierce debate has emerged about "colonial modernization," the argument that Japanese colonial rule created the basis for Korea's later economic development through the building of infrastructure, the fostering of education, and the development of industry. Leading scholars of this so-called New Right view are Ahn Byeong-jik and Lee Young-hoon of Seoul National University, who argue that colonial modernization not only refers to modernization of production facilities and infrastructure but also includes the modernization of the market economy, institutional modernization, and the modernization of law and other social systems. Progressives reject this argument, responding that even if Japanese rule contributed to modernization, it was done only to facilitate colonial rule and exploitation, with no benefits for Koreans. They also maintain that colonial modernization explains only economic modernization, not political, societal, or cultural modernization.

After colonial rule ended, a major task for Korean historians was to refute the colonialist view of Japanese rule—that is, that Japan modernized Korea through colonization. The new nationalist historiography portrayed Japanese rule as exploitative and distortive of Korea's path to the modern world. Accordingly, their research focus was to prove that Japanese rule had destroyed "sprouts of capitalism" and delayed Korean modernization. They also paid keen attention to the economic sufferings of Koreans.[12]

Beginning in the 1980s, however, this nationalist perspective was challenged and reexamined both inside and outside of the Korean academic community, especially by economic historians in Korea, Japan, and the United States.[13] These scholars sought to study the colonial period from more objective scholarly perspectives beyond the value-laden colonialist and nationalist views. Soon-Won Park lists four factors responsible for the change: (1) South Korea's success and corresponding self-confidence, (2) academic interest in examining Korea's colonial record, (3) the increasing importance of the colonial period in understanding the complex and diverse nature of the present-day South Korean economy, and (4) improvements in Korean higher education.[14]

In particular, this new scholarship focused on examining the socioeconomic changes from the intensive wartime industrial growth in the late colonial period. It reexamined the conventional interpretation of growth as enclave-style development, using more sophisticated social scientific research methods. The industrialization of this period was recast as colonial, dependent development, insufficient for full-scale modernization but sufficiently substantial to create an early state of economic growth during the 1960s. This colonial modernization perspective has rejected the dichotomies of development versus exploitation or suppression versus resistance by trying to offer more nuanced descriptions of socioeconomic changes under Japanese rule.

While this new perspective has gained much recognition by the 1990s, it also had provoked a strong reaction on the part of nationalist scholars. "Discussing the question of whether Japanese rule contributed to the modernization of Korea is like stepping into a minefield," writes Korean scholar Chulwoo Lee. "The pompous claims of Japanese colonialists that they were modernizing Korean society and the use of those claims to justify colonial rule are vivid memories for Koreans, as is the support many contemporary Westerners gave Japanese imperialism for bringing the blessings of modernity to Asia. Moreover, under the sway of modernization theory, postwar Western scholars have tended to credit Japanese rule for the material and institutional changes that occurred during the colonial period."[15]

These debates have become embroiled in parallel discussions among Japanese academics. There is growing interaction between Korean and Japanese progressives and between the Korean New Right historians and their colleagues in Japan. For instance, a group of Korean and Japanese economic historians collaborated to publish a book titled *The Economic Structure of Modern Korea*, which illustrates how the colonial period laid the basic infrastructure for Korea's modern economy.[16] In the United States, a group of scholars working on colonial Korea also challenged the nationalist master narratives through the larger framework of "colonial modernity." They sought to offer "more inclusive, pluralist approaches" to the study of colonial Korea so that they could recover "silenced voices and subjects of history held hostage by master nationalist narratives."[17] Thus, as in China, the debates on colonial modernity within Korea have become intertwined with those in Japan and even in U.S. academic circles.

## Cho Jeong Rae

A conversation with Cho Jeong Rae is a blur of activity. The Korean novelist leans over the table to address his interlocutors, his hands gesturing

Cho Jeong Rae

constantly. He laughs as he tells a story of his childhood and is animated as he discusses Japan's colonial rule of his country. His voice grows louder and punctuates his stories with oratory moments, his fingers banging against the tabletop for emphasis.

Cho does not hesitate to display a fierce nationalism and an undiminished animosity toward Japan. "The United States shouldn't feel guilty for dropping the atomic bomb on Japan," Cho pronounces, in a wide-ranging discussion of the war. "It was the best thing the U.S. has done."[18]

Cho's own life has been a similar blur of activity, a massive outpouring of literature that sought to communicate a powerful and sharply drawn vision of Korea's modern history. In a flow of writing that began in 1970 with short stories, Cho's output has included a trilogy of multivolume epic novels written over a twenty-year span, beginning in the early 1980s. They cover the sweep of Korean history from the colonial era, through the crucial five-year period between the liberation of Korea from Japanese rule to the Korean War, to the era of Park Chung-hee's rule in South Korea, which is covered in his most recent novel. "There is no nation that has a history as tragic and gruesome as we do," Cho says in an interview about his trio of historical books. "As a writer, I felt I should write about this 100 years of history," describing the span from the beginning of the twentieth century. For him, it is a "history of suffering."[19]

The most controversial of Cho's works dealt with the division of Korea and the events leading to the Korean War. Cho broke from the postwar South Korean narrative of a Manichean struggle between an evil Communist North that invaded a victimized and united South. Instead, he told the morally ambiguous tale of a country deeply split, even in the South, between advocates of social and political revolution and a conservative ruling elite, many of whom were part of the colonial system. His first epic novel, *Taebaek Mountain Range*, focuses on the struggles of a group of left-wing partisans in the mountains of southern Korea during the first years after the division of the country. Rather than a tale of North Korean invasion, the book portrays the main threat to the South Korean government at the time as coming from an indigenous Communist insurgency. Cho's clearly left-wing views got him into political hot water: he was accused of violations of the country's National Security Law for his account of the division of the country, which delayed publication of the book. Despite that, his trilogy set a publishing record for Korea—some ten million copies have been sold—and brought him numerous literary awards. *Taebaek Mountain Range* was made into a major film by one of Korea's most famous film directors, Im Kwon Taek.

Cho's tale of the Japanese colonial period appeared in 1995, written as a prequel to *Taebaek*. This tale of colonial rule, *Arirang*, is set in the Gimje plain, a rich rice-growing area in Korea's North Jeolla province. Cho portrays it as a "land of sorrow," exploited to grow food for the Japanese Empire. Cho stirred controversy internationally by asserting that the treatment of Koreans by the Japanese was in some ways even worse than the treatment of Jews by the Nazis.

Cho claimed that three to four million Koreans died at the hand of the Japanese. "The Jews were killed for three years," he writes in the introduction to the novel, referring to the period of the German "Final Solution," from 1942 to 1945. "But Koreans were killed during a period of more than ten times . . . that, 36 years. Which people suffered more?" And yet, he argues, the experience of the Jews is widely known, while that of Koreans is forgotten, even avoided. "When naked Jewish girls were dying in gas chambers, the girls of our people were getting gang raped in Southeast Asian jungles," he writes, referring to the sexual servitude of Korean women in Japanese Imperial Army brothels. "So how have we become such ignorant masses?" Jews, Cho continues, have used their suffering to secure their self-esteem, to develop their future as a people. Koreans, in contrast, are guilty of simply living in shame. But, he concludes, it is not too late "to know the history correctly."[20]

Cho's own personal history clearly informs his literary history. He was born at the Sonam Buddhist temple in Korea's South Jeolla province, a center of radicalism in the country. His father was a monk who had entered the temple at the age of sixteen, gaining the status of a full member at the age of twenty-four. Following the Japanese custom, he got married at the age of twenty-eight, in 1930. He had eight children—Cho was the fourth son, born in 1943. The liberation of Korea from Japanese rule in 1945 brought with it growing turmoil, especially in that region, as left-wing protests broke out against the conservative government of former exile leader Rhee Syngman. Cho's father, now a leader of his temple, was an active participant in those rebellions.

The protest culminated in the famous Yeosu-Suncheon Rebellion, which broke out in October 1948 as left-wing military refused to participate in the suppression of a Communist insurgency on nearby Jeju Island. Soon, civilian protestors joined, and it grew into a broader movement to establish a "peoples' republic" in the province, targeting the government's military and those accused of being collaborators with Japanese rule. Cho's father was arrested in the brutal crackdown that followed and released only after the intervention of fellow Buddhist monks. By Cho's account, his father retreated to a life as a poet and a teacher of Korean language and literature in a local middle school.

Cho absorbed the memory of this period from his family. When he reached his teens, he began to doubt what he was being taught in school and started collecting documents of his family history and the firsthand experiences of family members, already thinking about writing his own version of this history. As a student of Korean literature at Dongguk University, Cho was preparing to pen novels based on this family history. *Taebaek Mountain Range* was a direct product of that decision, though it cost him a great deal of psychological pain. A suit filed against him by a right-wing veteran's organization in 1994 for violation of the National Security Law was not resolved until eleven years later, in 2005.

For Cho, the history of modern Korea is rooted in the Japanese decision to annex the country in 1910 and the years of colonial rule that followed. Japan, in his view, pursued "one of the cruelest colonial policies" in the world. Japanese depredations, however, intensified after Japan embarked on its wider war with China in 1937. Pressed to mobilize the resources of its colonies for the war effort, Cho says, "the colonial government exercised a policy of destroying the cultural identity of Koreans," referring to the insistence on the adoption of Japanese names and the creation of so-called volunteer corps to mobilize labor, including comfort women, all of which occupy much of his novel about this period.

Cho is among those in Korea who believe that the country failed to confront the issue of the *chinilpa*, a Korean word for those who collaborated with Japanese rule. He believes the country should have embarked on a purge of all pro-Japanese collaborators and a redistribution of land confiscated from the Japanese and their collaborators. Cho is an advocate of "drastic measures" to resolve the problem of collaboration. He was an organizer of the Institute for Research on Collaborationist Activities, which published a two-volume dictionary of collaborators during Japanese colonial rule, the first volume in 2005 and the second four years later. The full list contained 4,776 names. The institute categorized the names into two groups—those who betrayed their country by being involved in the repression of independence movements and those who worked for the colonial government or propagated its activities in some way. "The dictionary is significant as a record of history—of who and what about the collaborators," says Cho, defending the controversial listing.

Among those whose names were on the list were former leaders of the country and well-known composers and educators. The most prominent name was that of Park Chung-hee, who was an officer in the Japanese Imperial Army's Kwantung forces based in northern China. Cho, in one of his novels, writes about Korean soldiers who were drafted into those forces and fought alongside the Japanese. Cho has no qualms about identifying Park as a collaborator but gives a nod, as he discusses in the third of his epic novels, to his role in leading the country to economic modernization.

"We should admit the dual dimension of his life," says Cho. "His pro-Japanese collaboration and later dictatorship should be punished, but his leadership and role in economic development and lifting the whole people from poverty should also be correctly recognized. This contrasting dual nature of his leadership is the reason why the controversy over him goes on without resolution."

Cho is equally unrelenting when it comes to the Japanese themselves. "We hope world leaders understand the depth of our animosity," he says. For Cho, Japan has yet to perform an act of apology for its rule that is comparable to the dramatic gesture performed by German Chancellor Willy Brandt when he knelt in contrition at a memorial to the victims of the destruction of the Warsaw Ghetto during a visit to Poland in 1970, a moment that remains iconic in Germany's attempts to achieve reconciliation with its former victims. Cho explains:

> As some have said, forgiveness is a gift for those who reflect on their wrongdoing. The acts of self-reflection and forgiveness are two sides of one coin. We cannot forgive those who do not reflect on their wrongdoing. Germany could be forgiven because of their full reflection and apology. Japan constantly avoids a formal apology. That is why Japan cannot be forgiven. I am ready to forgive Japan if it repeats what Germany did—like the emperor coming and kneeling down in front of Gwanghwamun [the rebuilt gate to the former Korean ruling dynasty's palace, destroyed during the Japanese invasion of 1592] or at Seodaemun Prison. But Japan will never do that.

## Lee Hong Koo

Lee Hong Koo is the very definition of a distinguished public servant in Korea. Among the first generation of Koreans to be educated in the United States after the Korean War, Lee returned to his country in the late 1960s to spend two decades at the elite Seoul National University. As a political scientist, the soft-spoken academic offered advice to the military regime but was also a confidant of American ambassadors and a quiet critic of the country's authoritarian rulers. With the advent of democracy in 1987, Lee served all of the governments that followed in the next decade, beginning with shaping policy toward North Korea as the Minister of National Unification under general-turned-politician Roh Tae-woo and then serving as a senior diplomat and as prime minister for conservative political leader Kim Young-sam from 1994 to 1995. Lee departed from his role as a mandarin to dip into politics and a seat in the parliament. But he returned to his favored status as a public official, representing progressive leader Kim Dae-jung as his ambassador to Washington from 1998 to 2000. In the years since, Lee has been Korea's senior statesman, called on to do everything from chair a

Lee Hong Koo

bid to host the World Cup with Japan to joining efforts with his colleagues from China and Japan to reduce tensions in the region.

Lee Hong Koo may have served presidents from across Korea's political spectrum, but he remains a part of the essentially conservative elite in the country, deeply rooted in its history and past and largely unmoved by the passions unleashed by democratic change, although he is a quiet architect of the transition from dictatorship to popular rule. He was born in 1934, in the city of Gaeseong, an ancient Korean capital that now lies north of the division between North and South Korea. His family came from the northern reaches of Seoul, the southern capital, and his line of illustrious ancestors can be traced back to King Seongjong, a late fifteenth-century ruler of Korea's Chosun dynasty. Lee was the *jong-son*, the eldest male in a family line that traced itself back some five hundred years. His family owned land; they were not at the top of Korea's feudal order but a respected part of the local well-to-do. At the time of Lee's birth, Korea was under the colonial rule of Japan, and his father made a living as a trader, mostly selling agricultural goods to Japan.

Lee's memories of Japanese rule are those of a relatively privileged child in the Japanese-run order. He attended a grammar school where all the instruction was in Japanese, though he and his classmates talked among themselves in Korean. His teachers were mostly Korean, though he somewhat fondly recalls a Japanese teacher in the third grade. "When the war broke out in 1941," Lee recalls, "everyone was excited because for the first few months, Japan was scoring such victories, one after another."[21] As he entered second grade, every student got a present of a small rubber ball, a product, they were told, of Japan's seizure of the rubber fields of British Malaya. But there were quiet voices countering the Japanese war propaganda. A family elder, who taught the children the Chinese classics, told Lee privately that this was not a march to victory: "No," he told him, "This is the end of Japan."

The old scholar's words surprised Lee, still enraptured by news of imperial triumph. "I said, 'Why?' And he explained. What he said was that the West was far more advanced in science and technology. Big ships, trains, and all these things were invented in the West, so that the West was far superior in terms of science and technology. Japan just learned this in the recent decades from the West. So there really was no contest. There was no way Japan could win the war eventually—so it may take time, but Japan was coming to an end. That's what he said."

Lee's father and his generation "were a little bit carried away when Japan was winning because they were indoctrinated by the Japanese and lived with the Japanese," he explains. "They basically functioned in the Japanese system every day. But in the older generation, like my grandfather's generation, people had a much better understanding of world history." Educated in the last days of the Chosun dynasty of independent Korea, before the Japanese annexation, they saw Japan as only a few steps ahead of Korea, thanks to its ability to westernize faster and modernize its army. But when it came to the West, "there was no contest between Japan and the West—it was a foregone conclusion."

As the tides of war began to shift against Japan, Lee heard more than just the insights of his elders. From 1943, "things began to change: we didn't hear too many pieces of good news, but we heard stories about how the entire Japanese contingent in some islands fought until the last moment, and everybody was killed—what they called a sort of collective suicide." Students began to speculate among themselves that Japan might not win the war and that Korea might gain its independence if Japan were defeated, though the word spread very quietly.

"Then August 15 came," Lee says, remembering the surrender. "I didn't hear the emperor's speech. This teacher came in, and he informed us that Japan just surrendered. And then he cried out loud—he was saying that this was the end of the Japanese Empire and it was such a shame that the war ended this way. He cried so much. What surprised me was that some of the older students also wept a bit. But to me, a city boy, it looked rather strange—I could see why the teacher was crying, but why [were] these students also showing such sympathy? Independence was already in our minds, so to me it was so strange that some students also wept."

By then, Lee had already heard the whispers about the resistance to Japan, including the name of the Communist guerrilla leader Kim Il-sung. By the day after the surrender, posters popped up in villages declaring a new Korean government led by the exiled leader Rhee Syngman. To this day, Lee remains an admirer of the man who led the republic from its formation in the South in 1948, through the Korean War, and until his overthrow by student-led protests in 1960. Lee served for five years as chairman of the commemorative commission for Rhee.

In March 1942, Rhee made a speech to Koreans in the United States, Lee says. "We play that speech every year on the day of his death, when we have the memorial service at the national cemetery. He said he was so glad that Japan started the war because this meant that the end of Japanese occupation was very close. You could almost feel how glad he was. Before too long, he said, the sea of fire would fall upon the Japanese islands. I don't think he knew about the atomic bomb, but he said, 'Tell every neighbor, every friend, that it is only a matter of time until we Koreans will regain independence.' Even now we could see that, as I said earlier, Rhee's generation from the beginning believed that Japan wouldn't last if they continued on that path."

Having grown up during the era of Japanese rule, Lee retains a more textured view of the question of collaboration. He is uncomfortable with the harsh, blanket condemnations of all who worked in some way with Japanese authorities as "collaborators," a view advocated by some progressive Koreans since the beginning of democratic rule. He is more sympathetic to those who argue for understanding the decision of many Koreans to work with the Japanese given the situation. "If a small boy like myself knew that we would regain independence, the greatest challenge facing the Korean population then was how to survive Japanese rule with the least damage," Lee observes.

Lee points to the role that Japanese-trained Koreans played in organizing its postliberation army, leading it in the war against the Communist invaders or in building the universities that were the foundation of Korea's postwar revival. With the clear exception of "those [who] worked for the Japanese police or Japanese military officers, who hunted down Korean independence movements," he has little patience for the current search for collaborators. The attempt to carry out a systematic investigation of this issue in the first years after the formation of the Korean republic in 1948 was, unfortunately, aborted by the outbreak of war, Lee notes, resulting in a "not-so-thorough job of sorting out these collaborations during the Japanese period. That is one reason, perhaps, why even today certain division still exists in this society." He admits that as a member of Korea's privileged class, which has its origins in part in those who benefited from Japanese rule, "I can't really say that I am completely objective."

Unlike many in Korea, this former senior public official sees little worth in continuing to plow through the ground of the wartime and colonial past with Japan. To normalize their relations, the two countries signed an agreement in 1965 that legally settled the issue of compensation for war crimes and damage, Lee says, a view shared by most Japanese officials as well. "Now the relationship between the two countries has reached a point that too much time has gone by," he said in an interview conducted in late 2009, just before the two countries marked the one hundredth anniversary of Japan's formal annexation of Korea. "After 100 years, that is it. There shouldn't be any problem with the position I have taken because Koreans should have gained sufficient confidence in themselves not to really dwell on this further. That is not the way to have a good relationship with your neighbor."

Lee points to the positive example of the two countries cohosting the 2002 World Cup. But even his tolerant voice points to the failure of the Japanese to consistently apologize for their wartime acts, expressing frustration at the continuing indulgence of Japanese nationalism by its leaders. Despite having been deeply engaged for decades in managing ties between the two countries, Lee says, "As I see it, Japan is a much bigger country than Korea in terms of population and economy. They could be much more magnanimous on these issues." Instead, when the problems of wartime and colonial rule come up, Lee says, Japanese leaders simply point to the need to pay heed to their nationalist culture and sentiments.

> Whenever Japanese politicians say that they have to say this and that to suit the Japanese people's sentiments, I don't know what the Japanese people are thinking. What I am asking for, and hoping for, is that the Japanese leadership and intellectuals come up with a much more clear-cut, historic, objective explanation of what had happened—that is, as a latecomer, Japan had to take extraordinary measures to modernize in a matter of two or three decades; that Japan had to rely on military strength, since all the imperial powers had great military power; that from the Meiji Restoration [in 1868] and those years of the age of imperialism, one thing led to another; that it is clear that Japan was carried away by these dynamics, and they committed these mistakes in their neighborhood and to the global community; and that they regret it, and they are sorry for all these mistakes.

## *Park Won-soon*

Seoul Mayor Park Won-soon was born a couple of years after the end of the Korean War in the remote and impoverished countryside of southeast Korea's South Gyeongsang province, in the county of Changnyeong, close to the port city of Busan. His parents were poor farmers, both of whom failed

Park Won-soon

to finish even elementary school. This poverty was fertile ground for Japan's colonial rulers who found needed workers here, many of them drafted as compulsory labor during the war years to fill the empty spaces at Japan's mines and factories. As a young man, his father was sent as a forced laborer to Japan, where he worked for seven years, returning before the end of the war and Korea's liberation from Japanese colonial rule.

The legacy of Japanese rule echoed, however, through the family. An uncle was sent to the coalmines of Sakhalin, the Russian island partially controlled by Japan, and never came back, marooned by the end of the war and return of the island to Soviet rule. His father did not return with money for his work, but he did gain an appreciation for what the Japanese had built. "Even though he was a forced laborer, he could witness what was going on in Japan," recalls Park. "So when he came back to Korea, he was determined to educate us, especially the sons," two of his parent's seven offspring.[22] Park and his brother were sent to Seoul to be educated, and he went on to enter the country's prestigious Seoul National University in 1975. His father sold fattened cows, and Park supported himself by tutoring other students.

His father's dreams for his sons soon clashed with the harsh realities of political repression, deepening under an increasingly beleaguered military dictatorship led by Park Chung-hee. On May 13, 1975, the regime enacted Presidential Emergency Decree for National Security and Public Order No. 9, a sweeping measure banning any kind of protest or criticism of the president and the system he had set up to ensure authoritarian rule, as well as allowing authorities to arrest and detain people without warrants. Park Won-soon's participation in a campus protest ended in arrest and expulsion from his privileged campus. "I had only attended class for three months," Park recounts. His father said nothing, in part relieved that his son was alive, but "you can imagine what the feelings of my parents and family members [were] like."

After his release from prison some four months later, Park embarked on a career as a human-rights lawyer, earning a university degree in history along the way. In 1994, he founded People's Solidarity for Participatory Democracy. As a lawyer and civil society activist, Park became a prominent voice on a range of issues, from the compensation of wartime forced laborers and comfort women to the promotion of democracy and the rule of law. In October 2011, Park shocked the political establishment in Korea by winning the election, as an independent candidate, for mayor of Seoul, a powerful platform that has catapulted past occupants to the presidency of Korea.

Park began his law career in 1983, under the tough rule of military leader Chun Doo-hwan, who came to power after the assassination of Park Chung-hee in 1979. Park Won-soon joined a group of human-rights lawyers who began their practice in the 1970s, seeking to defend victims of political repression. He took up cases of censorship and torture of political prisoners, some of them famous in the annals of the democracy movement that grew in strength during those years, culminating in the 1987 successful uprising against Chun and military rule. At the same time, Park pursued his passion for history, establishing in 1986 the Yoksa Research Institute, dedicated to modern Korean history.

In 1991, Park went to London to earn a degree in international law at the London School of Economics and Political Science. His thesis was on the role of human-rights nongovernmental organizations (NGOs) in Asia, but the biggest impact of his study was his encounter with a Japanese lawyer, Totsuka Etsuro, who was trying to use international law to bring the issue of the former comfort women to court. Totsuka sought to bring the case of the women to the United Nations (UN) Commission on Human Rights. Park joined his team.

"As a human-rights lawyer, I was very interested in the time limitations for prosecuting serious crimes because we had so many serious crimes against humanity in Korea domestically, such as torture and killing," recounts Park. "I was deeply interested in how to prevent the passage of time from being used to prevent the punishment of crimes against humanity." Park learned about United Nations conventions on the nonapplicability of statutory limitations when dealing with war crimes or crimes against humanity. Along with Totsuka, he filed suit in Japanese courts seeking redress for three Korean comfort women, based on the UN conventions and the Japanese constitutional requirement that international treaties and law could be applied as Japanese law.

The lawyers won a historic judgment in 1998 in a Japanese lower court ordering the Japanese government to pay compensation to the women. The court ruled that the women had become part of the wartime brothel system based on deception and "were confined and forced to have sex with the Imperial Japanese soldiers, and that even after the war, they physically suffered a great deal. In addition, they suffered much due to shame."[23] The court ruled that this was an ongoing human-rights issue that should be resolved.

As the lawyers anticipated, the ruling was overturned by higher courts on the grounds that the postwar treaties settled the issue of compensation. But they felt the case at least provided some political support to their cause in affirming, based on their testimony, the assertion that this was a system of sexual slavery and in giving further impetus to efforts to uphold the human rights of the victims. For Park, the lack of readiness of the Japanese government to accept responsibility for reparations, despite the legal arguments that it had settled these issues in the treaties to settle the war and normalize relations with Korea, is the true test of Japan's relations with its neighbors.

"Indeed," Park writes in a paper published by Duke University in 1997 on this subject, "this issue of reparations has been the major reason for other Asians' continued distrust of Japan and the primary impediment to their proceeding toward true reconciliation with Japan."[24] In his view, the Japanese official apologies for the war were far short of clear statements of responsibility. "Japan's continued ambivalence and hypocrisy toward its role in the war render apology impossible, and Japan's contempt for the East and its fawning admiration for the West remain firmly in place," he writes.

"These are the very conditions that first motivated Japan to commit atrocities in Asia."[25]

Park's view of wartime history is largely unrelenting in its sharp criticism of Japanese actions. He points to a long sweep of Japanese imperialism, driven by a sense of racial superiority that he traces back to the Japanese-attempted invasion of Korea in the sixteenth century. He sets the start of World War II in Asia, then, at 1910, when Japan annexed Korea, which he marks as the launching of a series of wars of imperial aggression.

Park holds the emperor of Japan responsible in part for the war, a subject he took up in a book published in Korea. "We cannot compare him with Hitler," he says, "but it is clear that he was the most responsible person in the war." He recognizes that an American decision to bring the emperor to trial would have made "peaceful occupation impossible." He points to a different approach to justice taken toward Japan than against Germany—but he holds Koreans and other Asians responsible as well. "In the European continent, the U.S. would not have been able to let the main criminals escape because of the pressure or awareness of people in the neighboring countries surrounding Germany," Park believes. "But in Asia, the awareness of ordinary people and of the governments was not enough to push the U.S. government."

When it comes to the American decision to use the atomic bomb against Japan, Park, as a human-rights advocate, concedes that under international law, "it was problematic." But, he says, as a policy maker, "I would have done it too." As Allied forces approached the Japanese home islands, they knew the Japanese were prepared to "resist until the last moment," so the use of the weapon was understandable. "I didn't say that it was a good thing. Even though it was inescapable, it is still a great tragedy."

Park has little problem with the postdemocratic pursuit of collaborators in Korea, having written about the comparison between collaborations in wartime France and Korea. "Even in France, they say that the issue of collaboration has not been resolved or cleared away," he observes. "But it was dealt with more seriously than in Korea. In France, the collaborators were brought to court and their social status was inhibited. Lawyers could not practice any longer. Even reporters could not work again. But in Korea, the collaborators were allowed to return to politics."

Park allows that there are arguments to be made about particular people. Asked about former ruler Park Chung-hee, who served as a member of Japan's wartime army, "I think that one person's life cannot be judged by one point," he says. "But when he was a soldier in the colonial times, he was clearly a collaborator." While France was occupied for only four years, Korea was occupied for thirty-six years. "Many people thought it was impossible to be liberated from Japan. Personally, I can understand that."

Still, for Park, the core question remains that of Japanese responsibility for the war and its colonial rule. "There can be no illusions," he wrote in 1997. "Japan cannot keep peace in Asia when it is not at peace with its own history."[26]

### Rhee Yong Hoon

Rhee Yong Hoon, with slightly graying hair and a studious appearance, carries himself with the calm demeanor of a scholar. He speaks the language of academia, with dense references to theory and long citations of research data. It is surprising, then, that Rhee has acquired the status of a controversial personality in Korea, the academic equivalent of a bomb-thrower who has chosen to assail some of the most sacred beliefs of postwar Korea.

On the surface, Rhee toils in the obscure gardens of academic research. He is an economic historian, the author of a series of studies of eighteenth-

Rhee Yong Hoon. Source: Courtesy Rhee Yong Hoon.

and nineteenth-century Korea and of the land policies of Japanese colonial rule. His work on the late Chosun dynasty in Korea is full of dense quantitative data exploring the growth of commercial activity and the structure of the economy. And from the early 1990s, he and his collaborators published detailed studies of the land surveys and policies of the Japanese, beginning during the first decade of their control of Korea.

The conventional and popular view among both academics and the general public was that the incipient development of Korea was strangled in its cradle by Japanese imperialism. In that account, Korea, during the late Chosun dynasty, was already undergoing the early stages of transition to a modern capitalist economy, experiencing the classic transition from an agricultural economy to an industrial economy, along the lines of what Japan itself was going through after the Meiji Revolution of 1968. Japanese colonial rule was built on a ruthless exploitation of Korean resources, including the seizure of at least half of Korea's land and rice production and the use of Korean labor in mines and factories.

Rhee and his colleagues challenged this historical account and precipitated a debate within Korea that has led to fists being thrown. For his school of thought, the evidence suggests that eighteenth- and nineteenth-century dynastic Korea was actually deeply stagnant, dominated by a backward agricultural economy that had failed to set the stage for industrialization. By the late nineteenth century, "Chosun Korea was in a full-scale crisis and unable to develop without an external shock," he writes.[27] Modern economic growth in Korea began, Rhee argues, only during the Japanese colonial period. The Japanese investment in the building of modern infrastructure, such as railroads, roads, and utilities, paired with the creation of labor and capital markets (made possible by the survey of the land, which allowed land holdings to be used as collateral for loans), "laid the basis for the development of the Korean market economy and industrial society," Rhee writes.[28]

Rhee, a Seoul National University scholar, went after some of the more essential beliefs about Japanese rule. His study of land ownership found that less than 10 percent of arable land actually came under direct Japanese control, and he found that rice was not seized by the Japanese rulers but bought in the marketplace. He sees the basis for postwar Korea's rapid modernization in the institutions created under Japanese rule: the civil service trained by Japan, the private companies that have driven Korean growth, and banking and fiscal systems. South Korea's ability to preserve those gains, unlike in the North, created the basis for its miracle, Rhee and his allies contend.[29]

These views have been broadly labeled in Korea as "colonial modernization theory," an argument about colonial rule that can be found in many other countries, such as India, where independence movements initially denied any positive impact of their former colonial masters. But this is not only an argument about Korea's past. Rhee and his allies, who became known as the "New Right," also laid the intellectual groundwork for asserting the legitimacy of the rule of Park Chung-hee, who embarked in the early 1960s on a development path that consciously aped Japan and embraced the legacy of Japanese-trained bureaucrats and other experts. As a group, Rhee and his colleagues in academia took on the neo-Marxism that predominated in Korean academia, particularly after the fall of the military regime. Among other things, they have fought for revisions of Korean textbooks that they have felt offered a distorted history of the country.

"We Korean people usually remember that period as a miserable time," Rhee says about the colonial era. "Imperial Japan usurped the land and took all our rice. They only exploited our lands and our people. That is the usual, conventional opinion of Korean people on that time period."[30] Rhee traces the rise of this "theory of exploitation" to the 1960s, when Park normalized relations with Japan, sparking resistance from Koreans. "In the 1990s, I and my colleagues began to investigate land surveys carried out in 1910. We learned that the exploitation theory did not have any empirical basis."

Following his writing in the 1980s on the Chosun dynasty, Rhee's original research on the land issues was published, over the objections of many other scholars, in 1992 and then in a book in 1997. The initial response, he says, was one of stony silence. "They just pretended as if they did not hear anything," he says of fellow scholars. In more recent years, he has become a widely known figure, getting himself into hot water for comments such as one calling into question the conventional view of comfort women as purely victims of Japanese forced labor, even suggesting that Korean brokers were more responsible for the women's service as prostitutes.

Contrary to his current image as a lion of the right in Korea, Rhee's own history fits far more easily with that of his ideological foes. He was born in 1951, during the Korean War, in Taegu, in the southern end of Korea. His father was expelled from his high school in 1944 on suspicion of sympathy for the anti-Japanese cause, and he traveled to Manchuria to attempt to join anti-Japanese guerrillas there. The family counts among its members, with great pride, relatives who served the exiled government in Shanghai. His father also embodied the complexity of the colonial experience: fluent in Japanese, he was a fan of Japanese literature and traditional Noh drama. "He often said that Japanese people are very kind, gentle, and bright," Rhee recalls.

Rhee grew up, however, in the "strong anti-Japanese atmosphere" of postwar Korea. As a student in the 1970s at Seoul National University, he joined the pro-democracy student movements and eagerly read Marxist literature that circulated clandestinely, much of it ironically written in Japanese. He was expelled from the university in 1971 for his role in organizing protests against fraud in the presidential election held that year. He fled the police, hiding in the mountains for six months before turning himself in. He was sent back to the university to await conscription for the military and finally returned to the university in 1976 to earn his degree and then his doctorate in economic history.

Rhee underwent an ideological transformation as a young professor at Hanshin Theological School. He began to read books about the realities of socialism in Eastern Europe and North Korea. "I learned it was only a totalitarian system. There was no liberty or hope. It was a very bureaucratic system," he recounts. "I began to know the miserable state of present socialism." His disillusionment with his youthful leftism deepened, and by the time of the 1997 financial crisis that struck South Korea, Rhee found that he had become an advocate of classical market liberalism "without even thinking about it."

Rhee's philosophical transformation was reflected in his work as an economic historian, animated by the belief that the empirical data should dictate the outcome of research rather than be guided by an ideological goal. He brings that same desire for precision and an aversion to broad judgment to his view of the war itself. Asked who was responsible for the war in Asia, he responds,

> Usually, we Koreans believe that the Japanese were responsible for the war in Asia and the Pacific War. But as a historian, I think it is a very difficult question. I think Japan and the U.S. have the same amount of responsibility. For example, the U.S. did not try to prevent the war. At that time, the chancellor Churchill in England appealed to the U.S. government that England did not

have enough power to be engaged in war in Europe and Asia, and, therefore, England would like to avoid the war in Asia. In the beginning, the U.S. tried to avoid war with Japan. I am not a specialist of that period, but some books and papers I read suggest that both the U.S. and Japan did not try seriously enough to avoid the war. . . . For most cases in history when war occurs, there must be good-enough reasons. At that time, the imperial race was going on, and the U.S. never admitted the hegemony of Japan in Asia. Japan tried to negotiate with the U.S., saying something like "We will retreat from China in twenty years. Give us twenty years." The U.S. rejected it and demanded Japan to retreat from China promptly. At that point, Japan decided to attack the U.S. But, because of that, we Koreans were liberated. That is the history.

Rhee does not hesitate to label Japan as the aggressor in the war, a product of its gradual imperial expansion into the Asian continent. Nor does he look away from the crimes committed in the course of that war. In the mid-2000s, at the behest of the Korean government, he carried out interviews with about sixty Koreans who were drafted into the Japanese army or were mobilized for labor in Japanese factories. He recounts tragic stories he heard, such as soldiers who were forced to carry out bayonet practice on live Chinese prisoners. But he also recognizes that many of the Koreans who participated in the Japanese war effort were conflicted in their feelings. "The Japanese army was very cruel, and the person who told me that story said he was ashamed of it," Rhee says. "Yet the Korean soldier also had some pride that once he was a Japanese soldier. He said the Chinese were weak and that they never won a battle."

Rhee, not surprisingly, was an opponent of the commission formed to investigate collaboration with Japan, including the publication of the dictionary list of collaborators.

"Most of the collaborators," Rhee argues, "did not believe in the possibility of liberation or emancipation from Japan. They believed that the expansion of the Japanese Empire was going to last forever. They believed that collaboration was necessary for the development of the Korean people into a modern nation. I understand that. Of course, I criticize those who collaborated in capturing and torturing the leaders of the liberation movement. But I can understand those collaborators who worked in education or business."

Park Chung-hee "was a collaborator," Rhee says without hesitation. But because of that experience, he was able to use the experience of those who were trained in Japan for the cause of economic modernization. For this Korean scholar, there is an overemphasis on the resistance to Japan and insufficient understanding of the process of building a modern nation in South Korea after the division of the peninsula.

Rhee shows a similarly iconoclastic outlook when it comes to the question of the decision to use the atomic bomb on Japan. Unlike almost all Koreans, including others interviewed for this book, the historian has mixed feelings about that decision, pointing to the large number of Koreans who also died as a result of the attack because they were living and working in those Japanese cities, a fact that Koreans have, at times, been reluctant to acknowledge:

> When the atomic bomb was dropped in Hiroshima and Nagasaki, about 200,000 people died promptly, and about 360,000 people were seriously injured. As far as I know, about 40,000 Korean people also died, and 30,000 were seriously injured. At that time, many Korean people resided in Hiroshima and Nagasaki. As a historian, my private opinion is that the dropping of the atomic bomb is also a tragedy in Korean history because so many Korean people were sacrificed, too. Usually, Korean people do not view it as a Korean tragedy and solely as that of Japanese. When the international peace movement for antinuclear weapons happened, Korean people did not participate. It is not good. I want to stress that so many Korean people also died. I do not have any opinion on whether the decision to drop the atomic bomb was good or bad. But so many people died. I visited Hiroshima and Nagasaki and also read many novels. I think the nuclear weapon must be banished forever. We Koreans must participate in the international campaign because we are one of the greatest victims, too. But we do not have such a kind of historical consciousness. That is the problem.

Perhaps for that reason, Rhee has little patience for the incessant demands on Japan to offer gestures of reconciliation to Koreans. "I think we Korean people must endeavor—we must overcome our history by ourselves," Rhee says with a sense of finality. "I do not think there is anything that Japan must solve. The problem is with us, Koreans."

## *Yang Mi Kang*

Every Wednesday, since 1992, a group of South Koreans have assembled across the street from the Japanese embassy in Seoul: long banners stretch

Yang Mi Kang

in front their ranks, calling on the Japanese government to finally provide justice to tens of thousands of women who were drafted into a particularly odious form of service by the Japanese Imperial Army during the wartime years. Among the ranks of the demonstrators are always a handful of surviving comfort women, who were recruited, many of them coercively by their colonial rulers, to provide sexual services to ranks of officers and ordinary soldiers who trooped into military-organized brothels set up across the vast reaches of Japan's wartime conquests.

The demonstrations are organized by a unique product of Korea's vibrant civil society: the Korean Council for the Women Drafted for Military Sexual Slavery by Japan. The Korean Council—a coalition of thirty-seven women's groups, most of them associated with Christian churches—was formed in November 1990. A few years earlier, a popular uprising overthrew decades of military-led authoritarian rule in Korea, unleashing passions and causes long bottled up by decades of military-led governments, including uncomfortable legacies of colonial rule. A few women began to unburden themselves in public of the deeply embarrassing tale of their sexual service.

With the backing of activists, these women put pressure on the Korean government to take up the issue—and the demand for both apology and compensation—with the Japanese government.

The council was created in frustration after the Japanese government failed to respond to an open letter from leaders of Korean women's organizations, which made these demands prior to the visit of the Japanese premier in October 1990. Some months later, in April 1991, the Japanese government finally responded to the open letter by stating that there was no evidence of forced drafting of Korean women for the brothels and, therefore, no question of an apology. That harsh response folded in the face of explosive revelations, in January of 1992 in Japan's leading liberal daily, the *Asahi Shimbun*, of documents, uncovered in official archives by a leading Japanese historian, that clearly demonstrated the Imperial Army's direct role in creating and staffing the brothel system.

The council continues to play a dual role in Korean society, as the voice of those who are unyielding in their demands both on Japan for official apology and compensation and on the Korean government to speak forcefully for them, as well as an orchestrator of public memory. The weekly demonstrations are a constant reminder that the memory of these women, their ranks thinned by 2014 to fifty-five survivors, will not be forgotten. To ensure that, in December 2011 the council erected a powerfully simple bronze memorial directly across from the Japanese embassy, where the demonstrators gather. The sculpture has two chairs: one is empty, suggesting those who are no longer present, and the second is occupied by a statue of a teenage girl dressed in traditional *hanbok*, barefoot and sitting with her hands folded in her lap, her face composed in a solemn gaze directed at the Japanese government presence across the street. Copies of this memorial have been placed around the world by Korean activists, in towns in Southern California, Michigan, and elsewhere, prompting, as did the Seoul memorial, the fierce protests of the Japanese government.

Yang Mi Kang, a remarkably upbeat and passionate leader among the Korean women in this movement, came into the leadership of the council in 1997. She has been a relentless advocate for these women ever since. But her role has extended beyond the council to engage the issues of textbooks and youth education, including as an organizer of the leading Korean NGO on this issue, the Asia Peace, History, and Education Network (APHEN). In that capacity, Yang has been active in forging partnerships with other civil-society organizations in Japan, China, and across Asia on these issues.

Yang was among a small group of progressive scholars from China, Japan, and Korea who launched a nongovernmental effort in 2001 to compile a common history textbook, an effort to counter a plan by Japan conservative groups to publish their own versions of history for use in Japanese schools. After several years of formal meetings and debates, drafting, and redrafting, the scholars published *History That Opens the Future*, a teachers' guide that focuses on World War II events and the unresolved history issues in East Asia. It appeared in all three languages, and a second volume on the modern history of the three countries was published in 2012. "It is possible to avoid the folly of repeating the same mistake," the authors of the first joint history guide write in their preface. "Our study of history too has the purpose of opening up the future by learning lessons from the past."[31]

There were, as the authors acknowledge, "numerous occasions during the three-year preparation when [their] views differed," but the book reflects a clear consensus about the wartime period, characterized in its table of contents as a "war of aggression and victimization of the people."[32] It frames the modern history of Northeast Asia largely as a response to the effort of Europe and America to force open all three societies, triggering movements for reform and resistance to Western imperialism. The decision of Japan to embark on its own imperial experiment, and the response of China and Korea to that historic shift, occupies a significant section of the historical narrative. The volume concludes with a look at the emergence of postwar East Asia out of the defeat of Japan, shaped by the nature of the American-led settlement of the war, and the emergence of the Cold War as defined by the division of Korea and the establishment of the People's Republic of China. The book's epilogue returns to the unresolved issues of the war, including compensation for war crimes to comfort women and the resurgence of Japanese defense of their wartime record.

The book sold well in all three countries, although it had its critics, particularly among some academics who saw it as a less-than-scholarly work. But perhaps the most significant achievement was the creation of a collaborative network of scholars from all three countries, most importantly from China. "The writers struggled through an intensive historiographical re-examination and debate, but, without knowing it, they laid a stepping-stone for a regional history in the future," observed historian Soon-Won Park.[33]

Yang's involvement in the teaching of history went beyond this dialogue. She launched a summer youth program that takes teens from all three countries through a joint exploration of wartime history. The program began as a Korea-Japan exchange, tied to the 2002 World Cup, which was jointly held in the two countries and sparked an upsurge in tourism and other exchanges. The youth were taken on field trips to museums and other memorials, including the House of Sharing in Korea, where surviving comfort women are cared for and a museum to their suffering has been set up. In Japan, Koreans were exposed for the first time to an understanding of the wartime bombings, marked by visits to the Hiroshima museum and visits with survivors. The visits had an eye-opening impact on the teens, says Yang. "In Korean history textbooks, there is no description of the Hiroshima bombing and its aftermath," she says. "In many ways, what we need is to write a common history together. We should first examine different narratives on our shared past and compare them."[34]

For an activist like Yang, the role of civil society is essential to both the construction of history memory and the creation of a pathway to reconciliation. "I believed that this kind of educational exchanges and dialogues are not possible at the level of governments," she says.

Yang arrived at this role via a personal path that began in 1960 in Korea's North Jeolla province, where she was the youngest of five children. Her father, a member of the colonial-era elite, was educated at a Japanese university and practiced law in Manchukuo and Korea under Japanese rule. Business troubles sent the family into bankruptcy in the early 1960s, but the children finished their university education, thanks in part to the efforts of siblings and supporting themselves through work.

Yang chose religious training, entering the graduate school at Hanshin Seminary. She became exposed to growing movements for social justice among workers and the poor that were organized by Christian theologians and activists. She later joined the Peace Institute for Christian Women and went on to earn her doctorate—her thesis focused on the role of women in the early period of Korean Christianity—and her status as a Presbyterian Minister. In 1994, just after her graduation from seminary, she married another minister, assigned to a church in Seoul.

This was, by her own description, a period of identity crisis. Frustrated at being consigned the role of the wife of a minister, rather than working as a minister on her own, in 1997 Yang took on the leadership of the Korean

Council that had been formed to advocate for comfort women. She became engaged with international organizations of women at the United Nations and elsewhere, which tied this issue to broader concerns about gender equality. She reached back to her undergraduate history studies to become involved in the wartime history discussions.

For Koreans, the colonial and wartime periods are not only a tale of victimization at the hands of the Japanese. They are also a source of controversy and painful self-examination in coming to grips with the extensive collaboration of Koreans with their Japanese rulers and the nature of colonial rule itself, not least the degree to which Japan contributed to the economic and structural modernization of Korea. Despite her activism on history education and her fierce criticism of Japanese self-portrayals, Yang is sensitive to the complexities of these issues for Koreans.

Japan's annexation of Korea in 1910 is, for example, still a disputed matter. Japanese official historiography regards it as legal act in which the Korean dynasty willingly signed away its independence. "I believe it was illegal because Korea never wanted it," says Yang, voicing the common view. "Nevertheless, it was an era of two separate logics of individual state versus international legal norms. In the eyes of the international law of the time, it was recognized as a legitimate act."

But there is little question that Yang embraces the progressive Korean narrative that rejects the legitimacy of the Japanese occupation, argues against those who point to the benefits of modernization under Japanese rule, and believes that the Japanese have failed to apologize and offer true contrition for their acts.

Yang led a joint Korea-Japan citizens' group to mark the one hundredth anniversary of the Japanese annexation of Korea in 2010. She acknowledged that the Liberal Democratic Party of Japan's government, led by Prime Minister Kan Naoto, issued an apology for colonial rule at the time of the anniversary. "But, Koreans still believe that such statements are not sufficient for the Japanese prime ministers to show their sincerity in reflecting on and apologizing for the past atrocities," she wrote at the time. "In fact, the Japanese leaders have been long on words but short on action. Koreans are fed up with Japan's rhetorical flourishes that have not yet been put into practice."[35]

Yang is equally harsh when it comes to those who argue that Japan played some positive role in the development of Korea under its rule. "For me," Yang says without hesitation, "the modernizing aspects of the colonial period were like the sudden affection shown by the rapist to buy food and clothing for the victim after the rape was committed." While the case of comfort women is different from that of the hundreds of thousands of Koreans who were recruited, and later compelled, to labor in Japanese mines and factories during the war, they are both bound by the issue of compensation and apology, in her view.

"Japan bears responsibility for legal reparation for these victims, but neither comfort women nor forced labor victims have received this," she says. "And it should be a reparation which the individual victims can satisfactorily accept." Yang led the council in rejecting the solution offered by Japan for the comfort women in the mid-1990s, the Asian Women's Fund, because the funds offered were private in their source and therefore did not constitute an official act of reparations. "The fund has been a scheme of the World War II aggressor, Japan, to avoid legal responsibilities for its actions," she told the *New York Times* in 1998.[36] For Yang, "the sincerity and moral character of the apology is what matters, and the Japanese failed in this."

When it comes to those who collaborated with Japanese rule, Yang offers this distinction:

> I think that many people, including my own parents, can be broadly categorized as collaborators. But there were those who played the role of leaders who were active in collaboration during the wartime period, compared to this broader public. I call them the core-collaborator group, and I believe they never came out and took responsibility for their acts during the late colonial period. This should be done sometime, inevitably, to make South Korean society more mature. After a historical or political trauma, no society can move forward unless there is a process of reconciliation, where the perpetrators confess their crimes and admit their responsibility.... In modern Korean society, the issue of collaboration remains a sensitive Achilles heel of society, of its ability to move beyond historical trauma and toward social healing.

Koreans, Yang admits, tend to have a victim mentality and avoid issues like collaboration that fall into the gray area between a black-and-white narrative of victims and perpetrators. The issues of collaboration and colonial modernization fall into that gray area, she says, and for Korea to finally grow up as a country, it must admit that these unhealed wounds exist and pursue true reconciliation.

FOUR

# Multiple Memories of War in Postwar Japan

Yasukuni Shrine, Japan's Shinto memorial to the nation's war dead, sits off a busy Tokyo boulevard, just north of the deep green waters of the moat surrounding the Imperial Palace grounds in the center of the city. Casual visitors to the shrine can easily miss its significance. A long stone pathway leads from the large steel *torii*, or gate, at the entrance to the shrine, past the statue of Omura Masujiro, the samurai-scholar who is considered the founder of Japan's modern military after the Meiji Revolution of 1868. Beyond the statue lies the main shrine, with its classical sloping tiled roofs, where Shinto priests in stiff robes move quietly within the inner courtyard. Except on holidays and in the spring when Tokyoites gather to sit below the blooming cherry trees that line the shrine's pathways, Yasukuni is a quiet place, attracting few visitors.

Yet Yasukuni holds powerful significance for the Japanese—and for its neighbors. Since its construction in the second year of the Meiji emperor's reign, the shrine has served to honor the almost two-and-a-half million people who died in a series of wars, from the internal struggles to create the modern nation to Japan's wars as an emergent great power, beginning with the Sino-Japanese War of 1894–1895 and ending with the disastrous conflict in the Pacific. Even though the shrine's formal ties to the Japanese state were severed after the war, it remains a highly symbolic evocation of the trilogy of emperor, Shintoism, and military prowess that were the centerpiece of Japan's wartime ideology.

Yasukuni Shrine has also come to emblemize the frictions over wartime memory between Japan and its neighbors, triggering serious tensions in the

A Zero Fighter displayed in the Entrance Hall of the Yushukan War Museum.
Source: © Guilhem Vellut (via Flickr).

first decade of this century between Japan and China, and between Japan and Korea. The memorial embodies a denial of war responsibility and of aggression, exemplified by the decision to include among the enshrined war dead some fifty thousand former colonial subjects, mostly Korean and Taiwanese, who were conscripted to serve their conquerors. The shrine also honors around one hundred thousand civilians from Okinawa, many of whom were dragooned into deadly service by the Imperial Army. Some were forced to commit mass suicide to prevent their surrender to the invading American forces.[1]

The most controversial expression of this denial of wartime responsibility was the decision of the shrine authorities, made in secret in 1969 in consultation with officials of the Health and Welfare Ministry, to honor by enshrinement the fourteen Japanese military and civilian leaders who were convicted as Class A war criminals, the highest level of criminal responsibility, and sentenced to death by the Tokyo War Crimes Tribunal. The actual enshrinement of the high-level war criminals, among them Japan's wartime leader Tojo Hideki, was not publicly carried out until 1978.[2] That decision prompted Emperor Hirohito, Japan's wartime emperor, to stop his visits to the shrine, which had been numerous since the end of the war, according to a memo written in 1988 by the Grand Steward of the Imperial Household Agency, Tomita Tomohiko.[3]

Although Yasukuni's formal ties to the Japanese state were severed by the occupation authorities, Japanese leaders began to visit the shrine at festivals to pay their respects to the war dead, beginning even before the restoration of sovereignty in 1952. The most sensitive visits were those that took place on August 15, the anniversary of Japan's surrender in 1945, a date with great symbolic import. To preserve the illusion that these visits had no official meaning, the prime ministers would usually declare themselves to be paying their respects, along with other prominent politicians, as "private citizens." In 1985, the nationalist conservative leader Nakasone Yasuhiro defiantly visited in his official capacity as prime minister, triggering a storm of protest from around Asia and effectively ending that practice. But Prime Minister Koizumi Junichiro revived the controversy by inaugurating a series of six annual visits, beginning in 2001, which triggered official protest from China, South Korea, and other Asian neighbors and sent Sino-Japanese relations into a virtual deep freeze for years.[4]

Conservative Prime Minister Shinzo Abe followed in these footsteps when he returned to power in 2012, visiting the shrine as an official visitor a year later, on December 26, 2013. The visit not only prompted angry protests from China and South Korea but also drew an unusual admonition from the U.S. government, which issued a statement on the U.S. embassy website declaring that "the United States is disappointed that Japan's leadership has taken an action that will exacerbate tensions with Japan's neighbors."[5]

Casual visitors to the shrine see no overt expression of this view of the wartime period. But the message is unavoidably clear at the shrine's Yushukan war museum, which is tucked off to the side and, until recently, was largely ignored. Yushukan was first established in 1882 to display the relics of Japan's wars, from the diaries of soldiers and samurai swords to the Zero fighter that occupies the entry of the museum. In the 1930s, as Japan embarked on war in China, the museum offered Japanese children a hands-on experience where they could sit in the cockpit of a bomber or fire an air rifle at a target. Millions of visitors, many of them students, came to the museum during those years.[6]

The war museum and its exhibition hall were shut down by the occupation authorities. A limited number of exhibits reopened in the early 1960s, but the entire museum was not opened to the public until 1985, after a restoration. In a visit two years after the reopening, the museum offered a somewhat subdued though clearly unrepentant presentation of Japan's wartime past. Outside the building, a one-man human torpedo, the Kaiten, was displayed. Inside, visitors could see Japanese weapons and models, including the Ohka, a rocket-propelled glider intended to be flown into enemy ships, celebrating, along with the Kaiten, the heroism of suicide attacks carried out by a desperate Japanese military in the waning days of the war. Wandering through the dimly lit stucco building, the visitor came to a large hall, used for the gatherings of groups of aging veterans, dominated at one end by a massive mural of Japanese fighter planes, the rising sun emblem on their wings glittering as they dove out of the sun at an invisible target, suggesting Pearl Harbor was below them.

Foreigners were largely ignorant of the reopened Yushukan. Even those who happened by accident on the building could not read the Japanese captions on the exhibit cases. All that changed in 2002 when a new, expanded, and more modern museum opened its doors, complete with well-lighted exhibition rooms and halls, the contents carefully explained in translated descriptions, though sometimes with sanitized language. The narrative of the war was now visible to foreign visitors, who were appalled to discover a version of history in which the enemy is virtually absent and Japanese actions, from the Sino-Japanese War to the war in the Pacific, are portrayed as acts of heroism and self-defense.

The lobby, partly open to the outside and surrounded by glass walls, is dominated by a Type 0 fighter, the Zero, the main aircraft of the Japanese Imperial Navy from the Sino-Japanese War onward. It is painted a shining dark green, with the large red insignia emblazoned on the wings and fuselage. To the right is a Japanese locomotive of the type that ran along the rail lines between Thailand and Burma in Japanese-conquered Southeast Asia. The description offers no hint of the tens of thousands of prisoners who died building those railways. Visitors wander through a series of exhibition rooms, beginning with *The Spirit of the Samurai*, moving through the early history of Meiji Japan and its internal struggles and then on to the Sino-Japanese War of 1894–1895, the Russo-Japanese War, the takeover of Manchuria in 1931, and then the "China Incident," as the start of the war in 1937 is so carefully labeled. An entire floor is dedicated to the "Greater East Asian War," the term used by the wartime regime. The final rooms are devoted to the display of "mementos of the Noble Spirits enshrined at Yasukuni Shrine," featuring the heartrending final messages that kamikaze pilots penned to loved ones before heading off to certain death.

Taken as one seamless narrative, Yushukan presents a history of glorious warfare leading up to the struggle with the United States and its allies. The museum presents the war as the inevitable product of Japan's efforts to forge a pan-Asian peace, even to liberate Asia from Western colonialism, in the face of outside encroachment. The annexation of Korea, in this version of history, was an effort to free that country from Chinese domination. As the Japanese insisted at the time, Japan's war with the United States is portrayed as a justified response to the hostile assault from the West—the "ABCD encirclement" of Japan by America, Britain, China, and the Dutch—that culminated in the economic embargo imposed by the United States.[7] Even Japan's defeat is presented in this light: "When the war ended the people of Asia returned to their homes. Those whose desire for independence had been awakened were no longer the obedient servants of their [Western] colonizers.... One after another, the nations of Southeast Asia won their independence and their successes inspired Africa and other areas as well," reads an exhibition placard.[8] The Allied judgment against Japan, delivered in the Tokyo War Crimes Tribunal, is largely dismissed—the museum features instead in its final gallery a tribute to Justice Radhibinod Pal, the Indian member of the Tokyo tribunal who offered a dissenting opinion pronouncing the Japanese innocent of war crimes and putting blame for the war on the aggression of American and British imperialism.

It is a sanitized history, comforting perhaps to some veterans and to those on the Japanese right who share this memory of the past, but disturbing to those who were the victims of Japan's colonial rule and wartime aggression, including the Japanese people themselves. "Neatly obliterated from the historical memory of Yushukan are the historical facts of Japanese war crimes, of Japanese colonialism and aggression, and of Japanese defeat," writes British historian John Breen.[9]

For many outside Japan, the Yushukan narrative is the principal, if not the dominant, narrative accepted in postwar Japan. Seen through the lens of media reportage, official statements, and even the writings of academics in the West and in much of Asia, this narrative justifies what one scholar calls "the orthodox interpretation of Japanese war memories."[10] According to this "orthodoxy," Japan was the clear aggressor in the war, it committed numerous atrocities on a scale comparable to Nazi Germany, and both its government and people have failed to acknowledge, much less address, its war responsibility. In that rendition of the war, the only acceptable Japanese response is guilt and contrition, one compatible with the Allied narrative of a "good war" fought to defeat evil foes.

Within that neat understanding, legitimate issues of historical and political debate are put to the side. Was Japan really solely responsible for the war in Asia and the Pacific? Can Japan's crimes, horrific as they were, be compared to those of the Holocaust? Has Japan, both as a state and as a people, truly failed to show contrition for its acts? The answers to those questions are far more complex than the orthodox view of Japan's war memory would allow.

At the root of the flawed nature of this orthodoxy is the assertion that the conservative war memory is the predominant one in Japan. This presumption is not surprising, given not only the impression formed by media and others but also the existence of largely monolithic war-memory narratives in Korea and China, where, at both the official and unofficial levels, the narrative is an undifferentiated tale of victimization by an evil invader and of heroic resistance. Scant reference is given to problems of collaboration with or support for the Japanese colonizer and invader, as such acknowledgment does not meet the more urgent need to use the past to shape national identity.

Japan does not present any such homogeneity of war memory. Since the first days of the American occupation of Japan—and in fact, even before that—the events of the war and how they should be recorded has been a heavily contested battleground.

Undoubtedly, Yushukan faithfully represents the conservative view of the war in Japan, one that can be found in the pages of right-wing media and is entrenched in the ranks of the ruling conservative Liberal Democratic Party (LDP), with scholarly gloss provided by members of the academic and literary intelligentsia. But if anything, they see themselves as something of a beleaguered minority in Japan, engaged in a decades-long war with their ideological foes on the left to reclaim a sense of Japanese pride.

Japanese progressives dominated early attempts to define Japan's war memory, taking their cue from Japan's occupiers. Amid the ruin and rubble of occupied Japan, they embraced the narrative of wartime responsibility embodied in the Tokyo War Crimes Tribunal. In those early years of occupation, amid the burst of democratic fervor and the rise of the long-suppressed Japanese left, Japanese anger was directed at the wartime regime, which was dominated by the military and its allies in the political elite and nominally headed by Emperor Hirohito.

The issue of war responsibility was heavily debated in the 1950s and 1960s, when progressive views held more sway. Liberal intellectuals such as Maruyama Masao argued that aspects of Japanese social structure and popular culture created fertile ground for the rise of militarism in the 1930s. He blamed the prewar imperial system for fostering the growth of ultranationalism and a lack of personal responsibility. Filmmakers such as Ichikawa Kon explored the grim realities of the war in *Harp of Burma* and *Fires on the Plain*, which offer stark portrayals of the bleak conditions of the Japanese army in retreat. Perhaps the most powerful critique of the war was Gomikawa Jumpei's *Ningen no joken* (The Human Condition), a trilogy of films (it also appeared in novel and manga forms) that offer an unremittingly harsh portrait of Japanese rule in northern China, including depictions of forced labor in the service of Japanese corporations, sexual slavery, and acts of brutality committed by soldiers against ordinary Chinese.

The retreat of the Japanese left in both political and intellectual life in Japan from the 1960s onward, propelled by the tides of the Cold War and the fading attraction of the Soviet and Chinese Communist systems, was reflected in a growing conservative voice on wartime memory issues. The counterattack focused in part on the educational system, with the right mounting a fierce critique of the left-wing Japanese teachers union for allegedly carrying a Marxist narrative about the past into the classroom. The intense battles over textbooks actually began in the 1950s, as the LDP began the campaign to revise textbooks, but they gained intensity in the 1980s, when textbook content became an issue of international contention between Japan and both China and Korea.

The progressive narrative lost much of its organizational power with the collapse of the Japanese Socialist Party as the principal opposition force, though the main opposition party, the Democratic Party of Japan, still partially reflects that view of historical responsibility. Still, this historical view remains a strong current of popular culture. To find the narrative in full form, one can visit another museum, far from Tokyo, perched on a cliff overlooking the Pacific Ocean on the southern Japanese island of Okinawa. Here, beginning in late March 1945, the war finally reached Japanese home territory in the form of the American-led invasion of Okinawa. The battle that ensued was a terrible one, fought for months in a "typhoon of steel" that altered the island's landscape and claimed the lives of upward of two hundred thousand people, more than half of them civilians.

The Okinawa Prefectural Peace Memorial Museum does not celebrate a heroic resistance. Its narrative is centered on Okinawa's civilians, the victims of both the American invaders and the brutal Japanese Imperial Army. Most famous among them are the young women and schoolchildren forced to commit suicide by the Japanese army rather than surrender to the Americans. "Some were blown apart by shells, some finding themselves in a hopeless situation were driven to suicide, some died of starvation, some succumbed to malaria, while others fell victim to the retreating Japanese troops," the museum brochure tells visitors. A display inside the museum offers graphic depiction of this. In a diorama, a grim Japanese soldier stands menacingly over an Okinawan family huddled in a cave, his bayonet glinting in the spotlight as the mother tries to smother the cries of her child. "At the hands of Japanese soldiers, civilians were massacred, forced to kill themselves and each other," the caption explains.

The main museum, a long, curving white building, graced by a series of red tile roofs typical of that tropical island, sits on a slight hilltop in the peace park in Mahbuni, where the last resistance to the Americans was mounted. Below, on a bluff overlooking the sea, semicircles of zigzagging black marble walls are inscribed with the names of all who died on the island, from the Allied soldiers and their Japanese army foes to the civilians. Modeled on the Vietnam Veterans Memorial in Washington, DC, the walls offer a poignant salute to the concept that Okinawa symbolizes: in the museum's own words (in its brochure), "the absurdity of war and atrocities it inevitably brings about."

The narrative of history offered in the Okinawa museum offers a very different view of who was responsible for this conflict. The exhibit *Road to the Battle of Okinawa* begins in the first exhibition room with an explanation of Japanese expansionism, which includes the annexation of Okinawa to the Japanese mainland, "aimed at making the Okinawans as faithful subjects of the Emperor." The Japanese Empire, as the museum tells visitors, set about building a strong army, invading neighboring countries, beginning with the Manchurian Incident and leading inexorably to this "last battle ground." For this museum, it is not the "Greater East Asian War" but rather "the fifteen-year war," a term of reference more popular among progressive historians, as it encapsulates the view of the war as a relentless imperialist venture beginning with the takeover of Manchuria in 1931.

The museum, which replaced a smaller, less imposing structure, was the creation of Ota Masahide, the preeminent Okinawan historian of the war, who was elected governor in 1990. Ota was conscripted as a high-school student into a unit called the Blood and Iron Student Corps and sent to work with pick and shovel to build airfields and fortifications for the Imperial Army. When the American forces landed, they were sent into the battlefield without any training. "Every day we were told that to give our life to the emperor is the best way to live as a human being," Ota recalls. "We believed that."[11] Ota was among the Japanese soldiers clinging to resistance at Mahbuni, pounded by American warships offshore and by the army onshore. Even after the resistance collapsed, Ota was among those who hid in caves, told not to surrender by commanders who threatened to kill their own soldiers. He did not emerge and give himself up to the Americans until October of 1945, unaware until then that Japan had surrendered in August.

As a college student in the early 1950s, Ota wrote his first book about the Battle of Okinawa, the first of many, a powerful collection of personal accounts of his high-school classmates who survived the war. Educated later in the United States, Ota dedicated himself to telling the story of the Battle of Okinawa for a general audience, initially as a journalist and popular writer. He went on to write a dozen books about the war, and after winning the governorship in 1990, he pushed to build a new museum that would reflect the Okinawan experience of war. But Ota, as a progressive, also dedicated himself to opposing the massive American base presence that has remained entrenched on Okinawa, even since the island reverted to Japanese administration in 1972.

The opening of the museum in 2000 was not without controversy. The victory of an LDP-backed candidate in the governor's election two years earlier led to change in the content to play down the displays depicting Japan's military aggression in Asia and the role of the Imperial Army in forced suicide. Popular protest fought back against these changes, as they did on several occasions when educational bureaucrats in Tokyo sought to remove references to forced suicide from textbooks.[12] The progressive narrative has faded somewhat in its influence, along with the organized Japanese left. What remains the dominant narrative in Japan, however, one that overlaps in certain respects with both the conservative and progressive narratives, is the pacifist narrative. In this version of the past, war itself is the enemy, an experience of destruction of the Japanese nation and, to a lesser extent, its neighbors, which should never be repeated. It is a narrative of victimization, one that condemns the act of war but rejects the notion of a "just war."

That antiwar narrative is ubiquitous in Japanese popular culture, in everything from novels to television and the cinema. Perhaps one of the most powerful expressions of that is the famous 1988 anime film, *Grave of the Fireflies*, by Takahata Isao, a collaborator of Miyazaki Hayao's Studio Ghibli. The film follows two orphaned children, a brother and sister, coping with the hunger and suffering of wartime Japan, facing the destruction of an unseen enemy far overhead in B-29 bombers. There is no sign of heroism, only the suffering of children in war. Indeed, the Japanese adults are portrayed as unusually cold and unwilling to help the children.

The film is loosely based on Takahata's own wartime experience of fleeing the firebombing of Okayama on June 29, 1945. "Of course, I had it in mind when I was making *Grave of the Fireflies* what I had experienced in that dawn bombing myself," explains Takahata.[13] He and his sister became separated from their parents. "All around, all around, Okayama was burning." They managed to flee and survive in the river running through the city, but when they came back, Takahata recalls, "all was dust; there was nothing there, and in front of the house, there were all the corpses of many people. It was such an experience, I can't tell you."[14] The film is rebroadcast annually in Japan, though it still draws the protests of rightists.

The most visible, and visited, expression of this pacifist narrative can be found in the Peace Memorial Museum built near ground zero in the western Japanese city of Hiroshima, the site of the first use of the atomic bomb in warfare. The graceful three-building structure is set at the entrance to a large park where every year the city holds a ceremony to mark the moment on August 6, 1945, when the bomb was detonated over the city. Up until then, Hiroshima had been spared from the horrific wave of airborne attacks on Japanese cities, including the March 9–10 firebombing of Tokyo that claimed some one hundred thousand lives.

The decision to use the atomic bomb remains a subject of intense debate among historians and military experts, not least in the United States. Was it truly necessary to end the war and to save lives of both the Japanese and the Allied soldiers gearing up for invasion of the Japanese mainland? Did a second bomb have to be dropped on Nagasaki? Wasn't Japan on the verge of surrender anyway? Did the bombing cause Japan to surrender, or did other factors, including the Soviet entry into the war two days later, force the decision? Were there other factors, such as the desire to limit the Soviet Union's postwar role, behind the American decision?

If those questions remain hotly debated elsewhere, there is no question of how they are answered for the millions who still visit the Hiroshima museum, by far the most visited war museum in Japan. The museum offers a brief nod to the Japanese aggression that preceded this moment. Following a renovation of the museum in 1994, new exhibits were mounted to acknowledge that Japan's aggression, including the slaughter of Chinese in Nanjing in 1937, started the war. The museum authorities understood that this was necessary to legitimize the message of victimization that is at the center of the museum's narrative.[15]

Visitors to the museum weave their way through several floors of exhibits, spread over two buildings, that offer an emotionally powerful tale of the enormous destructive power of the weapon. The museum takes you past artifacts of its effects, from a charred children's lunch box, bottles melted into bizarre twisted shapes, and the shadow of a victim who was sitting on some steps when the flash of heat whitened the stone around him. The terror of radiation, which claimed its victims for years afterward, is explored in detail. The death toll by the end of 1945 was estimated at over one hundred thousand, and perhaps as many more died within five years from the aftereffects of the bombing.

The historical message of the museum is unmistakable—it rejects the justification that the atomic bombing was necessary to save lives. It rather embraces the view, popular on the Japanese left and among revisionist historians in the United States, that the United States was looking past Japan's surrender to the postwar order and the coming contest for world domination with the Soviet Union. In an exhibit devoted to the question of why the United States decided to drop the bomb, the museum offers this version of history:

> After Germany's surrender, tension mounted between the U.S. and the Soviet Union regarding the disposition of postwar Europe. The U.S. began worrying

about the increased influence the Soviets would obtain if they joined the war against Japan in mid-August as planned. The U.S. believed that if the atomic bomb ended the war, the U.S. would establish postwar supremacy over the Soviets.[16]

That view leaves aside the arguments made by the United States at the time, though they were certainly disputed subsequently, that the use of the atomic bomb hastened surrender and saved lives. Perhaps more importantly, it isolates the atomic bombings as a singular event only loosely related to the decisions that set Japan on a path of colonialism and aggression and led to the war with the United States. Of course, Americans have also had difficulty with those who question the morality of the decision to use the bomb. As Notre Dame University scholar Benedict Giamo puts it,

> While the Smithsonian *Enola Gay* exhibit evades confronting the atomic bombings of Hiroshima and Nagasaki, the Peace Memorial Museum/Park severs historical consciousness of the Pacific War—and the question of responsibility—from the last acts themselves. In remembering the last acts of atomic victimage, everything that came before is mostly forgotten or simply rendered abstract.[17]

The evasion of responsibility has its origins, in part, in the decisions made by the American occupation of Japan. The most important decision was made even before the occupation began, when the United States accepted the surrender of Japan with the understanding that it would allow the emperor system in Japan to continue in place. Supreme Commander General Douglas MacArthur made a fateful decision to leave Emperor Hirohito on his throne, calculating with some degree of justification that the emperor could play a valuable role in persuading the Japanese people to accept foreign occupation. MacArthur compounded the impact of his decision by taking the emperor and his wartime role out of the deliberations of the Tokyo War Crimes Tribunal.

Whatever the rationale of that decision, it also allowed the Japanese themselves, who had been loyal subjects of the emperor, to avoid serious examination of their own responsibility. The exigencies of the Cold War further led the occupation to suppress the Japanese left in the late 1940s and to allow, if not encourage, the reentry into politics of key parts of the wartime establishment. Thus, the question of who was responsible for Japan's war in Asia and the Pacific remained a matter of debate, which is unresolved to this day in Japan.

The failure to resolve this question was the impetus for a special project undertaken by the conservative *Yomiuri Shimbun*, a daily with the world's largest circulation. The research institute of the newspaper carried out a massive historical research project aimed at answering the central issue of the war: "Who was responsible?" The results of that project, which involved documentary research, interviews, and other historical investigation, were published in the paper in a series of articles in 2005, tied to the sixtieth anniversary of the end of the war. The series was later published as a two-volume study and was translated into other languages.

The study was the brainchild of Watanabe Tsuneo, the aging but still powerful publisher of the *Yomiuri*. As a young man entering university in 1945, he was drafted and stationed on the coast to await the invading Americans. "Of course, we knew we'd lose," he recalls. "The military was always saying 'we'll win, we'll win,' but everyone knew for sure." Watanabe had witnessed the firebombing of Tokyo, and he saw Japan's defeat coming; he even welcomed it. "I didn't have feelings of enmity toward Americans," he recounts. "Japan had started the war by attacking Pearl Harbor. So everything was a matter of surrendering quickly. It was because the military wasn't surrendering, because the government wasn't doing so, that we ended up like this. I just wanted us to get defeated quickly. That's what I hoped for, though I would have been considered a traitor."[18]

In the early years of the occupation, Watanabe joined the Communists. "My main thought was to bring down the Japanese military and the emperor system, to raze them to the ground."[19] Today, Watanabe is a powerful member of the conservative establishment in Japan, able to meet with the emperor and empress and a supporter of the humanized, more democratic version of the monarchy. But even now, speaking in his Tokyo office, surrounded by photos of himself with presidents and prime ministers, Watanabe does not forgive Emperor Hirohito. "Millions were killed in his name—he bears that responsibility, that sin. I think he should have retired to Ise Shrine or somewhere. I still think that."[20]

Watanabe ordered the *Yomiuri* research and publication out of concern that the passing of the wartime generation would leave successive Japanese generations without a clear understanding of the war and what it meant for Japan. "After all, people now obviously have no experience of the war, never saw the bombing," he says. "That's the bulk of the people, and of course they cannot understand. But [it has] not even been a century since the time of the mess of the war that we created in Korea, China, and the Pacific region. I am not saying people should be suspicious of, or hate, or resent their parents, but they need to understand that this was the kind of political system it was. So textbooks should clearly say the government ordered these brutal invasions. They should teach the truth about it."[21]

Watanabe rejects the attempt to see the war as a product of imperialist rivalry between Japan and the United States and its allies, an argument embraced by some on the left as well as the right. "It was a unilateral act and invasion on the part of Japan," he says without hesitation.[22]

Watanabe and the *Yomiuri* research team sought to retry the Tokyo War Crimes Tribunal to identify those most responsible for the disastrous decision to go to war and its conduct. They do not disagree with the Tokyo judgments, including the Allied decision not to prosecute the emperor and the conviction of the fourteen Class A war criminals, led by Tojo. Indeed, Watanabe has crusaded against the Yasukuni shrine authorities for their decision to enshrine those men and joined with the editor of the liberal *Asahi Shimbun* in calling for the creation of a national war cemetery to replace Yasukuni.

But the *Yomiuri* goes beyond that, adding others to the list of those who deserve the opprobrium of responsibility for the war, among them Prime Minister Konoe Fumimaro, who held that post when the attack on Pearl Harbor was decided, and several others. The *Yomiuri* also criticizes the United States for the firebombing of Japanese cities and the dropping of the atomic bombs, while also putting blame on the Soviet Union for unilaterally revoking the neutrality pact with Japan and declaring war in early August 1945.

Ultimately, however, the *Yomiuri* decisively places responsibility on Japan itself and its wartime leaders. As Watanabe makes clear in the foreword to the volume on the project, without the Japanese taking responsibility, there is no hope for reconciliation:

> The *Yomiuri Shimbun*'s efforts were based on its belief that there can be no genuinely honest and friendly dialogue with those countries which suffered considerable damage and casualties in the wars with Japan, without correctly understanding Japan's past. To that end, we, the Japanese people, should follow our consciences in explaining on our own how barbaric the wars were and who should be held responsible.[23]

## Sakurai Yoshiko

Sakurai Yoshiko's Tokyo house stands a few steps down a stone pathway from the red lacquered posts and sloped tile roof of the Hikawa Shrine, a Shinto structure that was once the personal shrine of the shogun Tokugawa Yoshimune. The shrine and home are tucked away on a quiet side street of central Tokyo's Akasaka district, famous for its nightlife and for being the watering hole of Japan's political class. Behind a discreet stucco wall, Sakurai's home is a graceful combination of the modern and the traditional in Japanese life, with lustrous wood tables and antique *tansu* illuminated by recessed lighting.

It is a perfect setting for Sakurai, whose fiery commentary on current affairs and television has made her one of the most well-known voices of the contemporary Japanese right wing. She is a relentless defender of her vision of a traditional Japan but also one who can convey her views in fluent English. A proud alumnus of the University of Hawaii, she earned her spurs in journalism by working for the influential American newspaper the

Sakurai Yoshiko

*Christian Science Monitor*. After almost a decade of newspaper reporting, Sakurai began a career in 1980 as a highly popular television newscaster for Nippon Television, a post she held until 1996.

From that point, Sakurai embarked on a new career as a commentator, a champion of what some call the "assertive conservative right" in Japan, taking on issues ranging from history to contemporary culture. Talking in calm, polite tones over tea and traditional Japanese sweets in her home, however, Sakurai hardly conveys the image that leaps from the pages of the conservative magazines and newspapers.

In her writings, Sakurai constantly warns against the threat of a rising China and offers a torrent of criticism of Japanese governments for their toothless response to the Chinese menace. Sakurai's response to an incident in 2010 in the East China Sea, where a Chinese fishing-boat captain rammed his vessel into Japanese coast-guard ships trying to shoo the Chinese fishermen out of disputed waters, was typical. "There can hardly be anything more intolerable than the cowardice demonstrated by Prime Minister Naoto Kan and Chief Cabinet Secretary Yoshito Sengoku in their recent handling of the violation of Japan's territorial waters by a Chinese trawler ship near the Senkaku Islands," she wrote that fall.[24] She sees China using its growing power to assert hegemony over the region—and over Japan. "China is expanding the sphere of its orderliness with its strong will and ever-growing military power," she wrote later that year in a long essay in the right-wing daily *Sankei Shimbun*.[25] When the North Koreans carried out an artillery attack on a South Korean island in December of that year, Sakurai saw the hidden hand of China. "By not earnestly checking North Korea's reckless action, China is challenging the existing order of the present international community," she wrote in her weekly column.[26]

Sakurai's rhetoric is designed to touch the fears harbored by many Japanese that the country is inexorably fading and falling under China's influence. "Even today," she wrote later, after relations seemed to improve, "China is scheming against Japan under various pretexts. . . . One must not believe in China's sweet talk and smiles." Japan "must absolutely avoid relying excessively on economic relations with China," she continued, pointing to Chinese acquisitions of Japanese firms. Sakurai even warned against student exchanges and the flood of Chinese students into Japanese universities. "In no time," she wrote, "this has laid the groundwork for Japan to be infested with Chinese spies."[27]

Sakurai's writings and commentary on wartime history issues have been equally imbued with a spirit of Japanese patriotism, a sense that the portrayal of wartime Japan as the sole aggressor has been unfair. The desire to restore Japanese pride in the past animates her actions, as well. She has vigorously defended Japan against accusations of war crimes, such as the forced recruitment of women in conquered lands to serve as "comfort women" in brothels organized by the Imperial Army. Sakurai joins others on the right in Japan in denying the most horrendous war crimes, such as the mass murder of Chinese civilians in Nanjing in 1937, the infamous Nanjing Massacre. Like other "assertive conservatives," Sakurai defends Japan's record of colonial rule in Korea, Taiwan, and Manchuria and argues that Japan was forced into war with the United States in desperate defense of its interests in Asia. "It was not a war of aggression against the U.S.," she tells us, "though Americans may get mad."[28]

Sakurai became particularly engaged on the issue of comfort women, leading a response to a congressional resolution sponsored by San Jose Democrat Mike Honda that presented the tale of these women as one of coerced sexual slavery and called on Japan to compensate its victims and educate its youth about this history. She wrote strident attacks on the resolution, which Japanese rightists claimed was the product of lobbying by overseas Chinese and Koreans. In a full-page advertisement published on June 14, 2007, in the *Washington Post*, Sakurai and four other members of the self-styled Committee for Historical Facts presented what they claimed were the true "facts" about comfort women.

"Fact 1," the *Post* advertisement began, was the assertion that "no historical document has ever been found by historians or research organizations that positively demonstrates that women were forced against their will into prostitution by the Japanese army." It was unscrupulous brokers, who were later punished, who forced or tricked women into joining brothels to service soldiers. Faced with well-documented cases of women rounded up by the army, such as Dutch women prisoners in the East Indies, the group fell back on the contention that these were cases of "breakdowns in discipline." The final "fact," one that Sakurai frequently cites, is that these were not "sex slaves" but rather a commonplace system of "licensed prostitution," no different in kind from "comfort stations" set up in Japan under the American occupation to service American soldiers.[29]

"We were ashamed of this case [of comfort women]," Sakurai acknowledges, "but at the same time, I'd like American readers to realize the same thing happened when we lost the war.... So many Japanese women became prostitutes or mistresses of American soldiers. No one wants to talk about it. No suits have been brought in Japan or to the U.S. government. But it is an ugly side of war that women are used in this way. Not just by Japan."[30]

As we discuss elsewhere in this book (see chapter 6), the story of the comfort women, and of forced labor in general, is certainly more complex than some activists would admit. There is evidence of women who went off willingly, including from Japan, driven by conditions of severe poverty, to the Imperial Army's brothels. But there is also abundant proof, including material gathered by the Tokyo War Crimes Tribunal convened after the war, as well as documents in official archives uncovered by Japanese historians in the early 1990s, that this was a system set up under official auspices in which tens of thousands of women, many of whom never returned home to their families, were coerced into participation.

Sakurai is representative of Japanese historical revisionists who have downplayed, excused, or denied Japanese war crimes, most prominently the looting, rape, and mass murder of hundreds of thousands of the Chinese in the capital of Nanjing in 1937 in the early days of the Sino-Japanese War, the so-called Nanjing Massacre. Those disputes over Nanjing began in the 1970s but accelerated through the next two decades. In the 1990s, Japanese history textbooks for both middle- and high-school students generally acknowledged these crimes, including their scale, some citing the figures of two to three hundred thousand victims, the former the number given by the judgment of the Tokyo War Crimes Tribunal and the latter the number used by Chinese authorities. These frank admissions spurred conservatives to challenge those textbooks and call for their "reform." Denials of the Nanjing Massacre escalated after the publication in 1997 of *The Rape of Nanking: China's Hidden Holocaust*, authored by Chinese American author Iris Chang. The book relied heavily on the recently unearthed diary of John Rabe, a German businessman who ran the Nanking Safety Zone, where Chinese refugees were sheltered from Japanese assault. The book almost single-handedly revived the Nanjing Massacre as a global issue, but it was also riddled with errors and factual mistakes, making it a target of revisionist attack.

Japanese conservatives rolled out a series of volumes attacking Chang and her account of what one book typically termed "the alleged 'Nanking massacre.'"[31] Criticisms came from conservative academics such as Higashinakano Shudo, a professor at Tokyo's Asia University, who provided a detailed account of what he claimed were hundreds of factual errors in her book.[32] In the view of Japanese conservatives, the Nanjing Massacre was a creation of propaganda by Chinese Nationalists, who were amplified by the postwar tribunals to justify their judgments against Japan's leaders. Some dispute the numbers; others, the very nature of the crime—at most, they concede some deaths as a product of the chaos of conflict, caused in part by the Chinese defenders.

"It is impossible to find any information in available resources dealing with Nanking in 1937 to substantiate claims that a massacre was perpetrated in that city," concludes Higashinakano.[33] Like the professor, Sakurai cites documents that suggest a very different explanation for the events in that Chinese city. "These things make me not believe there was a massacre," she tells us. "I used to believe there was." She recounts an interview she had given some years ago in which she told the prominent Japanese conservative monthly *Bungei Shunju* that perhaps some ten to twenty thousand Chinese were killed by Japanese soldiers. "But now, I deny even that," she says.[34]

For revisionist conservatives in Japan, the struggle against the postwar judgment of Japan's leaders and their decision to go to war goes beyond specific crimes. It extends backward to a defense of Japan's colonial expansion into Korea and Manchuria, to a depiction of Japan as the liberator of Asia from Western imperialism, and finally to the core issue of whether Japan was the aggressor in the war with the United States.

Perhaps the most stunning expression of this view of the past in recent years was voiced by Tamogami Toshio, an air force general who, by the fall of 2008, had risen to the highest level in his service, the Chief of Staff of the Japan Air Self-Defense Force. A slight, somewhat unassuming officer who rose through the ranks as a commander of air-defense missile batteries, Tamogami became a national figure when he published an essay in a contest on history sponsored by a real-estate conglomerate known to be a promoter of right-wing history and politics. His essay, provocatively titled "Was Japan an Aggressor Nation?," won the contest and was published online.[35]

Hours after its publication, General Tamogami was forced into retirement for expressing views expressly contrary to the stated position of the

Japanese government. The incident triggered protest from China and South Korea, but it also catapulted Tamogami into rock-star status on the Japanese right, as he was invited to speak across the country and lauded for his stance. Tamogami's answer to the question in the title of his essay was a resounding no. In his view, Japan's advance into Asia was entirely legal and without the need for force. In our interview, he tells us:

> The 1910 annexation of Korea was much closer to a merger than to the creation of a colony. After all, Koreans were part of the Japanese military system—officers in the Imperial Army, even generals—and people from the royal family of Korea married into the royal family of Japan.... Japan did not oppress Korea or Taiwan or Manchuria. It developed those places and handled them in the same way it did the mainland of Japan.[36]

Tamogami, who worked closely with American military counterparts in the U.S.-Japan security alliance, goes even further to offer a classic revisionist account of the events that led to the decision to attack Pearl Harbor and begin war with America. "Japan was ensnared in a trap that was very carefully laid by the United States in order to draw Japan into a war," he writes in his essay. Echoing some American revisionists, Tamogami espouses the view that Roosevelt needed to maneuver Japan to take the first shot, and it was given no alternative after the ultimatum delivered by Secretary of State Cordell Hull in the fall of 1941. "The Tokyo Trials tried to push all the responsibility for the war onto Japan," he writes. "And that mind control is still misleading the Japanese people 63 years after the war."[37]

This was not the first time a postwar Japanese military leader expressed such views, but it was a first for someone holding an active position. Justice Minister Nagano Shigeto, a former chief of staff of the army, expressed similar views in May 1994, also prompting his resignation. "I still think it is wrong to define [the war] as a war of aggression," he told an audience. "Because Japan was in danger of being crushed, the country rose up to ensure its survival. We also sincerely believed in liberating Asia's colonies and establishing the Greater East Asian Co-Prosperity Sphere.... I think the Rape of Nanking is a fabrication."[38]

Sakurai, whose education and career took her close to Americans, is a bit more careful in rendering judgment on the war in the Pacific. For her, like many Japanese, the war seems less a morality play than a grave mistake, with its shared responsibility defying pronouncements of right and wrong.

"We committed our own crimes," she says. "You committed your own crimes. But we lost. If we're looking back all the time, we can't go forward."

## Takagi Kenichi

Japan began its wars in Asia as a relatively rich nation, vastly more powerful than the victims of its aggression. When it needed laborers to work in the mines, forests, and factories of its far-flung empire, Japan could lure them with high wages. That is how tens of thousands of Koreans, their nation occupied by Japan as a colony since 1910, came to the otherwise forbidding island of Sakhalin, whose resource-rich southern half had come into Japan's hands after its defeat of Russia in 1905.

But by 1940, Japan's fortunes of war had soured. The mighty empire was sunk into a quagmire of a war in China, a struggle that ate up resources in blood and treasure with no victory in sight. And a war with China's allies— the United States, Britain, and other Western powers—loomed closer and closer. Desperate for resources, the empire no longer bothered with offering

Takagi Kenichi

bounteous wages to Koreans willing to work in Sakhalin's coal mines or the mines and factories on Japanese home islands. Instead, it resorted to forced labor—coerced recruitment at very low wages, many of which were never paid but only recorded on paper.

As the tides of war swung heavily against Japan, Koreans were simply conscripted into labor. At its high point, some 150,000 Koreans worked on the island of Sakhalin alone, and many times more worked in Japan itself. When the Soviet Union took back control of this remote corner of Russia at the end of the war, about 400,000 Japanese were repatriated home from the island along with a large number of Koreans, who went to Japan or, in some cases, to the northern half of Korea, which was then under Soviet occupation. That left, by later estimates, about 43,000 Koreans from the southern part of Korea, which was controlled by the United States until 1948. As the Cold War deepened, propelled by the Korean War, those Koreans were left in legal limbo—Japan, which had brought them to this remote land, denied any responsibility for them, but they were unable to return home because there were no relations between the Soviet Union and South Korea.

"What I really can't understand is that after the war, the Japanese went home, and we were just abandoned here," Chung Teong Young plaintively told a rare visiting group of Western journalists gathered in a small meeting hall in the provincial capital of Yuzhno-Sakhalinsk in the fall of 1989. In 1943, at the age of twenty, Chung had been dragooned from his village in the southern part of Korea and sent to the mines of Sakhalin.[39]

Many of the Koreans left on Sakhalin abandoned any hope of returning home, opting for either Soviet or North Korean citizenship. But about seven thousand of them remained loyal to their motherland, declaring themselves stateless persons and demanding to be repatriated (many Koreans who found themselves in Japan at the end of the war chose the same status). The Japanese government took the position that it bore no legal responsibility for those who became caught up in wartime forced labor, so it would not repatriate them to Japan.

Into this forgotten corner of debris left from Japan's defeat stepped Takagi Kenichi, a human-rights lawyer who had begun his career in the late 1960s defending student radicals who had once been his comrades at Japan's elite Tokyo University. Takagi was born in the closing days of the war in Japanese-occupied Manchuria, on May 15, 1944, where his father worked as an architect for the Anshan mines. His father was taken prisoner by the

Soviet armies that entered the war in its closing days, and he was sent to Siberia where he spent three years in forced labor. "I didn't hear much about the content of my father's experience other than it was a great struggle," Takagi recounts.[40] His father returned to work after the war to rejoin an American architectural firm. His bosses told Takagi later that his father "was a different man after the war." Takagi's father died as his son entered university.

Despite his father's experience, Takagi had very little sense of the war, only a vague desire to work "on behalf of the weak people in society." Soon after becoming a lawyer in 1973, the leader of the association of Korean Kyoto residents came to his office. The association leader was famous for his challenges to Japan to take responsibility for marshaling Koreans as forced laborers during the war. He asked Takagi to help him with a suit to force Japan to take responsibility to return the Koreans from Sakhalin. Takagi agreed, launching a legal crusade that lasted for more than fifteen years and led to a career of taking up the causes of other victims of the war, including Koreans who suffered in the atomic bombings, Japanese prisoners of war in the Soviet Union, and women from the Philippines who were forced into sexual slavery.

The first task in the Sakhalin case, Takagi recalls, was to find some plaintiffs. Through former Korean workers who had Japanese wives and were repatriated to Japan, he was able to make contact with a handful of Koreans in Sakhalin and recruit them to join the suit. He got in touch with their families in Korea and consulted them, as well. Takagi skirted around the problem of returning them to Korea by arguing that since they had been in Japan before being sent to Sakhalin, they should be returned there—they could go on to Korea after that, he reasoned. "I argued that the Japanese state should take responsibility for these people because the most basic human right recognized by the world was the right of people to return to their own home. This was not a matter of citizenship but of the place where people resided," he says.

The suit was launched in 1975 to compel the Japanese government to guarantee their return to Japan. The Japanese government argued that the decision lay in the hands of the Soviet authorities. The suit wandered through the courts for more than a decade, a long process that is not uncommon in the Japanese courts, particularly with controversial matters. Takagi understood that the goal was not a court ruling but a decision in the court of public opinion. "The media started covering it, and there was pressure on the government, and public opinion was energized," he says.

With the coming of change in the Soviet Union, particularly after Mikhail Gorbachev came to power and eased restrictions on Jewish emigration, the attitudes in Moscow softened. Takagi was able to help Koreans get immigration permits and bring them to Japan. Japanese volunteers met them and took them to Tokyo to hold tearful reunions with family members from Korea. In two and a half years, from 1988 to 1990, Takagi brought one thousand people out of Sakhalin. Families who had been separated for forty-five years were rejoined: children with parents, wives with husbands. "I was there," Takagi reflects, "and it was a huge joy for me."

The Seoul Olympics in 1988 led to Soviet recognition of South Korea, as well. And in 1987, Takagi and other allies organized a group of members of the Japanese parliament to support their cause. Starting in 1991, the parliament provided funds in cooperation with the South Korean Red Cross to run charter flights directly to Seoul, bringing about twenty thousand Koreans back to their homeland in the end. Takagi dropped the suit, finally, in 1988.

The next war issue for Takagi, who was a member of the Human Rights Committee of the Japan Bar Association, was the plight of Koreans who had suffered radiation exposure from the American atomic bombings of Hiroshima and Nagasaki. There was no treatment available for them in Korea, and the Koreans were not eager to publicize the plight of victims of the atomic bombing, an act supported by almost all Koreans. The Japanese government had provided funding for the Koreans to come to Japan for treatment, but the Korean government refused appeals to continue that arrangement. "The Korean government said no, that's just propaganda to make the Japanese look good, and our treatment is as good as yours anyway," Takagi recalls. "So the result was to support the treatment in Korea." Ultimately, in 1988, Takagi persuaded both governments to build a Japanese-funded treatment facility in Korea. "Sometimes it's strange like that."

Takagi's most voluminous work has become one of the most delicate and difficult issues remaining from the war: compensation to individual victims. He filed a suit in 1990 on behalf of Sakhalin Koreans seeking compensation for their labor and demanding legal responsibility by the Japanese government. The suit was withdrawn when the Japanese government offered to negotiate, ultimately paying to construct assisted-living facilities in Korea for the aging former forced laborers. But it was the first case seeking compensation for individual victims of forced labor and conscription. A few years later, Takagi was asked to take on the case of Filipina comfort women. In 1991, he had gone as a representative to what became a series of meetings of the Asia-Pacific Area War Compensation Forum, which brought together representatives from ten countries, including China, Korea, Hong Kong, Indonesia, Singapore, and Malaysia. He recalls,

> Going to all these places, islands in the Philippines and so on, I had the feeling that I was retreading the traces of the war. I had the sense that these victims had just been left untouched, that Japan must therefore give compensation. That view of mine has never changed. But I also learned that not all the Japanese did was bad, as is the general view. I learned, for example, in the Philippines, that there were Japanese military men who tried to save the comfort women—very human stories. These facts must be known in Japanese society, too.

The question of compensation remains an ongoing source of tension between Japan and Korea and between Japan and its wartime foes, including China and the Western allies. From American prisoners of war seeking compensation for forced labor in coal mines in Kyushu to the Chinese and Koreans brought to work in Japan, victims of the war—the few that are still left—seek recognition in the form of a Japanese admission of responsibility to compensate them. Many point to the example of Germany, which accepted its responsibility to compensate some individuals beyond reparations paid to states, mostly for Jewish victims of the Holocaust. Germany argued for a long time, including in American courts, that it was not responsible for compensation to all those employed as forced laborers in the camps and factories during the war. But under pressure, and with the encouragement of the U.S. government, Germany changed its stance and in 2000 formed a fund, the Foundation for Remembrance, Responsibility and Future, or the so-called Fund for the Future, with money from both the German parliament and corporations, to pay compensation to all individuals of any nationality who served in forced labor.[41]

In the case of Japan, the principle of individual compensation has never been accepted. After the war, Japan paid reparations to the nations that were the targets of its aggression, and the San Francisco Peace Treaty, signed in 1951, considered those reparations to have resolved the issue. Communist-controlled China, the People's Republic, and the two Koreas were not, however, signatories to that treaty. When Japan normalized its relations with China in 1972 and with South Korea in 1965, it agreed to massive economic grants and loans that were considered to be forms of delayed reparations. On this basis, the Japanese government's response to claims for individual compensation is that these were settled by those treaties and that Japan no longer has any legal obligation to pay money to those individuals. When the issue of the comfort women emerged in the early 1990s, the Japanese government tried to solve the problem by creating a nongovernmental Asian Women's Fund to provide compensation, a structure that allowed it to keep intact its legal position. The U.S. government, in response to suits filed in American courts, has backed the Japanese interpretation of the San Francisco treaty.

Takagi has challenged the Japanese government's position, arguing repeatedly in court and in print that the state cannot deprive individuals of the right to seek compensation, particularly from nongovernment entities like the Japanese companies that employed the forced laborers. He points to the contradictory stance taken by the Japanese government in supporting the right of those Japanese whose property was seized by Canada during the war to seek compensation. Similarly, Japanese prisoners of war in Siberia, such as Takagi's father, were supported in their claims against the Soviet Union. So far, the Japanese courts have ruled against Takagi's suits. But he remains committed to the cause. The shelves of his small Tokyo office remain jammed with the files of wartime claimants. He remains determined, fueled in part by the sense that the Japanese people have yet to come to grips with their own responsibility for the injustices of the past.

In his view, the origins of this failure go back in part to the decisions made by the Allies about postwar justice. That begins, for Takagi, with the decision of the United States not to hold the emperor individually responsible. "All was done in the name of the emperor," he says without a hint of qualification. "Even if the military carried it out, they used his name to do so, and he knew it and let them. The fact that America allowed him to remain in place was America's biggest crime. . . . He should have been tried."

That decision was compounded by the matter of who was tried in Tokyo. In contrast to Nuremberg, where not only wartime leaders but also German businessmen, scholars, and others were put on trial for the crimes against humanity of the Nazi regime, the Tokyo trial was focused solely on crimes against peace, and only a handful of military and civilian leaders were tried.

126  NATIONAL MEMORIES

War crimes were tried only in the subsidiary trials held out in Asia—in China, the Philippines, or the Dutch East Indies where the atrocities and mass murders carried out by the Japanese military were aired. "I think that's because America and England didn't even have in their line of sight the Asian victims at all," Takagi states. As a result, the Japanese people did not really confront, as Germans were forced to do, those crimes in Asia. "The postwar compensation issues—that Japan should pay compensation to the victims in Asia—is the first effort to deal with this issue of the war here in Japan," Takagi says. "I was the one who coined the term 'postwar compensation' back in the first case in 1993, I think it was. For forty-five years, nothing was done at our instigation, and I think it is important that it be done at *our* instigation, as it had been in Germany."

## Takahata Isao

Until the last year of the war, the Japanese living on the home islands were largely insulated from the direct experience of warfare, other than the growing shortages created by the demands of the military and the slow

Takahata Isao

strangulation imposed by American submarine warfare. In November 1944, the American air forces were finally able to launch long-range bombing raids from the captured Marianas Islands in the Pacific. Even then, the raids were small, concentrated against Japanese aircraft production, with bombers dropping their loads in daytime attacks carried out from very high altitudes that usually missed their targets.

All that changed on the night of March 9–10, 1945. Under the command of General Curtis E. LeMay, a new American strategy of air warfare against Japan's cities was begun that night over Tokyo. Large formations of B-29 Superfortresses flew in at a low altitude, which allowed them to carry heavier loads of incendiary bombs designed to set Japan's wooden cities on fire. On that early spring night, 1,667 tons of incendiary bombs were dropped on Tokyo's most densely populated districts. The resulting firestorm killed, by the estimate of the United States Strategic Bombing Survey, some 185,000 people. Other estimates are somewhat lower, but no matter which number is used, the death and destruction wrought on Japan in that single night's attack was greater that what took place five months later in the atomic bombings of Hiroshima and Nagasaki.

Over the intervening five months, General LeMay's nighttime bombing campaign destroyed nearly half of the area of sixty-six cities. Incendiary bombs were particularly effective against Japanese cities because of their wooden houses and narrow streets. Half of Tokyo was wiped out, and even more of the port city of Kobe and a third of the western Japanese center of Nagoya. More than 330,000 Japanese were killed and almost a half million injured, most of them by burns from the ferocious fires that consumed homes, schools, and workplaces.

The fire bombings of Germany, most notably the destruction of the medieval city of Dresden in February 1944, are much better documented, not least through Kurt Vonnegut's influential novel *Slaughterhouse-Five*. Yet only some twenty-five thousand people died in what many consider an epochal moment in the European theater, along with about forty thousand victims of the firebombing of Hamburg. The far vaster massacre of civilians in Japan's cities in firebombings is barely noted, at least outside of Japan. The attack on Tokyo is still marked there every year with a solemn ceremony that brings together a dwindling group of survivors to share their experiences with fellow Japanese, most of whom have no personal memory of these events.

The most powerful reminder of those dark days comes, however, in the form of an animated film, *Hotaru no haka*, or, as it is titled in English, *Grave of the Fireflies*. First released in 1988, the film is shown every summer on Japanese television to mark the anniversary of the war's end. It has been watched almost universally by Japanese schoolchildren for decades. It has been compared to Steven Spielberg's *Schindler's List* for its profound emotional impact and its status, in the view of critics, as one of the greatest war movies ever made. It has been remade at least twice as a live-action film for television and the cinema.

Based on a novel of the same name by Nosaka Akiyuki, the film takes place in those final months of Japan's war, telling the gripping and profoundly sad story of two children, the pre-teen boy Seita and his younger sister Setsuko, in the city of Kobe. The film takes the form of an extended flashback to Japan during the firebombings, narrated by the spirit of Seita. The flashback begins in Kobe with the B-29s flying almost invisibly overhead. The children had been left to guard their house and the family's belongings while their mother, who was suffering from heart problems, had been moved to a bomb shelter. The firebombs strike their neighborhood, destroying their home. Though the children survive without injury, their mother dies from burns she suffers in the attack. Their father is serving as a sailor in the Imperial Navy—and, they learn later, probably dead.

The orphaned boy and his sister suffer at the hands of an aunt who becomes increasingly resentful and angry with them as food supplies dwindle. Seita is bullied by mean kids but swallows his pride to save himself and his sister. The children flee to create a home in an abandoned dirt bomb shelter dug out of the side of a hill. They fill it with fireflies to provide light, but this moment of joy passes when Setsuko awakens to find them all dead. She buries them in a little grave, wondering out loud why the fireflies, and her mother, are now dead. Their situation grows increasingly dire as they run out of food, spurned by the adults around them, dressed in rags and suffering from malnutrition. At the moment when news of Japan's surrender reaches him, Seita has used all his remaining resources to buy food for his dying sister, only to have her die in his arms. He carries Setsuko's ashes in a fruit tin, given to him by his mother, along with the photo of his father until the day he dies—in September, just weeks after the war's end. The film ends with the images of the spirits of the two children, now healthy and well-dressed, sitting side by side as they gaze down on the modern and rebuilt city of Kobe.

*Grave of the Fireflies* is the singular creation of one of Japan's greatest animated film directors, Takahata Isao, who both wrote and directed the movie. He is a longtime collaborator of Japan's most famous animated filmmaker, Miyazaki Hayao, whose Studio Ghibli and films have been compared to Walt Disney's. In the studio's offices, located down a quiet side street in a Tokyo suburb, Takahata, dressed in a green striped shirt, grey flannel pants, and a gray denim jacket, his hair flecked with gray, explains that the film draws directly from a personal experience. It remains, he says, "the biggest event in what is now my long life."[42] The story comes pouring out of him without hesitation, punctuated only by emotions undiminished by the passage of time.

Takahata was born in 1935 in the town of Ise in Japan's Mie prefecture, home to one of Japan's most sacred Shinto shrines, which is dedicated to the goddess Amaterasu, worshipped as the primordial ancestor of the imperial family. Takahata recalls how, when he was a small child, the train lines were cleared for the arrival of special trains carrying the imperial family coming to worship at the shrine. He recalls sword-carrying police guarding the rail line when he and his friends would run to look, though he was left only with an impression of "the very grave importance of the emperor." In his elementary school, the emperor's photograph was kept in a special place. The schoolchildren would gather, and the principal would open a door with a creak, revealing the god emperor. "I remember thinking there was something very odd about how the principal would open that door, and everyone would bow. Why were we doing this?"

Takahata's father was himself the principal of a girls' middle school in the nearby city of Okayama, where the family was living in the last months of the war. In the predawn hours of June 29, 1945, American bombers struck the city. "I was the youngest—I was nine years old—and I woke and saw red all around me. I was wearing my pajamas, and I went running outside just like that. I saw all the people were running away, in front of my house, and my big sister, the one just older than me in age, came running out, too. We wondered why the rest of our family wasn't outside there, so we waited for them. But so many people were streaming, we were scared we'd been left behind, so we just went along with the crowds."

Takahata's father had, in fact, already left to rush to his school. He abandoned his family, Takahata explains, because, as principal, he was bound to fight the fires, and "he had to protect the photograph of the emperor. At that time, for the photograph of the emperor to burn was the greatest humiliation a principal could experience." Takahata and his sister were thus separated from both of their parents. "All around, all around Okayama was burning," Takahata recounts, his memory as clear and crisp as if this had taken place only days before, rather than sixty-five years earlier. "What they did was bomb the perimeter [of the city]. Everyone was running toward the center of the city, and that's what we did. On the way, there were shelters and basements people were going into. I was so small, so I suppose I could have gone in, but I was so scared to go into those dark and narrow places."

Instead, Takahata and his sister headed, terrified, for a river that ran down the middle of Okayama. "The B29s—it was just the way we showed in the movie. The fire literally came down that way and you could be hiding somewhere, but wherever that fire struck, it would just burst into flames." If you could avoid the fire, however, there was a chance to survive. "As I was running, more and more all around me, something would get hit, so the running became more and more confusing. I'll go this way, I'll go that way, and then something was bursting into flames all around. It was all happening right next to me. It was a very intimate, close experience."

The firebombs rained down as the children fled down the narrow streets, seeking safety. The explosion of one of the bombs knocked his sister down. "I got her up, and she regarded me as having saved her life. She had shrapnel in her, and later in life she had surgery for that. In any case, we ran, and there was nowhere to go, because all around us it was burning. There were places where they kept water to put out fires, and you'd pour it on yourself. But it would dry instantly. So what were we to do? Finally, there was an adult who ran across. We followed, and we broke through the fires and got to the river. When I ran out of the house, I was not just in my pajamas, but I was barefoot. All the way, I was stepping on the melting asphalt, and everything there was—all the glass—got into my feet. Later on, it became infected, and it was really a terrible thing. But in any case, I got away, and my life was saved."

Meanwhile, Takahata's mother and the rest of his family had their own harrowing escape from death. They found their way into a narrow canal. The fires created a wind tunnel down the canal, and many people died.

Somehow, the family managed to keep themselves in the water and were saved. His father's school was burned completely. After the fire died down, his parents returned to the house to look for their children. "They looked among the piles of children's corpses and asked themselves, 'Is it this one, or that one, that child?'"

The children sat out the firebombing in the river, a black rain of ashes falling on them as they shivered in the water. A family friend found them and somehow got in touch with their family. "When we met, when we re-encountered each other, we did it in a typically Japanese way," remembers Takahata. "We didn't embrace each other. I didn't go running to them, and they didn't come running to me and hold me, either. We—neither of us approached each other or embraced each other. That still remains inside of me, emotionally or spiritually. Why couldn't we run to each other at such a moment and embrace each other? What was the embarrassment or the something that stopped our feelings from pouring out at that moment?" Later, he channeled this feeling into his most famous film, *Heidi*, in a scene in which Heidi is reunited with her grandfather: "I have her go *running* into his arms."

Takahata recalls the moment of Japan's surrender. "At the time of the emperor's broadcast on the radio, my older siblings were crying. It seemed to me as if they had to cry. The people of the time had to express themselves this way. I had no such inclination at all. I was nine years old. I wasn't happy; I wasn't sad."

After the surrender, they were warned about the rapacious Americans who were about to land on their shores. But when Takahata encountered the Americans in their jeeps and trucks riding through the streets, "there was nothing like that." Instead, "they seemed so splendid." Takahata didn't join other children in running after the GIs, seeking handouts of candy and chewing gum. But near his school, "they'd be playing softball—not baseball but softball, with this big ball—and I was watching. I was really jealous of what they were like. Wow, they're playing with such a beautiful thing." From their incredible baseball gloves to the powerful jeeps, which could tear right up the sides of a nearby mountain, "it was amazing to look at, and you'd think, 'My god, we went to war with *that*!'"

After the war, Takahata went to Japan's prestigious Tokyo University, graduating in 1959 at the age of twenty-three. An admirer of French animated films, he got a job at the Toei film studio, Japan's largest, to edit and ultimately direct animated films. By working on everything from cheap television series to full-length films, he moved his career steadily ahead. But that day, June 29, of the last year of Japan's disastrous war was never far from his thoughts. It became the inspiration for *Grave of the Fireflies*, but the film was not borne out of anger or a sense of Japan's victimization at the hands of the distant enemy. "The motivation was not to make an antiwar film," Takahata insists. "I felt another type of expression was possible in children's tales." He wanted to start with the death of the two children and then tell the story of how it came to be. "I thought if you want to be antiwar, the important thing is to show the beginning of the war. It's no use being antiwar to just talk about the tragic end of the war."

The film was shown in a double feature with Miyazaki's most famous film, *My Neighbor Totoro*, a delightful fantasy very different in mood from Takahata's somber tale. Still, Takahata was worried about how children would respond. "I decided that it was okay to show the kids [the war]," he explains. "Kids these days are much too distant from death, and it would be okay to be close to a trauma of that kind." The children of today are not so distant from the experiences of Seito and his sister, who deal with bullies and struggle to be independent. Even the coldness of the adults in the film has some resonance. "I wanted to warn the children that at any time a person might become that kind of cold person. Nowadays, we're so materially blessed, [and] everybody can be good and generous, but would we be that way in materially hard times?" Takahata's portrayal of Japanese society during wartime goes against the romantic images of a wartime in which everyone banded together. "I wanted to do precisely that," he insists. "It's not that all the beauty of wartime that people talk about wasn't there, but there would be no meaning in showing that."

Even now, *Grave of the Fireflies* draws the ire of Japanese conservatives. The annual showing of the film is protested even now. But Takahata is hardly cowed. He participates in a civic movement to preserve Japan's constitutional bar to the use of force, Article 9 of the postwar constitution. He worries about a Japan that would be freed to use weapons, including nuclear weapons, without justification. "Japan doesn't want to become the kind of country that does that," he says. "And it is because I worry that I participate in the movement to protect Article 9."

Japan, the filmmaker concludes, still needs to promote reconciliation with its past victims. "Japan's development over this past half-century is *built* on regret for the way Japan acted. It's built on that remorse for the war, but it hasn't communicated that. Communication means not just apologizing. It means at the same time showing how we have brought our country to this place on the basis of the regret or remorse we feel."

## Togo Kazuhiko

Togo Kazuhiko is a third-generation Japanese diplomat, the scion of a family intimately intertwined with the history of modern Japan: the rise of Japan as a great power, its march to war, its defeat, and its resurrection. His grandfather, Togo Shigenori, was the foreign minister in General Tojo Hideki's cabinet when Japan launched its ill-fated attack on the United States. He was called back to service in the desperate days of the spring of 1945, tasked with negotiating an end to the disastrous war. Togo Kazuhiko's father, Fumihiko, already a young diplomat by the time the war started, participated in his own father's defense during the Tokyo War Crimes Tribunal and translated and edited his posthumously published account of his

Togo Kazuhiko

role in Japan's war. No longer a serving diplomat, Togo Kazuhiko now occupies himself as a historian still struggling to come to terms with a war and its aftermath. The wartime era "was the narrative of my family, coming from my very youngest years," he says without a hint of drama.[43]

The war was headed into its final months when Togo and his twin brother were born on January 10, 1945. The family had fled the tribulations of Tokyo for the mountain resort of Karuizawa, a favorite escape for the Japanese elite. His father, Fumihiko, joined the foreign ministry out of the elite Tokyo Imperial University in 1939. He was married to the daughter of Togo Shigenori and adopted into his family, as was the custom in Japan. Togo Kazuhiko's grandfather, the offspring of a samurai family from the powerful Satsuma clan in western Japan, began his diplomatic career in 1913 as a consular officer in Mukden, a cockpit of Japanese involvement in Manchuria in northeastern China.

Togo Shigenori's diplomatic career followed a path that touched almost every key locale in Japan's arc, from the close of World War I through the second global conflict of the century. From Manchuria, he made his way to Europe, reopening Japan's embassy in Berlin after the war. There, he met his bride, a German, which was an unusual choice in Japan's traditional society. After returning home in 1921, Togo took on responsibility for relations with Russia, an assignment that led him (and later his grandson) into a lifelong career of dealing with the Soviet Union. After duty in Washington and again in Germany, Togo came home in 1933 amid the growing crisis triggered by Japan's takeover of Manchuria (creating the puppet state of Manchukuo) and rising tensions with the West, China, and the Soviet Union. Togo's first task as director of the European American bureau of the foreign ministry was to suggest a way to extricate Japan from this crisis, one exacerbated soon after his arrival by Japan's withdrawal from the League of Nations.

Togo, already firmly identified as an advocate of negotiation and compromise, offered a voice against the forces of Japanese militarism, whose appetite for expansion and aggression had only been whetted by their success in northern China. "It is essential," he wrote in a memo at the time, "that for many years to come, while we are striving for the proper development of Manchukuo, we avoid conflicts with other countries, unless conflict be forced upon us." He cautioned in particular against any clash of interests with the United States. "As the United States does not welcome the exercise by Japan of a hegemony over the entire Far East, Japan on her part should not make this her policy in the foreseeable future." Failure would lead, he warned, to an arms race, a Japanese-American war, and ultimately "a world war," the result of which would hardly favor Japan.[44]

"Japan did not follow the road pointed out by Mr. Togo," writes Togo Fumihiko, in understated fashion, in the introduction to his father's memoir, coedited by the American lawyer who defended him at the war crimes tribunal.[45] For the next five years, as Japan fell under the spell of the militarists and embarked on a wider war with China, Togo Shigenori was occupied with Soviet affairs. In late 1937, he was dispatched again to serve as ambassador to Berlin, inheriting a policy of alliance with Nazi Germany that was personally distasteful to him, apparently so evidently that he was abruptly transferred to Moscow in 1938. There, he occupied himself by preventing border clashes from escalating into full-scale war and negotiating a neutrality pact between the two countries.

The signing of the Tripartite Pact with Nazi Germany and fascist Italy in September 1940, a moment of triumph of the proto-totalitarian forces in Japan, led to Togo's recall from Moscow and pressure for him to resign from the foreign service. He refused but was left to sit, effectively unemployed, in Karuizawa. Privately, he urged negotiations with the United States to head off a war in the Pacific. Those negotiations began in 1941 but went nowhere. The formation of a new cabinet in July led to the movement of Japanese armed forces into Indochina, which triggered Roosevelt's freeze of Japanese assets and the imposition of an oil embargo. Togo continued to preach the need for negotiations, causing the Kempeitai, the military police, to visit him regularly. In October, General Tojo, the minister of war, was asked to form a new government and requested that Togo join the cabinet as foreign minister. Togo initially refused, arguing that he would not join if the army refused to compromise on the war in China and on American demands for Japanese withdrawal. Tojo assured him that he was prepared for real negotiations, and the navy seemed also to side with that course, which persuaded Togo to enter the cabinet for a last-ditch effort to avert war.

Perhaps Togo was deluding himself, as he seems to suggest at moments in his memoir, published in English as *The Cause of Japan*. But whatever illusions he had were shattered by the delivery of the Hull note, the outline of a proposed agreement delivered by Roosevelt's Secretary of State, Cordell Hull, to the Japanese ambassador on November 26, 1941. Hull's demands left little room for anything but a Japanese retreat from its imperial adventures—withdrawal of all its forces from China and from Indochina, recognition of the Nationalist government in China, and abrogation of Japan's commitment under the Tripartite Pact.

This moment is central to the narrative of the Togo family, as told to Togo Kazuhiko by his mother. Togo recalls that she recounted to him many times the evening of November 27, 1941, "when my grandfather came back from the foreign ministry after receiving the Hull note. Till that evening, my grandfather was in full vigor, full of energy, determined not to let the war happen. But the mood completely changed when he saw the Hull note. His mood was so gloomy. He lost hope that the war could be avoided." In the Togo family narrative, this is a tragic moment in which the United States bears the burden of a failure of will to compromise. "At the last stage, the failure came from the U.S.," says Togo Kazuhiko. "Because at this point, the U.S. had already abandoned their wish to compromise."

Togo tells the story as it was narrated to him by his mother on her deathbed:

> My mother said, "Kazu, do you know what your grandfather used to say about what is the most important factor in diplomacy?" I said no. He used to say that the most important point in diplomacy is to be prepared to give 51 percent to your counterpart, and be prepared to accept 49 percent. And that was a bit of a surprise, because my grandfather was known to be a person who stuck to principle and tried to get to the end without compromise. That was the image created about him. So, at first, I couldn't understand. Then my mother said, "Usually we say in the foreign service that winning too much is not good for one's country. If you win too much, the other side will become frustrated, and that leaves the seeds for future conflict. So the best result is fifty-fifty—no winner, no loser. But your grandfather said a little more. He said that mutually satisfactory results would emerge if a negotiator thinks truly about the other side, even to the point of contemplating giving 51 percent to the other side, a little more than the position of one's own country. Why? This is the most difficult part. There are so many forces pressuring you to think about the immediate interests of your own country. Someone has to think about the position of the other side, and that is the way to secure, ultimately, the best interests of your country. That is the challenge and the art of diplomacy."

In this family narrative, Foreign Minister Togo tried to come in the last days of negotiation to fifty-one–forty-nine, but at the end, as his grandson puts it, "there was no one in the U.S. thinking in this way."

By his own account, Togo Shigenori understood that the United States was not prepared to compromise on its fundamental demands—and that those were unacceptable to Tokyo. He thought about resigning but realized it would change nothing. "In the conditions of November 1941," he wrote later in prison, "it was unthinkable that a cabinet which would capitulate abjectly to pressure of the United States could be established." He decided to stay for a bit. "I therefore made up my mind to remain in office to try to obtain the United States' reconsideration, to fight for peace to the last moment, and if war did come to devote myself to working for its early termination, for the sake of Japan and of the world."[46]

Ultimately, however, when the decision to go to war was made in the following days, Togo, too, felt there was no alternative. But rather than spending time on the decision to go to war, his memoir concerns itself more with defending his role in the infamous surprise attack on Pearl Harbor. Togo insists that he was not informed of the attack plan until very late and that he demanded that the declaration of war be made before the attack commenced. The botched effort of the Japanese embassy, which conveyed the declaration only after the beginning of the air assault, remained a stain on Togo's conduct of the war.

In the early months of war, when Japan's forces made striking advances across the Pacific, Togo remained in the cabinet. In September 1942, he clashed with Tojo over the plan to create a greater East Asia ministry, aimed at consolidating Japan's wartime empire and putting relations with occupied Asia outside the purview of the foreign ministry. Togo resigned and retreated to Karuizawa, watching from a distance as the war turned against Japan and concluding that defeat was only a matter of time.

By the spring of 1945, Tokyo, along with all other major Japanese cities, was under brutal aerial bombardment. American troops had retaken the Philippines and landed on Iwo Jima and Okinawa, where bloody battles took place for the first time on Japanese soil. Germany's last defenses were crumbling in the face of the Red Army advancing from the east and the British and American armies attacking from the west. In April, a new Japanese government was formed. Admiral Suzuki Kantaro, the designated prime minister, called on Togo to come back as foreign minister. He told Suzuki that he would come back only if the goal was to end the war as soon as possible. Suzuki failed to give him a satisfactory response, and Togo at first turned down the request. But at the urging of senior officials around the emperor, Togo changed his mind. In the months that followed, Togo devoted himself to searching for a route to peace. The Imperial Army and Navy wanted Togo to focus on keeping the Soviet Union from entering the war against Japan; Togo took that as an opportunity to explore using Moscow as a mediator to negotiate terms to end the war.

While the Japanese military still wanted to fight on, Togo and key civilians with close ties to the emperor sought only to guarantee the continuation of Japan's constitutional monarchy following surrender. Togo's efforts to enlist Moscow's help failed. On July 26, Joseph Stalin joined U.S. president Harry Truman, British prime minister Winston Churchill, and China's Nationalist leader Chiang Kai-shek in issuing the Potsdam Declaration, which set the terms for Japan's surrender. While Togo urged a careful response to the declaration, the military pressed the premier to reject it, a fateful decision.

Only days later, on August 6, the United States dropped the atomic bomb on Hiroshima, incinerating the city with a single weapon. It was a stunning event for Togo, who, in an audience with the emperor two days later, urged immediate surrender. The emperor agreed, but the Supreme War Council of six key government leaders, including Togo, was deadlocked. On August 9, the Soviet Union finally entered the war, quickly sweeping aside the Japanese army in northeast China. For Togo, this marked the absolute last straw (curiously, in his memoir, he makes no mention of the bombing of Nagasaki on the same day). In his mind, the Soviet declaration of war was a personal failure, a betrayal of the Soviet-Japanese Neutrality Pact he had negotiated and a reflection of his inability to grasp Soviet intentions. In the family narrative that was recounted to Togo Kazuhiko by his mother, it was *konchikusho*—an obscene expression that conveys "the feeling of betrayal and anger on the part of Togo Shigenori." Togo Kazuhiko reflects, "[That feeling] stayed in my DNA and became the underlying psychology of dealing with the Soviet Union after I joined the foreign ministry."

For most Western historians, Soviet entry into the Pacific War was, if anything, overdue, a long-sought realization of the wartime alliance against Nazi Germany and its allies. But in the view of many Japanese, up to this day, the Soviet entry was a stab in the back that conjured up feelings of outrage reinforced by the harsh treatment of Japanese prisoners of war by the Soviets after the war. But it is an inescapable reality that the combination of the atomic bomb and the Soviet decision to enter the war finally allowed the emperor to intervene and break the deadlock in the government. Without it, the war might have continued and led to an American invasion of the Japanese home islands and the death of hundreds of thousands, if not millions, more Japanese. As Togo Shigenori wrote in prison five years after the end of the war,

> I carried with me, and carry still, the memory ineradicable of those days. As I think today of that time, vividly before my eyes is the scene of the Imperial Conference at which the Emperor decided for surrender, and my feeling of then returns to me: that while the future of Japan is eternal, it is a blessing beyond estimation that this most dreadful of wars has been brought to a close, ending our country's agony and saving millions of lives; with that my life's work has been done, it does not matter what befalls me.[47]

Despite his efforts to engineer Japan's surrender, Togo's role as foreign minister at the start of the war earned him a spot high on the list of war criminals sought for trial by General Douglas MacArthur and the American occupiers. "For MacArthur, the most critical issue was Pearl Harbor and the sneak attack," Togo Kazuhiko says. His grandfather was arrested in the fall of 1945, and when the trial began in December 1947, the family anticipated the death sentence. Togo Kazuhiko's father, Fumihiko, was assigned by the foreign ministry to be the liaison to the defense team. He attended every day of the trial, along with Foreign Minister Togo's wife and daughter.

The family narrative "is full of memories of the Tokyo trials," says Togo Kazuhiko. "My grandfather prepared throughout how to defend his cause to the world. He was full of vigor; he was at his best in explaining. The impression my mother had was that he was an elderly person whose health was completely fading, yet he managed to pull himself together and tell the world the truth he saw." Togo Shigenori insisted that he had done everything he could to prevent war but that there was no choice after the delivery of the Hull note. In filing their charges against him, the prosecutors did not consider his role in ending the war.

When the verdict of the tribunal was delivered in late 1948, it came as a shock. Among the twenty-five Japanese leaders convicted as Class A war criminals, seven of them were sentenced to death, with Tojo among them. The majority of the accused, sixteen of them, received a life sentence. Only

Togo and Mamoru Shigemitsu, who served after him as foreign minister during the war, received lighter sentences. Togo Kazuhiko recounts the words of his mother about that moment:

> I can never forget the day when the sentence was pronounced. As usual, I was with your grandmother at the court. When the sentencing began, there was utter silence in the courtroom. But each time the death sentence was pronounced, all who were in the courtroom breathed in so deeply that those sounds are still vivid in my ears. But you know, Kazu, when the verdict was pronounced for your grandfather—twenty years of imprisonment—deeply in my heart, I told myself, "We won!" Yes, twenty years seems to be a harsh sentence now, particularly for someone who did everything to prevent the war from happening and who contributed so much to ending the war, but he was the foreign minister at the time of Pearl Harbor. His situation was very precarious. Every one of us was fighting. Yes, twenty years—that was a victory for us.

Togo's grandfather died in the early hours of July 23, 1950, in Sugamo Prison, as a convicted war criminal. But for the family, the task of coming to terms with Japan's past in the postwar world remained in front of them. Togo's father, Fumihiko, rose rapidly in the foreign ministry as a leading architect of Japan's alliance with the United States. As a younger officer, he drafted the revised 1960 security treaty that sought to create a more equal partnership. In the late 1960s, he was the lead negotiator of the agreement to return Okinawa, still occupied by the Americans since the war, to Japanese sovereignty. His career culminated in service as the Japanese ambassador to Washington in the latter half of the 1970s.

Togo Kazuhiko was a high-school student, influenced, as many were in those days, by left-wing ideology, at the time of the security treaty, whose revision triggered massive antigovernment demonstrations in 1960. "My father was always angry when I mentioned it," he recalls. "Why can't they understand that this is a treaty which would let Japan become an equal?" his father would tell him. At the elite Tokyo University, which he attended during the turbulent days of student revolution in the 1960s, Togo at first pursued a career as a scholar but ultimately could not resist the temptation of following his grandfather and father into the diplomatic service. Like his grandfather, Togo ended up specializing in relations with the Soviet Union. "Historical memory was not on the surface," Togo says, "just in the background."

The war leapt to the foreground when Togo, then the director general of the foreign ministry's European affairs bureau, organized the visit of the emperor to the Netherlands in May 2000. For the Dutch, the issue of Japan's wartime conduct was still a sensitive issue, not least because of the treatment of 140,000 Dutch interned by the Japanese as prisoners after the seizure of the Dutch East Indies (Indonesia). The brutal treatment of the prisoners, including the forced prostitution of Dutch women in brothels organized by the Japanese Imperial Army—comfort women to serve Japanese troops—was the subject of postwar trials held in Indonesia and resulted in payment of reparations to the Dutch, agreed to in a special protocol to the San Francisco Peace Treaty. For the first time, Togo admits, he became aware of the comfort women issue, including the payment of "atonement money" to some seventy Dutch women out of the Asian Women's Fund, a nominally private fund created in the early 1990s to try to deal with the outrage of Korean, Chinese, Dutch, and other groups seeking redress for this long-buried and often denied wartime outrage.

With the emperor's visit, the first since the war, the Dutch government signaled to Togo that "a still clearer message and apology was necessary." What moved Togo the most, he says, was reading the personal testimony of ten Dutch comfort women. Togo came to understand that even though the Japanese government had formally apologized for the war, most notably in the statement issued by Prime Minister Murayama Tomiichi in 1995 on the fiftieth anniversary of the end of the war, "I needed words to directly link his statement to the Dutch." The meetings before the emperor's visit were "very tense negotiations because we needed to find language to satisfy the Dutch without antagonizing the Japanese right unduly." For the right, the emperor's words were the most important statement, and they heavily resisted any utterance of contrition by him.

In his address in the Netherlands, Emperor Akihito, the son of Japan's wartime emperor, declared, in typically stilted fashion but with clear reference to the lingering tensions, "It grieves our hearts to think that so many people were victimized in their respective ways during that war and that there are still those who continue to bear unhealed scars from it."[48]

For Togo, the experience led him to reimmerse himself in the problem of Japan's historical memory of the war, a memory that took him immediately to the story of his family. He retired from the ministry in 2002 and went to the University of Leiden to work on a history of Japanese foreign policy after the end of the war, which was published a few years later. The book is laced with passages about his family history. Togo feels strongly that "some aspect of what we did [in the war] was so atrocious that we must make clear we are sorry." He became vocal in arguing that Japan should back away from its past. "Clearly, I don't think my grandfather had that kind of feeling," Togo admits. While "not everything Japan did before World War II was wrong," the country was fractured, and in some ways, Japanese society fell apart. The crimes of Japanese soldiers in China were a product of that breakdown, but there is no trace in his grandfather's writings of any specific objections to the war in China. "He doesn't pin down which actions went beyond the permissible," Togo says. "In that sense, he doesn't criticize the major decisions to go to war."

Togo has now become active in the debates on wartime memory in Japan, penning more books and articles as well as participating in international conferences and discussions about how to come to terms with the past. He carries into these discussions the weight, and somewhat tragic history, of his family's intertwinement with this past. He objects strongly to the idea that the Japanese avoided the horrors of what Japan did during the war. "We wanted to know the truth." What consumes him now, says Togo, "is that these things aren't taught to the younger generation."

## *Watanabe Tsuneo*

Watanabe Tsuneo's spacious office is filled with the trappings of power, befitting a figure whose status as the ultimate insider in Japan's political life is legendary. Photos of Watanabe, the publisher of Japan's largest daily newspaper, the *Yomiuri Shimbun*, in the company of prime ministers and presidents line the walls along with baseball memorabilia from Japan's most popular professional baseball team, the Yomiuri Giants, which is also under his sway.

Watanabe is a media baron who has shaped conservative politics in Japan for decades, quietly advising leaders of the longtime ruling conservative Liberal Democratic Party. The pages of his influential daily, and its television network partner, maintain a relentless attack on the Japanese left. Under his leadership, the paper led the charge for revision of the American-imposed pacifist constitution, thereby becoming a force for a more assertive Japanese role in the world.

So it came as somewhat of a surprise to many in Japan, when, in June of 2005, the *Yomiuri* issued an editorial condemning the visits of then prime

Watanabe Tsuneo.
Source: Associated Press.

minister Junichiro Koizumi to Yasukuni Shrine, the Shinto memorial to Japan's war dead. The prime minister should not visit a shrine, the paper warned, where Class A war criminals are memorialized. It called for the construction of a secular national memorial for the war dead, along the lines of the Arlington National Cemetery in Washington, to replace the tainted role of Yasukuni.[49]

A couple of months later, in August, at the sixtieth anniversary of the war's end, the *Yomiuri* launched a remarkable yearlong series of articles to explore the issue of who among Japan's military and political leadership was responsible for the war and Japan's disastrous defeat. The articles, collected in a two-volume set in Japanese and later published in other languages, were based on a four-month study conducted by an in-house team. The *Yomiuri*, Watanabe explains, felt an obligation to tell the Japanese people who was responsible for starting the war and why the country fought "until many of its cities had been almost completely reduced to ashes."[50]

The study not only reaffirmed the judgment of the Tokyo War Crimes Tribunal but added names of those it thought should have faced trial. In the introduction to the English edition of the war-responsibility study,

Watanabe laments the loss of memory in modern Japan. "Many Japanese continue to worship at Yasukuni Shrine," he writes. "If things are left as they are, a skewed perception of history—without knowledge of the horrors of war—will be handed down to future generations."[51]

Sitting in a square leather chair, fiddling with a rack of pipes and stuffing them with tobacco, Watanabe slips easily into his own memory of war, one that continues to motivate him more than six decades after the end of the conflict. He was born in Tokyo in 1926, as one of five children of a well-to-do family, the son of a banker who enjoyed the company of Japanese elite intellectuals. The military police and the Kempeitai (the thought police) made their presence felt during the war years, forcing him and his friends to hide leftist writings. Around his dinner table, however, Watanabe listened to his parents and their friends talk about how the war was lost, despite the propaganda claims of victory.

Watanabe and his fellow students shared antiwar feelings and a disdain for the military. Even in the late 1930s, the traces of Japan's Taisho democracy lingered, and in his high school, there was still a tradition of individual freedom. "I couldn't abide absolutism," he tells us.

In the final year of the war, Watanabe was called to military service out of university. "Usually, university students went for officer training," he recalls, "but I thought that would be stupid in a war that couldn't be won." Instead, he went off for infantry training, thinking that when the Americans came, "I would be able to get away and surrender." He carried with him a little English dictionary and some precious books, all wrapped in a bundle of the *Japan Times*, an English-language newspaper.

Before he left for duty, Watanabe witnessed the firebombing of Tokyo. "I saw all of Tokyo on fire," he recalls, but he emerged unscathed when the advance of the flames was halted by a river and a railroad line. "I didn't have any feelings of enmity toward the Americans," he says. "Japan started the war by attacking Pearl Harbor. So everything was a matter of surrendering quickly." But the military refused to accept defeat.

Watanabe's service was brief but brutal. "I got beat up a lot. . . . There wasn't enough food. And for no reason at all, I'd get beat up by my superiors. I thought, at the time, it was like being a slave." His unit was stationed on the coast, equipped only with artillery shells and dummy weapons. "Draftees were supposed to dig a hole in the sand and hide in it, and when the U.S. soldiers came, we were supposed to jump out and blow them up." They had no rifles. "So stupid. All I thought about was running."

When the atomic bombs were dropped, Watanabe was given a one-day leave and went home. "All of my friends from high school got together," he recalls. This time, they thought, "there's no way we can resist. The war will surely end by September." For the victims of Hiroshima and Nagasaki, he says, "of course, I feel so sad for those who were killed there. But if they hadn't been, I know I would have been killed myself."

When surrender came, it was a moment for celebration. To this day, Watanabe curses the military for a mindless sacrifice of Japanese lives in those final months of fruitless struggle, not least in the atomic bombings. "Obviously, America would have to come after Japan because we were the ones who had attacked them. So we were the ones in the wrong. I still think so," he says with a stunning absence of ambiguity. His position is no less clear in his mind today than it was in 1945.

Watanabe returned to the university at the end of the war with one burning passion. "The main thing I thought was to bring down the Japanese military and the emperor system, to raze them to the ground." His consuming cause led him to the door of the Communist Party, which emerged from the underground of Japanese life as the only party that clearly called for an end to the emperor system. "So I joined the Communist Party because I hated the military and the emperor." Watanabe enrolled in the party in December 1945, but his toleration for Marxist absolutism proved no greater than for the ideologists of wartime Japan. He was expelled two years later for his deviations from the party line but found a new calling at the *Yomiuri*, whose editor at the time, Yasuda Shoji, was a "true liberal" who impressed Watanabe with a campaign calling on the emperor to step down from the throne and leave the moat-girded palace in the center of Tokyo.

Watanabe's career in the *Yomiuri* mellowed his view of the emperor system and of the emperor himself, whom he came to know and even to like. At the time of the war, he explained, under the Meiji constitution, the emperor was treated as God and worshipped by the right with cries of "*Tenno heika banzai*," or "Long live the emperor." "So I opposed the system. But once [the emperor] was human and renounced his divinity and became, with the empress and their family, a symbol of democracy with no political power as an individual," Watanabe accepted the system. Amid a scandal-ridden political system, he argues, "I think it's good to have someone who is above all the dirt, for unity, so the emperor is useful as a symbol."

In the war-responsibility series, the *Yomiuri* dealt carefully with the issue of Hirohito's personal responsibility. Watanabe himself thinks for a moment before answering a question about whether the Americans were wrong not to hold Hirohito responsible for the wartime decisions. "The emperor came to think the war was bad from about the midpoint on," he says, "but he rejoiced at the news from Pearl Harbor. Of course, he got only certain information, and he probably didn't have great mental powers, but millions were killed in his name. He bears that responsibility, that sin. I think he should have retired to Ise Shrine or somewhere. I still think that."

In the declining years of his life, Watanabe feels the weight of his memory of war, and of his responsibility to the younger generation, even more. "Yasukuni is still there, and it's a totally militaristic view of history. It really needs to stop, so I won't go there. I won't pay my respects there. The fact that war criminals are enshrined there means we haven't put it behind us."

Watanabe looks at the younger Japanese generation with a wariness that is shared by many who experienced the horror of war. "After all, people now, obviously, have no experience [of war]—never saw the bombing. That's the bulk of the people, and of course they cannot understand. But it [has] not even been a century since the time of the mess of the war that we created in Korea, China, and the Pacific region. I'm not saying people should be suspicious of, or hate, or resent their parents. But they need to understand that this was the kind of political system it was. So textbooks should clearly say [that] the government ordered these brutal invasions. They should teach the truth about it."

Watanabe launches into a recollection of his time as a Washington correspondent for the *Yomiuri*. He lived in northern Virginia and experienced the still lingering and divided memories of the Civil War. In Maryland, his friends celebrated Lincoln's birthday, while in Virginia, "[Robert E.] Lee was the hero and Lincoln was the enemy." In his child's school, the textbooks described the Civil War as a contest between the industrial north and the agrarian south, in all of two pages, and didn't mention slavery. "Now people write a lot about slavery, and America can begin to be a place of racial equality."

For Watanabe, the path to Japan's reconciliation begins with the truth about a disastrous war that brought death to his doorstep and animates his life to this day. "I am," he says with a sense of finality, "the last of the generation to have experience of the war."

FIVE

# The Uncomfortable War:
# The Pacific War in American Memory

Visitors to Hawaii's Pearl Harbor Naval Station, on the island of Oahu, usually make their way to the visitor center on the shore of the sparkling azure bay. There, they board a small launch for a short ride to a swooping white marble building, set crossways over the sunken hull of the USS *Arizona*. The building is a memorial to the men who died in the Japanese surprise attack on Pearl Harbor on December 7, 1941, with the ship itself containing the watery graves of more than one thousand sailors who died that day. At one end of the building, in a shrine, a wall is inscribed with the names of all the American military personnel who died on the *Arizona*.

When it opened in 1962, the USS *Arizona* Memorial, along with a small museum onshore, offered little in the way of explanation of the events that led to this tragic day in American history. For the U.S. Navy, the message was simple: a reminder to be prepared to defeat America's enemies with the might of a powerful military. When the Park Service took over the memorial in 1980, the message was broadened slightly to focus on the victims along with the facts of the attack.

For almost all of the postwar period, the American historical memory of the war in the Pacific was reduced to the powerful iconography of Pearl Harbor, a metaphor for the perfidy of our enemies and the need for preparedness, which endures and has been reinforced by such events as the terrorist assault of 9/11. The question of why the attack on Pearl Harbor took place has been largely left to history tomes gathering dust on library shelves. The other enduring legacy of the Pacific War remains locked in memory as

Plaza of the Presidents at the National Museum of the Pacific War

a powerful image—the mushroom clouds thrusting above the Japanese cities of Hiroshima and Nagasaki in August 1945.

The brutal fighting that took place between these signal moments, stretching across the Pacific and waged at sea or on jungle-covered islands leading up to the assault on Japanese territory itself, is largely confined in American memory to a handful of old Hollywood movies shown late at night on television. The only triumphal image of the war in the Pacific is the enduring symbol of the flag being raised by a group of marines on Iwo Jima, itself associated with one of the most horrific battles of the war.

In a broad sense, Americans associate World War II with the idea of sacrifice for a higher cause, carried out by the "greatest generation." But within that paradigm, the war in the Pacific remains for Americans an uncomfortable war. In contrast to the moral clarity and nobility of purpose associated with the war in Europe and the defeat of Nazi Germany, the path to war with Japan and its conclusion are far less clear. In the American mind, it seems that Japan's attack came out of nowhere, without reason and perhaps reflecting the failure of American readiness. The battles themselves were dirty and brutal, a racially tinged struggle against a fanatical enemy, and are perceived almost as subhuman. And the war begins with defeat, not only at Pearl Harbor but also in the Philippines, the scene of the largest surrender of American forces in its history.

The sense of discomfort is deeply rooted in the morally questionable decision to use atomic weapons against Japan, killing hundreds of thousands of Japanese. For most Americans, that act was justified to force Japan's surrender and avoid a much broader slaughter that would have accompanied a grinding invasion of the Japanese home islands. Still, feelings of doubt and guilt tug uncomfortably at the corners of the American mind. In the mid-1990s, the curators of the Smithsonian National Air and Space Museum mounted an exhibit of the *Enola Gay*, the B-29 bomber that carried the bomb to Hiroshima. A proposed accompanying explanation that dared to broach the idea of a legitimate debate over the decision to use the weapon triggered a firestorm of criticism from veterans and their defenders in Congress, which forced the museum to beat a hasty retreat.

Only in recent years can we find evidence of a willingness to explore a history of the Pacific War beyond a simple tale of unprovoked aggression and American resistance. One sign can be found at the Pearl Harbor memorial itself, in a new museum exhibit onshore, called *Road to War*, that seeks to provide the background of events that led to the war. The exhibit offers images and descriptions of Japan in the 1930s, from scenes of Babe Ruth on a tour of Japan to the political and economic turmoil that accompanied the Depression there. The attack on Oahu is described as "the culmination of a decade of deteriorating relations between Japan and the United States over the status of China and the security of Southeast Asia." Beginning with the Japanese seizure of Manchuria in 1931, Japan is described as ignoring American protests over its aggression, escalating in 1937 to full-scale attack on China, triggering diplomatic and economic pressure and culminating in an embargo on oil shipments.[1]

"By the summer of 1941," the museum tells visitors, "both countries had taken positions from which they could not retreat without a loss of national prestige. Although both governments continued to negotiate their differences, Japan had already decided on war."[2] It is a view that does not relieve Japan of the burden of responsibility for war but does seek to offer some explanation of the chain of events that led to the day of infamy at Pearl Harbor.

To find a more comprehensive narrative of the Pacific War in the United States, one must travel through the low rolling hills of the Texas Hill Country to the small town of Fredericksburg. There, more than a thousand miles from the shores of the Pacific, visitors come upon a remarkable exploration of this period in American history—the National Museum of the Pacific War. The museum has its roots in the decision of the town's leaders to honor its most famous citizen, Chester W. Nimitz, who rose to fame as the commander of the war effort in the Pacific. Admiral Nimitz, to his credit, told the town's leaders that he would only allow his name to be associated with the project if it also honored all those who served in the theater of battle. From a tale of the town, the Nimitz family, and Nimitz's naval career, the museum slowly expanded to include exhibits of submarines and other weaponry and artifacts. In 2009, around the same time the museum at Pearl Harbor was renovated, Fredericksburg opened a modern complex that uses sophisticated curating techniques to powerfully tell the story of the war, including a detailed accounting of every military engagement across the Pacific.

Unusually, the National Museum of the Pacific War begins with a discussion of the "seeds of conflict" in the complex historical contest between the West and Japan over the future of China. It starts by showing how nineteenth-century China, a great power of Asia, was victimized by European powers and by its own internal problems and explores how Japan, seeking to avoid the fate of China, responded to the challenge of the West with its own rapid modernization and military development. The exhibit traces the growth of Japanese contempt for Korea and its growing disrespect for a weakened China. The narrative describes the emergence of "A new threat—Japan" and its "road to empire." From the response to anti-immigrant restrictions in the United States to the civil war in China, Japan is depicted as moving step by step toward a confrontation with the West.

Pearl Harbor emerges from this narrative as the product of Japanese imperial expansion and the flawed belief that Americans lacked the will to fight. From the early days of Japanese victories to the turning of the tide of battle and the relentless American and Allied advance toward its shores, the war's arc is laid out by the museum. The museum's exhibits artfully take visitors through each battle of the war, beginning with the Japanese conquest of the Philippines and Bataan Death March, in which at least seven thousand prisoners died after their surrender.

The museum offers a vivid account, with maps, photos, artifacts, and videos, of the mounting American retaliation for the Japanese surprise attack, beginning with the Doolittle Raid on Tokyo in April 1942. From the great naval victory at the Battle of Midway in June 1942 through the island-hopping campaigns across the Pacific, the China-Burma-India theater, and submarine warfare, this beautifully designed museum in the heart of Texas takes American visitors through a history they have largely ignored, if not forgotten.

The darker side of the war is not entirely unexplored. The museum notes the fearful decision to intern Japanese Americans in camps, and it acknowledges the terrible cost in lives from the firebombing of Japanese cities that killed "at least 330,000 civilians and left up to 15 million homeless"; more than 100,000 were killed in one night in March 1945 in Tokyo. The museum offers, in defense of these actions, the words of General Curtis LeMay, the architect of the strategic bombing of Japanese cities: "No matter how you slice it, you're going to kill an awful lot of civilians, thousands and thousands. But if you don't destroy Japanese industry, we're going to have to invade Japan. And how many Americans will be killed in an invasion?" That same logic is offered for the decision to incinerate two entire Japanese cities—Hiroshima and Nagasaki—on August 6 and 9, 1945. The museum sums up that choice with the words of its city's native son, Admiral Nimitz, who described it as a weapon that was "indecent . . . but necessary."

American history textbooks offer a similar narrative of a Japan bent on aggression and expansion in Asia, moving relentlessly toward a clash of blows with the United States. "As French, Dutch, and British colonies lay unprotected in Asia, Japanese leaders leaped at the opportunity to unite East Asia under Japanese control by seizing the colonial lands," a widely used American history textbook, *The Americans*, tells students. "By 1941, the British were too busy fighting Hitler to block Japanese expansion. Only the U.S. and its Pacific islands remained in Japan's way."[3]

The final negotiations between Tokyo and Washington are portrayed as an almost tragic slide into war. The State Department insisted that Japan withdraw from its ill-fated invasion of China, recounts *The American Pageant*, the most widely used textbook for college-bound high schoolers. "Japanese imperialists, after waging a bitter war against the Chinese for more than four years, were unwilling to lose face by withdrawing at the behest of the United States. Faced with capitulation or continued conquest, they chose the sword."[4]

This account of the events leading to the attack on Pearl Harbor was challenged even before the war was over. Proponents of the "back door to war" school accused President Franklin D. Roosevelt of provoking the Japanese to attack in order to overcome American isolationism and be able to come to the aid of a beleaguered Great Britain. Revisionist historians like Charles Beard and Charles Tansill penned books articulating this theory in the early years after the war. Conspiratorial versions of this view referred to deliberate suppression of intelligence predicting the Japanese attack. Such views were even aired in a special congressional investigation of the Pearl Harbor attack in late 1946, the majority report of which exonerated the Roosevelt administration of having maneuvered Japan into launching the first strike of the war. Still, the revisionist attack on even this aspect of the war in the Pacific resurfaces now and then, though not with the ferocity of belief found in those earlier years.

More than this recurrent questioning, the dimension of the war in the Pacific that makes it distinctly uncomfortable for many Americans is its racial nature. Racism was a powerful part of the Nazi ideology, most clearly in the anti-Semitism that drove the Holocaust but also in the attitude toward Slavic peoples and the attempt to exterminate minorities such as Gypsies. Americans, however, did not perceive the war in Europe as a struggle for racial superiority. The war in Asia, however, was overlain on both sides with propaganda that depicted the enemy in crude racial stereotypes, though Americans are more conscious of Japanese racism than of their own. The one exception to that myopia is the stain of the decision to intern 122,000 Japanese, most of them American citizens, by moving them from the West Coast to camps inland on the grounds that they could be spies or saboteurs—an act for which the U.S. government formally apologized decades later.

The American historian John Dower dug deeply into this reality in *War Without Mercy: Race and Power in the Pacific War*, one of the most influential studies of the war. "In the United States and Britain, the Japanese were more hated than the Germans before as well as after Pearl Harbor," Dower writes in his seminal work. "They were perceived as a race apart, even a species apart—and an overpoweringly monolithic one at that. There was no Japanese counterpart to the 'good German' in the popular consciousness of the Western Allies. At the same time, the Japanese themselves dwelled at inordinate length on their own racial and cultural superiority."[5]

In Dower's account, this racial imagery contributed to the merciless nature of the fighting. "Prejudice and racial stereotypes frequently distorted both Japanese and Allied evaluations of the enemy's intentions and capabilities," he writes. "Race hate fed atrocities and atrocities in turn fanned the fires of race hate."[6] Dower's study makes frequent reference to the war films churned out by Hollywood during the war, filled with imagery of fanatical hordes rushing madly into battle with cries of loyalty to the God emperor on their lips, to mobilize the American people against their foe.

Postwar films continued to portray the war largely through depiction of a fanatical enemy. Films devoted to the mistreatment of prisoners of war, a dominant charge in the postwar war crimes trials, remain among the classic films of the war shown again and again, such as David Lean's 1957 *The Bridge on the River Kwai*, about a Japanese prisoner-of-war (POW) camp in Burma.

That imagery persists today. Hollywood giants Tom Hanks and Steven Spielberg have become the most important chroniclers of World War II, almost single-handedly shaping the memory of that war for many baby boomers and their children through films such as *Saving Private Ryan*, *Schindler's List*, *Empire of the Sun*, and the stunning miniseries *Band of Brothers*. The first and last have come to define the modern war film and probably are more widely viewed than any other films about the war in Europe, because they are shown and reshown on television.

Spielberg and Hanks were determined to do for the Pacific War what they had done for that European theater. That project yielded a companion miniseries to *Band of Brothers*, also broadcast initially on the HBO network, simply titled *The Pacific*. Like its European theater version, *The Pacific* offered an account of the war through the eyes of ordinary soldiers rather than the commanders' view of the war. *Band of Brothers* is based on Stephen Ambrose's classic tale of one company of the 101st Airborne Division and follows the unit from training through the landing at Normandy and all the way to the defeat of Germany, including a memorable episode depicting the liberation of a concentration camp.

The Pacific theater provided no such comparable unit. It was a theater where naval warfare was central and ground campaign was episodic in nature. The producers of *The Pacific* settled on telling the story of the war through the Marine Corps and their campaign across the Pacific islands, based on the wartime memoirs of marine veterans Eugene B. Sledge and

Robert Leckie and the tale of marine hero Sergeant John Basilone. In overlapping fashion, their combat experiences stretch from the early days just after Pearl Harbor to the first great battle of the war, in Guadalcanal, and the brutal retaking of island fortresses such as Peleliu, Iwo Jima, and, finally, Okinawa. The naval war was left to the side, and the atomic bombing appears only as a distant event that allows the men to return home.

*The Pacific* offers little of the romance of war or the nobility of combat. There is brotherhood, but what emerges most clearly is a sense of the brutality of war and its effect on men. "We thought the Pacific War was so emblematic of what war is, in and of itself," explains Kirk Saduski, who oversees nonfiction productions for Playtone, the film- and television-production company established by Hanks, which oversaw both war series. "The nature of combat on these islands, as Sledge said in his book, is like two scorpions in a bottle. It was war stripped of all pretense of civilization and nicety and rules."[7]

In the short documentary film that was made to explain the background of the film series, Hanks and the producers argue that there was a "culture of cruelty" among the Japanese soldiers. "The Japanese culture was without mercy, without compassion," the documentary asserts. This view is expressed by some of the marine veterans who were interviewed for the making of the film. "You soon learned that with the Japanese you had to meet brutality with brutality," recalls Sidney Phillips, a veteran of combat with the First Marines. "The Marines quickly became every bit as brutal as the Japanese, or more so."[8] This is conveyed in scene after scene of this film series, where the heat and dirt of jungle warfare seems to emanate through the television screen and the enemy appears repeatedly in engagements in which they prefer to die in hopeless battle than to surrender and live.

While *Band of Brothers* hardly offered an apologia for the Germans, there was clearly some separation of the actions of the regular German army and their Nazi political leadership, though the producers are quick to agree that, ultimately, there was no moral difference. And when it came to casualties, the death toll from combat in Europe was almost double that of the Pacific theater. But there was a certain difference between the films in how they portrayed the enemy. "The nature of the Japanese army was different than the nature of the German army," says Saduski. "Brutality seemed to be a policy of the Japanese army, where it wasn't a policy of the Wehrmacht."[9]

Historians who consulted with the producers on the film made the point that the atrocities of the Holocaust were still largely unknown until the end of the war. In contrast, Japan's war atrocities were widely publicized before and during the war. "We knew about Nanjing before the war," Saduski points out, referring to the Japanese massacre in China in 1937. "So that was already in the mix." Then came infamous moments like the Bataan Death March. "We became very aware of the brutality of Japanese policy."[10]

*The Pacific*, which first aired on HBO in 2010, was a critical success. But it has never achieved the status of *Band of Brothers*, a classic that is repeatedly aired and widely known. The reason, even the producers admit, lies in precisely the uncomfortable feelings that arise from *The Pacific*'s stark depiction of the warfare itself. It is, simply put, difficult to watch.

Even more difficult to watch, apparently, is the atomic bombing. Given its historical importance, it would seem inevitable that this, too, would be a subject for American filmmakers to take up. Certainly this has been the case in Japan, where the dropping of the bombs, their impact on Japan's decision to surrender, and, of course, the destruction that took place and the its aftermath effects on the lives of victims have been explored countless times in films for cinema and television. American filmmakers have portrayed the tremendous efforts to build the bomb in the Manhattan Project, the difficult decision to drop it, and even a biopic of the flight crew of the first bomber, the *Enola Gay*. But they have never chosen to confront what happened on the ground and its aftermath. "If you are looking for a movie of the effects on the ground in either Hiroshima or Nagasaki afterwards, I don't know what that movie would be for America," says Saduski. "It is not just because we just don't want to look at what we did. . . . [T]here has to be some commercial viability, and I just don't know how many people would to go a movie about somebody that's slowly dying from radiation poisoning."[11]

Hollywood is not the only institution in American life that finds this end to our war in the Pacific a deeply uncomfortable moment. In the mid-1990s, a searing controversy erupted over the mounting of an exhibit of the *Enola Gay* at the Smithsonian National Air and Space Museum in Washington, DC, timed to the fiftieth anniversary of the dropping of the bomb. The Smithsonian has been the depository for the aircraft since 1949, but its restoration and plans to display it did not begin seriously until the 1980s.

In 1993, work began on a script for an exhibition of the aircraft intended to grapple with the events that led to the use of the weapon and the questions that arose about the necessity for the bombing. According to the script for the exhibit, which was aired by opponents led by the Air Force Association (AFA), the principal veterans group, the exhibit's purpose was partly "to show how different the Pacific war was for Americans—no quarter was given and few prisoners were taken—as well as for the Japanese, who increasingly felt compelled to make the ultimate sacrifice to defend the emperor and the nation."[12]

The proposed exhibit would have centered on the atomic bombings, with artifacts from Japan showing the destruction displayed along with the aircraft. As for its historical judgment, "neither the atomic bomb nor an invasion was probably needed to end the Pacific war, but this is more obvious in hindsight that it was at the time,"[13] a view certainly held by many American historians of the war. The exhibit, to be titled *The Crossroads: The End of World War II, the Atomic Bomb, and the Origins of the Cold War*, was scheduled to run from May 1995 to January 1996, overlapping the anniversary of the use of the bomb. Meanwhile, a small group of veterans calling themselves the Committee for the Restoration and Proud Display of the *Enola Gay* lobbied for the Smithsonian to mount a very differently conceived display and requested the AFA's support. The group collected signatures asking the museum "to display the plane proudly, or give it to a museum that will."[14] The AFA got copies of the proposed script in the summer of 1993 and went on the assault. The AFA insists, to this day, that it was open to a critical, even controversial, treatment of the subject. "However, the museum's plan was not a critical analysis," the AFA claims in a report issued in 2004. "It was a one-sided, antinuclear rant." The script did acknowledge that the use of the bomb played "a crucial role in ending the Pacific war quickly." But the Air Force veterans pointed to what became an infamous two lines in the proposed exhibit script: "For most Americans this war was fundamentally different than the one waged against Germany and Italy—it was a war of vengeance. For most Japanese, it was a war to defend their unique culture against Western imperialism." For the AFA, that "seemed to suggest that the Japanese were the victims rather than the aggressors in World War II."[15]

The battle over the Smithsonian exhibit of the *Enola Gay* moved into the media and, finally, into the halls of Congress, where cries to block the institution's plans grew into a major political issue. Historians issued statements critical of the AFA and in support of the original plans. Multiple revisions of the script took place, each one rejected by the AFA, which said it would not support any exhibit that portrayed the Japanese as victims; that characterized the Americans as ruthless invaders, driven by racism and revenge; that suggested moral equivalency between Japan and the United States; and that in any way argued that the United States "acted dishonestly, dishonorably, or immorally in its decision to use the atomic bomb."[16]

In January 1995, the Smithsonian canceled the elaborate exhibit in favor of a simple display, allowing the aircraft and its crew to speak for themselves with a limited rendition of the facts surrounding the dropping of the bomb. A group of historians wrote a letter of protest in July 1995, arguing that "unfortunately, the Enola Gay exhibit contains a text which goes far beyond the facts."[17] The historians pointed to low estimates for the deaths caused by the bombs, an assertion that the use of the weapons clearly led to the immediate surrender of Japan and prevented the invasion. They contested the exhibit's assertion that Japan would not have surrendered without such an invasion.

Stanford historian Barton Bernstein, one of the signatories to the letter and a scholar of the decision making on the bomb, remains scarred by the controversy. He points to mistakes on both sides of the battle but believes the AFA simply would not tolerate a critical presentation of this war memory. "They wanted a celebratory presentation," says Bernstein.[18] The controversy remains a powerful warning to anyone seeking to question the necessity of that act. The suggestion that President Barack Obama might visit the bombing sites early in his administration was considered so politically inflammatory that consideration was quickly quashed.[19]

American historical memory of the Pacific War is thus still largely frozen into the twin images of Pearl Harbor and Hiroshima, with a hazy sense of the grim combat that bridges those two moments in our past. The discomfort associated with the Pacific War has left it strangely unexplored, a distant cousin to the more celebrated battles of Europe and the triumph over Nazi Germany. Americans remember Pearl Harbor but have forgotten the sweep of events in Asia that led to that fateful moment and the nasty but necessary warfare that followed in its wake.

The aftermath of the war in the form of the occupation and rebuilding of Japan under the leadership of General Douglas MacArthur served, however, to wipe out some of the dark memories associated with the conduct of the war, including its ending. In the end, as historian Dower documents so powerfully, the United States and postwar Japan became intensely entangled with each other, a condition that remains true today. "It was a war of extraordinary hatred," Dower says, "but when the war ends, that hatred disappears."[20]

## Iris Chang

One of China's most visited museums does not display the treasures of its dynasties or the heritage of its celebrated culture. It is a memorial to death, to the victims of the worst atrocity of World War II in Asia, the 1937 massacre of hundreds of thousands of Chinese by the invading Japanese army in the former Chinese capital of Nanking, or Nanjing, as it is now known. Remodeled in 2007, the Nanjing Massacre Memorial Hall features modern well-lighted exhibits and visual presentations, and its exterior is graced by striking bronze statuary and inscribed granite walls set amid pools and gardens.

Statue of Iris Chang at the Nanjing Massacre Memorial Hall. Source: © Adam Howarth (via Flickr).

Sitting in an inner courtyard, just outside the offices of the museum, stands a tribute to a young American woman who is rightly credited with having made this museum and its message of victimization possible. Visitors come upon the bronze statue of Iris Chang, her right arm outstretched in a thoughtful gesture, and her left arm cradling a book, its English title clearly visible, etched into the metal—*The Rape of Nanking*. The statue is unusual recognition by the Chinese Communist authorities that they owe a debt to a Chinese American, the daughter of supporters of the defeated Nationalists who fled to Taiwan and later immigrated to the United States.

Since its publication in 1997, the book not only became a best seller; it single-handedly elevated a little-known wartime event in Asia into what Chang audaciously labeled "the forgotten holocaust of World War II." Based in part on previously unknown Western diaries and other eyewitness accounts, Chang asserts that the events in Nanjing constituted a crime on the scale of the most horrific mass killings of the modern era, that the Japanese government and people have systematically covered up those crimes, and that the West has consciously chosen to ignore the suffering of Asians. Citing a range of deaths of noncombatants from the Allied war crimes tribunal estimates of 260,000 to figures above 350,000, Chang's volume details accounts of cruelty that range from the rape of tens of thousands of women to the machine-gunning, bayonetting, and burning alive of young men in an orgy of violence committed after Japanese troops seized the capital. "Using numbers killed alone," Chang writes, "the Rape of Nanking surpasses much of the worst barbarism of the ages." In language that often reaches the hyperbolic, she does not hesitate to associate the Japanese acts with those of the worst crimes of the European war, not least the Holocaust itself, and with the mass murders associated with Stalin's rule. "These deaths were brought about over some few years," she argues. "In the Rape of Nanking the killing was concentrated within a few weeks."[21]

For Chang, the killings in Nanjing were merely the first stage of a "terrorist" campaign to crush resistance from Chinese forces. It led, she claimed, to a policy that aimed to "exterminate everyone in the northern Chinese countryside."[22] She accuses the Japanese, with the exception of a few lone progressive voices who, she says, operate under threat of death, with covering up these crimes. Japan's refusal to acknowledge its criminality was compounded by the United States and other Western powers that, in the service of Cold War necessity, did not force Japan to either apologize or pay reparations for its crimes, and which left these events obscured in the history books. "Whatever the course of postwar history, the Rape of Nanking will stand as a blemish upon the honor of human beings," Chang writes in the epilogue of her book. "But what makes the blemish particularly repugnant is that history has never written a proper end for the story. Sixty years later the Japanese as a nation are still trying to bury the victims of Nanking—not under the soil, as in 1937, but into historical oblivion. In a disgraceful compounding of the offense, the story of the Nanking massacre is barely known in the West because so few people have tried to document and narrate it systematically to the public."[23]

Chang's work, the first book-length treatment of this subject in the postwar era, unleashed a veritable cottage industry of Nanjing remembrances, from documentary films and books to full-length movies, produced not only in China but also in the West. For the Chinese Communist regime in Beijing, Chang's work emerged precisely at the time when it was embracing a full-throated turn toward patriotic ideology to replace the discredited themes of communism. The events in Nanjing became central to a tale of victimization at the hands of the Japanese and other foreign invaders, and of Chinese resistance. The fact that the battles in Nanjing represented a Chinese defeat, one led not by the Communists but by their Nationalist rivals, was largely swept under the rug.

Despite the official embrace of Chang, the source of her work had nothing to do with the Beijing government's newfound patriotic meme. Rather, by her own account, and those of her parents provided after her tragic death in 2004 at her own hands, Chang's inspirations were twofold: the tales of her Nationalist grandparents and her own émigré parents, and the activism of overseas Chinese in the United States and Canada who felt that the Chinese government had engaged in its own cover-up of these crimes for the sake of seeking economic largess from Japan.

Chang was born in 1968 and spent almost all of her childhood in the quiet academic community of Champaign-Urbana, Illinois, where her parents were professors of physics and biology. Her parents were born in China during the war, the children of supporters and officials of the Kuomintang, the Nationalists. "I was born in 1940, the hardest year during the Japanese invasion," recalls her mother, Ying-Ying Chang, who spent her early years in the Nationalist wartime capital of Chongqing. "My earliest memories were when I was three or four—the siren of bombing continuously. They just kept on bombing, sometimes once or twice a day."²⁴ She grew up on the stories of her parents, who had fled from Nanjing.

"My mother and father didn't witness the 1937 Nanjing Massacre, but they witnessed the tragedy of mass killing, the brutality of the firebombs to destroy civilians' houses, hospitals, schools, everything," continues Ying-Ying Chang. "My mother saw a mother try to rescue her boy, and then all [his] body was charred, and they smelled the stench of flesh, and they saw the limbs dangling on the trees and wires. All those things they told us."²⁵ Iris's parents and her grandparents, who joined them from Taiwan when she was young, shared these stories with their American girl. "Iris was curious when she was in grade school," her mother recalls. "She asked us why we had to end up in the U.S., why we came. . . . I wanted her to be proud of the Chinese. Although she is American, she should know her roots. Everybody should know where she or he comes from. And I wanted her to appreciate Chinese culture and civilization in addition to what she would receive in the U.S."²⁶

After graduating from college in the late 1980s, Iris Chang embarked on a career in journalism. But she soon turned, after her marriage, to a career as a book writer. Her first work, *Thread of the Silkworm*, published in 1995, tells the story of the father of China's missile program, a scientist driven out of America's space program. She had begun to look for a subject for a second book in 1994 and was exploring the tales of the war she had heard in childhood. That brought her into contact with a group of Chinese emigrants trying to preserve the memory of the victims of Nanjing. She met them at a conference in Cupertino, a Silicon Valley suburb, which was the founding event of an association of mostly Asian émigré organizations with the grandiose title of the Global Alliance for Preserving the History of World War II. "She didn't know anything about us," says the group's leader and founder, Ignatius Ding, a Silicon Valley tech engineer.²⁷ In the conference hall, Chang found a huge poster of gruesome photos of the massacre, of decapitated heads, bellies ripped open, of rape victims displayed in grotesque poses by their abusers. "She had heard all the stories of our family, but they never prepared her to see such cruel tragedy," her mother says.²⁸ "Iris that night became cofounder [of the alliance] because she helped to write the mission statement that evening," says Ding. "We formed a committee, and we worked with her from that point on."²⁹

The activists helped Chang begin her search of archives, including the diaries of American missionaries and others who had worked in Nanjing's international settlement to protect the Chinese from the Japanese military. Chang eventually got access to perhaps her most significant new discovery—the diary and notebooks of John Rabe, a German businessman and Nazi supporter who was the head of the Nanking Safety Zone, where he is credited with sheltering some two hundred thousand Chinese. She also went to Nanjing to carry out interviews with survivors. "When she came back, she was like a changed person," Ding recalls. "When you really meet a survivor, and listen to them whisper, you can't forget that. I think when she came back with those interviews, that [became] really like a mission."[30] After *The Rape of Nanking* was published, Chang went around the country and the world, promoting this cause of remembrance. "She became de facto spokesperson for the whole issue," says Ding.[31]

Chang's role as a historical researcher and writer came under serious criticism, however, from professional historians who questioned her historiography, the linkage of this atrocity to the Holocaust, her inability to explain Japanese actions, and her characterization of a systematic refusal to acknowledge the massacre in Japan. They credit her for bringing new attention to these events but question her credibility as a historical writer. "Iris Chang's book is seriously flawed," writes historian Joshua Fogel, an expert on the Nanjing Massacre, in a review in the *Journal of Asian Studies*. "For all its apparent good intentions, it is full of misinformation and harebrained explanations. . . . This book begins to fall apart when she tries to explain why such a horror took place. It is a book that is more of a polemic than a history," Fogel concludes.[32]

Fogel and other historians took issue with her assertion that the deaths were the product of a flawed Japanese character and of a master plan for butchery conceived at the top of the Japanese state, which were views drawn mostly from Chinese documents and conspiratorial theories of Japanese wartime actions. The view of most historians is rather of an army that suffered a serious breakdown in discipline and sought to terrorize their foes to overcome far more serious resistance to their advance into China than anticipated. "Despite Chang's shocking description of events in Nanjing, she gives the reader little reason to conclude that what happened there should be compared to the systematic killing of the Holocaust, an episode that was surely the spawn of Hitler's purposeful policy—not an incident of war or the mere excrescence of individual cruelty or the result of a poorly disciplined army run amok," writes Stanford historian David Kennedy in the *Atlantic*.[33]

Kennedy, one of the premier historians of the United States, also questions the idea that the Nanjing events were entirely lost to American view. "The Western world in fact neither then nor later ignored the Rape of Nanking," he writes. American attention was "riveted" on the area in late 1937 after the sinking of the American gunboat *Panay* by the Japanese in the course of their attack. As he points out, American newspapers carried "extensive and lurid coverage of the Rape of Nanking," complete with banner headlines and first-person reporting. The massacre "later became a staple of wartime anti-Japanese propaganda," such as Frank Capra's *Battle of China*, part of a series of wartime films that were widely shown to both troops and the general public.[34]

Perhaps the most controversial part of Chang's book is a long section that seeks to portray Japan as a nation that has denied its past and where the few voices that raise such issues are threatened with the loss of their careers and even their lives. "The most disturbing element of Chang's work is her insistence that postwar Japan continues to hide its past," writes Fogel. "Would that it were so simple."[35]

In reality, he points out, there is an extensive body of Japanese scholarship on wartime atrocities, from the enslavement of women in army brothels to the butchery of the Sino-Japanese War. The most comprehensive work on the massacre, based on extensive interviews with victims and perpetrators, was done by Japanese historians and writers, including the investigative journalist Honda Katsuichi, whose searing series of articles on the subject appeared in the 1970s in the *Asahi Shimbun*, the second-largest circulation newspaper in Japan. Chang claims that Japanese textbooks do not discuss the Nanjing Massacre and other crimes, which is an inaccurate assertion.[36]

Chang is not wrong, however, in pointing to the voices among Japan's revisionist conservatives who are members of the so-called denial school, insisting that the mass killing never took place, a view echoed to this day by prominent Japanese politicians and public figures on the right. Her book served the purpose, ironically, of generating a wave of activity by members of that camp, who issued books and other publications in a desperate attempt to counter the impact of her work. Books like *The Nanking Massacre: Fact Versus Fiction*, written by historian Higashinakano Shudo, presented detailed rebuttals of the account presented by Chang. In another work, *The Alleged "Nanking Massacre*," the authors, Japanese academics Takemoto Tadao and Ohara Yasuo, claim that Chang was simply mouthing the propaganda of the Chinese Communist regime, part of an effort to encourage anti-Japanese attitudes in the United States.

Such attacks on Chang did little to dampen the impact of her work. Among other effects, *The Rape of Nanking* generated multiple films, including a biopic about Rabe, and it continues to shape American perceptions of the events. Chang herself tried to turn away from the subject of the war, devoting her next book to an account of the Chinese experience in America. But at the time of her suicide, Chang had turned back to the war, conducting interviews with survivors of the Bataan Death March with the intention of writing a book about yet another dark corner of wartime historical memory seemingly lost from view.

Chang's mother, in a sad but loving memoir of her daughter's short but impactful life, *The Woman Who Could Not Forget: Iris Chang Before and Beyond "The Rape of Nanking,"* admits that she wondered whether her death could have been a result of depression from delving into these subjects or even from the threats to her life from critics of her work. But she and others finally attribute it to a horrendous side effect, now recognized, of the psychiatric drugs she was taking. Chang's mother took solace in the end by celebrating Iris's "pursuit of historical truth and social justice," as she writes at the conclusion of her memoir.[37]

"It's precisely this spirit which has inspired people worldwide," writes Ying-Ying Chang. "*The Rape of Nanking* galvanized the global Chinese communities and vitalized the international redress movement in forcing Japan to reflect on its actions during the Second World War."[38]

## *John Dower*

The history of war should not be confused with military history. Military historians delve into the narrative arc of combat, how wars are planned and fought, and the role of commanders and the experience of soldiers on the battlefield. Historians of war paint a much broader canvas, trying to understand what drives societies toward war, why states and their leaders chose the use of force over other pathways, and, of no less importance, how peace is constructed in the aftermath of war.

John Dower is a historian of war but certainly not a military historian. In his early days studying Japanese history at Harvard, Dower began with the goal of understanding the relationship between prewar and postwar Japan.

John Dower.
Source: Courtesy John Dower.

That interest grew into a study of war and peace in Japan and of the forces that shaped the relationship between the United States and Japan and, even more broadly, between Asia and Japan. Through a long career in academia that ended at the Massachusetts Institute of Technology, Dower has come back again and again to what he called in a recent book "the cultures of war."[39]

For students of Japan, John Dower's work is a prerequisite to understanding that country's modern history and certainly the impact of World War II and its aftermath. His first book, based on his PhD thesis, was a lengthy political biography of Yoshida Shigeru from his prewar days as a Japanese diplomat to his postwar role as prime minister and the architect of Japan's reemergence from defeat. This book, aptly titled *Empire and Aftermath*, took Dower into a lifetime exploration of the war itself. He is best known for his pioneering exploration of the war in the Pacific as a racial conflict in *War Without Mercy: Race and Power in the Pacific War*. He followed this a little more than a decade later with a study of the American occupation of Japan and the Japanese response, *Embracing Defeat: Japan in the Wake of World War II*, a tour de force that earned him the Pulitzer Prize and the 1999 National Book Award for nonfiction.

As Dower explains it, the two works on the war actually began with a desire to write a book about the occupation. But "a paragraph became a chapter [and] then became a book in itself." He started with the idea that "what takes place in Japan after the war was remarkable when you consider what a merciless, violent, racist war the war in the Pacific was." He was then moved to explain "how it was racist, why it was merciless, how much hatred there was."[40] That became the book-length *War Without Mercy*, which offers a detailed comparison of how the war appeared in Western eyes with how it appeared in Japanese eyes.

What Dower found was a clash of imagery, conveyed through wartime propaganda, in literature, film, posters, art, and the media, that saw the war in distinctly racial terms and fueled a sense of hatred that went beyond what was present in the European theater of the global conflict. The Japanese were routinely depicted in Western imagery as monkeys or apes, sometimes as "little men" or "lesser men," whose capabilities were inferior. As members of the "yellow race," the Japanese were seen as a mass described in "sweeping racial clichés," writes Dower, such as "regimented," "treacherous," "fanatic," and "bestial."[41] The Japanese attack on the United States was merely, in the view of wartime propaganda, the latest step in a quest for world domination that began with the infamous Tanaka Memorial, a plan for expansion alleged to have been submitted to the emperor and compared to Hitler's *Mein Kampf*, though it was later revealed to be a hoax.

Japanese wartime propaganda routinely portrayed Japan's Western foes—mainly the British and Americans—as demons, drawing from Japanese mythology. For Japan, it was the non-Axis West that was bent on world domination and had been so for centuries, driven by a culture of greed and self-gratification. Japan's conquest of Asia, in contrast, was a mission of liberation of fellow Asians from Western imperialism and oppression, a "struggle between races," as a wartime manual told soldiers.[42]

Dower documented the manner in which these racially tinged images lent themselves to a war fought with unusual savagery and brutality that was distinct from the European theater (a distinction, however, that ignored the war fought on the eastern front between the Axis and the Soviet Union). As reports of the torture, and even murder, of prisoners began to emerge in 1943, this sense of the war in the Pacific as a struggle against bestiality deepened. Stories like the execution of several fliers captured after the famous early bombing raid on Tokyo led by Jimmy Doolittle and the release of the diary found on a Japanese soldier killed in New Guinea, which described in florid detail the beheading of a captured airman, inflamed Americans.

The enemy in Asia was different, the famous war correspondent Ernie Pyle told his readers after transferring to the Pacific in February 1945. As Dower recounts in his book, Pyle wrote, "In Europe, we felt that our enemies, horrible and deadly as they were, were still people. But out here I soon gathered that the Japanese were looked upon as something subhuman and repulsive, the way some people feel about cockroaches or mice."[43]

This history of the war broke new ground. Dower's first work about Yoshida had been a more traditional history, drawn from documents and archives, memoirs, and the letters of prominent people. But *War Without Mercy* was, in his own description, a sociocultural history deeply routed in popular culture: "There was a visceral, emotional dimension here that the formal documents can't convey."

Dower was born in 1938, raised in a middle-class neighborhood in Providence, Rhode Island. The war raged during his childhood, but it "really had very little impact" on him. Rather, his work as a historian reflected his almost accidental fascination for Japanese culture, combined, as the 1960s unfolded, with his powerful rejection of the American war in Vietnam. In his junior year in college, in 1958, Dower spent a summer in Japan, chosen "because it was far away." Japan's visual aesthetics and culture drove him to return later to pursue studies in literature and design, and he married a Japanese woman and returned to Harvard in 1965 with the intention of earning a PhD in Japanese literature.

During the next seven years at Harvard, Dower became a participant in the growing dissent among Asian academic specialists over the Vietnam War, organized by the Committee of Concerned Asian Scholars. He and others were determined to overcome the fate of the previous generation of scholars in Asian studies, who, accused of being sympathizers of Communist China, were practically driven out of the field by the anti-Communism of the 1950s. "And if you have any sense of history, which I had gotten by this date," Dower recounts, "America was in its third war in Asia—first the Asia-Pacific War, then the Korean War, and now Vietnam. The violence and destructiveness in each of those conflicts was appalling, and the contradictions were, to me, something I had to puzzle out." For Dower in the late 1960s, the parallel between Japan in World War II and the war between American and Vietnam jumped out, not least the racial element that seemed to be part of both wars.

Dower began to question the depiction of the Pacific War as yet another expression of the "good war," a moralistic struggle between dark and light. "The Manichean images of World War II were all disintegrating in the 1960s," he says. At the point when he began to work on *War Without Mercy*, Dower was attuned to the need to understand how the wartime imagery of Japan, which persisted to the present day, had been formed in American popular consciousness. "This does not mitigate the horrors of what the Japanese did, but you've got to understand war in a broader context, and you've got to bring out more critical perspective on Western behavior."

Dower's *War Without Mercy* ends with two questions that formed the crux of *Embracing Defeat*: "After such a merciless war, how can one explain the peaceful nature of the Allied occupation of Japan, and the genuine goodwill that soon developed between the Japanese and the Americans in particular? How could the race hate dissipate so quickly?"[44]

As the title of *Embracing Defeat* implies, Dower found that the Japanese, in stunningly rapid fashion, turned from preparation for a final battle to an embrace of their defeat. Almost within moments of the arrival of American troops on Japanese soil, they discovered that the enemy were not demons, ready to rape, plunder, and murder, as wartime propaganda promised would take place. The Japanese both were exhausted by war and had a capacity for adaptability that proved remarkable.

Liberated overnight from war and the regimentation of the military-led regime, the Japanese response was far more "diverse and spirited" than American planners anticipated. "Because the defeat was so shattering, the surrender so unconditional, the disgrace of the militarists so complete, the misery the 'holy war' had brought home so personal, starting over involved not merely reconstructing buildings but also rethinking what it meant to speak of a good life and good society," Dower writes in *Embracing Defeat*.[45] The shock of defeat, coupled with the discrediting of Japan's economic and political leadership, unleashed tremendous forces of change, from radicalized left-wing labor movements to passions for previously banned Western culture. "The mystique of racial and social solidarity that had saturated wartime propaganda and behavior seemed to disappear overnight," he writes.

"Before the victors ever set foot in Japan, defeat had profoundly altered how people thought and behaved."[46]

This was the setting for the idealistic vision of transformation of Japan into a peaceful democracy that animated at least the early stages of the American occupation. "It was in this atmosphere of flux and uncertainty that the Americans proceed[ed] to dismantle the oppressive controls of the imperial state," Dower recounts.[47] With its ranks filled by liberal New Dealers, the occupation authorities proceed to overhaul everything from education and labor relations to land reform and women's rights, not least pushing through a redrafting of Japan's constitution to cement these changes and to impose a concept of Japan that would forever renounce war as an instrument of national policy. The ability to force such change was due in part to the fact that the United States was the sole occupying power—unlike in Germany. Under the singular leadership of the supreme commander, General Douglas MacArthur exercised absolute final authority for an unusually long time. Full Japanese sovereignty was not restored until 1952.

*Embracing Defeat* provides the first comprehensive account of the postwar occupation by an American historian. But it also delves into those aspects that were in some ways the postwar expression of the uncomfortable nature of the Pacific War. Dower details the retreat from reform, under the growing pressures of governance; the rise of Cold War anti-Communism; and the need to maintain order against a rising tide of rebellion. More importantly, Dower details the fateful decisions that limited the pursuit of postwar justice by exonerating the emperor of all war responsibility, which were motivated, as he documents, by both anti-Communism and the belief that the emperor's support for the occupation would ensure a more pliant populace.

The first fateful decision, Dower argues, was for the victors to rule indirectly, through the existing Japanese government and its bureaucracy. The orders of the occupiers were carried out through the Japanese system, leaving them intact to pick up the reins of power when the Americans departed. "For ideological purposes, MacArthur also chose to rely on Emperor Hirohito, in whose name all of Asia had been savaged," Dower writes. "He went so far as to secretly discourage queries about Hirohito's abdication that came from the emperor's own entourage while publicly praising him as the leader of the new democracy."[48] When the war crimes tribunals were organized after the war, modeled on the Nuremberg trials in Germany, MacArthur went even further in deciding to remove the emperor's culpability from serious review. Not only was the emperor himself not to stand in the dock, but, Dower's research showed, MacArthur and his aides secretly encouraged the Japanese leaders on trial to paint a picture of the emperor as a force for peace whose main role was to force Japan's surrender.

The question of the emperor's precise role remains a subject of historical debate, and Dower does not join some who claim that he was an active leader of the war rather than its symbol. "His moral responsibility, in any case, was transparent," Dower concludes. "And in choosing not merely to ignore this but to deny it, the Americans came close to turning the entire issue of 'war responsibility' into a joke. If the man in whose name imperial Japan had conducted foreign and military policy for twenty years was not held accountable for the initiation or conduct of the war, why should anyone expect ordinary people to dwell on such matters, or to think seriously about their own personal responsibility."[49] This decision is at the root of Japan's historical amnesia about war crimes, Dower believes, which is a view shared by some other historians and by activists both within and outside of Japan. This was compounded by the focus at the trial of the top Japanese leadership, at the International Military Tribunal for the Far East (commonly known as the Tokyo War Crimes Tribunal), on Japan's war of aggression against the Western Allies and, less so, on the crimes against Asians. No Korean served as a judge or prosecutor, Dower points out, "although hundreds of thousands of colonized Korean men and women had been brutalized by the Japanese war machine—as 'comfort women,' as laborers forced to work in the most onerous sectors of mining and heavy industry in Japan, or as lowly conscripts in the military."[50] As the Cold War emerged, the American prosecutors opted not to indict many Japanese wartime leaders who later emerged as powerful figures in the pro-American conservative governments that ruled Japan after the end of the occupation. Nonetheless, Dower celebrates the transformational nature of the postwar occupation, crediting the desire of the Japanese people for change as much as the early idealism of the victors. Japanese nationalism was effectively channeled into the quest for economic recovery in a structure of democracy and law, even if it was flawed. The postwar elites who led Japan's impressive recovery were largely imbued, Dower writes, with an understanding of the stupidity of the decision to go to war against a far more powerful foe and a determination not to repeat that mistake. They were sensitive to the need not to arouse suspicions of a return to military power, and they were ready to express their remorse for Japan's wartime acts.

Unfortunately, Dower worries in the conclusion to *Embracing Defeat*, the wartime generation is now passing from the scene, "leaving behind a miserable record when it came to offering a clear and unequivocal acknowledgement of and apology for the depredations committed during the first two decades of Hirohito's reign."[51] The flawed nature of the postwar settlement of accounts leaves open the door to a retreat from that legacy of the war, he argued in the late 1990s.[52]

Ironically, and painfully, a few years later, *Embracing Defeat* was cited by the Bush administration as a blueprint for the occupation of Iraq and its transformation into an American-style democracy. Dower was appalled at the idea. "The occupation of Japan offers no model whatsoever for any projected occupation of Iraq," he wrote in the beginning of April 2003, as the war had just begun. "On the contrary, it should stand as a warning that we are lurching toward war with no idea of what we are really getting into." The real lesson of the war in the Pacific, he counseled to no avail, is the danger of leaders who take the road to war believing that no other solutions exist, that their prowess will prevail, and that "each new escalation, each new extension of empire, [is] essential to the national interest." Looking back, he concludes, it is still difficult to say when realism turned to insanity. "But it was, in the end, madness."[53]

## Mike Honda

In the dry lands of southeastern Colorado, where the Arkansas River, its banks lined with cottonwood trees, runs through the desert, sits the town of Granada. There, in 1942, the U.S. government built a sprawling barbed-wire enclosed camp, Camp Amache, to house families of Japanese Americans from the West Coast who were interned under Executive Order 9066, issued by President Roosevelt in the early months after the Japanese surprise attack on Pearl Harbor. On the grounds of protecting the United States against enemy espionage and sabotage, nearly 122,000 men, women, and children of Japanese ancestry on the West Coast were relocated into such camps in the interior of the West. Most of them were American citizens.

Among them was Mike Honda, who was not even one year old when the order was issued in February 1942, a third generation Japanese American

Mike Honda. Source: © Patricia Montes Gregory (via Flickr).

born in the California agricultural community of Walnut Grove. He was four years old when he left the camp; his experience there was imprinted on his mind and character less by his hazy memories of the dusty camp than by the tales of his father and other family members and the sense of injustice they felt over this act. It was an experience that would shape a long career in public life, from local politics to California's state legislature to the U.S. Congress, where he still sits—a career marked by a passion for human rights and a desire to right the wrongs of wartime history.

Honda's family ran a dry-goods store in Walnut Creek, now a bedroom community of the San Francisco Bay area but then a levy town on the Sacramento Delta. The family rented rooms to Chinese, Japanese, and Filipino farmworkers, ran a Japanese bathhouse out back, and hunted and fished in the wetlands by the Delta. His grandparents were immigrants from the western Japanese main island of Kyushu, from which many Japanese fled poverty for the farmlands of California or Hawaii. Though Honda's father was born in 1914 in California, his parents sent him to study at Meiji University in Japan in the 1930s, and he came home with excellent Japanese and a facility for languages. Honda's father told him stories about the shock of the roundup for the camps, the train ride with blinds drawn, not knowing where they were going, the first gathering at the Merced fairgrounds in central California and then the move to Amache. They were told that they were there for their own security, Honda recounts. "My father always used to raise the question: If that is the case, why were the machine guns pointed inward?"[54]

Honda's father was not among those Japanese Americans who were eager to prove their loyalty by volunteering for military service. Instead, he turned his language skills to the war effort, teaching Japanese to naval intelligence officers at the famous Japanese training program in Boulder, Colorado, and after that at Northwestern University near Chicago. After the war was over, Honda and his mother joined him in Chicago, where he began to learn the lessons his father took away from his wartime experience.

Honda tells the story of playing in the street while his father was at a friend's apartment: "We were playing war, and he heard me yell out, 'Okay, we'll be the good guys, and you guys be the Japs.' And I heard his voice, 'Michael, come upstairs.' I said, 'Whoa, I didn't do anything.' 'Michael, come upstairs. I want to talk to you.' So I went upstairs to my father's friend's house, and he sat me down and asked us, 'Do you know what you were doing?' I said, 'Yes, we're just playing.'" His father repeated the words he had heard from Honda. "And he says, 'Do you know what that means?' And then at that point, he taught me some derogatory words. Then I started realizing that at school being called a 'Jap' was not really nice."[55]

As he grew up in those years, Honda became aware of the subtle racial messages he was absorbing. The Flash Gordon serials shown at the movie houses featured a blond-haired, blue-eyed hero fighting the evil Emperor Ming, a sinister Asian figure. In 1953, the family returned to California, and his father tried to pick up the strands of a life lost more than a decade earlier. Attempts to return to farm life failed, and ultimately his college-educated father became a mailman in the Bay Area suburb of Sunnyvale, later part of what became known as Silicon Valley.

Honda went to college in San Jose, joined the Peace Corps in the idealistic days of the 1960s, and eventually became a schoolteacher. His long career as an educator led to a career in elected public office, beginning with the school board in 1981 and followed by the county board of supervisors in 1990, the California State Assembly in 1996, and the U.S. Congress in 2000, where he filled the seat vacated by his mentor, another Japanese American politician, Norman Minetta. Over the course of this career in public life, Honda had a growing interest and engagement in the cause of wartime justice. He became involved with the Japanese American Citizens League (JACL), the largest and best-known of such organizations, which was formed in 1929 to deal with the anti-Japanese immigration laws of that time. In JACL, Honda became a protégé of the Japanese American civil rights leader Edison Uno, who led the postwar campaign to give remembrance to the wartime incarceration of Japanese, to prevent any future such acts, and to seek compensation for those who were detained, many of whom lost their property. He was considered the founding father of the redress movement, which he led until his death in 1976.

The campaign, which Honda helped lead after Uno's passing, had to overcome the reluctance of Japanese Americans to revisit the painful past. "They didn't want to talk about it," Honda recalls. "They said, 'It's water under the bridge.'"[56] But the issue gained support in the community, and the organization came to lead the push for redress for this wartime injustice. In 1980, President Jimmy Carter signed a law creating the Commission on Wartime Relocation and Internment of Civilians to conduct a study of the wartime orders. Two years later, the commission issued findings that concluded that the internment was not justified by military circumstances and that the decision was a manifestation of "race prejudice, war hysteria, and a failure of political leadership."[57] Based on its recommendations, the Civil Liberties Act of 1988 was passed, formally repealing the original executive order, and the next year appropriations were made to accord each surviving internee a reparations payment, along with a letter of apology. Honda, as a member of the California State Assembly, authored a bill in 2000 that established February 19—the day the order was issued—as a Day of Remembrance in the state. He also was among the leaders of efforts to establish national parks at some of the former internment camps, with exhibits that explained what had happened. As Honda wrote at the time,

> I became a leader in a movement to call for an apology and reparations. It was not a call for money—though the payment of reparations retains symbolic significance. It was not a call to embarrass the government or punish those that conspired to rob us of our dignity. It was a request to acknowledge the truth and to allow us to begin the process of healing our communal wounds.[58]

The settlement succeeded, in Honda's view, in bringing closure for Japanese Americans. It established that the internment was unjustified and recognized the suffering of that community of Americans at the hands of their own government.

In the 1990s, Honda became aware of the issue of Japanese war crimes and the demands for Japan to more clearly atone for its crimes and offer its own reparations. He saw a parallel between the Japanese American redress movement and those demands being made on Japan, especially by Asian victims but also by American POWs. In 1999, Honda sponsored a resolution in the California State Assembly, Assembly Joint Resolution No. 27, that called on Japan to offer a "clear and unambiguous apology for atrocious war crimes committed by the Japanese military during World War II" and to immediately pay reparations to the victims, including American POWs, survivors of the Nanjing Massacre of 1937, and the "comfort women" forced into sexual slavery. The resolution called on the U.S. Congress to adopt a similar resolution. Honda's sponsorship of this resolution was opposed by others in the Japanese American community, including a fellow legislator who feared it would feed anti-Japanese sentiment. But Honda saw this as a similar fight to the one over redress, pointing to not only the need to overcome the reluctance to take a stand but also the importance of solidarity with others in the Asian community in the United States.

Honda rejected the criticism that Japan had already offered apologies and that the issue of reparations was legally settled by the San Francisco Peace Treaty to end the war. "The issue is not whether Japan can on technical grounds elude responsibility," he wrote. "The question is whether justice has been done." He argued that Japan's acceptance of responsibility had been a "mixed bag," with contradictory statements, including recent ones denying war crimes, by Japanese officials. "At worst, it has been described as institutionalized national amnesia." Honda understood this as continuity with his earlier cause. "I have watched my community suffer as a result of internment," he said in a speech to Asian Americans. "I have seen the value of an apology and symbolic reparations." Those acts "lifted the burden of the injustice.... I ask no more for the victims of Japan's war atrocities than I asked for my own community: to bring closure."[59] His resolution was adopted in August 1999. The following year, Honda was elected to Congress by his Silicon Valley constituency, a post he has held since.

Soon after his arrival on Capitol Hill, Honda took up the causes of wartime justice again. He sponsored legislation to seek reparations for POWs who had worked as slave laborers in Japanese mines and factories, and he joined a group of representatives in sponsoring a resolution on the issue of sexual slavery and comfort women, similar to the one he got through the California legislature. The resolution, House Congressional Resolution 195, introduced in 2001, called on Japan to "formally issue a clear and unambiguous apology for the sexual enslavement of young women during colonial occupation of Asia and World War II, known to the world as 'comfort women.'" The resolution also called on Japan to pay reparations, to educate future generations about this "horrible crime against humanity," and to refute claims that deny that it took place.

This and several subsequent attempts at similar resolutions were effectively bottled up in congressional committees, never coming to a vote, in part because of the strenuous efforts of the Japanese government to lobby against them. Often with the tacit, if not explicit, backing of the U.S. State Department, the Japanese government argued, quite effectively, that such a resolution would harm relations, especially at a time when Japan was actively supporting the United States in the War on Terror. Honda's efforts to bring this issue to a vote and to gain support among his fellow members of Congress gained an unexpected boost when conservative Japanese politician Abe Shinzo became prime minister of Japan in the fall of 2006. Abe had long argued against the official statement issued by Japanese Chief Cabinet Secretary Kono Yohei in 1993, which accepted the widely held view of historians that the Imperial Army had organized the coercive recruitment of hundreds of thousands of women, most of them from Korea but some of them from other occupied territories such as the Philippines, the Dutch East Indies, and Taiwan, to serve in brothels during the war. Abe had sought to reverse that statement, particularly the insistence on official involvement and the coercive nature of the brothel system.

Honda reintroduced the resolution, now labeled House Resolution 121, on January 31, 2007. The text referred to a system of "forced military prostitution by the government of Japan" and linked it to the broader issue of sexual violence and human trafficking that had gained recognition internationally and nationally as a serious crime. While the resolution recognized the efforts of the Japanese government in the 1990s to create an Asian Women's Fund to extend "atonement" to the surviving victims, it noted that the fund had been disbanded, and it pointed to more recent efforts, in textbooks and elsewhere, to downplay the tragedy and other war crimes. Like the 2001 congressional resolution, it called for a clear official apology and the need to educate future generations. Honda managed to organize hearings on the resolution in February 2007, bringing three former comfort women to testify. Among them was Jan Ruff O'Herne, a Dutch woman who, as a teenager, was taken from a Java prison camp in 1944, in the Dutch East Indies, and forced to serve the sexual needs of Japanese officers. "They are pretty credible," Honda told a reporter at the time. "I can't tell a woman she wasn't multiply gang-raped. If she said it happened, it happened. The big fight is over whether it was military organized."[60]

This resolution, too, would probably have suffered the same fate had it not been for the inflammatory response of Prime Minister Abe. Reacting to the resolution and the hearings, Abe told the Japanese parliament in early March that he had no intention of issuing such an apology. Moreover, he repudiated the essential conclusion of Kono's statement regarding official involvement in a coercive system. "There was no coercion such as kidnappings by the Japanese authorities," Abe said, adding that the statements made by former comfort women could not be considered "reliable" on this point.[61] Abe's remarks galvanized support for the resolution from Asian American community organizations, particularly those of Koreans and Filipinos, who began to lobby heavily in Congress. Abe tried to calm the issue during an April visit to the United States, telling reporters at a joint press conference with President George W. Bush that "my heart goes out in sympathy to all those who suffered extreme hardships as comfort women, and I express my apologies for the fact that they were forced to endure such extreme and harsh conditions."[62] The Japanese leader carefully sidestepped the issue of official responsibility for the system and its coercive nature.

The Japanese lobbied hard in Congress to block the resolution. The Japanese ambassador sent a letter to members of Congress warning that "this measure will almost certainly have lasting and harmful effects on the deep friendship, close trust and wide-ranging cooperation our two nations now enjoy."[63] He pointed to the Japanese deployment of forces to Iraq, hinting that such cooperation would be jeopardized. On a less elevated level, Japanese conservative media close to the government launched a concerted personal attack on Honda, accusing him of being in the pay of Korean American and Chinese émigré groups and even hinting that he was somehow doing the work of the Chinese government. Honda, in an interview published in Japan, struck back angrily, pointing to the contributions he got from all sorts of people—including Japanese Americans and African

Americans—and denying receiving any money from foreign governments. "If people who are saying this had any guts," he said, "they would ask me straight. They don't have any guts. They would rather lie or give disinformation to smear my character to the media."[64] This assault backfired completely when the *Washington Post* ran an advertisement on June 14, 2007, put out by a right-wing Japanese group, the self-styled Committee for Historical Facts and the Society for the Dissemination of Historical Fact. The advertisement was signed by a long list of Japanese parliament members, most of them from the ruling conservative Liberal Democratic Party, along with professors, members of the media, and others, many of them close supporters of Prime Minister Abe. Titled "The Facts," the advertisement laid out in clear view for American readers, not least members of Congress, the views of those in Japan who denied such a war crime had even taken place. The advertisement asserted that there was no historical evidence that proved women were forced against their will into prostitution by the Japanese Imperial Army. At most, unscrupulous brokers, against the instructions of the army, tricked women into prostitution. In reality, the ad concluded, the women who were "embedded" with the Japanese were not sex slaves but willing prostitutes, pursuing their profession out of their own free will, earning income and being treated well. Backers of this view even compared the system to brothels that serviced American servicemen in Vietnam. This denial outraged members of Congress, who with almost no dissent voted the resolution out of the Foreign Affairs Committee on June 26. The committee chairman, California congressman Tom Lantos, who had previously been reluctant to push the resolution through, stated,

> The true strength of a nation is tested when it is forced to confront the darkest chapters in its history. Will it have the courage to face up to the truth of its own past, or will it run from that truth in the foolish hope that truth will fade with time? . . . Post-war Germany . . . made the right choice. Japan, on the other hand, has actively promoted historical amnesia. The facts . . . are plain. There can be no denying that the Japanese Imperial military coerced thousands upon thousands of women, primarily Chinese and Koreans, into sexual slavery during the Second World War.[65]

The resolution was sent to the floor of Congress, where it was overwhelmingly passed on July 30, 2007.

Mike Honda does not dwell at length on the history of the war or seek to explore the intellectual meaning of these issues. For him, this begins and, in some sense, ends with his earliest days in the internment camp and the quest for justice for himself, his family, and the larger society that seemed to flow from that experience. The goal, he says, is reconciliation, and apology is a means to that end. "You apologize sincerely, and you accept historical facts, and you do something about it after that—providing compensation. You put it in the books, and you make sure children don't make the same mistakes."⁶⁶

## Mark Peattie

Mark Peattie was a boy of eleven, living in the peaceful California coastal community of Santa Barbara, when war entered his life and never left. Some seven decades later, he still remembers the moment on Sunday, December 7, 1941, with great clarity. "I was passing through the living room, and my older brother said, 'The Japanese have just attacked Pearl Harbor.' I rushed in and told my parents, and they said, 'Go away, and don't bother us. That's just Orson Welles doing his *War of the Worlds* thing again.' They said, 'It's just a publicity stunt.' Of course, it wasn't, and I went back, and we

Mark Peattie. Source: Courtesy Walter H. Shorenstein Asia-Pacific Research Center.

all listened in very carefully."⁶⁷ President Roosevelt's Day of Infamy speech to Congress the following day also remained fixed in Peattie's memory, as was the day the war ended, almost four years later. During the war years, Peattie's bedroom was covered with a huge map of Europe and the Pacific. He marked Allied advances with colored pins, collected articles on the war, and posted photos on the walls. "I was fascinated with the U.S. Navy, and I collected lots of photographs and articles about American and Japanese warships," he recounts.

Peattie's experience of the war set him on a path to becoming one of the preeminent American historians of the war and the events leading up to that great conflict. He was the author of the first comprehensive studies of the Japanese Imperial Navy and its air forces as well as of the biography of the Japanese military leader Ishiwara Kanji, who was the architect of the Japanese seizure of Manchuria and its drive into northern China. Peattie delved into Japanese colonial rule, from its the early days in Micronesia to its rule of Southeast Asia. His expertise on the military history of the Sino-Japanese War led him to lead an effort at dialogue among Chinese, Japanese, and American historians about those events.

In his work as a historian, Peattie was moved by another wartime experience—not that of a boy charting the movement of armies and navies but of the son of two American writers who struggled against the rising tide of hatred at home. At the time the war began, the family employed two Japanese women at their home in Santa Barbara. "One was a housekeeper who was born in Japan, grew up in Japan, and had been in the United States for about ten years," he recalls. "And she was very, very, very conflicted about [the war]. She burst into tears and collapsed into my mother's arms. The other one was a young Japanese girl who had just graduated from high school and who worked for my father as a secretary. She was very Americanized. Her reaction was—she said she couldn't understand it. She thought 'the Emperor must have had ants in his pants.' I quote her literally." In addition, the father of the secretary was a gardener on the estate where the Peattie family rented a home. The gardener and the family shared a love of plants.

Within hours of the attack on Pearl Harbor, Peattie's father was on the phone to the local radio station, asking for a few minutes on air to urge tolerance for their fellow Japanese American citizens. It was a message he carried in the early months of the war, lecturing to social clubs and professional associations who would listen to him "asking for fair play for Japanese American citizens," as his son recounts. In 1942, after Roosevelt issued an executive order to relocate Japanese from the West Coast, authorities came to the estate where the Peatties were living to haul off the father of his secretary, the gardener. "My father was broken up about it, and Yunida [the gardener] turned to my father and he said, 'Don't be upset, Mr. Peattie. Wherever they take me, it will still be America,' which was pretty decent of a guy who was going to be thrown in the slammer for something he didn't do." Peattie's father worked hard to move Yunida's daughter and their housekeeper to keep them out of the relocation camps.

The wartime propaganda portrayed an insidious trio—Hitler, Mussolini, and Tojo—but of the three, the Japanese leader was almost a racial caricature in Peattie's memory. "It was sort of a stereotypical Japanese with a small mustache and Coke bottles for eyeglasses that were perfectly round. I think most Americans really didn't know much about [the Japanese] except that we should hate them. I didn't hate them. I wanted us to win, but I can't remember any deep-seated animosity to[ward] the Japanese. My father certainly hated what the Japanese leadership had done to its own country."

After college, Peattie went off to earn a master's degree in American history at Stanford University. But when the Korean War came along, he volunteered for military service, training in counterintelligence but serving in Germany. He came home in 1954, and, after a break, embarked on a career in the U.S. Foreign Service as an information and cultural affairs officer, serving in Cambodia before being sent in 1957 to the northern Japanese city of Sendai, where he was the sole official American presence. Peattie embraced the country he had known only in the context of war, studying the language and engaging in Japanese society. In the early 1960s, running the American cultural center in Kyoto, Peattie confronted the left-wing drift of Japanese intellectuals who were highly critical of American foreign policy. When it came to discussing the war, Japanese students would tell him, "'You know, come on, we know why you went to war with us. It was all about profit and trade; that's why you went to war with us.' The phrasing was always 'You went to war with us.' They never said, 'We went to war with you.'"

Peattie became eager to exit the role of being a defender of the United States and opted to return to academia, heading to Princeton to earn his PhD in Japanese history. He brought with him not only a new facility in the language but his old interest in the Japanese military. Under the guidance of the great Japan scholar Marius Jansen, Peattie decided to write his thesis about Ishiwara Kanji, the leader of the Kwantung Army, spearhead of Japan's takeover of Manchuria, and stronghold of radicalized Army officers who advocated a military-led state—a form of state control of the economy and an aggressive takeover of the Asian mainland. General Ishiwara was the architect of the infamous Mukden Incident in 1931, the pretext for the creation of the Japanese puppet state of Manchukuo, a step that put Japan on the path to the wider war with China and, ultimately, with the United States.

Peattie's interest was grounded in his own wartime reference point. But he was also motivated, under Jansen's influence, to go beyond the stereotypes of prewar and wartime Japan and gain a deeper understanding of the individuals who made the key decisions. "I've always been impressed by the fact that despite all that's been written in modern Japanese history, [so] few of the generals in modern Japan have ever been written about." Even figures such as the emperor tend to be studied, he points out, as institutions and not as individuals. This flows in part, he argues, from the tendency to see Japan as a collective society and to downplay the role of individuals.

As a military historian, Peattie's passion was naval history, evident in his two significant works for the Naval Institute Press. He wrote the history of the Japanese Imperial Navy and of the rise of Japanese naval air power, which, of course, played the central role in the war, beginning with the attack on Pearl Harbor. As he writes in a reflective essay on the fiftieth anniversary of the end of the war, the Pacific War "was without doubt the greatest naval war in history." With the exception of the campaigns of Genghis Khan, "no modern war has been fought over such vast distances" or employed such a variety of weapons and tactics. "It opened with an attack on what was supposed to be the prime element of sea power—the battleship—and ended with that element eclipsed by a new element—the aircraft carrier." The war featured great carrier battles and was the testing ground for amphibious warfare, and thus it is a case study of "the economic strangulation of an island enemy by submarine warfare." Of course, the two atomic bombs that ended the war "transformed strategic planning for the rest of the twentieth century." Because of the changes this war brought about, ironically, perhaps, "that kind of naval war seems destined never to be repeated."[68]

Peattie's approach yielded an early appreciation for the often tortured nature of Japanese decision making, the absence of what wartime propaganda contended was a master plan, and the profound strategic mistakes that led to Japan's destruction and defeat in the war. He was increasingly fascinated with the question of why the Japanese lost World War II, beyond the fact that the United States enjoyed an overwhelming material advantage. While not denying the unequal nature of the struggle in the Pacific, "the Japanese made a whole lot of mistakes," Peattie reflected toward the end of his career. "The main mistake was letting the military have an almost unfettered hand in decision making."

Japanese military officers were trained to think of their careers in terms of "the importance of personal glory" and a belief in taking the offensive. "That's why the Japanese so underestimated the importance of logistics," Peattie reasons. In the Japanese navy, those who failed were put in charge of logistics and, to some extent, of intelligence. In December 1941, the Japanese naval leadership had very precise information on Allied military strengths and weaknesses in Asia. "What they were absolutely clueless about was the psychology of the American people. If they had any understanding of the psychology of the American people, the idea of the attack on Pearl Harbor would have been dumped immediately." No Japanese military planner "took into account the emotional public American response to the attack," he says.

For Japanese military planners, Peattie argued, Pearl Harbor was actually a sideshow for the invasion of Southeast Asia. The Japanese decided that the way to keep the United States at bay was to attack the main fleet base in Hawaii to prevent American battleships from moving across the Pacific and attacking their invasion of Southeast Asia. It was, in Peattie's words, "a stupid decision." Had Japan confined itself to attack British and Dutch colonial possessions in Southeast Asia, where it hoped to find the oil and other resources lost because of the American embargo, President Roosevelt would have found it very difficult to persuade the American people to go to war, he believed.

Japanese war planning was full of strategic holes, the result of the failure to "think a whole lot of things through." This included the vulnerability of their shipping lines back to Japan, which ultimately were severed by American submarine and naval power. But this lack of thought was already evident in the Japanese invasion of China that preceded the Pacific war. The conventional view, strongly held during the war itself, was that the expansion of Japan into the mainland was a carefully plotted series of moves and that "Japanese aggression in Asia worked like a smoothly oiled machine in which every part worked flawlessly to crush all opposition." But the record shows, Peattie argues, that "actually the opposite is true." Japanese foreign policy in the 1920s and 1930s "lurched from one pole to another" as Japanese civil and military leaders were split and the military itself was split into cliques and factions that worked against each other. Japanese policy making was "chaotic and brutal, sometimes almost rudderless and incoherent." When it came to China, where the Japanese believed that they would conquer the country in a matter of months, "the Japanese military blundered into that war with a whole lot of wishful thinking about the Chinese," Peattie contends. The Japanese had a very accurate view of Chinese factions and rivalries, as they had their advisors serving with many of the warlords. But again, they had very little sense of what the Chinese were feeling and how their actions were perceived. "The biggest problem that Japan faced in China was the emerging sense of outrage by the Chinese people over decades of Japanese humiliations, atrocities, and general bullying, which the Japanese had brought about. They had no sense of that whatsoever."

Peattie's multiple studies of Japanese colonial rule reveal a similar pattern of self-delusion. Japanese leaders portrayed themselves as the liberators of Asia from Western colonialism who would bring enlightenment to Asia under Japanese leadership, clothed in rhetoric about the equality of peoples. In reality, the Japanese replicated the racism of the West, clearly perceiving other Asian peoples in Korea, China, and elsewhere as subordinates, often in the most extreme racist terms. Japanese officials saw China as a "cesspool" to be cleaned up by Japan of its filth, Peattie says. Many Japanese deeply believed their own propaganda, however; among them was Ishiwara, who was brought to testify at the Tokyo War Crimes Tribunal as a witness for the Allied prosecutors. There, Ishiwara reminded the Americans of how Japan was forced to open its doors to the world in 1853 by an American naval flotilla commanded by Commodore Matthew Perry. Peattie, his biographer, sums up the encounter:

> He turned on the American prosecutor and said, "Obviously, you haven't read history, that's your problem. We Japanese were alone, isolated in our islands [and] minding our own business and along comes Perry with his black ships

and at the point of a gun [he] said, open up your doors or we're going to blow you out of the water. And we looked around the world and we saw that this is the way that big powers behave. So we just took your country as a model." And that's why he turned to the American prosecutor and said—"I propose that you summon Perry from the other world and try him as a war criminal."[69]

Peattie contrasts the Japanese, in this sense, to the Germans. "The Japanese deluded themselves into thinking a lot of the things about the world that simply weren't true. It wasn't a totally cynical undertaking for them. They really did believe this stuff, where I think the Nazis did not."

In his later years as a historian, Peattie became engaged with an effort led by the great Harvard East Asian scholar Ezra Vogel to bring professional historians together to create a military history of the Sino-Japanese War, long neglected in Western historiography—a history that reflected the research efforts of scholars in the region and could create a more balanced and textured mutual understanding of those events. This project organized two international conferences, with scholars from Japan, China, and the West, in an effort that was part historical research and part diplomacy as it aimed to create opportunities for dialogue and collaboration between Chinese and Japanese scholars. The dialogue was difficult, at times tortured. Chinese and Japanese scholars exchanged barbs, but American scholars were also irritated by the Chinese claims about their role in winning the war against Japan. Still, the effort co-led by Peattie yielded two books, the most important of which was *The Battle for China: Essays on the Military History of the Sino-Japanese War of 1937–1945*, the most comprehensive account of the war published in English.

As tensions continue to rise between China and Japan, Peattie reflected on the importance of this war in shaping the mutual perceptions of these two Asian powers. In an essay published in 2007, Peattie discusses the poisoned well created by the war and the fifty years of animosity that flowed from those events. "One can liken the twelve hundred years of Sino-Japanese relations, prior to the twentieth century, to a well filled by China's universal culture, from which Japan drank deeply and respectfully," he writes. But that well became poisoned, he continues, "beginning first with the imbalance between a decaying imperial bureaucratic empire and a modernizing, aggressive nation at the end of the nineteenth century, and ending with a clash of nationalisms in the 1930s."[70]

In this essay, Peattie discusses the competing historical narratives in China, Japan, and the United States about this war:

> That historical animosity is indeed at the core of the current unstable relations between China and Japan. I believe that a freer, less partisan *public* discussion of both countries' memories and myths can help to reduce that animosity. . . . To detoxify the poisoned well that they now share will take prolonged, consistent, and concerted efforts by both peoples to rise above their corrosive national myths and prejudices to find a common humanity in their tragic pasts. It will require the people of China to forgive—if not forget—and the Japanese to remember, and to make that memory part of the permanent public record.[71]

This did not, as Peattie predicted, happen in his lifetime. But he left a legacy as a historian whose work may contribute to that eventual accomplishment.

## *Lester Tenney*

Lester Tenney, a garrulous twenty-one-year-old from Chicago, arrived in the Philippines on the newly proclaimed Thanksgiving Day of November 20, 1941, and headed to a U.S. Army base next to Clark Field. A little more than a year earlier, Lester enlisted in the 192nd Tank Battalion, Company B of the Illinois National Guard. At the time, by his own account, Tenney hoped

Lester Tenney.
Source: Courtesy Lester Tenney.

to spend a year in the guard and fulfill his military service, moving on with his search for a career in business. Instead, his guard unit was inducted into federal service that November, putting him on a pathway that led to a shattering experience of war, captivity as a prisoner of war, service as a slave laborer in the coal mines of Japan, and, ultimately, to his belated decision to lead a campaign for justice and reparation for himself and his fellow POWs.

Even as a young Jewish man growing up during the Depression, Tenney, or Tenenberg, as he was legally known then, did not think much about the storm clouds of war gathering in Europe and in Asia. "That was in the late 1930s," he recalls. "We were more interested in our own life than we were in what was happening somewhere else. I never had any idea of Japan."[72] The reality of impending conflict only hit once he was on the ship heading west from Pearl Harbor to the Philippines, as blackouts were ordered on word that Japanese warships were in the area. "It was probably my first time thinking about Japan as a nation," Tenney says.

When the Japanese struck Pearl Harbor, in the Philippines it was in the early hours of December 8. By eight in the morning, the tanks in Tenney's unit were positioned to defend the airfield, the main air base on the islands. Little more than four hours later, Japanese bombers struck the field, leaving devastation in their wake. Months of battle against the invading Japanese Imperial Army followed, much of it on the Bataan Peninsula protecting the city of Manila. It was a hard fought but ultimately hopeless defense, ending in surrender on April 9, 1942. Almost one of out every five American military deaths in World War II took place in the Philippines. What followed is forever memorialized as one of the most horrific events in American military history—the so-called Bataan Death March, the marching by Japanese conquerors of 105,000 American and Filipino prisoners from Bataan to POW camps. Of the 12,000 captured American soldiers who were on that march, only 1,700 ever made it home; most of them died in the camps. An estimated 7,000 to 10,000 American and Filipino prisoners died on the march, starved of food and water, beaten mercilessly, murdered by gun and sword, and sometimes forced to bury their own dead along the way or shot for their inability to pick up a shovel.

Tenney witnessed one after another of these atrocities. In his first encounter with his captors, a Japanese soldier asked for a cigarette, and Tenney signaled that he had none. "[The soldier] smiled and then a second later hit me in the face with the butt of his gun. Blood spurted from my nose and from a deep gash on my cheekbone. He laughed and said something that made all of his buddies laugh, too . . . laughing at the defeated and weak Americans." As Tenney wrote later, there was

> no sympathy, no concern for us as humans, no burials—the Japanese were treating us like animals. We had thought that the first few hours of captivity would probably be the most dangerous, but the horrors we witnessed continued well after the surrender. For the Japanese, the sweet taste of victory should have overshadowed the bitterness associated with their strenuous fighting on Bataan, but it was obvious to us that the Japanese soldiers were committing acts of revenge.[73]

Tenney survived the Bataan Death March and spent the next months in a prison camp, interrupted by an escape to join a group of guerrilla fighters, only to be recaptured within weeks. On September 5, 1942, Tenney was jammed into a rusting freighter with some 500 other prisoners—a "human cargo of slave labor" destined for the coal mines of western Japan, in Kyushu. From then until the end of the war, Tenney was held at Camp 17, with what eventually totaled 1,700 prisoners, mostly American but also Australian and Javanese soldiers captured in the Dutch East Indies. They labored in the mine, owned by Mitsui, one of Japan's well-established conglomerates, and were often subjected to beatings at the hands of their civilian overseers. "They were the ones who would get furious at us, and we never knew why," Tenney recounts. "But we slowly realized that it was different events of the war that would cause them to become very upset. A man comes down the mine, and he just got word that his brother was killed by an American torpedo from a submarine, and he's mad at America."

Tenney was beaten frequently by his overseers, sometimes with pickaxes, hammers, and shovels—causing injuries that required months in the hospital after the war to repair the damage. But he also showed a facility for language that allowed him to become an intermediary for his captors and to establish a valuable black-market trade with his guards. By the winter of 1944, however, conditions worsened. Food was in short supply as the U.S. forces grew nearer and nearer to the Japanese main islands. "The guards and the civilians in the mine found all kinds of excuses to beat us," poundings that worsened in response to the growing crescendo of American bombing raids on Japan. In late June 1945, American fighters strafed the Japanese guardhouses. On August 6, their Japanese captors, with suddenly softened attitudes, quietly informed them that the Americans had dropped a big bomb. The mine and camp were located only thirty-five miles from the Kyushu port city of Nagasaki, the target of the second atomic bombing. On August 9, as they set out to the mine, "we saw what appeared to be a large floating cloud, with a large stem-like cloud at the bottom.... We later learned that we had witnessed the rising cloud of the second atomic bomb." Tenney remains convinced that without this bombing, all the American prisoners would have been killed by their captors in the event of a ground invasion. "As far as Camp 17 was concerned, there is no doubt that dropping this devastating bomb saved our lives, as well as the lives of millions of our Allies and our enemy, the Japanese. Although about two hundred thousand civilians were killed in both Hiroshima and Nagasaki," he later wrote, "the benefit to us prisoners was immediate."[74]

More than any other charges of wartime criminality, the treatment of prisoners by the Japanese drove the postwar trials of Japanese military and civilian leaders. There was a widespread belief that Japanese treatment of prisoners was distinctly harsher than that of their German and Italian allies, a belief that was reinforced by a statistic that emerged in the trials. While only 4 percent of American and British servicemen taken prisoner in Europe died in captivity, the death rate at Japanese hands was 27 percent. Tenney did not emerge from the war necessarily consumed by hatred. Indeed, as he explains in a 2010 interview, he did not buy the wartime propaganda that portrayed Imperial Japan as bent on global conquest, in lockstep with Nazi Germany and Italy. Instead, he offers this more nuanced view of the events that led to his ordeal in the Philippines and beyond:

> The Japanese were invading China. They were slaughtering Chinese, and the United States felt that they had to do something, and so they started to deny the Japanese raw materials. That upset the Japanese, but that was okay. They could deal with it, and all they had to do was buy it from somebody else, until the United States froze all their assets. When the United States froze all their money, ... they couldn't even buy it from anybody else. So that was the straw that broke the camel's back, and the Japanese said, "The United States are our enemy." They and Germany joined forces together, [but] I think Germany was the one that influenced the Japanese. I think Germany wanted the Americans to be fighting on two fronts. Germany felt that if they could get the U.S. to fight on two fronts, they could get the United States to be willing, not to surrender but to stop the war. They were surprised.... The Japanese felt it was the right time. They never expected to win the war. I'm convinced in my own mind that

they never expected to win a war. They never expected to land on American soil and control America. All they wanted to do was get raw materials and get some of the land they were fighting for, and then they were willing to say to the United States, "We'll accept a treaty." They weren't going to stop to surrender. They wanted just to accept a treaty. And so that's what happened. That's my opinion of the war.

Tenney came home in October 1945. His brother Bill questioned him intensely about his experience, taking detailed notes in those first months home. Tenney brought home notes of his own that he wrote in prison camp and recorded many of his own memories in writing in those early months. All of this remained locked away for almost fifty years, as Tenney eagerly embraced a normal life, going on to teach finance and insurance at Arizona State University and San Diego State University. Tenney, ashamed of his surrender and captivity, never talked about the experience with the rest of his family. Finally, at the request of his children, he began to write his memoir in 1994. "Sometimes I would write two or three sentences and cry," he said about the process. "Sometimes I could write fifteen or twenty pages, but there was an awful lot of emotions." He finished in five or six months, initially intending the manuscript to be read only by his family. But it came out as a powerful book, *My Hitch in Hell: the Bataan Death March*, the following year.

Tenney was also motivated by a growing sense of anger. He worried that the history of the Pacific War, and of the sacrifices of those who fought in the Philippines, was slipping from memory. He felt "humiliated again by the Japanese," whose leaders in the 1980s had begun to voice denials of their wartime crimes as fabrications. "I cannot allow these attempts by government officials to justify the Japanese aggression and inhumane treatment of soldiers and civilians to go unchallenged and unanswered," he writes in the preface to his book.[75]

Tenney became active, for the first time since the early days after the end of the war, in veterans groups such as the American Defenders of Bataan and Corregidor Memorial Society. Ultimately, he became the most widely recognized spokesman for former POWs, giving speeches, testifying before Congress, writing op-eds, and agitating for justice for forgotten crimes. Tenney focused on the quest for an official apology from the Japanese government and from Japanese firms for their treatment of American POWs, including demands that they be paid, as the Geneva Convention requires, for their forced labor.

The compensation of wartime forced labor took on new visibility in 1998, when class-action suits were filed in U.S. courts against twelve German firms on behalf of those who were used as wartime slaves in their factories and mines. The German firms eventually settled those suits and the court actions led, with the involvement of the U.S. and German governments, to the creation of a German fund in 2000 to compensate all forced laborers used by German firms during the war, as well as to support public education on the issue.

California passed a law in July 1999 that gave the state's courts the jurisdiction to hear such cases against the former Axis powers and extended the statute of limitations for such litigation. Lester Tenney became the first person to employ this law against Japanese firms in August 1999, filing suit against the Mitsui Mining Company and other Mitsui conglomerate firms, seeking compensation for his work in their mines. For Japanese firms, which also faced suits filed by Chinese and Korean slave laborers who numbered in the millions, this represented a serious problem. Unlike the Germans, the Japanese government and firms never fully acknowledged their responsibility for compensation, and records of their service (and even of payments held in accounts in Japan) have been very difficult to pry loose from Japanese archives. "My fight against the Japanese company that abused and tortured me is not about money," Tenney wrote later in a newspaper op-ed. "It has never been about money. It has been about honor, dignity and responsibility. Like the great country of Japan, we too take pride in our honor and dignity, but it was taken from us, and now we want it restored."[76]

The Japanese government position on such suits, one echoed by the firms, is that the claims for reparation were settled by the San Francisco Peace Treaty of 1951. Plaintiffs have argued, however, that the while the U.S. government and others may have agreed to not seek further reparations from Japan, that did not remove the rights of individual victims to seek compensation, particularly from private firms. In the German case, the suits were a public-relations nightmare for the firms, fed by the ongoing horror over the Holocaust. Perhaps reflecting the political pressures generated by these cases, the U.S. government was largely supportive of the plaintiffs and actively intervened to mediate the broader settlement that led to the creation of the German fund.

When the Japanese case reached federal courts, however, the U.S. State Department was active in leading the opposition to the suit filed by Tenney, who was joined by other former POWs. Based almost entirely on the U.S.

government's intervention, a federal district judge rejected Tenney's suit, a decision ultimately upheld by the U.S. Supreme Court. "We were turned back, turned back by our own State Department, which chose to defend the Japanese actions," Tenney recalls, the event still a source of bitterness for him and other survivors of Japanese POW camps. "The real problem that continues is the lack—the total lack of responsibility of the private companies, who have said absolutely nothing, not one word, not one breath, nothing," he says. "They owe us an apology, not just because they put us in forced labor but because they didn't do the things that would be considered human."

This quest for justice did, however, achieve one milestone: after much personal effort on his part, Tenney was rewarded with the first official statement of apology for the ordeal of those who fought and were imprisoned in the Philippines. On March 30, 2009, the Japanese ambassador to Washington, Fujisaki Ichiro, came to the annual convention of the American Defenders of Bataan and Corregidor Memorial Society to offer, for the first time, a direct apology to seventy-three surviving POWs. "As former Prime Ministers of Japan have repeatedly stated, the Japanese people should bear in mind that we must look into the past and to learn from the lessons of history," Fujisaki said. "We extend a heartfelt apology for our country having caused tremendous damage and suffering to many people, including prisoners of wars, those who have undergone tragic experiences in the Bataan Peninsula, Corregidor Island, in the Philippines, and other places. Ladies and gentlemen, taking this opportunity, I would like to express my deepest condolences to all those who have lost their lives in the war, and after the war, and their family members."[77]

Tenney, who, as president of the association, introduced the Japanese ambassador, called it a historic day. "After sixty-seven years of searching for justice, of being a former POW of the Japanese, today is the culmination of those years of searching," he told the audience.[78] The following year, Tenney and five other former POWs visited Japan under an official Japanese government program to foster reconciliation—the first time such a visit had been organized for Americans. Tenney had been to Japan five times before, but many in the group were there for the first time since their captivity.

"I offer my deep, heartfelt apology for the inhuman treatment you suffered," Foreign Minister Okada Katsuya told the group.[79] For Lester Tenney, then ninety years old, this was a step toward reconciliation but not yet the end of his search for justice.

PART THREE

*Divided Memories: The Major Controversies*

SIX

# Japanese Colonial Rule, Forced Labor, and Comfort Women

In December 2011, a bronze statue in memory of former "comfort women" was installed across the street from the Japanese embassy in Seoul. Japanese officials have asked the Korean authorities to remove the statue, and a Japanese activist even visited the site with the intention of doing so himself, enraging the Korean public. Japanese leaders have said that their formal apologies, expressions of remorse, and admissions of responsibility regarding the treatment of comfort women, including an offer to establish a private fund for victims, should be sufficient. But many Koreans disagree, contending that the Japanese government should unequivocally acknowledge its wrongdoings and pay reparations to the victims. In May 2012, South Korea opened a new "museum of war and women's rights" for the purposes of "memory, commemoration, record, and reconciliation" with regard to Korean comfort women.[1]

Across the Pacific, tensions between Japan and South Korea over the legacy of comfort women have spilled over to the United States. Controversies surrounding a monument dedicated to comfort women in New Jersey's Palisades Park became the focus of international media in 2012, when members of Japanese parliament carried out several attempts to remove the small copper plaque. Japanese delegations, including one led by the Japanese consul general in New York, even offered to plant cherry trees in the borough, donate books to the public library, and provide other services in order to get the monument down. Many have viewed these attempts as Japan's efforts to erase history—or, at least, to make it quietly fade from memory.

The Japanese government was unsuccessful in taking the monument down; however, right-wing Japanese lawmakers and activists have successfully rounded up more than twenty-five thousand signatures for a petition on the White House's "We the People" website, asking the Obama administration to force the Palisades Park local government to remove the monument. The petition claims that "false accusations regarding the South Korean comfort women issue have disgraced the people of Japan for decades. Over the past few years it has come to light that many of the original charges were false or completely fabricated."[2] As one *New York Times* article aptly points out, this episode only "deepened animosity between Japan and South Korea over the issue of comfort women, a longstanding irritant in their relations."[3] In fact, this controversy has made Koreans around the country even more determined to build more monuments to the comfort women elsewhere. In early 2014, the first comfort women statue in America was erected in the city of Glendale, California, supported by the Korea-Glendale Sister City Association and the Korean American Forum of California, followed by the second such statue in Southfield, Michigan, in August 2014. The Fullerton City Council and the San Francisco Board of Supervisors of California have also approved the erection of the next such statues, and more statues are being discussed elsewhere in the United States, such as in Milpitas, California. These efforts are led by Asian American communities—most prominently, the Korean American and Chinese American communities.

A few years earlier, the U.S. House of Representatives passed House Resolution 121, which criticized the Japanese handling of the comfort-women issue. Introduced in 2007 by Representative Mike Honda, a Japanese American legislator, it called on the Japanese government to "formally acknowledge, apologize, and accept historical responsibility in a clear and unequivocal manner for its Imperial Armed Forces' coercion of young women into sexual slavery, during its colonial and wartime occupation of Asia and the Pacific Islands from the 1930s through the duration of World War II." Although nonbinding, the resolution urged Japan to "educate current and future generations about this horrible crime while following the recommendation of the international community with respect to the 'comfort women.'" Although none of the countries involved would deny that forced labor and the exploitation of comfort women did exist during the colonial and war years, disputes over the scale, nature, legality, means of compensation, and reconciliation remain as intense as ever.

This chapter discusses how the forced-labor and comfort-women issues have produced divided memories of colonial aggression and war atrocities in the Asia-Pacific region, with particular attention to the main themes of the book as outlined in the introductory chapter: imbalance in focus, contention and diversity, and the transformation of wartime memories. These two subjects are more important to historical memories for Korea and Japan than for China and the United States, showing cross-national variation in memory formation. In addition, within each nation, there exists a good amount of variation in views. In Korea, for instance, while nationalist views are still dominant, recent years have seen the rise of feminist and human-rights approaches to the questions of forced labor and comfort women. In Japan, the government has not taken full responsibility but established a private fund for the victims, and some liberal scholars have been leading concerted efforts to find historical documents to prove Japan's responsibility. Thanks to the rise of diverse views, memories of the two issues have gradually changed over time. Koreans have tended to be less nationalistic in recent years, and Japan's position has changed from denial to acceptance, even if reluctant. In recent years, however, under renewed conservative rule, there is a move to reverse even those steps toward acknowledging that dark history. Even in the United States, as evidenced by the construction of monuments in cities across the country, the comfort-women issue has been disputed.

## *Japanese Colonialism, Forced Labor, and Comfort Women*

Colonialism originated from Europe, and both World Wars began there, too, but colonialism and war also constitute important elements of history and memory in Asia. After its victory in the Sino-Japanese War of 1894–1895, Japan took Taiwan from China to become the first and only non-Western colonial power. A decade later, Japan made Korea its protectorate, and five years afterward annexed Korea into its expanding empire. In 1937, Japan invaded China and extended its empire into Southeast Asia. In 1941, imperial Japan went to war with the United States, engaging in a series of battles with Western allies known as the Pacific War in Asia. During these years of colonialism and war, Japan committed a number of atrocities; forced labor and the exploitation of women as sex slaves known as comfort women are the results of Japanese aggression toward the end of its imperial era.

From 1939, labor shortages resulting from the conscription of Japanese males for the military efforts in China and elsewhere led to organized official recruitment of Koreans to work in mainland Japan, initially through civilian agents and later directly, often involving elements of coercion. By 1942, as the labor shortage grew more severe, Japanese authorities extended the provisions of the National Mobilization Law to include the conscription of Korean workers for factories and mines on the Korean peninsula, Manchukuo, and the involuntary relocation of workers to Japan itself as needed (some of them were killed during the atomic bombings of Hiroshima and Nagasaki). It is in this context that Korean women and others were taken as sex slaves to Japanese military bases.

The lack of detailed information concerning the forced recruitment of Korean and Chinese laborers and comfort women makes it difficult to estimate the exact figures and almost impossible to resolve the substantial discrepancies in the statistics and estimates that are available in each country. Estimated figures of the number of comfort women range from 8,000 to approximately 200,000 Korean women alone.[4] Some scholars contend that the number was as high as 410,000 women, including those from Vietnam, Malaysia, the Philippines, and elsewhere. But most international media sources turn to Japanese historian Yoshiaki Yoshimi, who conducted the first academic study of the comfort-women issue.[5] Based on his studies, about 200,000 young women were recruited or kidnapped by soldiers to serve in Japanese military brothels. The BBC writes of "200,000 to 300,000," while the International Commission of Jurists quotes "estimates of historians that 100,000 to 200,000 women were made to serve as comfort women."[6]

Regarding forced labor, about 670,000 out of the 5.4 million Koreans conscripted by the Japanese are estimated to have been taken to mainland Japan (including Karafuto Prefecture, present-day Sakhalin, now part of Russia) for civilian labor, and about 60,000 are estimated to have died between 1939 and 1945 as a result of harsh treatment, inhumane working conditions, and Allied bombings.[7] However, figures vary: some reports estimate the total number of Korean forced workers in Japan during the war to be at about 700,000, whereas other researchers claim that more than 1.5 million Koreans were forcibly recruited.[8] The total number of deaths of Korean forced laborers in Korea and Manchuria is estimated to be between 270,000 and 810,000.[9] Chinese sources indicate that around 40,000 Chinese were forced to work in Japan during World War II and 7,000 of them died there.

But according to a joint study by historians including Zhifen Ju, Mitsuyoshi Himeta, Toru Kubo, and Mark Peattie, more than 10 million Chinese civilians were mobilized by the Kōa-in (Japanese Asia Development Board) for forced labor.

*Bringing the Issues to the Fore*

Until the 1980s, both the forced-labor and comfort-women issues were not well known to the public. Silence may have arisen from social and psychological trauma, which made people unable or unwilling to speak openly of their experiences, either because social receptivity was lacking or because the psychological trauma was too great. Also, there existed no organized activism to bring these issues to the public at the national or international level. Instead, authoritarian regimes suppressed discussion of the issues. When the Park Chung-hee government signed the Japan-Korea Basic Treaty in 1965, it set aside historical issues to focus on economic assistance from Japan. Japan and the United States took the position that the San Francisco Peace Treaty of 1951 resolved these issues, including that of reparations for victims. It was not until the late 1980s that these issues, especially the issue of comfort women, became highly charged and politically significant in Korea.

With democratization, Korean activists and nongovernmental organization (NGO) leaders began to bring the issue of comfort women to the public. After political liberalization in 1987, Korea saw the development of a contentious civil society that addressed many social, historical, and political issues that had been ignored or repressed during the authoritarian years.[10] During this period of growing civic activism, the Korean Council for the Women Drafted into Sexual Slavery by Japan was formed in South Korea in November 1990. A year later, Kim Hak-sun, a former comfort woman in Korea, broke the forty years of silence by testifying in public about her experiences and brought her case against the Japanese government to court. Later, a group of former comfort women organized themselves to seek redress for past injustices and suffering; they gather every Wednesday in front of the Japanese embassy in Seoul, demanding an apology and compensation from Japan. With the help of NGO groups, they began to speak out and obtain redress for historical injustices.

On December 21, 1991, the South Korean foreign ministry made public a U.S. Army document containing a report on the role of the Japanese

Imperial Army in the recruitment of Korean women and girls to serve as comfort women. The report claimed, "A 'comfort girl' is nothing more than a prostitute or 'professional camp follower' attached to the Japanese army for the benefit of the soldiers."[11] However, the report failed to mention that the "camp followers" did not follow by choice but were taken and held by force. Nonetheless, the document confirmed that Japanese military authorities were involved in a campaign to promote the establishment of a sex trade to Japanese businessmen and requested permission for such a program from the Japanese government. The authorities provided free transportation for the women and girls to military encampments.

The Japanese government initially responded to the charges by saying that the "comfort women" were prostitutes who had worked voluntarily for private entrepreneurs and that, therefore, the government and the military would not accept any responsibility in the matter.[12] However, in January 1992, the Japanese newspaper *Asahi Shimbun* published a front-page article based on incriminating documents from the Japanese Defense Agency archives demonstrating military involvement in the running of comfort stations.[13] Following the revelations, the Japanese government withdrew its previous denial, with Prime Minister Miyazawa offering the first official apology during his trip to Korea on January 17, 1992. On July 6 and August 4, 1993, the Japanese government issued two statements acknowledging that "comfort stations were operated in response to the request of the military authorities of the day." It also recognized that "the Japanese military was, directly or indirectly, involved in the establishment and management of the comfort stations and the transfer of comfort women" and that the women were "in many cases . . . recruited against their own will, through coaxing, coercion, etc."[14] However, it continued to deny any legal responsibility for the victims and contended that the brothels were not a "system," a war crime, or a crime against humanity.[15] When socialist leader Murayama became prime minister in 1994, he took up the historical issue more seriously. On the occasion of the fiftieth anniversary of the war's end, he acknowledged that "through its colonial rule and aggression, [Japan] caused tremendous damage and suffering to the people of many countries, particularly to those of Asian nations." He then expressed "feelings of deep remorse" and a "heartfelt apology" and announced the establishment of the Asian Women Fund, a private fund for victims of sex slavery.[16] Slowly but gradually, Japan appeared to be accepting responsibility for its unfortunate past, but as late as 2013, Prime Minister Abe sought to rebut the 1993 Kono Statement that acknowledged Japan's responsibility for wartime aggressions including sex slavery, provoking domestic as well as international outcry, especially from the United States.[17]

China was slower than Korea or Japan in taking up these issues. Still, following in the steps of their Korean counterparts, a group of former forced laborers began to raise awareness of their suffering during the war years by filing numerous lawsuits against Japanese companies. As a result, a local court in Tokyo ruled in July 2001 that the Japanese government should pay twenty million Japanese yen ($250,000) in compensation to the siblings of deceased forced laborer Liu Lianren. But two higher courts later rejected the verdict. In the end, Japanese courts have rejected all compensation claims in fifteen lawsuits filed by Chinese forced laborers since the 1990s, claiming that the individual rights of Chinese nationals for war reparations were discarded under the 1972 Japan-China joint statement. Nonetheless, two Japanese companies agreed to offer 378 million yen in compensation payments to Chinese forced workers and their families in April and October of 2009. As Liu Huanxin points out, "Some Japanese companies have shifted in their attitudes to acknowledge history and assume their responsibilities,"[18] but this is far from what former forced workers from China wanted from Japan as compensation.

The U.S. government took the position that these were matters to be settled among Asians. Accordingly, the United States took few steps to address the issues of forced labor and comfort women until 1994, when the International Commission of Jurists published a special report asserting that "it is indisputable that these women were forced, deceived, coerced and abducted to provide sexual services to the Japanese military. . . . [Japan] violated customary norms of international law concerning war crimes, crimes against humanity, slavery and the trafficking in women and children."[19] In July 1999, the California legislature unanimously enacted section 354.6 of the California Code of Civil Procedures, also known as the Hayden Act. In effect until 2010, it allowed World War II forced-labor victims or their heirs now living in the United States to bring a lawsuit against the entity for which the labor was performed. The law effectively extended the statute of limitations for claims relating to forced labor performed between 1929 and 1945. Subsequently, Korean and Chinese victims filed lawsuits against the Japanese government and companies in American courts.

In 2000, however, Judge Vaughn Walker of the federal district court for Northern California dismissed all cases filed by former Allied POWs, saying that the plaintiffs' claims were barred by the 1951 San Francisco Peace Treaty. In the cases of victims from such countries as Korea and China, which were not signatories to the Peace Treaty, Judge Walker ruled that they also should be dismissed based on his interpretation that the California statute was unconstitutional because it infringed on the federal government's exclusive power over foreign affairs. Thus, efforts to bring the cases to U.S. courts did not fare any better than in Japan.

## *Mainstream Narratives: History Textbooks*

As expected, there are significant variations in the official narratives of forced labor and comfort women as described in history textbooks. In both China and the United States, descriptions of both subjects are relatively brief. With regard to forced labor, the *Chinese Modern and Contemporary History* textbook mentions that "the Japanese invaders obtained Chinese resources and labor through force with no restraint. The general guideline of the Japanese invaders was to turn the economy in the occupied areas into its own dependency."[20] Similarly, the U.S. world-history textbook, *World Civilizations*, claims that "during World War II, the Japanese military police forcibly conscripted increasing numbers of Korean youths for labor gangs and troops to support their expanding war effort, and the population was exhorted to join the Japanese people in 'training to endure hardship.'"[21] Neither the Chinese nor the U.S. history textbook, however, discusses the issue of comfort women.

In sharp contrast, both Korean and Japanese textbooks discuss the issues in detail, offering contending views of forced labor. The *Keumsung Contemporary Korean History* textbook describes the situation at length:

> With the start of the Pacific War, an aggressive campaign waged by Imperial Japan extended to whole parts of Asia. To carry out its reckless war, Imperial Japan proclaimed the so-called National General Mobilization Orders. In need of strength, Imperial Japan induced young Korean men to go to war as volunteers in 1938. In 1943, Imperial Japan even sent students out as cannon fodder by initiating a student "volunteer" system. Finally, in 1944, a conscription system was established, and two hundred thousand young men were conscripted in the time leading up to Imperial Japan's surrender. Imperial Japan also forcibly

commandeered the labor necessary for the war based on the National General Mobilization Orders. Commandeered Koreans were downtrodden like slaves or were killed in coal mines, metalliferous mines, construction sites, and munitions factories. Their wages were only half those of Japanese laborers and were deducted from for various reasons. The conscription of manpower targeted farmers in rural areas. Thus, agricultural production decreased remarkably from 1939 due to the decline of rural populations."[22]

This textbook then discusses legal efforts by victims for compensation: "Sixty years of lawsuits for taking back delayed payment for forced labor from Imperial Japan: Kim Kyung-Seok, who was one of many Koreans forcibly conscripted as a laborer at the end of the colonial period, won a lawsuit for taking back delayed payment for forced labor from Imperial Japan. It is expected that his case could bring about tremendous ripple effects in similar cases that will be advanced."[23]

The *Yamakawa Japanese History B* textbook also describes the conditions under which Korean and Chinese laborers were brought to Japanese factories, but it mentions little of the sufferings of forced laborers: "The National Mobilization Law was enacted in April 1938, and the government was authorized, without the approval of the Diet, to mobilize the materials and labor force necessary for conducing war."[24] As a result, "hundreds of thousands of Koreans and tens of thousands of Chinese in occupied regions were forcefully brought to the main islands of Japan and put to work in mines and at civil work sites."[25] The textbook acknowledges the "forced" nature of this labor and even notes the lack of compensation given to the laborers, but it does not contain the vivid depiction of the suffering of these workers found in the Korean textbooks.

With regard to comfort women, the Korean and Japanese textbooks show even greater differences. The *Tokyo Shoseki Japanese History B* textbook mentions in passing that "many women from Korea were sent to Japanese factories as volunteer corps or the battlefront as comfort women. Further, to make up for inadequate war potential, a conscription system was implemented in Korea and Taiwan in the wake of an enlistment system."[26] Even this brief note was made only in the 1990s after strong protest from Korea. In contrast, Korean textbooks not only describe what happened to the comfort women but also explain why and how it occurred. For instance, a government-produced *Korean National History* textbook explains the situation as follows: "Imperial Japan, as it extended its wars of aggression after 1932, took Korean, Chinese, and Taiwanese women to its military bases under the pretext of 'preventing rapes committed by soldiers, checking for venereal infections, and stopping leaks of military secrets.' Deprived of their human rights, the comfort women were forced to perform sexual work throughout Imperial Japan's occupied territories, including Manchuria, China, Myanmar, Malaysia, Indonesia, Papua New Guinea, various islands in the Atlantic, Japan, and Korea."[27] It also describes what happened to those women after the war: "Those who did not return to their native countries after the war were left deserted in the fields, forced to commit suicide, or slaughtered. The comfort women who were lucky enough to return home had to suffer from a sense of shame, a weakened physical condition, and social alienation."[28]

Another Korean history textbook, the *Keumsung Contemporary Korean History* textbook, offers a similar but more detailed description of the Japanese action:

> The most immoral crime committed by Imperial Japan during its aggressive war was the conscription of women. Though it began by recruiting female labor on a voluntary basis, Imperial Japan enacted the "Comfort Women Law" toward the end of the war (1944). Some women were sent to munitions factories in Japan and Korea, while others were sent to battlefields and forced to become sex workers for soldiers. Imperial Japan, which had already employed military "comfort" institutions as early as the 1930s, systematized these institutions and conscripted a great number of Korean women. Though the number of Korean women conscripted toward the end of the war is assumed to be in the hundreds of thousands, an exact figure has yet to be determined. Whereas some comfort women returned to Korea after the war, some had to remain abroad and could not come back to Korea due to personal reasons. Most of the returnees, too, could not overcome mental and physical damage for a long time and have lived miserable lives.[29]

Then, toward the end of the section, this textbook charges the Japanese government with a lack of responsibility: "But an international solution for comfort women has not yet been arrived at, since the Japanese government has not made clear the responsibility that it will take for the issue."[30]

## Contending Views Inside Korea and Japan

As shown, the issues of forced labor and comfort women have received considerably more attention in Korea and Japan than in China or the United

States. For China, the main area of contention is the Japanese invasion, particularly the Nanjing Massacre (see chapter 2). For the United States, the primary issues with respect to the Pacific War involve the Japanese attack on Pearl Harbor in 1941 and the U.S. decision to drop atomic bombs in order to end the war (see chapter 4).

In Korea and Japan, however, the two subjects—particularly that of comfort women—have received an enormous amount of public attention and become an enduring source of tension between the two neighbors. There exists a mainstream view in both nations on these two contentious issues as presented in the textbook descriptions. However, even within each country, there is significant variation among viewpoints, especially in Japan. As noted in chapter 1, one must recognize imbalances in focus in memory formation and internal diversity of views in order to adequately understand the politics of memory with regard to colonialism and the war in Asia.

In Korea, the dominant view has been a nationalist one. It condemns the inhumane and brutal nature of Japanese colonialism and aggression, and it would be very difficult to find any Korean who disagrees with such a view. However, in recent years the country has seen the rise of other views, though not necessarily contradictory ones. Perhaps the most important new perspective comes from feminist activists who have been engaged in history redress movements. Korean feminists frame the matter of comfort women primarily as a gender issue and have collaborated with international (including Japanese) feminist groups in raising awareness of sexual slavery and demanding a Japanese apology and compensation. For instance, in September 1995, the United Nations (UN) Fourth World Conference on Women, in Beijing, adopted a resolution supporting former comfort women, and in January 1996, the UN Special Rapporteur on Violence Against Women, Radhika Coomaraswamy, issued a detailed report on crimes against comfort women to the UN Commission on Human Rights. In December 2000, Asian feminist NGOs, including Korean and Japanese groups, organized the Women's International War Crimes Tribunal on Japan's Military Sexual Slavery in Tokyo. In an interview with us, Korean activist Yang Mi Kang attributes the relative success of the comfort-women movement to its collaboration with international groups: "Unlike the forced labor issue, the comfort women issue was able to be internationalized because of its nature as a wartime gender issue. The forced labor movement was organized solely by the male victims themselves, and it was true that it did not have support from other activism groups, like the global gender movement groups."[31] By taking feminist rather than nationalist positions, these Korean activists were able to make their cause transnational and have worked closely with international feminist groups in redressing gender violence committed against comfort women.

Some Koreans advance a perspective that could challenge the grain of dominant nationalist narratives. Still a minority view, but with a growing voice and important implications for historical reconciliation, is one that pays close attention to Korean collaboration in the cases of forced labor and comfort women. It is now well known that there was widespread collaboration in Europe vis-à-vis German atrocities,[32] and some Korean scholars and activists have begun to take up the question of Korean collaboration with the Japanese. In an interview with us, the progressive historian Chung Hyun Baek contends that "there were some Koreans who were involved in the mobilization of girls. Without these Koreans, so many young girls could not have become a part of the comfort-women service. We have to raise questions of this kind of responsibility, as well. We should ask the Japanese government to apologize, but at the same time, we should raise the question of Korean collaborators during the colonial rule in relation to the comfort-women issue."[33] This view, while a new development in South Korea, is expected to gain recognition and increase the diversity of views of Japanese colonialism and aggression toward Korea and Koreans. By admitting some responsibility on the part of Korean collaborators rather than placing all the blame on Japan, there is room for reconciliation with certain Japanese views, though it is still politically difficult to do so.

A greater level of diversity of historical memory can be found in Japan, however. Outsiders often have the impression that Japan has monolithic historical amnesia and denial, which is said to explain its inability to come to terms with its past aggression. Such episodes as the one at Palisades Park only reinforce the negative perception of Japan in the minds of the public. Nonetheless, the Japanese have diverse views of the issues of comfort women and forced labor: the left perceives these issues as war crimes that Japan, as a nation, should take responsibility for, whereas the right considers them to be instances of lawful conscription because these people were Japanese subjects. In fact, it was the progressive historians Yoshiaki Yoshimi and Hirofumi Hayashi who discovered, in the archives of the Tokyo War Crimes Tribunals, seven official documents suggesting that imperial military forces such as the *Tokeitai* (the naval secret police) directly coerced women to work in frontline brothels in China, Indochina, and Indonesia.[34] However, such efforts provoked a neonationalist backlash that accused progressive historians of spreading masochistic views among young Japanese. In response, those on the right advanced a self-glorifying view of history by organizing symposiums, publishing books, and even compiling textbooks of their own, including the controversial *New History Textbook*.

Our interviews with Japanese opinion leaders clearly suggest the existence of diverse views of the past. At the risk of some simplification, and based on our interviews, we find three areas of contention with regard to forced labor and comfort women.

The first point of debate concerns the nature of Japanese atrocities. An extreme view considers the comfort-women issue to be a complete lie. As Japanese historian Ito Takashi contends, "Wherever there are military bases, prostitution houses gather all around that base, and wherever the military goes, prostitution houses follow. They were voluntary." He makes a similar point with respect to forced labor: "They were people who were gathered, hired, and brought to Japan under the force of law. They weren't slaves; they were paid wages. They were not coerced; they were recruited."[35] Conversely, others stress the structural condition under which Koreans were coerced into service, with little in the way of choice. For instance, *Asahi Shimbun* editor Wakamiya Yoshibumi notes that the main issue in the controversy over comfort women is "not so much that they were rounded up as a group and hauled off, but that they were in a situation in which they were pulled into this condition. This is what [Yohei] Kono as chief cabinet secretary called the system of being forced in a public sense: there is a forced quality to it, even where there isn't physical forcing. By its nature, the very condition of being a colony is to be in a condition of coercion. So it is nonsense to say otherwise."[36]

Yet there exist views between these two poles. Some stress the elements of deception and controlled recruitment, while others focus on the role of Korean collaboration in the recruitment of comfort women and forced laborers. For instance, human-rights lawyer Takagi Kenichi argues,

> That young women, ordinary people, would volunteer to be comfort women is not possible. I talked to many comfort women, and they were not coerced, like snatched off the streets and loaded onto a truck, but they were deceived, and

that was how it usually was: they were told they'd do laundry for the military in exchange for education, and when they got off the boat, that's the situation they found themselves in. Not coerced or mass kidnapped, but not voluntary. The military was using its smarts. What we do know is that the Korean women were taken to China and the islands to give sex to Japanese military; that's clear, and that they couldn't escape is clear, too. So I think it's wrong to make the debate be about whether it was forced or not and then conclude in the way of the Abe administration that it was all voluntary.

As for forced labor, he describes different stages of recruitment:

Around 1940, it was what you might call controlled recruitment. The government-general gets an order calling for one thousand laborers. Then it goes to each village and says, "Send us an allotment of five men." And the village has to. Some raise their hands, maybe—if someone has to go, I'll go—but if [there were] not enough of such people, others would get sent: you have an extra son, so send him. The police or the elders say so. So they do so. That can't be called voluntary. Then there's the Kan-assen era, when it's not just an allotment, but a stronger police and military use the family registers and know who's where, of what age, and make a much more direct kind of recruitment using their power. And then from 1944, it's a conscription postcard: show up at the station on such and such a date. This is completely in its most basic meaning "forced"; of course, it was happening in Japan, as well. But even the allotment at the beginning was forced. There are various kinds, but all are forced labor. Even the government of Japan has recognized this.[37]

On the other hand, Sakurai Yoshiko emphasizes the role of Korean brokers in recruiting Korean women as sex slaves. As she says,

I've done lots of interviews about Korean people and comfort women and Japanese, too. In 1992, when it became a hot issue, I read about it and the documents. There are no official military documents forcing comfort women. Also, there are so many witnesses on the part of the women, too, that they went for business. So many brokers, and Korean brokers. And newspaper articles remain that the Japanese government will punish the brokers who cheat the women by using the name of the Japanese government, which means our government was aware that the Japanese military name was used. [These brokers were] advising or tricking the women to work for something else and bringing them to prostitution houses. Of course, the Japanese military welcomed these women, but it did not coerce them. There was the collaboration of brokers, women, and a welcoming military.[38]

In stressing the element of Korean collaboration, Sakurai arrives at the same conclusion as the Korean historian Chung, though perhaps with a different intent in mind.

The second area of contention is whether comfort women and forced labor are specific to Japan or are more general phenomena during times of colonialism and war. Here again, one extreme view advances the argument that there is nothing exceptional about the case of Japan, as prostitution and forced labor can be found elsewhere, including in the United States, and that the victims were not only Korean or Chinese but also Japanese. On the other hand, some view state involvement in recruiting sex slaves for the military as unprecedented and maintain that Koreans were in a very different situation than the Japanese victims.

Ito Takashi, for instance, insists that

> [from] reading many memoirs of military people, in Burma and such, [it is clear that] the prostitutes would follow them literally to the front. And they'd stay with them. And in their writings, the soldiers would express their thanks to those who stayed with them to the very end and were so committed. When Korean troops went to Vietnam, they took their own comfort women with them. But there weren't enough, so they had a lot of relations with Vietnamese women, and there were lots of children born there.[39]

Referring to the post-1945 situation when Americans came to occupy Japan, Sakurai Yoshiko also points out that "many Japanese women became prostitutes or mistresses of American soldiers. No one wants to talk about it. No suits have been brought to Japan or the U.S. government. But it is an ugly side of war that women are used in this way. Not just Japan. Any other country doing a similar thing—Cambodia, Kosovo, Germany."[40] Conversely, Takahata Isao argues, "I think Japan bears responsibility [for forced labor]. There might have been noncoercive aspects as well. That kind of thing happens in the world, too, but that doesn't matter. You cannot say that there was zero coercion. And in that case, I think if they say, 'Apologize,' we have to apologize."[41]

In addition, some argue that even Japanese, not just Korean or Chinese citizens, suffered and that there was no difference in that regard. Togo Kazuhiko, for example, says,

> Japan had a total war, and the colonies were a part of Japan, and military leadership squeezed out every last effort from Japan, Korea, and Taiwan. As a result of

thirty-five years of colonialism, there were at least some Koreans who *willingly* participated. There were those who really resisted, but the mood of the society was a kind of mirror of what happened inside Japan. Can't say much regarding forced labor. But the Korean kamikaze pilot stories were a formal part of [the] empire—no particular discrimination there. Koreans were part of the Imperial Army and had Japanese names and volunteered as Japanese kamikaze.[42]

However, others maintain that Japan and Korea cannot be treated equally, as one was a colonizer and the other the colonized. As Sakurai says, "Even if Japan says they were equal, I'm sure there were discrepancies, and we should not deny that."[43] Wakamiya notes that there was "social coercion" for the Japanese, too, but he adds that the same condition cannot be said to have applied to both Japan and Korea. In his view,

> You can say, of course, that Japanese people—when they received their draft notice and said *banzai banzai*, I'm so happy, I'm going to get to go die for the emperor—in their hearts they were not happy receiving this. So there's a kind of social coercion, the thing that makes you say *banzai*. Or maybe those in Japan, too, had to become comfort women for their livelihood, so it isn't just Koreans in this position. But there's a completely different position between those who are dominated and those who are not, and those who are dominated suffer a particular kind of humiliation. So the people who say it was the same for Japan—they were Japanese, and the Japanese suffered the same conditions—that argument doesn't stand.[44]

Finally, the Japanese debate the extent of Japan's responsibility and the proper forms of compensation. Obviously, those who believe that the claim of comfort women is a complete lie, or that the same standard applied to Japan and its colonies as part of the Japanese empire, or that there is nothing exceptional or unique about victims of Japanese aggression and war do not feel strongly about Japan's responsibility toward victims or the need for compensation. However, others perceive matters differently, though they often point to the complexity of the question of compensation.

Japanese historian Kawashima Shin, for instance, believes that the issue of forced labor should be brought to court but acknowledges the difficulties of resolving the issues through legal channels: "The Japanese Supreme Court made a ruling in 2007 that changed the way this was handled. This ruling declared that in the 1952 Sino-Japanese Peace Treaty [with the Republic of China, including Taiwan], China had renounced both national and private reparations. Until then, the interpretation had been that although the nation had denounced reparations, private compensation was still possible [and] could still be sought in court. Therefore it's virtually impossible with China and very difficult with Taiwan as well."[45] However, he acknowledges that Korea is different from China and Taiwan, suggesting better hopes for Korean cases "because it's not part of the 1952 treaty." For Koreans, Kawashima argues,

> the issue is that the suits are about prewar behavior, and under the prewar imperial constitution, the nation couldn't be called to account or brought to court. Also, there's the issue of statutes of limitations [of fifteen years]. So if the Koreans bring suit against not the nation but the private sector, and if the statutes of limitations don't apply—in the case of forced labor by companies, say, and if they can show that there wasn't the opportunity to bring suit before, so the statute of limitations doesn't apply—then there's a chance of winning. The same could be true with comfort women.[46]

Besides legal complications, Kawashima notes the complexity of the domestic politics of compensation. In his view, "There's some number of victims in the colonies, and you calculate how much you'd give to them, but there's a huge number of victims in Japan. . . . So if you start giving too much to comfort women over there, it will lead to everyone demanding their share over here. . . . The government would be overwhelmed. So to save itself, it simply doesn't go there. This is a problem of demographics, really. When they've all died off, then the government can approach this."[47]

On the other hand, Americans tend to believe that Japanese actions cannot be defended as general phenomena of wartime situations and that Japan should set the record straight beyond mere monetary compensation. In the view of Kirk Saduski, for instance, the military involvement of the comfort-women system was unprecedented. He argues, "The difference is that they institutionalized it. I don't think any other militaries have done that, no. So I think that is unique—to that level of it being official policy."[48] As to compensation, American experts like John Dower feel that monetary compensation is not enough. Dower argues, "The monetary compensation was a tiny fraction of the shared monetary, let alone emotional, cost to those people, the monetary dimension of it. Where all the focus goes is not the key. The key thing is to get the record straight, to acknowledge these ills, to apologize—and it's a huge moral question. I think it's appropriate to pursue these things."[49] Mike Honda, too, believes that compensation is not merely a monetary issue. He contends, "You apologize sincerely, and you accept historical facts, and you do something about it after that—providing compensation. You put it in the books, and you make sure children don't make the same mistakes."[50]

## Contentions Continue

In August 2014, the leading Japanese newspaper the *Asahi Shimbun* reported that its sixteen articles from the 1980s and 1990s contained false accounts of comfort women, based on testimonies of Seiji Yoshida, who claimed that he had kidnapped hundreds of Korean females and forced them to work in military brothels; the paper retracted those stories. The *Asahi*'s retraction provided political ammunition to nationalistic right-wing lawmakers and media who had denied that Japan should be held responsible for the suffering of comfort women. As a result, it added fuel to anti-Japan sentiment and the history debate in neighboring countries, especially South Korea. A number of scholars and practitioners in the United States have also expressed displeasure and concern about the consequences of such a retraction. Japanese rightists argue that Yoshida's false remarks and the *Asahi*'s articles based on his unverifiable testimonies largely contributed to the 1996 UN Human Rights Commission report, which helped to propagate a misunderstanding in the international community about whether the forcible recruitment of comfort women took place, and to the passing of the 2007 U.S. House of Representative House Resolution 121, which asked the Japanese government to apologize to former comfort women and include curriculum about them in Japanese schools. On the other hand, some experts, including Larry Niksch of the Center for Strategic and International Studies, who participated in the drafting of the resolution, have denied that Yoshida's testimonies and the *Asahi*'s articles had any impact on the drafting and passing of the resolution or the UN report.

Many members of the Japanese public, particularly young people, have also been displeased with recent efforts by South Korean citizens to build memorials and statues in the United States in dedication to the comfort women. On the contrary, Korean American and Chinese American communities' efforts to bring the comfort-women issue into public awareness in the United States continue to grow, and the United States has become more and more a psychological, political, and even physical battlefield for the history wars among Asian countries.

Thus, the issues of comfort women and forced labor remain contentious between Japan and its Asian neighbors today, even with the recent deal between Korea and Japan, and it is clear that the United States cannot simply stand outside the fray, as exemplified in legal cases and in the New Jersey monument incident. However, it is wrong to assume that the people of each nation hold a monolithic view of these issues. While each nation has its official position on the two subjects and promotes that position through formal education and diplomacy, there also exist diverse and frequently contending views within each nation. Such is especially true in the case of Japan, contrary to outside impressions. Unfortunately, the Japanese attempts to remove the monument from the Palisades Park in New Jersey and to revise the Kono Statement have only reinforced popular perceptions of Japan, doing great harm to the nation's ability to move past the events of the war.[51]

Seeing past these actions of the government and recognizing internal diversity, which has been overlooked in the past, is important to understanding wartime memories and may be a first step toward reconciliation. The existence of diverse views within society gives hope that there might be some common ground among nations with regard to historical memory and ways of coming to terms with historical injustices in the Asia-Pacific region. In this context, it is encouraging to see that Korean and Japanese feminists, sharing concerns about gender issues, have worked together toward redress for gender violence committed against Korean comfort women. Furthermore, by addressing the question of Korean collaboration with the Japanese, Koreans can become more self-reflective regarding their past, which may create some space for reconciliation with certain Japanese views. All said, colonial and wartime memories remain divided and contentious, but the emergence of diverse views within each nation alongside political liberalization increases the chances for more open and constructive discussions of historical events.

SEVEN

# The Sino-Japanese War and Japanese War Crimes

The war between China and Japan is perhaps the most contested ground in the formation of historical memory about the wartime period. Almost everything about this conflict is the subject of argument, sometimes intense, not only between the countries involved but also within them. The disputes begin with the definition of the war itself—when it began and even what name to call it. And the contest over this past extends to the deeper issues surrounding this war—why Japan went to war in China, what the strategic intention of Japan was, and how the fighting in China affected the war being fought in the Pacific between Japan and the Allies. And last, but hardly least, there remain huge controversies over the nature of Japan's conduct in the war in China, from the brutalities that took place in the capture of China's capital, Nanjing, in 1937 to broader charges of war crimes.

## *When Did the Sino-Japanese War Begin?*

The roots of the war between China and Japan can be traced back to the nineteenth century, to the decay of the Qing dynasty in China and the emergence of a modernizing, industrial Japan following the Meiji Restoration in 1868. China's fall and Japan's rise are the engine of a love-hate relationship in which Chinese revolutionaries such as Sun Yat-sen looked to Japan as a model for the modernization of China, admiring its ability to reform itself and resist the rapacious Western imperial powers. But that admiration turned to hatred, or at least fear, when Japan joined the ranks of the imperial powers and moved to seize its own pieces of the decaying corpse of imperial China. The first Sino-Japanese War was actually fought in 1894–1895, when Japan moved to rip Korea out of the Chinese sphere of influence, eventually formally annexing it in 1910, and gained control of the island of Taiwan, which remained a Japanese colony until the end of World War II. With the successful war against Russia, in 1904–1905, the Japanese empire acquired Russian territorial rights and access to Manchuria, giving it a foothold on the Chinese mainland.

Some historians and popular renditions of history portray these events as the first steps in one long sweep of Japanese aggression, leading inexorably to the Japanese invasion of China, making that the first theater of what became the global conflict known as World War II. For most historians and those who have shaped historical memory about the wartime period in Asia, there are two distinct and different candidates for the starting point of what is widely called the Sino-Japanese War.

One candidate for the war's beginning is September 18, 1931, when a bomb exploded on a railway line near the Manchurian city of Mukden. The Japanese Kwantung Army, which had been stationed in the region since 1905, immediately declared that the blast was the work of the Chinese and that they had to act to protect Japanese lives and property. Within hours, trainloads of soldiers rolled in from Korea, and within weeks, the Kwantung Army had seized Manchuria, a territory the size of France and Germany combined, with a populace of thirty million people. As we found out later, the bomb was in fact set by the Japanese military, part of a plot by the leaders of the Kwantung Army to lead the Japanese empire onto a path of conquest in northern China, without the knowledge of Japan's civilian leaders at the time, though they acquiesced to what amounted to a coup.

The Manchurian Incident, as it is known in the West, marks the starting point of the unraveling of the post–World War I order, symbolized by Japan's withdrawal from the League of Nations in protest over its condemnation of the puppet state of Manchukuo. The Japanese militarists were soon joined on the path of conquest by Italy and Germany. As Chinese leader Chiang Kai-shek struggled to unify the country under the rule of the Nationalist Kuomintang, fighting for control with warlords and the emerging Communist Party, the Japanese military continued over the next years to probe and eat away at Chinese control in the north and in the central Chinese metropolis of Shanghai.

For most observers, however, the starting point of the Sino-Japanese War was the second famous incident—a minor firefight between Japanese and Chinese troops that took place on the night of July 7, 1937, at the Marco Polo Bridge outside of Beijing. A month later, serious fighting flared in Shanghai, as Japanese troops undertook a frontal assault on Nationalist positions, transforming a crisis into a major war that raged on for eight years, taking fifteen to twenty million lives.

The debate over the starting point for the war is one part of a larger discussion about whether and how the war in China is connected to the broader global conflict known in the West as World War II. This debate is often reflected in the terminology used to describe the war. Progressive historians in Japan, who emphasize Japanese aggression in Asia, talk about "the Fifteen Years War," a term that frames the conflict as beginning in 1931 and ending in 1945. Conservatives in Japan cling to "the Greater East Asian War," the name given to the conflict by the wartime regime, reflecting its claim to be constructing a Greater East Asian Co-Prosperity Sphere. That term fell into disfavor under the American occupation and was replaced by the term "Pacific War," one that put greater emphasis on the war with the United States and Britain than on the ill-fated invasion of China.

Ogata Sadako, who began her career as an academic with a study of the diplomatic history of the Manchurian incident, sees the Sino-Japanese War as the moment when Japan turned away from the West and decided to expand into Asia. For Ogata, who went on to an illustrious career as a diplomat, leading the United Nations' efforts on relief and Japan's own development aid organization, this was a fateful decision that led to the disastrous choice to go to war with the United States, a sequence of mistakes in which the Manchurian takeover was the "turning point."[1]

Ito Takashi, a prominent conservative historian who led the movement to revise Japan's textbooks to correct what he saw as their liberal bent, places the start of World War II as a global conflict in 1941, the moment when the war in Europe and the war in Asia became tied together. As for the war in China, Ito separates the Manchurian Incident as an earlier moment in the long process of Japan's involvement in China. The Sino-Japanese War began, in his view, in 1937, with the Marco Polo Bridge Incident.[2]

For most Americans, the war began in 1941 with the Japanese surprise attack on Pearl Harbor. But that is not a universal view. "I always regarded 1931 as a really important date," says Michael Armacost, the former U.S.

ambassador to Japan and a prominent scholar of U.S.-Japan relations. "From an official standpoint, the Pacific War commenced on Pearl Harbor Day. But the events that set that into motion began with the events a decade before."[3]

Mark Peattie, among the foremost American military historians of the war, takes a different approach from most Americans, shaped by his scholarly focus on understanding Japanese military strategy. For Peattie, the conflict began in the summer of 1937, and he dismisses "Pacific War" as an American term. For Japan, the locus of the war began and remained in Asia. He prefers an entirely different term—"Japan's War in Asia, because I think it was primarily Japanese responsibility."[4]

The Chinese term for the war is itself revealing—in official discourse, repeated in everything from textbooks to museums and popular television dramas, it is the "War of Resistance Against Japan." Chinese scholars differ, however, on when this war began; they are divided between those who think it started on September 18, 1931, in Mukden and those who date it to the events in 1937. Prominent historians have been more willing, in recent years, to break from a more orthodox view that the war began in 1931, acknowledging the role of the Nationalists, rather than the Communists, in leading the war against Japan.

"I agree with the view that the national War of Resistance began in 1937 with the Marco Polo Bridge Incident—that it wasn't a full-scale war before that," says historian Yang Tianshi, the most prominent Chinese scholar on the history of the Nationalists and the wartime period, one of the few of his stature never to join the Communist Party. "The War of Resistance was, of course, part of World War II—a very important part. My own view is that if we are talking about World War II, it began when Hitler attacked Poland," Yang says.[5]

Historian Bu Ping, who led the Chinese side of the official Japan-China history dialogue formed in 2006, shares the belief that the war began in 1937. "In China, a lot of people, especially in the northeast, where I used to live, believe the war started in 1931," he acknowledges, "but in the research institutes, from an academic perspective, the majority thinks it was 1937. Although there was a war in 1931, the two sides did not formally declare war. Nevertheless, because Japan occupied the northeast in 1931 and established Manchukuo, many people suffered at that time. People feel very strongly about this. 'We suffered so much; how can you say that the war didn't start until 1937?' Popular sentiment is very important [in] this issue."[6]

## Why Did Japan Go to War in China, and What Was Its Strategic Goal?

The differences over the starting point of the war lead directly to the disputes over Japan's motivation for war among historians and shapers of historical memory. At one extreme is the view that Japan embarked on a grand strategy of empire building, in which every conquest from the late nineteenth century onward was part of a plan that led, inexorably, to war with the Western imperial powers—Britain, the Netherlands, France, and the United States—that stood in its way.

Chinese textbooks still cite the infamous Tanaka Memorial, an alleged Japanese strategic plan to take over the world, with the seizure of Manchuria, Mongolia, and China as the first steps in a march toward global conquest, to be followed by the takeover of Southeast Asia from the European colonial rulers and, finally, the defeat of the United States itself. The document was published in China in the late 1920s, and although it was later considered to be a forgery, it was a staple of not only Chinese but also American wartime propaganda.

Despite its continued presence in Chinese schoolbooks, this conspiratorial rendition of Japan's global strategy is not widely believed. Most historians tend to agree that it would be a mistake to view Japanese policy in China as one integrated plan, devised over years and implemented smoothly in a series of aggressive moves. The Japanese empire, driven by economic crisis at home and the closure of global markets during the Depression, certainly was eager to expand from Korea to northern China and then turned south in search for oil, rubber, and other vital resources. But even that move to the south was hotly debated and argued against within Japan, particularly by Japanese military leaders such as Ishiwara Kanji (the subject of an extensive biography authored by American historian Peattie), who saw the Soviet Union as the main threat to Japan.

The war in China was based on massive miscalculations by the Japanese military and civilian leadership, who stumbled into a wider war that, they were convinced, would be won in a matter of months. Instead Japan found itself mired in a quagmire of a war, unable to defeat the Chinese and pouring huge amounts of manpower and resources into a battlefield that left it weakened when facing a far more powerful foe, the United States.

Chinese historians now concede that the events that triggered the war in July 1937 were not necessarily part of a detailed plan. But they still argue that these events were products of the strategic intentions of the Japanese empire. Historian Bu Ping, who led the official dialogue with Japan on these events, places the widening of the war in 1937 in this broader context:

> Japan definitely had a goal, which they had begun formulating long before, since the Meiji Restoration. Japan, as an island nation, was very weak and needed access to resources. They believed they must have a sphere of influence as a lifeline to support the homeland. They thought China's northeast, the region they called Man-meng, including Korea, was the most important area in which they needed to establish a sphere of influence. Once this objective was determined, in order to extend their interests, they began to advance step by step into the region. I now believe that, although in this process there were many random factors that shaped events, had Japan not had an ultimate objective, these random events would not have developed into a war. Korea was controlled by Japan following the Russo-Japan War of 1905; after the September 18 incident, it was China's northeast; from 1937 [Japan expanded] southwards; and after 1941, they went still farther south [into Southeast Asia]. This happened step by step. But, of course, there was not a single person or policy outlining how Japan should go to a particular place in a particular year. The Marco Polo Bridge Incident took place on July 7, 1937. That it happened on that date was random. It didn't happen on that day because someone planned it that way. From that perspective it was random. There was, however, an extremely strong desire on Japan's part to control that region. So, after the events took place, Japan quickly sent over more troops to strengthen their army. I think the actual events were random, but behind [them] were factors that made escalation of the incident inevitable. It provided an opportunity for them to send a huge number of troops to China. Had that incident not taken place, perhaps they would have found another [opportunity].[7]

Chinese military historians such as Zhang Zhenkun, the author of the officially sanctioned history of the Sino-Japanese War, acknowledge that some Japanese military planners were still committed to an attack on the Soviet Union. But Zhang points to the arrogant belief on the part of Japanese military leaders that the campaign against China would be brief, allowing them to pivot toward the Soviet Union and to the south against the American, British, and Dutch holdings in Southeast Asia:

> They certainly had other targets. They thought that invading China would be very straightforward and did not expect to meet such determined resistance from the Chinese. Senior military leaders had estimated that they could defeat

China within three months. They thought that once Nanjing had fallen, there would be nothing left to fight. Other cities had fallen so quickly, and all the wealthier parts of China had just let themselves be occupied. What was left was just a vast area of barren land—what or who was there to resist them? They had not predicted that China would go on fighting; they thought it would be easy to defeat China and that they could then turn to other targets. They aimed to invade Southeast Asia and expand towards India. In Southeast Asia, Britain and Holland occupied many places, and the United States occupied the Philippines. This was a big obstacle. So they had to fight the U.S.[8]

Japanese historians offer a more nuanced understanding of the events that led to the Sino-Japanese War and its conduct. They see a Japan where the civilian and military leadership were at odds, and there was a deep split between those who saw the Soviet Union as the principal enemy and those who saw the West, particularly Britain and the United States, as the barrier to Japan's imperial expansion. The initial move into an alliance with Nazi Germany and Fascist Italy, the so-called Tripartite Alliance, was conceived as a coalition against the Communist movement globally. But those views lost favor after a huge border clash with Soviet forces in 1939 at Nomonhan, in which the Kwantung Army suffered a stunning defeat at the hands of the Red Army, one largely kept secret from the Japanese public. Strategy shifted toward the south and led to the move into Southeast Asia, driven in part by the quagmire of the China war and the need for resources to replace those embargoed by the United States, particularly oil.

Diplomatic and military historian Kitaoka Shinichi, who headed the Japanese side of the official Japan-China history dialogue, sees a Japanese military and political leadership that was increasingly unable to make decisions, with each step into a deepening war leading to more mistakes:

> The biggest problem was the way of thinking of the military. They wanted a perfect defense, a perfect security. They wanted to secure the Korean peninsula in order to have the security of Japanese islands. It was the mind-set in the Meiji period. And after getting Korea, they wanted to have Manchuria, and after Manchukuo, they wanted to secure the southern part of Manchuria.... And then the Marco Polo Bridge Incident was an accident.[9]

"There were growing tensions in Northern China," says Kitaoka, which set the stage for the clash. The Kwantung Army leadership, looking north toward the Soviet border, was opposed to expansion at that time. But once the fighting started, the Japanese military was desperate to avoid defeat and rapidly expanded its strength on the continent. The Chinese leadership under Chiang Kai-shek tried to shift the battlefield south, to Shanghai, where they believed they were stronger, says Kitaoka. The fighting in that urban setting was terrible and included heavy use of aerial bombardment by the Japanese air forces. Attempts to find a negotiated solution, including through a pro-Japanese regime set up in Shanghai by the Nationalist Chinese leader Wang Jingwei, foundered, in part because the Japanese could not retreat from their commitment to control China. "The quagmire of the Sino-Japanese War is the starting point for the decisions that led to Japan's ultimate defeat," argues Kitaoka. "Japan could not win the war; therefore, they wanted to unite with Germany, and because they were unable to win the war, they wanted to go south, and that's why they got into war with [the] United States. So, in that sense, the Sino-Japanese War was almost everything for Japan."[10]

Americans embraced an almost romantic idea of Chinese resistance to Japan during the wartime years, fed by Hollywood movies depicting a united China, almost American in character and love for democracy, waging a noble war against an evil Japan. The Japanese were depicted as relentless conquerors, brutal in their actions and on a path of total takeover of Asia. American historians, however, offer a more complex view of Japanese actions, one closer to that shared by Japanese historians such as Kitaoka. "It would be a mistake to see Japanese policy in China working as a smoothly running juggernaut, guided by a single, clearly fixed plan devised over the decades," writes historian Mark Peattie.[11] He points to the often chaotic events, particularly in 1937, in which Japanese commanders tried to resolve disputes only to see them escalate, often prompted by the actions of both the Chinese and Japanese governments. Chiang Kai-shek, accused by both Chinese warlords and the Communists of surrendering to Japan, was forced to abandon his preoccupation with battling the Communists and take a more aggressive posture, Peattie observes.[12]

As Peattie also recounts, not all Japanese military leaders were seeking a larger war with China. Preoccupied with the perceived threat from the Soviet Union in the north, some argued against escalation with China, while others felt the need to secure their rear before confronting the Soviets. In the end, Peattie argues, the long sweep of events drove the two sides toward what turned into not months but eight years of war, one that left an awful legacy that persists to this day. "In the long perspective, there can be little doubt that the Sino-Japanese war was the result of nearly thirty years of Japanese aggression toward China," Peattie writes. "However, in the chaotic summer weeks of 1937, the decisive steps toward total conflict were taken as much by China as by Japan, initiatives that are understandable in the light of the three decades of humiliation that preceded them."[13]

Left aside in this discussion is the issue that has preoccupied the Chinese themselves—who really fought the Japanese? The resistance to Japan was enormously complicated by the civil war between the Nationalists and the Communists, both of which blamed the other for failing to shoulder their part of the burden of warfare and for being more interested in prevailing in their internal struggle for power than in building a national front against Japan. These issues remain fiercely debated within China.

## Did China's War with Japan Have a Decisive Influence on the Outcome of the War?

It may not be a surprise, given the differences over the war already presented, that the role of China in the final outcome of World War II is perhaps the most contested ground of all. This was true not only in the aftermath of the war but during the war itself, when the British and American backers of the Nationalist Chinese regime in Chongqing were constantly questioning the worth of their Chinese allies and the aid being supplied them, often at massive human and material cost, and, ultimately, the value of the Chinese contribution to the overall war effort. The American commander in wartime China, General Joseph Stilwell, was quite public in his caustic and less-than-complementary view of the leadership of Chiang Kai-shek. Indeed, Barbara Tuchman's prize-winning book *Stilwell and the American Experience in China* largely shaped a postwar view of the Nationalists as hopelessly corrupt, ineffective, and undeserving of credit as one of the architects of victory over Japan. This was paired with romantic accounts of the Communist-led guerrillas by wartime journalists such as Edgar Snow, who portrayed Mao Zedong and his fellow Communists as far more committed to the fight against Japan.

Beyond the issue of who carried the brunt of battle, Chinese historiography in the modern era, under Communist Party rule, was fiercely bound to a narrative of heroic resistance and victory over Japan. In that account, not only was China considered a key theater of World War II; it may have been the decisive front that changed the outcome of the entire global war. As the official history tended to tell it, the Chinese decisively defeated the Japanese armies on the continent. But also, by engaging them in a long drawn-out contest after the global war started, the Chinese tied down a million men who would have been deployed otherwise against the United States and Great Britain. Without the sacrifice of China, Japan would have driven successfully into India, these historians argue, ultimately linking up with Germany in the Middle East. In the earlier era of Communist China, when the influence of the Soviet Union and Marxist historiography was still strong, the victory was attributed to China and to the late Soviet entry into the war, all part of a struggle against fascism.

The Chinese military historian Zhang Zhenkun makes a less bombastic argument about the role of China, acknowledging, as most sophisticated war observers in China now do, that the battle in the Pacific was the most decisive factor. But his account still places the Chinese contribution as a central factor in the outcome of the Asian theater of World War II:

> It is widely believed among the Japanese that Japan was defeated by the U.S.—that they lost to the U.S. and not to China. Conversely, in China, we say that China defeated Japan. In my opinion, Japan surrendered because they could not withstand the U.S. attack, not because they could not withstand the Chinese attack. Nevertheless, China still played a major role in defeating Japan that must be acknowledged. I've heard that Western writings generally do not say much about China's role in resisting Japan during World War II and sometimes omit it altogether. I think this is not right. China clearly played a role in several respects. First, they resisted Japan. So many Japanese troops were tied down in the Chinese theater and were unable to be redeployed to fight elsewhere. There are statistics to prove this. Second, China directly attacked the Japanese. Although China was much weaker than Japan, and many more Chinese died than Japanese, some Japanese were nevertheless killed by the Chinese. This was a direct contribution to destroying Japan. I think these are the most important. A third aspect is that they participated in the alliance or supported it. China's keeping Japanese troops in the Chinese theater helped the U.S. to fight in the Pacific theater. More importantly, China also sent troops to Burma and not only aided Britain but actually saved a lot of British troops. This contribution should not be underestimated.[14]

Some Western historians today echo at least the broad theme of this Chinese view. In his recent widely praised book *Forgotten Ally: China's World*

*War II, 1937–1945*, British historian Rana Mitter goes to great lengths to document China's contribution to the war effort and to remind Western readers of a scale of sacrifice on that front that was second only to much more well-known losses suffered by the Soviet people in the defeat of Nazi Germany. "China remains the forgotten ally," Mitter writes, "its contribution only slowly being remembered as its experience fades out of living memory."[15] He sketches that cost of that war—fifteen to twenty million dead, eight to one hundred million refugees, an economy destroyed, and a society that upturned, ultimately leading to the Communist victory in the ensuing civil war. The Chinese were the only forces in East Asia to continue to oppose the Japanese through the end of the war, he writes, maintaining some four million Nationalist troops and a large Communist guerrilla force in the field, "helping to tie down some half a million or more Japanese soldiers who could have otherwise been transferred elsewhere."[16] Without that resistance, China would have become yet another Japanese colony, allowing Tokyo to turn its attentions to expansion in Southeast and South Asia. "Without the 'China Quagmire'—a quagmire caused by the refusal of the Chinese to stop fighting—Japan's imperial ambitions would have been much easier to fulfill."[17]

Even some conservative Japanese historians, such as Ito Takashi, concede that Chinese resistance steadily weakened Japan, leaving it less able to turn back the American assault across the Pacific. But Ito vigorously denies the popular Chinese belief that they won the war against Japan. "Japan was not defeated by China but by America," he says. "And yet, even though they weren't victorious, they were considered part of the victorious countries, and they became known as the winners."[18]

Japanese military historian Tohmatsu Haruo offers a more developed analysis of the war in China and its relation to the larger war in the Pacific but one that is no less harsh, and perhaps harsher, in its dismissal of China's claim to victory over Japan. Tohmatsu contends—and his views are echoed by most Western military historians—that the relationship was actually the reverse: the Allied activity in the other theaters had a clear impact on the China war. The Japanese divisions that remained in China at the war's end, he writes, were not there because of the Chinese resistance but because the Allied attack on Japanese shipping was so successful that there was no way to move those troops to the fronts in the Pacific where the Japanese army was losing ground day by day. Japan was brought to the brink of surrender by that stranglehold on Japan's resources—by the last months of the war, Japan did not have the fuel to send its ships into battle—and by a ruthless assault on the homeland from the air.[19]

Japan launched a final massive offensive in China at the beginning of 1944, Operation Ichigo, that was intended to drive south and link Japan's hold over northern and central China to the areas occupied in Southeast Asia, as well as to attack airbases that the Allies were using for attacks on Japan. The latter goal became the central aim, which the Japanese assault was largely successful in accomplishing. But by the end of Ichigo, the Americans had captured bases that were closer to the Japanese mainland and easier to use in the Pacific islands. China's value to the war effort, writes Tohmatsu, was, by the end, "primarily political." Japanese and Chinese forces were locked in a stalemate from the end of 1941 to 1944, a period during which the United States and its Western allies fought fierce battles across the Pacific, heavily using naval forces. "In conclusion, from the end of 1941 to the summer of 1945, the China theater executed no substantial influence on the development of the Japanese-American war," Tohmatsu states definitively.[20]

Neither the Chinese nor the Japanese are comfortable with this understanding of that war. Both would prefer to see meaning in the sacrifice that took place or, in the case of the Japanese, to bury the events as a sideshow to the defeat in the Pacific. Each side attributes a decisive strategic purpose to this struggle when the evidence suggests there was a lack of strategic thought on both sides. The American military historian Ronald Spector refers to the "paucity of strategic planning by either Japan or China." From this starting point, he writes, "Japan stumbled into the war in 1937. From 1937 to 1944, the Japanese priority was to pacify the countryside by any means possible—brute force, intimidation, the use of terror, subversion, and bribery—an objective that involved Japan's armies in a constant struggle to consolidate its control over territories that it had conquered during the first year of the war. For Nationalist China the minimum acceptable 'victory' was simply the survival of China as a nation and, it hoped, a place at the post-war treaty table."[21]

Out of this quagmire of a war, so aptly described by Spector, emerged a record of savagery and criminality that remains the most lasting legacy of the war and the subject, in the end, of the most intense controversy.

## Japanese War Crimes in China

The history problem that now sours the relations between Japan and China certainly rests on the disconnected perceptions of the series of events that led ultimately to the Sino-Japanese War. But the differences over the strategic intent and the premeditation behind Japan's war are far less significant in their effect on way the two peoples perceive the past, and each other, than on the issue of Japanese atrocities committed during the war.

The list of crimes that Japan is accused of carrying out is well known. It includes a campaign of aerial bombardment of Chinese cities—attacks on civilian populations clearly intended to terrorize the populace and put pressure on the Chinese government to surrender or to negotiate under pressure. These air attacks were often tied to stalemates on the ground, beginning in 1939 with the repeated raids carried out against the wartime capital of Chongqing. Incendiary raids caused massive fires and huge casualties.

While the Chinese frequently cite the experience of Japanese aerial bombing during the war, these acts were not the focus of the Allied war crimes tribunals. Undoubtedly, this omission was at least in part a reflection of the fact that the Allies also engaged in the same tactics of targeting cities and causing the deaths of large numbers of civilians. The American attacks on Japan's cities, not least the horrendous firebombings of Tokyo, Nagoya, and other large urban centers, caused hundreds of thousands of deaths, a scale far greater than the Japanese bombings in China, although the Japanese acts certainly preceded them. And, of course, there is the case of the atomic bombings of Hiroshima and Nagasaki—carried out with the same political aim of forcing surrender.

A more celebrated case is that of the now infamous Unit 731, a covert operation of the Kwantung Army to carry out research on biological and chemical weapons. Operating in the northern part of China, the covert group used Chinese and Russian prisoners as fodder in human experimentation. Known officially as the Epidemic Prevention and Water Purification Department of the Kwantung Army, it was responsible for perhaps as many as twelve thousand deaths. Controversially, although the Soviet Union tried some of the unit's personnel for war crimes at the trials it conducted in Khabarovsk after the war, the United States decided to give the unit's commanders and personnel immunity in order to gain the value of the biological and chemical warfare information they had garnered.

None of these crimes, however, comes close to the attention given, not only by the Chinese but also by international observers, to the "rape of Nanjing." As discussed in chapters 2 and 4, this single moment in the war is the center of a hot debate that has gone on for decades and continues to rage. The debate tends to settle on the scale of the killing that took place after the Japanese Imperial Army took control of the Chinese capital of Nanjing in 1937. But more than the number of casualties, the core issue is one of intent—was this the product of the normal conduct of war, the collateral effect of a fierce struggle carried out by both sides, or was it a deliberate case of mass murder by the Japanese? And beyond that, was this an isolated event, or the most visible symptom of a conduct that the Japanese forces replicated in towns and villages across China?

The starting point of this event is at least clear. After an intense and highly destructive campaign to take control of Shanghai, the start of the Sino-Japanese War for most military historians, Japanese army divisions moved up the Yangtze River valley toward Nanjing, where the forces of the Nationalist army were concentrated to resist them. The Japanese had already suffered surprisingly high casualties at the hands of the Chinese—42,200 died in the capture of Shanghai. Chinese leader Chiang Kai-shek decided to leave the capital in the face of advancing Japanese forces, and when he left the city, the shattered Chinese forces collected there under the command of General Tang Shengzhi. Nanjing was not a militarily significant target, but it was important as a symbol of the Chinese government. As the Japanese advanced on the city in mid-December, General Tang finally gave orders to his divisions to abandon Nanjing.

What ensued remains a source of ongoing controversy. Unexpectedly, the Japanese troops engaged in widespread killing of both captured Chinese soldiers and civilians. Historian Rana Mitter describes what happened:

> From the first hours of the occupation, the Japanese troops seem to have abandoned all constraints. For the next six weeks, until the middle of January 1938, the soldiers of the Japanese Central China Area Army embarked on an uninterrupted spree of murder, rape, and robbery. Far from establishing a new, if temporary, order in the city, the army seemed determined to reduce Nanjing to utter chaos.[22]

The scale of the killing is itself an ongoing controversy. The International Military Tribunal for the Far East (commonly known as the Tokyo War

Crimes Tribunal) put the deaths at a maximum of two hundred thousand, including some twenty thousand Chinese civilian men falsely called combatants, another thirty thousand soldiers whose bodies were thrown into the river after they were killed, and large numbers of civilians. The tribunal judged that there were twenty thousand cases of rape in the city during the first month of occupation. The Chinese place the casualty figures at three hundred thousand, a figure literally carved in stone at the memorial museum to the event erected in Nanjing.

For Chinese historians, there is little question of what happened, and this is echoed in Chinese movies and novels. "The Nanjing Massacre exposed the savage nature of Japanese imperialism," says historian Yang Tianshi. "Nanjing was not the first time the Japanese carried out such a massacre during the war," he explains, citing events as early as the late 1920s. "Furthermore, the massacre of 1937 was not just limited to Nanjing."[23]

American military historian Mark Peattie offers what may be a balanced judgment about the atrocities carried out during Japan's invasion of China. "Nanjing was not an isolated event," Peattie writes.[24] The Japanese army had an established strategy: "to crush Chinese resistance by what became known as the tactics of 'Kill all, burn all, destroy all.'" But he also points out that the Chinese army frequently engaged in its own barbarities during the war, including some against Chinese populations and some associated with the ongoing civil war with the Communists.[25]

The most intense debate about Japanese crimes, and about Nanjing, takes place within Japan itself. Japanese conservatives and those who defend Japan against charges of criminality first of all challenge the numbers—many believe the deaths totaled, at most, twenty to forty thousand. But they also take aim at the description of the deaths as a deliberate massacre. For them, it was, at worst, a product of the chaos and indiscipline of both the Chinese defenders and some of the Japanese troops. They deny the idea of a "Nanjing Massacre." Conservative historian Ito summarizes this view:

> There was a war. That's what I say. And there was a battle to take Nanjing. And the military leadership of China fled all at once to the inland, and the Japanese pursued them, so there was a war battle. I don't believe there was a Nanjing incident as such, the way the Americans and Chinese say took place. The reason I say that is because Matsumoto Shigehara, the man who founded International House, was a wire service reporter, a little on the left, and he went into Nanjing two to three days after the invasion. When I interviewed him many years later,

he said, "I went into Nanjing, and I saw no sign of massacre. Absolutely, there were signs of war." So I think there must have been many signs of war and many deaths that occurred on account of war. We can't know how many people died. There is no way to know, I believe. They say three hundred thousand died, but that was the entire population of the city at the time. And very shortly after the Japanese occupation of the city, the people who'd run away came back, and very soon the number was past three hundred thousand.[26]

In this Japanese view, this was at most a singular event—at worst, a case of troops getting out of control and the excesses of war. It was not reflective of the way Japanese troops carried themselves in China through the war.

But this is not the only, or even the dominant, view in Japan of what happened on the Chinese battlefields. Most famously, the *Asahi Shimbun* reporter Honda Katsuichi wrote a series of articles in the 1970s based on interviews he carried out in both Japan and China, detailing the atrocities committed by Japanese soldiers. He was assailed for this reporting, but he was not alone in Japan in revealing Japanese atrocities.

The Japanese writer Hosaka Masayasu devoted his life to writing about the war, mainly based on extensive oral history interviews and documentary research. Hosaka talked to some four thousand people, from high officials to ordinary soldiers who served at the front. He published a series of books drawn from this material, none of it translated into English, and has notebooks filled with accounts that he has kept unpublished, awaiting the death of the interviewees. Based on what he has learned, Hosaka has no patience for those who deny what happened in Nanjing:

> I call it the Nanjing Massacre, and I think the fact that there's any denial of the atrocities is itself extraordinary. I don't think they killed upwards of two hundred thousand people, as [some] say, but they did kill a lot of people. I have heard about it directly from a number of soldiers. One officer said people say they didn't do this; they won't talk about it to the media, but they say it among themselves. I have had people who've told me their superiors ordered them to fire on the civilians who were tied up, and when I'd go to the superior and say, your past subordinate or colleague or fellow officer told me that you did this, the superior would say to me, "Who told you?" And I said, "I heard it from one of your past comrades." [The superior] responded, "Please don't write this while I'm alive, and you mustn't use my name because it would be terrible for my son or grandson. But all of this is true, and I have lived with these terrible things that they did at my orders, but don't ever name my name. Don't let people know, because of my grandson."[27]

Hosaka recounts the tale told to him by an old man whom he interviewed about his service in China. The man worked in a small business and asked him to come to his office on a Saturday, when the store was closed, to talk. There, the man told him a horrendous story that he kept secret from his own family and that Hosaka himself has yet to publish:

> This is painful to me, so I'll talk about it, but I've never been able to embrace my children or my four-to-five-year-old grandchildren. The reason is that when we were setting Chinese homes and places on fire, the children would come running out, crying. We would ask our officers what we should do about the children. We were told, "Finish the situation; finish it off," and then I'd kill the child. How many did I kill? And so I've never been able to embrace my grandchild, and when I see a child on the train, I move to another seat, because it's so painful to be near children.[28]

Hosaka is still unsure what to do with these recollections. "I have heard this so many times, and now the problem is on me—how to handle leaving these records. I believe these records need to be left in history, but is it right or wrong to leave the names? Is it good or bad to think about the child or grandchild or not? I haven't yet determined."[29]

The Japanese writer is dismissive of those who see the events in Nanjing as a singular moment:

> When you talk about the Nanjing Massacre, it makes it seem as if all the bad things just happened in one place. But they happened one after another after another. Of course, the generation that did these terrible things should acknowledge what they did and pay the reparations, and that should happen in that generation, but they haven't, and so it's left to my generation. . . . Why do people deny this? I think there are two reasons: one, they don't have the courage to look at the facts, and two, they are putting interpretation before evidence, making the evidence fit the interpretation.[30]

Thus, the Sino-Japanese War remains a subject of combative interpretations, refighting the contest that took place on the battlefields decades ago, over and over again. As we have seen, there are real shifts in elite opinion that have, in turn, driven changes in public perception. Those changing views of the past offer some hope that a movement toward elite consensus among the former combatants could eventually lead to reconciliation.

EIGHT

# The War in the Pacific

There is no dispute about when the war in the Pacific began. In the dawn hours of Sunday, December 7, 1941, in Hawaii, the air forces of the Japanese Imperial Navy swooped down on the battleships and war vessels of the American Pacific fleet anchored in Pearl Harbor and struck what Japan hoped would be a decisive and paralyzing blow. Within days, Japan launched a vast offensive in Southeast Asia, attacking British possessions in Hong Kong and Singapore and invading the American colony, the Philippines. For nearly four more years, Imperial Japan and the United States and its Allies fought a protracted and often brutal war across a geographic expanse unprecedented in modern history.

Historical consensus about the Pacific War extends only, however, to this moment of inception. Beyond that, the war is no less a contested narrative battlefield than the Sino-Japanese War. Historians remain absorbed by, and continue to argue over, the circumstances that shaped Japan's fateful decision to attack the most powerful nation in the world at that time, the United States. The chain of events that led to this decision remains controversial, both within Japan and between Japan and the United States. Why Japan went to war, whether that choice could have been averted, and who was responsible for the attack that made the war in Asia an inextricable part of a global conflict—all these subjects remain contentious.

Even the course of the war itself, as it unfolded on battlefields across the Pacific, generates clashing narratives. Military historians continue to dissect the fateful moments in the war, from the great naval battles that turned the tide of war against Japan to the combat in the jungles of the Pacific and Southeast Asia, overlain with brutality and racial struggle. It is a war remembered as much for its atrocities as for its heroism, most infamously for the mistreatment of prisoners of war but also for aerial attacks against Japanese cities that killed hundreds of thousands of civilians, culminating in the atomic bombing of Hiroshima and Nagasaki.

As we have discussed elsewhere, different events dominate the memories of the four nations. The Pacific War barely exists for China and Korea. The Chinese are absorbed by the experiences of the Sino-Japanese War, while Koreans focus on the depredations of decades of colonial rule under Japan. Their textbooks and films give scant reference to the four years of war the Allies fought in the Pacific.

The Pacific War is central, however, to the wartime memory of Japan and the United States, its principal combatants, as well as that of Allies in Great Britain, Australia, and the Netherlands and former colonies in Southeast Asia such as the Dutch East Indies, the Philippines, and Vietnam. Where, then, do American and Japanese memories of the Pacific War converge, and how do they differ? That is the focus of this chapter. We must begin with "the road to Pearl Harbor," as the great American historian Herbert Feis so memorably titled his account of the process that led to Japan's decision to launch this war.

## *The Road to Pearl Harbor*

The road to Pearl Harbor began in China. Japan's decision to expand its empire beyond its control of Korea, Taiwan, and Manchuria and launch a wider war with China in 1937 set it on a path that led to war with the United States. Led by President Franklin D. Roosevelt, the United States had been the staunch opponent of Japanese aggression in China, going back to Japan's creation of the puppet state of Manchukuo in 1931. In 1937, Roosevelt assailed the Japanese for violating the 1922 Nine-Power Treaty of Washington that called on its signees, including Japan, to respect the sovereignty and territorial integrity of China. American newspaper headlines pointed a finger at the role of American supplies in helping Japan "rain death" down on the helpless Chinese. In a famous speech in Chicago in October of 1937, Roosevelt spoke of a "quarantine" of aggressors, hinting that the United States was ready to cut off the supplies of oil, scrap iron, and machinery that were vital to the Japanese war effort. But the president, acknowledging the reality of American isolationism and the fear of being sucked into war, did nothing. "The last good chance to work out a stable settlement between China and Japan was lost in 1937," Feis writes in his masterpiece.[1]

As the war in China dragged on, Japanese policy makers debated between two strategies to bolster their imperial expansion. Some advocated a move north against the Communist enemy in the Soviet Union, a backer of the Chinese resistance and a historic foe of Japan. Others argued for a strike south at the resource-rich colonies of France, Britain, and the Netherlands. The powerful Kwantung Army assembled some seven hundred thousand troops in Manchuria with plans to occupy the Soviet Far East and much of Siberia. But the move north hit a wall in 1939 in a series of clashes along the border of Manchuria and Soviet-allied Mongolia between units of the Japanese Kwantung Army and the Soviet Red Army. These clashes culminated in a decisive Soviet victory in August 1939 known as the Nomonhan Incident. Within weeks, Stalin signed the peace pact with Nazi Germany, buying time to prepare for war in Europe now that he was confident that he would not face a two-front war.

For Japan, both the defeat in battle and the decision of its German ally to make a deal with the Soviet Union left it little choice but to turn south. As the war in Europe erupted, leading to the German conquest of France and the Netherlands and the weakening of Great Britain, the colonies of the Western imperialists were ripe for the taking. In September 1940, Japan seized northern French Indochina. Emboldened by the victories of Germany, the Japanese government signed the Tripartite Pact on September 27, 1940, with Germany and Italy, which became known as the Axis alliance.

At least among some Japanese leaders, both military and civilian, the events in Europe had a powerful influence on their thinking. "We were still muddling along in China, and they believed they could join hands with Germany and between them create a new world order, with Europe and Africa under German control, and Asia under Japan," says war historian and writer Hosaka Masayasu.[2]

Japanese historians tend to agree that the origins of the Pacific War lie in Japan's inability to extract itself from the quagmire of China. From this starting point, however, Japanese and American narratives of the path of events that led to Pearl Harbor begin to diverge. American accounts overwhelmingly portray Japan as locked into a course of aggression and as opting for escalation when faced with growing pressure from the United States. A minority American view, more visible in the years right after the war when isolationists were still a powerful voice in American life, offered a theory of provocation and manipulation by Roosevelt, who, in their view, maneuvered Japan into striking the first blow to allow him to gain approval for entry into the war in Europe.

Views within Japan are also divided. The extreme right-wing Japanese, as discussed later in this chapter, embrace the conspiracy theories of American isolationists and add elements of their own to justify their denial of Japan's aggressive nature. The dominant narrative in Japan, however, accepts responsibility for the decision to go to war in the Pacific. But it offers a more nuanced account of the events leading up to the attack, emphasizing Japan's desperate diplomatic efforts to avert a war and suggesting that, to some degree, American intransigence led to the fatal choice of war. Current Japanese accounts continue to reference the popular term of wartime Japan—the "ABCD (American-British-Chinese-Dutch) encirclement" of Japan.

The common American understanding of how the Pacific War came to pass is neatly summed up by strategic historian Jeffrey Record in his examination of why Japan attacked America in 1941, provocatively titled, *A War It Was Always Going to Lose*. Record writes that the war arose simply from Japan's "determination to subdue all of East Asia" and that, like Germany, "Japan was undeterrable."[3] The American narrative of the sequence of events that led from China to Pearl Harbor is captured succinctly in the American high-school history textbook coauthored by Stanford historian David Kennedy and Harvard historian Lizabeth Cohen and widely used across the country:

> Japan's position in the Far East had grown more perilous by the hour. It was still mired down in the costly and exhausting "China incident," from which it could extract neither honor nor victory. Its war machine was fatally dependent on immense shipments of steel, scrap iron, oil, and aviation gasoline from the United States. Such assistance to the Japanese aggressor was highly unpopular in America. But Roosevelt had resolutely held off an embargo, lest he goad the Tokyo warlords into a descent upon the oil-rich but defense-poor Dutch East Indies. Washington, late in 1940, finally imposed the first of its embargoes on Japan-bound supplies. This blow was followed in mid-1941 by a freezing of Japanese assets in the United States and a cessation of all shipments of gasoline and other sinews of war. As the oil gauge dropped, the squeeze on Japan grew steadily

more nerve-racking. Japanese leaders were faced with two painful alternatives. They could either knuckle under to the Americans or break out of the embargo ring by a desperate attack on the oil supplies and other riches of Southeast Asia. Final tense negotiations with Japan took place in Washington during November and early December of 1941. The State Department insisted that the Japanese clear out of China, but to sweeten the pill offered to renew trade relations on a limited basis. Japanese imperialists, after waging a bitter war against the Chinese for more than four years, were unwilling to lose face by withdrawing at the behest of the United States. Faced with capitulation or continued conquest, they chose the sword.[4]

The comparable Japanese high-school history textbook covers the same ground in much greater detail, with a description of events that suggests that both Japan and the United States were responsible for the drift toward war in the Pacific. The Japanese history textbook published by Yamakawa, used in more than two-thirds of Japanese schools, takes its readers from the Sino-Japanese War into the outbreak of World War II in Europe. At the time of the beginning of the European war in 1939, the Japanese government was reluctant to join ranks with Germany and stuck to a policy of nonintervention, the book recounts.[5] Since the Sino-Japanese War began, the economic bloc controlled by Japan—its colonies and occupied parts of China—was not adequate to supply its war industry, and Japan was still reliant on the West.

As Japan moved to form a "New Order in East Asia," the Yamakawa history textbook continues, "the U.S. regarded this as a serious challenge to its own East Asia policy, and the volume of trade between Japan and the U.S. began to decrease."[6] When Japan started to form a military alliance with Germany, the United States began to curb trade, beginning with the repeal of a trade treaty in July 1939, which, when it came into effect the following year, made it more difficult for Japan to procure war materials. The decisions of the Japanese military leadership generated resistance, the textbook tells Japanese students, but Japan was too weak to change the course of events:

> Germany overwhelmingly dominated in Europe, and Britain alone continued to resist. Led by the army, demands suddenly emerged in Japan for strengthened ties with Germany, to advance toward Western colonies in the south knowing that a war against Britain and the U.S. was inevitable, to draw up plans for the establishment of the "Greater East Asia Co-prosperity Sphere," and to seek out

raw materials such as petroleum, rubber, and bauxite. There was an air of resistance against this in the Diet and top echelons of the political world, but they were without the power to turn the tide, and the southern advance contrarily invited further strengthened economic sanctions against Japan.[7]

The formation of a new government under Prime Minister Konoe Fumimaro in July 1940 set a course toward the south and alliance with Germany, culminating in the seizure of northern French Indochina and the formation of the Tripartite Pact in September 1940. The United States responded with bans on the sale of aviation gasoline and scrap metal to Japan and imposed full-scale economic sanctions. The United States, the authors state, was now set on an "anti-Japanese posture."[8]

At this point, the Japanese textbook moves into a historical account of what it describes as "the beginning of the Pacific War." The Konoe government "initiated Japan-U.S. negotiations to circumvent a conflict between Japan and the United States," including back-channel negotiations that developed into talks between the Japanese ambassador in Washington and Secretary of State Cordell Hull. The signing of a neutrality pact with the Soviet Union in April 1941 is described as an attempt to secure the north for the drive to the south and to balance worsening ties with the United States. When the Germans invaded the Soviet Union two months later, the Japanese war councils decided to continue their southward expansion but to be prepared to strike north if the Soviet Union seemed ready to fall to the German invaders.[9]

In this Japanese narrative, the decision for war is a response to the tightening of the noose by the United States, which escalated when the United States froze Japanese assets following the occupation of the southern part of French Indochina in July 1941. When the United States underlined its intention to contain Japan's southern expansion and establishment of the New Order in East Asia, Britain and Holland followed suit. The Japanese military felt a deepened sense of crisis and asserted that war was the only available course for responding to the pressure of the ABCD blockade.

Still, the Japanese textbook authors recount, Japan tried to negotiate peace, including overtures for a summit between Konoe and Roosevelt. Only when Hull issued his famous note on November 26—which was, according to the textbook, "equal to an ultimatum that demanded total and unconditional withdrawal from China and French Indochina, the renouncement of the Manchukuo and Wang Jingwei governments [the latter being the Japanese puppet regime in China], substantive annulment of the Tripartite Pact, and a return to the state of the region prior to the Manchurian Incident"—was it clear that "negotiations were hopeless." The December attack on Pearl Harbor and the British colonies then followed, the Yamakawa textbook concludes.[10]

## The Roosevelt Trap

The American and Japanese narratives of the road to Pearl Harbor offer similar timelines that both trace back to the faltering war effort in China. But they clearly differ concerning the role of American pressure and demands in forcing Tokyo's hand, which the Japanese emphasize. Nevertheless, both these conventional narratives sharply diverge from the conspiratorial view held by American historians of an isolationist persuasion and by Japanese revisionist conservatives, both of whom lay blame at the feet of Roosevelt, who is depicted as a mastermind who maneuvered Japan into firing the first shot in order to drag the United States into the world war in Europe.

The American revisionists began to voice their views even before the war was over and in the years immediately after 1945. Men like the historian Charles Beard and others wrote books, echoed in congressional hearings, weaving a theory that accused Roosevelt of having prior knowledge of the Japanese attack, based in part on intercepts of secret communications but deliberately keeping this information from our military commanders. Some went farther to accuse Roosevelt of conspiring to provoke a Japanese attack in order to maneuver America into the war in Europe, a path blocked until then by isolationist sentiment in Congress. These views continue to surface now and then, despite the lack of "a shred of convincing evidence," as historian Record puts it.[11]

Such conspiracy theories are consigned to the fringes of American wartime history memory. That is not the case, however, when it comes to their Japanese counterparts. One of the most recent examples of the prominence of such views in Japan is the case of General Tamogami Toshio, the chief of staff of the Japanese air force, who penned an award-winning essay for a right-wing group in 2008 asking the provocative question "Was Japan an aggressor nation?"[12] General Tamogami's elaborated answer in the negative created a storm of controversy that led to his dismissal, but he remains a prominent figure, earning significant votes in a run for the governorship of Tokyo and emerging as the deputy head of a new right-wing political party.

During his long years of service in Japan's air forces, some of it spent commanding antiaircraft missile batteries on the island of Okinawa, Tamogami worked closely with his American counterparts stationed in Japan. But by his own account, he kept his views of Japan's American allies to himself, concealing a dark view of the United States as the architect of the Pacific War. As he writes in his essay,

> There are some who say that it was because Japan invaded the Chinese mainland and the Korean peninsula that it ended up entering the war with the United States, where it lost three million people and met with defeat; it committed an irrevocable error. However, it also has been confirmed now that Japan was ensnared in a trap that was carefully laid by the United States in order to draw Japan into a war. . . . Roosevelt became the President on his public pledge not to go to war, so in order to start the war between the United States and Japan it had to appear that Japan took the first shot. Japan was caught in Roosevelt's trap and carried out the attack on Pearl Harbor.[13]

Echoing imperial Japan's wartime propaganda, Tamogami sees the war as a historical struggle against Western imperialism, in which Japan's own expansionism is excused as an act of liberation:

> From the fifteenth century, England, France, Holland, Spain, and later America went out into the world, and, increasingly, [other places] became their colonies—the people of the world were living in very bad circumstances. Only Japan and Thailand remained independent, and . . . it was hard to say that about Thailand because it was pressed between England and France. So only Japan remained autonomous. But, increasingly, it, too, felt the pressure of all the powers surrounding it. If Japan had done what America wanted and not fought the war, it, too, would have ended up subjugated. It was because Japan fought and in the first six months drove the Americans out of the Philippines [and] the English out of Burma [and] defeat[ed] the Dutch in Indonesia—it was because of all this that the Asians were able to wake up and form their own independence movements. In that way, Japan hastened the era of racial equality.[14]

In this account, the United States was the primary actor, driving the ABCD encirclement and embargoes against Japan to the point that Japan would be compelled "to act somewhere, somehow." "America wanted to draw Japan into war because of the war in Europe. Churchill ha[d] been seeking FDR's help, . . . but he couldn't declare war on Germany because of campaign promises not to do so. But because of the Axis alliance, Roosevelt thought that if [the] German ally Japan were under sufficient pressure, it would surely do America the favor of attacking, and that would be the way for America to get into the war."[15]

The instrument of American provocation was the Hull note, the ultimatum delivered in late November. Even mainstream historians concur that this note was the last nail in the coffin of negotiation. But Tamogami and those who share his view add another twist to this conspiratorial tale—they attribute this note and the strategy behind it, including turning back the last-ditch Japanese efforts to negotiate a settlement, to alleged Soviet spies among Roosevelt's close advisors.

In a throwback to the Anti-Comintern Pact signed with Germany and Italy in 1936, Japanese revisionist conservatives assert that Japan was the victim of a vast Communist plot. "In fact, America was also being manipulated by the Comintern," Tamogami writes in his 2008 essay. Citing the so-called Venona files documenting Comintern activities in the United States, he accuses Harry Dexter White, the assistant secretary of the treasury, of being a Soviet spy. Tamogami credits White with authoring the Hull note and working through Treasury Secretary Henry Morgenthau, a well-known advocate of tough response to Japanese aggression.[16]

Tamogami is hardly alone in such assertions. In our interview, the prominent conservative Japanese historian Ito Takashi, one of the founders of the movement to reform Japanese history textbooks in a more revisionist direction, embraces that same theory. "If American and Japanese negotiations [referring to peace feelers in the year before the war started] were successful, something could have come of it," Ito says. "So when [Prime Minister] Konoe finally said [that] we should have a summit meeting in Alaska or somewhere, Roosevelt initially agreed. But now we know, from recent papers that have come to light, that there were a lot of Soviet spies in the state department" who blocked this path.[17]

The conservative revisionists also eagerly embrace American isolationists' assertions that Roosevelt was in possession of intelligence information on Japanese preparations for war and kept it secret, even encouraging the Japanese to believe a blow would be successful. "I believe that America forced Japan to act, sought the attack," says Tamogami. "America knew [Japan would attack], and if anything, Japan lost the intelligence war. America had full information, knew what would happen, [and] was seeking to make it happen, and Japan didn't have as much."[18]

*Pearl Harbor and War Responsibility*

At its core, the revisionist argument is a somewhat desperate attempt to deny Japanese responsibility for the decision to initiate the Pacific War. Behind that desire to deny responsibility lies a deeper question: Why would Japan launch a war in which its chance of victory was so evidently small, if not completely absent? In the historical memory of this moment, how do the Japanese and Americans explain the profound strategic miscalculation of the war?

A few outspoken Japanese leaders warned against the decision to strike the United States, anticipating the outcome of an inherently uneven struggle between resource-poor Japan and the rich United States. Among them were military leaders such as the great Japanese naval strategist Admiral Yamamoto Isoroku, the planner of the Pearl Harbor attack. Only two months before that attack, he famously predicted the outcome:

> It is obvious that a Japanese-American war will become a protracted one. As long as the tides of war are in our favor, the United States will never stop fighting. As a consequence, the war will continue for several years, during which [our] material [resources] will be exhausted, vessels and arms will be damaged, and they can be replaced only with great difficulties. Ultimately we will not be able to contend with [the United States]. As a result of war the people's livelihood will become indigent . . . and it is hard not to imagine [that] the situation will become out of control. We must not start a war with so little chance of success.[19]

There were those who harbored delusions about American weakness and decline, who thought that Japanese martial spirit could triumph over the material advantages enjoyed by the United States. But most Japanese decision makers were far from convinced of success. Paralyzed by their own internal rifts, they drifted into a fateful decision because of their inability to face the bankruptcy of their war in China.

"Japan's fateful decision to go to war can best be understood as a huge national gamble," Japanese historian Eri Hotta writes in a study of the decision making in 1941.[20] Believing that war was inevitable, the Japanese took a huge risk, gambling that by dictating the timing of events and banking on German victory in Europe, they could somehow force the United States to offer the terms of peace it had offered in the preceding months—essentially, to accept Japanese domination of East Asia.

Many Japanese reject the attempt to evade responsibility by putting an emphasis on the American pressure tactics. Watanabe Tsuneo, the powerful publisher of the *Yomiuri Shimbun*, the most widely circulated paper in Japan (and the world), who was drafted in the final months of the war, commissioned a major project on this subject of war responsibility at the time of the sixtieth anniversary of the war. It was published in a series in the paper, and later in two volumes, and reached the clear conclusion that the decision to go war was a huge and disastrous mistake on the part of the leadership of Japan. Watanabe himself, in our interview, is even more unwilling to give credence to a narrative of self-defense or even interimperialist rivalry as the cause of the war:

> I believe that the base cause of the imperialist war in Asia, in Korea, in China, [and] in Southeast Asia had nothing to do with the United States. It was a unilateral act and invasion on the part of Japan. But let me add that if only the American Hull note had been sent ten years earlier, that idiotic mammoth war need never have happened, because without oil, we couldn't have gone to war. What happened was America cut off the oil, and Japan advanced to the South and to Indonesia and eventually to all of the Pacific. But if the embargo had taken place much earlier, Japan would never have been able to go to war without the oil. That much, surely, the military would have understood—that it couldn't prosecute the war without the oil—and an idiotic war could have been avoided.[21]

Whether that could have happened, history cannot tell us. As we know from archival records of Japanese war councils, the attack on the U.S. fleet at Pearl Harbor was a product of the decision to move into Southeast Asia and seize the resources of that region for the Empire. Once that die was cast, Japanese military planners like Yamamoto believed that a move against the United States was necessary to secure their flanks against what was thought to be an inevitable American attack. As American military historian Mark Peattie puts it in our interview,

> The attack on Pearl Harbor was a sideshow. It was not the main purpose. The Japanese invasion of Southeast Asia from the Japanese perspective was what was

important. The Japanese had made a decision that the way to keep the United States at bay was to kick us in the teeth at our main fleet base in the Pacific. That would prevent all those battleships from moving across the Pacific and attacking them, attacking their invasion in Southeast Asia and their flank.[22]

Instead, the Pearl Harbor attack served only to enrage and mobilize an American population that had been reluctant to become involved in the wars in Europe and Asia. "The Japanese made a fundamental miscalculation," observes former U.S. Ambassador to Japan Michael Armacost. "They underestimated the facts of an aroused and mobilized American economy and society. Thoughtful Japanese understood that."[23]

Ironically, if Japan had confined itself to an attack on British and Dutch possessions, Roosevelt would have faced a tough task to persuade the American people to come to their rescue. In contrast to the conspiracy theories of the Japanese revisionists and their American isolationist cousins, contemporary historiography in the United States and in Japan is convinced that Roosevelt was actually trying to avoid war with Japan for fear that such a war would undermine the more important effort to come to the aid of Britain in Europe. As Jeffrey Record puts it,

> The Roosevelt administration was committed to stopping Hitler in Europe above all else, and by October 1941 was not only engaged in an undeclared shooting war with Nazi submarines in the North Atlantic but also wedded to a "Germany-first" strategy in the event of war with all the Axis powers. The last thing Roosevelt wanted was a war in the Pacific. The administration was unwilling to go to war over China and mistakenly believed that it could deter or retard a Japanese advance into Southeast Asia via the retention of powerful naval forces in Hawaii, the imposition of economic sanctions, and the deployment of long-range bombers to the Philippines. It presumed realism and rationality on the part of the Japanese and failed to understand that the sanctions it imposed upon Japan in the summer of 1941 were tantamount to an act of war.[24]

## *From Midway to Okinawa: The Long War in the Pacific*

The victories of the Japanese military in the early months of the Pacific were impressive in their speed and scope, establishing a line of control that stretched from the Aleutian Islands in Alaska to the borders of British India. In March 1942, General Douglas MacArthur, the commander of Allied forces in the Philippines, fled the islands, leaving tens of thousands of

American and Filipino soldiers behind but vowing to return. The defenders surrendered in May, only to be treated with savage cruelty in the infamous eighty-mile Bataan Death March to POW camps. It was, as Kennedy and Cohen's American history textbook notes with equanimity, "the first in a series of atrocities committed by both sides in the unusually savage Pacific War."[25]

Despite its early success, the tide of war began to turn against Japan within a matter of months. In a series of naval battles, beginning in the Coral Sea in May 1942 and then at Midway in June 1942, the Japanese expansion was halted. By August, the United States seized the initiative in the Battle of Guadalcanal Island, the first of the long campaign of attacks on Japanese-held islands in the Pacific. The battle became emblematic of the ugly nature of warfare in the Pacific War, from coping with disease and jungle to the disproportionate scale of casualties. "Japanese losses were 20,000, compared to 1,700 for the Americans," write Kennedy and Cohen. "That casualty ratio of more than ten to one, Japanese to American, persisted throughout the Pacific war."[26]

The American leapfrog across the Pacific is memorialized in the American memory as a series of land battles, such as those at Tarawa, Peleliu, Saipan, and Iwo Jima, and naval engagements that culminated in the clash in the Leyte Gulf in October 1944, when Allied troops returned to the Philippines. With the capture of Saipan and other islands in the Marianas, the United States was positioned to begin widespread bombing raids on Japanese cities and other targets. Kennedy and Cohen's textbook does not shy away from what that meant for Japanese people: "The massive firebomb raid on Tokyo, March 9–10, 1945, was annihilating. It destroyed over 250,000 buildings, gutted a quarter of the city, and killed an estimated 83,000 people—a loss comparable to that later inflicted by the atomic bombs."[27]

As the Allied advance crept closer to the Japanese mainland, the fighting became even fiercer. The struggle for the tiny but strategic Japanese island of Iwo Jima, the first major fight on Japanese soil, is forever carved into American memory by the iconic image of American soldiers raising the flag over Mount Suribachi, the highest point on the island. More than twenty thousand Japanese soldiers gave their lives to defend the island, digging into caves and tunnels where they would fight to the end rather than surrender. Some six thousand U.S. Marines died to take Iwo Jima. The savage, unforgiving character of this battle was powerfully portrayed by the American film director Clint Eastwood in a pair of movies, *Flags of Our Fathers* and *Letters from Iwo Jima*, which offered views of the battle through the eyes of both the American invaders and the Japanese defenders.

## The Battle for Okinawa

The horrendous scale of casualties and the desperate nature of the battle for the southern Japanese island of Okinawa that followed served to certify for Americans that an invasion of the Japanese homeland would be a bloodbath. A widely adopted American history textbook offers this narrative:

> In April 1945, U.S. Marines invaded Okinawa. The Japanese unleashed more than 1,900 kamikaze attacks on the Allies during the Okinawa campaign, sinking 30 ships, damaging more than 300 more, and killing almost 5,000 seamen.... Once ashore, the Allies faced even fiercer opposition than on Iwo Jima. By the time the fighting ended on June 21, 1945, more than 7,600 Americans had died. But the Japanese paid an even ghastlier price—110,000 lives—in defending Okinawa. This total included two generals who chose ritual suicide over the shame of surrender. A witness to this ceremony described their end: "A simultaneous shout and a flash of the sword ... and both generals had nobly accomplished their last duty to their Emperor." ... The Battle for Okinawa was a chilling foretaste of what the Allies imagined the invasion of Japan's home islands would be. Churchill predicted the cost would be a million American lives and half that number of British lives.[28]

From this American perspective, the decision to drop the atomic bombs on Japan seems almost unquestionable. This narrative of the Pacific War occupies many pages of the American textbooks, which are full of maps of the tides of war, photos, and descriptions of the battles that took place, and leads, finally, to victory. Perhaps not surprisingly, the main textbooks in use in Japanese high schools do not dwell on the war in any similar detail. The American march across the Pacific occupies a few paragraphs, major battles are given no more than a line, and there is no mention of the mistreatment of prisoners. The Yamakawa textbook sums up the last big battles of the war:

> In October 1944 (Shōwa 19), the American military landed at Leyte Island with the intention of retaking the Philippines, and occupied the island after a pitched battle. In March the following year (1945, Shōwa 20) the U.S. military occupied Iwo Jima (Iōtō), and in April finally landed on the main island of Okinawa,

which was occupied after fighting a battle that involved the island residents for close to three months.²⁹

The American air raids on Japan receive much more extensive coverage in the Japanese historical narrative of these final months of war:

> Beginning in the latter half of 1944 (Shōwa 19), mainland air strikes by U.S. planes flying out of bases in Saipan intensified. The air strikes initially aimed for the destruction of munitions factories, but soon began to drop incendiary bombs on cities so that citizens would lose the will to fight. In the cities, [efforts such as] the forced demolition of architectural structures, digging of bomb shelters, movement of munitions factories to the countryside, and the evacuation of relatives and mass evacuation of national people's school students (student evacuation) were initiated. . . . In the Great Tokyo Air Raid of 10 March 1945 (Sh wa 20), some 300 B29 bombers dropped roughly 1,700 tons of incendiary bombs primarily on the congested area of Shitamachi, and about 100,000 people burned to death in one night. The air raids also [targeted] mid- and small-sized cities throughout the country; 1.43 million homes were destroyed by fire, there were as many as 200,000 deaths and 270,000 casualties, and primary production facilities were destroyed.³⁰

The Battle of Okinawa remains a source of controversy within Japan. The deaths of huge numbers of Japanese civilians, the forced mobilization of young Okinawans to serve in the last-ditch defense of the island, and incidents of mass suicide by civilians, ordered by the Japanese military, continue to be contested memories in Japan. Conservative historians have tried numerous times to remove from the Japanese curriculum references to them, such as this one, from a more progressive Japanese textbook:

> In March U.S. forces landed at Okinawa. Because the Japanese military regarded the Battle of Okinawa [as a means] to gain time to prepare for the decisive battle on the mainland, a ground war, in which general citizens were caught up, was conducted for more than three months. Many common citizens were sacrificed due to the fierce bombardment by the U.S. forces, which was referred to as a "storm of steel" and because the Japanese military abandoned the Shuri [Castle] command center and troops retreated to the evacuation zone for general citizens on the southern tip of the main islands at the end of May. Many men who were ineligible for military service were mobilized as defense units to conduct auxiliary military services, and male students were mobilized into the Tekketsu Kinno Tai (Blood and Iron for the Emperor Service Units) and female

students into nursing units (Himeyuri Tai). The number of war dead in the Battle of Okinawa on the Japan side was roughly 188,000, among which more than 120,000 were Okinawa residents. . . . Further, normal citizens were forced to commit mass suicide since Japanese forces were forbidden from surrendering according to the Field Service Code, and citizens were slain for being spy suspects or getting in the way of battle.[31]

The text includes a footnote on the Field Service Code:

> Instructions delivered to army officers and soldiers by Army Minister Tōjō Hideki in January 1941. It expounded that [soldiers should] choose death rather than be taken prisoner, and is one cause for the bringing about honorable deaths and the suicides of officers, soldiers, and citizens during the war.[32]

In the early years after the end of the war, such accounts emerged from Okinawans themselves and were published widely in Japan; they were made into movies that had huge audiences. While still a college student, in 1953, Ota Masahide, who had a subsequent long career as a journalist and popular historian of the Battle of Okinawa and later served as governor of the island, penned a memoir of his experience as a high-school student drafted into the war. In 1955, the book was made into a film, *Student Soldiers of Okinawa*, that was very popular then. Other films portrayed the mass suicide of the girls of First Girls High School, an incident that became famous as an example of how the Imperial Army had mistreated Okinawans.

Ota, in our interview, conducted more than six decades after the war, still recalls his experience with clarity and passion for what he believes is a truth that remains hidden from most Japanese. As a nineteen-year-old high-school student, he was mobilized into the Battle of Okinawa, initially to build airfields and other defense facilities and later to destroy them when the U.S. forces invaded the island.

> Boys were ordered to organize the Blood and Iron units for the Emperor. Girls were given short training for nurses and assigned to the field hospitals—all the girl students, without any laws. In Okinawa, there was no law—mobilization law allowed to send kids to the factory but not to the battlefield. But in Okinawa, we were mobilized and sent to the battlefield. We had two hand grenades and one rifle with 120 rounds of ammunition. We had military uniform[s] and [were] sent to the battlefield.[33]

Even after Japan surrendered, Ota and his comrades were ordered to keep fighting, hiding in caves in the southern part of the island. He was assigned as messenger, carrying orders and news to units. "We were attacked all the time," he recalls. "But every day we were told [that] to give your life for the emperor was the best way to live as a human being." They were told not to be captured, not to surrender—an order that continued even after Japan surrendered on August 15. Ota did not give up until late October, fearful of capture by the Americans but even more so of being killed by Japanese soldiers.

> Those imperial soldiers—they shot civilians from the back when they tried to surrender. Okinawans had two enemies. At the front you had U.S. soldiers, and at the back you had [the] Japanese Imperial Army—friendly soldiers became the enemy. [The] Imperial Army kicked people out of caves—they used them for themselves. Young kids cried. Soldiers were afraid U.S. forces would find the cave. So they ordered the mothers to kill their kids. The mothers cannot kill their own kids, so soldiers did it. I saw this myself. Up until that time, I trusted the Imperial Army, as we were told. But to see this, I changed my mind, and I changed my thinking about war. So when I was saved, I made up my mind: Why did this kind of thing happen? I have to find out. Ever since war was over, I have been collecting all kind[s] of materials to tell what the war was. I visited the National Archives in Washington to collect the U.S. materials; we have collected the Japanese soldiers' stories from the archives and local stories.[34]

Ota has authored numerous books about the war, including a defining history of the Battle of Okinawa.[35] Still, decades later, Japanese conservatives such as Tamogami deny that such forced suicides and similar atrocities took place. Conservative historian Fujioka Nobukatsu argued in a column in 2007 that such accounts were based on "false testimony," and he commended textbook screening that instructed publishers to note that there was not definitive proof that the Imperial Army gave such orders.[36] The textbook review triggered mass protests in Okinawa, forcing the education ministry to allow wording that would acknowledge the army's "involvement" in the suicides.[37] The extent of the Imperial Army's involvement in these atrocities remains an unresolved issue in Japan.

## Stupidity or Immorality

The differences between Japanese and American narratives about the Pacific War are abundant, as are the divergent views within each country. But the issue is more than disputes over detail or even the natural clashes of perspective that arise from the sharply opposed experiences of the victor and the defeated. At the core of the issue is the nature of the war itself—for Americans, a clash of civilizations, and for the Japanese, a disastrous mistake.

For Americans, the war remains essentially a moral contest. "World War II is an important subject because there was such a stark distinction between good and evil," observes American filmmaker Kirk Saduski, who worked with Tom Hanks in the production of two memorable series about the war in Europe and in the Pacific. "I think Tolkien wrote that Mordor in the Lord of the Rings was Nazi Germany. But it's the real thing. I think that's why we're so fascinated by World War II—not only is it starkly good and evil, but there are real heroes. And again, when the enemy is evil incarnate, of course you're going to keep going back to that."[38]

Whereas there are Japanese who place the war with China in a moral framework, there are few Japanese, from any part of the spectrum, who see the war in the Pacific in those terms. Even for those Japanese who accept their responsibility for starting the war and who place the main blame for events on their own leadership, the war is a case of strategic miscalculation, of a monumental mistake in strategic thinking and judgment.

"To do this war at all was irrational," says Wakamiya Yoshibumi, the longtime editor of Japan's great liberal daily, the *Asahi Shimbun*. "If you look at it objectively, there was no way we could win." The breakdown in negotiations in the final days before Pearl Harbor can be laid at the doorstep of both Japan and the United States, he says. "But in any case, as a strategy of going to war with the U.S., it was an incredibly idiotic act. More than the legality or the morality of the war is the sheer stupidity of it all."[39]

NINE

# The Atomic Bombings of Japan

In August 2012, Clifton Truman Daniel, a grandson of former U.S. President Harry Truman, visited the Hiroshima Peace Memorial Museum to attend a memorial service for the victims of the atomic bombings. His visit was the first by a member of the Truman family and came two years after the U.S. government first sent a representative—the American ambassador to Japan, John Roos—to the annual commemoration of the atomic bombings. Such visits are positive steps toward reconciliation between the two countries over the tragic events but are still far short of removing the historical thorn that exists between the two allies.

The decision by President Truman to attack the Japanese cities of Hiroshima and Nagasaki with nuclear weapons remains controversial even today, and the bombings have become a major aspect of Japan's victim consciousness. Japan was a major aggressor in Asia but also the only nation subjected to nuclear attacks. Victim identity has led to historical amnesia among the Japanese, which explains their reluctance to come to terms with the past. This is one crucial factor that separates Japan from Germany, a major aggressor in Europe, in dealing with historical injustice and reconciliation.

Why did the United States decide to use nuclear weapons against Japan? Was the decision justified? What motivated the Japanese surrender—the bomb, the Soviet entry into the war, or other factors? Should the United States apologize for the atomic bombings? How have they affected the formation of wartime memories in Japan and influenced the country's relations with the United States? How have they shaped Japanese attitudes toward historical reconciliation in general?

## The Atomic Bombings

World War II in Asia, better known as the Pacific War, lasted several years. It began with the Japanese surprise attack on Pearl Harbor in 1941 and ended with the Japanese surrender in the summer of 1945. It caused both the Allied Powers and Japan tremendous damage, including human casualties, economic deprivation, and resource scarcity. Toward the end, the battles became fiercer. Four years into the war with Japan, in July 1945, leaders of the United States, the United Kingdom, and the Nationalist Government of China together issued the Potsdam Declaration, demanding that Japan surrender unconditionally or face "prompt and utter destruction."[1] When Japan rejected this ultimatum, Truman decided to launch the first nuclear attack in history against Hiroshima, an important military base with a population of approximately 350,000.

At the time, President Truman was advised that U.S. casualties could range from 250,000 to one million men in the scenario of a planned land invasion of Japan. A study conducted by the joint chiefs of staff in April 1945 had also produced figures of 7.45 casualties and 1.78 fatalities per thousand man-days. This implied that the two planned campaigns at the time to conquer Japan would cost 1.6 million U.S. casualties, including 380,000 deaths. For Truman and the U.S. military leaders, the nuclear option was seen as necessary to hasten the end of the war with fewer casualties, both Allied and Japanese.

*Little Boy*, America's first atomic bomb to be used as a weapon, was dropped on the city of Hiroshima and wiped out 90 percent of the city, immediately killing eighty thousand people and injuring seventy thousand. (Tens of thousands more died later of radiation exposure.) Three days later, on August 9, 1945, a second atomic bomb, *Fat Man*, was dropped on the city of Nagasaki. Although a major portion of the city was protected by Nagasaki's hills, about 44 percent of the city was destroyed, and an estimated forty thousand people were killed in addition to the sixty thousand injured. Together, the two bombs eventually killed an estimated two hundred thousand civilians.[2] On August 15, six days after the bombing of Nagasaki, Japan announced its unconditional surrender to the Allies and signed the Instrument of Surrender on September 2, officially ending the Pacific War.

Decades after the end of the war, the influence of the bombings on Japan's surrender and the bombings' ethical justification remain a subject of fierce debate around the world. Discussion has primarily focused on the role of the bombings in Japan's decision to surrender and the United States' justification for using the bombs, based on the premise that the strikes precipitated the surrender. Supporters of the bombings argue that the use of nuclear weapons was critical to bringing about Japanese surrender and thus preventing massive casualties on both sides. The end of the war also liberated millions of laborers working in harsh conditions under forced mobilization by the Japanese government. But opponents of the bombings contend that the nuclear strikes were militarily unnecessary. They argue that Japan was already defeated and was ready to surrender even without the attacks; therefore, the bombings were not only immoral but unjustified.

This chapter discusses how the atomic bombings of Japan are viewed and remembered among those countries directly or indirectly affected by the events, with emphases on the imbalances of various national focuses, contention and diversity, and the transformation of memories over time. The debate over the atomic bombings of Hiroshima and Nagasaki is obviously one primarily relevant to the United States and Japan, and the two countries tend to view the bombings as more important memories of the war than others do. As with other issues of the war, there are cross-national variations in memory formation: even with over twenty thousand Korean lives lost in the bombings, Korea rarely touches on these events in its textbooks or in academic or general publications. This chapter also discusses how the atomic bombings and various views and memories of them have affected the process of historical reconciliation in the Asia-Pacific region.

## *Legacy, Memory, and Controversies*

A majority of American leaders, including the final decision maker, President Truman, maintained that these bombings were necessary to defeat the Japanese military while minimizing American (and Japanese) casualties and hastening the end of the war. Truman wrote, "I regarded the bomb as a military weapon and never had any doubt that it should be used."[3] Following his visit to General Douglas MacArthur's headquarters in Tokyo a month after the bombings, Karl T. Compton, a nuclear physicist who had taken part in the Manhattan Project, declared, "If the atomic bomb had not been used, evidence like that I have cited points to the practical certainty that there would have been many more months of death and destruction on an enormous scale."[4] Winston Churchill likewise supported the bombing, saying, "There were those who considered that the atomic bomb should never have been used at all. I cannot associate myself with such ideas. . . . I am surprised that very worthy people—but people who in most cases had no intention of proceeding to the Japanese front themselves—should adopt a position that rather than throw this bomb we should have sacrificed a million American and a quarter of a million British lives."[5]

However, a number of notable individuals and organizations have criticized the nuclear attacks, characterizing the bombings as war crimes, crimes against humanity, and state terrorism. Early critics of the bombings included Albert Einstein, Eugene Wigner, and Leo Szilard, who had together spurred the first nuclear bomb research in 1939. Szilard, who had gone on to play a major role in the Manhattan Project, argued,

> Let me say only this much to the moral issue involved: Suppose Germany had developed two bombs before we had any bombs. And suppose Germany had dropped one bomb, say, on Rochester and the other on Buffalo, and then having run out of bombs she would have lost the war. Can anyone doubt that we would then have defined the dropping of atomic bombs on cities as a war crime, and that we would have sentenced the Germans who were guilty of this crime to death at Nuremberg and hanged them?[6]

The 1946 United States Strategic Bombing Survey, written by Paul Nitze, also concluded that the atomic bombings were unnecessary to the winning of the war. After reviewing numerous documents and interviewing hundreds of Japanese civilian and military leaders after Japan's surrender, he reported,

> There is little point in attempting precisely to impute Japan's unconditional surrender to any one of the numerous causes which jointly and cumulatively were responsible for Japan's disaster. The time lapse between military impotence and political acceptance of the inevitable might have been shorter had the political structure of Japan permitted a more rapid and decisive determination of national policies. Nevertheless, it seems clear that, even without the atomic bombing attacks, air supremacy over Japan could have exerted sufficient pressure to bring about unconditional surrender and obviate the need for invasion. It was the Survey's opinion that certainly prior to December 31, 1945, and in all probability prior to November 1945, Japan would have surrendered even if the atomic

bombs had not been dropped, even if Russia had not entered the war, and even if no invasion had been planned or contemplated.[7]

In 1963, the bombings were the subject of a judicial review in *Ryuichi Shimoda et al. v. State*.[8] On the twenty-second anniversary of the attack on Pearl Harbor, the Tokyo District Court declined to rule on the legality of nuclear weapons in general but found that "the attacks upon Hiroshima and Nagasaki caused such severe and indiscriminate suffering that they did violate the most basic legal principles governing the conduct of war."[9]

While Japan and the United States have maintained a tacit understanding that both parties should avoid issues that could undermine their bilateral security alliance, that approach has failed to remove the historical thorn that exists between the two countries. For instance, in 1995, the Japanese government undertook a project called the Peace, Friendship, and Exchange Initiative to promote reconciliation by inviting former POWs and their families to Japan to meet Japanese individuals involved in wartime events. By 2004, 784 former POWs had been invited to Japan from Britain, 425 from the Netherlands, and 56 from Australia. Until 2010, however, American POWs were excluded from the initiative, and the atomic and carpet bombings were the primary reasons for this exclusion. As former Japanese senior diplomat Togo Kazuhiko notes, "There seemed to be popular sentiment about whether there was any need for further reconciliation with the American soldiers who were prisoners-of-war, for they had killed many Japanese citizens with their atomic bombings, carpet bombings, and other operations. Such seemed to have been taken into consideration."[10]

In addition, the bombings produced victim consciousness among many Japanese. It is widely argued and taught in Japan, as witnessed in its history textbooks, that the atomic bombs were used against Japan for nonmilitary motives—that is, to pressure the Soviet Union or demonstrate power, to end the war before the Soviet Union could enter, to test the power of the atomic bomb, and to exact revenge for Pearl Harbor. Professor Sadao Asada of Doshisha University in Japan has found that anger and suspicion of the United States' reasoning behind bombing Japan are especially strong among younger generations. Asada argues that the Japanese sense of victimization is most bitterly expressed in the racist interpretation of the bombings, as about half of students sampled at Doshisha responded that they felt that American leaders would not have dropped atomic bombs on

Germany, even if the bombs had been ready in time, but that they were dropped on Japan because of racial prejudice and discrimination against Asians.[11] Asada reveals that one of the students responded, "The United States dropped the A-bomb on Japan because of its racial prejudice. Looking down upon the yellow Japanese as having less human value, Americans used the Japanese to test their new weapon."[12] Almost immediately after the atomic bombs were dropped, people like Kiyose Ichiro, who later emerged as a major defense attorney in the Tokyo War Crimes Tribunal, publicly speculated that racist contempt for Japanese "monkeys" explained why the Americans used the atomic bombs against Japan but not Germany. Even so, many American historians, including John Dower, feel that the atomic bomb would undoubtedly have been used against Germany if it had been ready by early 1945.

This notion of American guilt and Japanese victimhood persists as a prevalent theme in Japanese education and popular culture. Besides descriptions in the history textbooks noted later in this chapter, the inscriptions at the Yushukan Museum at Yasukuni Shrine, prepared in the early 2000s, for example, make no reference to invasion, aggression, massacres, or atrocities committed by Japanese troops. Instead, they blame American President Franklin D. Roosevelt for provoking war with Japan. As Jeff Kingston writes, "Japanese suffering is the only suffering on display."[13] While less explicit than the Yushukan Museum language, even historical museums dealing with the atomic bombings present a view that questions America's justification for the strikes and leaves open the question of general responsibility for the war. Descriptions at the Hiroshima Peace Memorial Museum, for instance, assert that "the atomic bomb had cost 2 billion dollars and mobilized, at its peak, over 120,000 people. Linking this weapon to the end of the war would help justify that expenditure. In addition to the desire to force Japan's surrender, these considerations led the U.S. to proceed with the atomic bombings."[14] This accusation is backed by depictions of U.S. behavior immediately following the bombings and characterizations of perceived American insensitivity to the resulting damage. At one point, the exhibits devote several captions to the suggestion that the horrific casualties had inspired a U.S. reaction more attuned to scientific research than medical and humanitarian aid.

Japan's victim consciousness largely stems from its status as the only nation ever attacked with atomic weapons. That the victims of the attacks were not only Japanese, however, is not widely known in Japan or elsewhere—not even in Korea, despite the fact that as many as 70,000 Koreans, or 10 percent of the Hiroshima and Nagasaki victims, were Koreans working in the two cities at the time of bombings. Most of the Korean victims were forced laborers in Japanese military factories. Approximately 20,000 Korean victims are believed to have returned to Korea after the war was over, and of these individuals, approximately 2,600 individuals are still alive. For a long time, the Japanese government did not acknowledge the suffering of these overseas *hibakusa* (victims of the atomic bombs). Especially for Korean victims, Japan has argued that war-related compensation issues concerning South Koreans were "settled completely and finally" under the 1965 Agreement Concerning the Settlement of Problems in Regard to Property and Claims and on Economic Cooperation between Japan and South Korea, which was signed when Tokyo and Seoul normalized diplomatic relations.[15] Moreover, because they were not Japanese citizens, these Korean victims were refused access to Japanese-funded health benefits for atomic survivors, even if they remained in Japan following the nation's defeat. The Korean government likewise neglected to bring this issue to the forefront of history education or negotiations with Japan.

In 1978, after decades of Korean struggles for compensation and medical treatment from Japan, the Japanese Supreme Court made the landmark decision that Son Jin Doo, a South Korean victim who had entered Japan to obtain medical treatment, must be provided equal treatment. However, Son's case was only a Pyrrhic victory, as the Japanese Health Administration limited medical treatment and pension payments to victims living in Japan. Although the rule restricting benefits to residents of Japan was also overturned in 1998 in a lawsuit by Korean survivor Kwak Kwi Hoon, and since March 1, 2003, Korean victims have been able to receive an officially recognized victim's passbook that ensures access to medical assistance, compensation has been restricted to medical treatment and small pension payments. Other benefits, such as the 198,000 yen given to victims for their funeral expenses, have not been extended to Korean victims.

In addition, Korean victims have demanded that medical treatment and pension benefits be offered to second- and third-generation victims with medical conditions caused by the bombings. In 2006, 2,500 members of the Korean Atomic Bomb Victims Association filed a petition with the Korean Constitutional Court, claiming that the government's passive attitude toward resolving the dispute with Japan was a violation of their basic rights. The court ruled that the basic rights of the persons in question had indeed been violated by the inaction of the South Korean government and judged that the government's failure to pursue these matters adequately with Japan was in violation of the country's constitution.

*Mainstream Narratives: History Textbooks*

Variations in the views of the atomic bombings and the question of their justification also become apparent in history textbooks. As expected, in Chinese textbooks, discussions of the subject and its role in bringing the war to a close are very brief. However, they do devote some energy to claiming that China played a part in precipitating the Japanese surrender: "In August, the U.S. attacked Hiroshima and Nagasaki with atomic bombs, and the USSR declared war against Japan and surrounded and annihilated the Japanese troops in northeastern China. At the same time, anti-Japanese military forces in China launched a general counterattack on Japanese troops. On August 15, Japan announced its surrender."[16]

Korean textbooks do not include a single line describing how the war ended—other than simply noting that Japan was defeated—and make no mention of the atomic bombs used against Japan. The Korean reluctance to endorse the image of victimization by the Japanese is clear, but this lack of coverage is surprising given that as many as seventy thousand Koreans were victims of atomic bombings in Japan (including a Korean prince of the Chosun dynasty, Yi Wu, who died in the bombing of Hiroshima). Although a considerable number of Koreans—making up close to 10 percent of the total victims—were killed by the two bombings, Koreans, other than the victims themselves, have not actively fought for recognition as atomic-bomb victims and have not been taught in schools about the sufferings of their national fellows.[17]

In contrast, but as expected, both Japanese and U.S. textbooks discuss the subjects in great detail, providing context of the war situation at the time of the bombings and putting forth contending views of the use of the bombs and their impact. U.S. textbooks describe the situation at length, offering quite earnest accounts of what was being debated at that historical moment, as in this passage from *The Americans: Reconstruction to the 21st Century*: "Many advisors to President Truman, including Secretary of

War Henry Stimson, had the point of view that the only way to end the war against Japan was to bomb the Japanese mainland. They felt the bomb would end the war and save American lives. Two other concerns pushed Americans to use the bomb. Some people feared that if the bomb were not dropped, the project might be viewed as a gigantic waste of money. Some officials believed that a successful use of the atomic bomb would give the U.S. a powerful advantage over the Soviets in shaping the postwar world."[18]

While mostly stressing that U.S. leadership hoped to conclude the war as quickly as possible and therefore resorted to the bombings, U.S. textbooks also give voice to both sides of the debate. The authors of *The Americans* write,

> A petition drawn up by Dr. Leo Szilard, a Hungarian born physicist who had helped President Roosevelt launch the project and who had a major role in developing the bomb, and signed by 70 other scientists argued that it would be immoral to drop an atomic bomb on Japan without fair warning. Many supported staging a demonstration of the bomb for Japanese leaders, perhaps by exploding one on a deserted island near Japan, to convince the Japanese surrender. Supreme Allied Commander General Dwight Eisenhower agreed. He maintained that "dropping the bomb was completely unnecessary" to save American lives and that Japan was already defeated. Ike told Stimson, "I was against the bomb on two accounts. First the Japanese were ready to surrender and it wasn't necessary to hit them with that awful thing. Second, I hated to see our country to be the first to use such a weapon."[19]

Another U.S. textbook suggests other motives: "Some scholars, notably Gar Alperovitz, have further charged that the atomic holocausts at Hiroshima and Nagasaki were not the last shots of World War II, but the first salvos in the emerging Cold War. Alperovitz argues that the Japanese were already defeated in the summer of 1945 and were in fact attempting to arrange a conditional surrender. President Truman ignored these attempts and unleashed his horrible new weapons, so the argument goes, not simply to defeat Japan but to frighten the Soviets into submission to America's will and to keep them out of the final stages of the war and postwar reconstruction in Asia."[20] As apparent from the first and third examples above, U.S. textbooks also dedicate a few lines to describing the state of U.S. relations with the USSR just before Japan's surrender.

Japanese textbooks, in general, are suspicious of the motives of the United States' decision to use atomic bombs against Japan. The authors of the *Tokyo Shoseki History B* textbook write, "In order to secure its leading role in the postwar government [of Japan] by forcing Japan to surrender before the Soviet Union's participation in the war, the United States dropped atomic bombs on Hiroshima on August 6 and Nagasaki on August 9 (altogether more than 200,000 people perished)."[21] In the note section of the book, the authors argue, "While Japan's declaration, in response to the Potsdam Declaration, that it would 'continue the war undaunted' has been cited as the official reason for the United States' dropping of atomic bombs, the U.S. had already decided to drop atomic bombs regardless of the Japanese government's declaration."[22] The *Yamakawa World History B* textbook also asserts, "The military maneuverings of the United States and Soviet Union *just prior* to Japan's surrender were an attempt to seize the initiative in the postwar world."[23] As seen, Japanese textbooks refer as well to the role of the USSR, especially with respect to that country's breaking of the Soviet-Japanese Neutrality Pact. All three Japanese textbooks that we reviewed contain this phrase: "The Soviet Union, ignoring the provisions of the Soviet-Japanese Neutrality Pact, declared war on Japan on August 8, 1945."[24] Only the Japanese and U.S. textbooks provide detailed figures of how many people died or were injured as a result of the bombings.

Descriptions of how the war came to an end in Japanese textbooks reveal Japan's victim identity, based on the ideas that (1) the first-ever atomic bombs were used against its people, and (2) Japan was a victim of the U.S.-Soviet rivalry. These textbooks argue that Japan was ready to surrender and that it had notified the Allied Nations on August 10 that it would accept the Potsdam Declaration (in contradiction to its official response to the Potsdam Declaration that it would "deliberately ignore [the declaration]")[25] if the emperor system would be preserved; however, the United States, being aware of Japan's intent to surrender, responded instead by bombing Hiroshima and Nagasaki in order to take the lead in the postwar world as well as to accomplish the original objective of Japan's unconditional surrender.

### Contending Views Inside the United States and Japan

Debates over whether the use of bombs was militarily—not to mention morally—necessary and whether such an act can be justified are at the heart of the ongoing discussion surrounding wartime history, not only cross-nationally but also within involved nations. While justification that the bombings were necessary to bring about Japan's immediate surrender and thus minimize casualties on both sides has been generally accepted in China, Korea, and the United States, many Japanese survivors and leaders of the Japanese military, along with a few U.S. leaders, hold somewhat different opinions. These varying opinions tend to address three issues: (1) whether the bombings were necessary and effective; (2) whether they constituted a justifiable act or a war crime and, if the latter, whether the United States should have been tried at the Tokyo War Crimes Tribunal; and (3) whether the United States should accept the Japanese invitation for the U.S. president to visit Hiroshima or Nagasaki for the commemoration of victims. Unsurprisingly, opinions of elites in China and Korea did not show much variation regarding these questions, so our discussion here focuses on Japanese and American views.

Most of those whom we interviewed in Japan and the United States agreed that the atomic bombings were a significant factor in leading Japan to capitulate. However, not everyone thought that the use of the bombs was the only choice left for the United States to bring about a timely surrender. Many Japanese and American opinion leaders we interviewed felt that Japanese surrender was already imminent when the bombs struck the two cities. Kawashima Shin argues, "Japan was already turning toward surrender by the 6th and 9th of August. If the A-bomb hastened the surrender, it was only by a matter of days, maybe a week. America wanted to end the war quickly but at the same time demonstrate its new weapon to the Soviet Union, etcetera."[26] Togo Kazuhiko espouses a similar view: "The Suzuki Cabinet was formed with a view to end the war.... There was a tacit consensus among the top six to end the war, which led to sending the Konoe cable to Moscow. So there was an accumulation of will, without bombs and the Soviet attack. But this was not taken seriously by either Stalin or Truman."[27] Sakurai Yoshiko confers: "It is not at all acceptable that the U.S. people say this was necessary, just as to Americans it's not acceptable that Pearl Harbor was inevitable. We were already seeking how to end the war through the Soviet Union. But the Soviet Union, on the other side, had already [broken the Soviet-Japanese Neutrality Pact in order to emerge from the war as a victor]. So I'm sure that, at some point, the war would have ended even without nuclear weapons, because Japan had no more power to fight."[28] And Takahata Isao argues, likewise, "I cannot think that it was the case that America dropped the bomb because it thought it would save many lives, including those of Japanese people. It dropped the bomb because that would work to its advantage in the postwar hegemony."[29]

Some American leaders and scholars also expressed doubts about the necessity of the use of atomic bombs. Scholars like Barton Bernstein argued that the use of the bombs was unnecessary but that the Truman administration leaders did not seek to avoid using them. Bernstein argues, "There was not an effort to avoid the use of the first atomic bomb—and certainly not the second. They believed that its military use might produce a powerful bonus: the intimidation of the Soviets. Because American leaders expected that the bombings would also compel the Soviet Union to loosen its policy in Eastern Europe, there was no incentive to question their intention to use the atomic bomb."[30] Lester Tenney, by contrast, argues that the bombings were militarily necessary by that point. He notes, "We already tested the fact that they were not going to surrender with the firebombing of Tokyo. That's three or four days of thousands of planes bombing every day, and they still would not surrender."[31] Mark Peattie takes this view further, contending that even if the Japanese were ready to surrender prior to the bombings, "the dropping of the atomic bombs obviated the necessity for them to make a decision."[32]

Some individuals question the United States' intentions in bombing Nagasaki, when, they believe, one bomb on Hiroshima would have sufficed. Sakurai Yoshiko suggests that the United States' deployment of two different kinds of bombs against Hiroshima and Nagasaki raises the issue of whether the true intention of the United States was to end the war quickly or to test the bombs that it had developed. Wakamiya Yoshibumi, similarly, asserts, "I believe the war could have ended with just the bombing of Hiroshima, but here were two different bombs, and they tried it two different times, and in that sense went too far. I certainly have that suspicion."[33] Bernstein agrees: "Whatever one thinks of Hiroshima, bombing Nagasaki was almost certainly unnecessary."[34] Tenney, on the other hand, counters by saying that the bombing of Nagasaki served its purpose well. "The advantage of the second bomb was that the Japanese did not know for sure how many more atomic bombs we had," he says. "It convinced them that we had more."[35]

However, even if the bombs precipitated Japan's surrender and were militarily justified, the question of whether their use on cities—that is, on civilians—was morally justified, from a human-rights perspective, becomes significant. The second contentious issue regarding the nuclear strikes deals with whether the use of the bombs was a war crime and, if so, whether the United States should have been tried at the Tokyo War Crimes Tribunal. As discussed in more detail in the chapter 10, the tribunal focused only on "crimes against peace" and did not address "crimes against humanity." Not surprisingly, the majority of the Japanese opinion leaders we interviewed say that the use of nuclear weapons against Hiroshima and Nagasaki constituted a war crime and, in particular, a crime against humanity. Takagi Kenichi asked, "Maybe the bombs saved a lot of Americans, but was it therefore just to kill hundreds of thousands of Japanese? The weapon is a war crime itself."[36] Similarly, Takahashi Akihiro, the former director of Hiroshima Peace Memorial Museum, asserts, "Atomic bombs are different. Regular bombs happen if you're in a war. But this was radiation, and that's different, even in a war. It's simply wrong to annihilate civilians."[37] John Dower, an American, holds a similar view: "We've crossed the moral Rubicon in which deliberately killing noncombatants was accepted as both necessary and just. And looking back now, I would say that we moved into the area of atrocities and war crimes in doing this."[38] Kirk Saduski, in contrast, says, "I think it was justified, and I think civilians were intentionally targeted, but civilians had been targets on both sides for years by that point. Obviously, what should have been the primary concern is American servicemen dying—and think of the Japanese casualties if we had actually had to invade Japan. Okinawa was the precursor to what it would have been like, but only how many more times worse."[39] Kawashima Shin agrees: "If indiscriminate killing of civilians is a war crime, then yes, it was. But as to indiscriminate bombing—whether atomic or firebombing—Japan did it first in Nanjing and in Shanghai, etcetera."[40]

Finally, a new debate has emerged recently, drawing international attention over the legacy of the atomic bombings and whether that legacy might in some way serve as a locus of historical reconciliation between Japan and the United States, and perhaps indirectly for the region at large. The atomic bombings enabled many Japanese to absolve themselves of responsibility for Japanese atrocities on the grounds that they, the Japanese, were now the victims. For this reason, there has been a growing discussion, especially in light of the ongoing—and, in fact, worsening—historical disputes in the region, about whether it would be appropriate for the United States to apologize to Japan or for the U.S. president to visit one of the two memorial sites in the bombed cities and pay respects to the victims of the tragedies. In recent years, the call for a U.S. presidential visit to Hiroshima or Nagasaki has gained new momentum, given President Obama's Prague speech advocating a nuclear-free world. Nagasaki Mayor Tomihisa Tanoue recommended such a visit at a meeting of NGOs under the preparatory committee for the Non-Proliferation of Nuclear Weapons Treaty Review Conference held in May 2009. Hiroshima Mayor Tadatoshi Akiba made the same request at his meeting with democratic members of the U.S. House of Representatives. Survivors' and citizens' groups of both cities have sent letters to President Obama, calling for him to visit the sites of the bombings.[41]

Again, opinion leaders in China and Korea have shown little variation in their views. The vast majority of them felt that Japan should visit the memorial sites in China and Korea to pay respects and apologize to the victims before demanding that the United States do so in Japan. Within Japan and the United States, opinions were split about whether such a visit by the U.S. president would be an option worth considering. The historian Ogata Sadako says, "I wouldn't insist, but such a visit would be appreciated. But it's not expected either."[42] Takagi, recalling his meeting with U.S. congressman Mike Honda, who led the passage of the U.S. congressional resolution regarding comfort women, recalls,

> I said to him that I would like Obama to come to Hiroshima and Nagasaki in August and make an apology, and with America having done that, Japan would be able to as well—it will become much easier for [then Prime Minister Yukio] Hatoyama to address Asia and do compensation, to create something like what was created in Germany on behalf of the victims. . . . If Obama shows by visiting Hiroshima or Nagasaki that this is how a country demonstrates its national values, it would become easier to argue that Japan has to follow suit. He has said he is antinuclear, so if he says the natural thing that everyone already knows—that is, to use nuclear weapons is a war crime—and says that America must recognize this, [it would be appreciated].[43]

Tamogami Toshio, on the other hand, asserts, "I don't think he should, and I don't think he will. For America, that would be a big problem. Sure, there are many people who'd like him to apologize for Hiroshima, but for the military who died fighting for America, that would be very inexcusable, a betrayal. And if they did that, of course there would be tremendous reactions everywhere. What kind of result would there be, for America, for Japan, for China—there would be an enormous reaction everywhere, entirely unpredictable."⁴⁴ Sakurai Yoshiko argues along the same lines: "If Obama brings the idea from his side, fine, but we should not ask him to do that, for it would not be constructive for [Prime Minister] Hatoyama to go to Nanjing."⁴⁵

## Should the U.S. President Visit the Sites of Bombings?

Given the debates over the merits of an American presidential visit to the sites of the nuclear attacks, it is important to assess such a visit's potential benefits and drawbacks. While many have proposed such a visit, the Japanese journalist Fumio Matsuo has been a most eloquent and persistent advocate. In his view, many Japanese feel uneasy about the lack of "true closure" between the two countries over the war, and this lack of closure should be addressed. He envisions a step-by-step process of historical reconciliation, led by U.S. action: "As a starting point, Japan must face up to its past and its unfortunate war with the U.S. After we remove that remaining thorn, Japan will have to . . . [admit] the simple truth to the rest of Asia that Japan started the war. From that start, we can begin to remove the thorns, one by one, between Japan and its neighbors, just as we are asking the Americans to pay respects to our war victims, and bring closure to a sad chapter in our history."⁴⁶ Referring to the "Dresden moment," in which the military leaders of Germany's former enemies attended the fiftieth anniversary of the Allied bombings of that city, Matsuo suggests that the U.S. president should visit and lay a wreath at the Hiroshima Peace Memorial, followed by similar actions on the part of Japanese leaders vis-à-vis Japan's Asian neighbors.⁴⁷

It appears that, in fact, a U.S. presidential visit to Hiroshima nearly took place. Citing a source from the U.S. embassy in Tokyo, the Japanese newspaper the *Mainichi* reports that the United States considered having President George W. Bush stop in Hiroshima before or after the Asia-Pacific Economic Cooperation (APEC) meetings held in November 2005 in South Korea. However, Japan's relations with China and South Korea were chilly at that time because of then prime minister Junichiro Koizumi's repeated visits to the Yasukuni Shrine, and the United States reportedly forwent the Hiroshima visit to avoid any misunderstanding that it had in some sense sided with Japan.⁴⁸ The U.S. government had considered a similar visit in 1995, the fiftieth anniversary of the end of the war, but President Bill

Clinton was forced to cancel his participation in the APEC meetings that year because of a crisis over the passage of the nation's budget. He visited Japan the following year but did not travel to Hiroshima.[49] Still, a few years ago, the time seemed ripe for reciprocal visits by the leaders of the United States and Japan when Obama and Hatoyama were in power. The visit fit nicely with President Obama's vision for a nuclear-free world, and his official visit to Hiroshima or Nagasaki could have been seen as an important step toward demonstrating his leadership in implementing nuclear-free policies. It also aligned with Prime Minister Hatoyama's vision of creating an East Asian community.

An American presidential visit would certainly enhance the United States' international image as a champion of human rights and peace—an image that has been tainted as of late, resulting in a sharp rise in anti-American sentiment in many parts of the world. It would certainly aid in removing the historical thorn that exists between the United States and Japan.

Despite these potential benefits, an American presidential visit must be carried out with great caution and care. It should be made clear from the outset that such a visit would not be meant to vindicate Japan's victim identity or support rightist views that hold the United States responsible for wartime atrocities. It should serve as an occasion to acknowledge human sufferings of nuclear attacks and thus the importance of creating a nuclear-free world, as President Obama has proclaimed in his Prague speech. If a Hiroshima visit were construed as an official apology, it would draw strong resistance from conservatives in the United States[50] and be counterproductive to achieving reconciliation. It could even have the unintended consequence of validating Japan's victim consciousness and bolstering the historical amnesia that overlooks Japan's own responsibility for wartime atrocities toward its Asian neighbors.

Most importantly, an American presidential visit should not merely be an effort to strengthen the U.S.-Japan bilateral relationship. Rather, the primary reason for the visit should be to activate a larger process of historical reconciliation that includes Northeast Asian nations as well as the United States. Most Japanese who support a U.S. presidential visit see its merit mainly in terms of removing the historical thorn that exists between the United States and Japan. However, if such a visit were taken only to reaffirm the U.S.-Japan alliance, it would create grave and widespread concerns, particularly among Chinese and Koreans, that the United States sides with

Japan over historical issues. It was for this reason, as noted above, that the U.S. government did not pursue a possible Bush visit to Hiroshima in 2005. As Fumio Matsuo suggests, for such a visit by a U.S. president to be successful, it should be followed by similar actions on the part of the Japanese toward their Asian neighbors; for instance, the Japanese prime minister could undertake a similar visit to Nanjing to pay tribute to the victims of the 1937 massacre. Only when a U.S. presidential visit occurs in a larger regional context can the United States avoid alienating China and South Korea and play a constructive role in facilitating historical reconciliation in Northeast Asia.

TEN

# The United States and Postwar Settlements

At the state level as well as at the individual level, the extent and forms of compensation for the victims of Japanese colonial and wartime aggression have been by far the most contentious issues of the war between Japan and its neighbors. In seeking a settlement between the victims of Japanese aggression and those responsible for crimes against them, various attempts have been made, and litigation has been adopted as a major tactic in redressing historical injustices. Unlike in the West, however, its efficacy has proven to be very limited. Almost all lawsuits that Asian victims have filed in Japanese and U.S. courts have been either thrown out or left unresolved on the basis of the San Francisco Peace Treaty of 1951, though courts have recognized the fact of the victims' suffering.

Yet, more fundamentally, Japan has failed to apologize unequivocally to its neighbors for its aggression, and this can be considered a key legacy of insufficient postwar settlements. Despite Japan's various efforts to "apologize" for colonial and wartime atrocities, these efforts have not been backed up by actions to reinforce the apologies; instead, they are often coupled with ambiguous wording and counterproductive statements and behavior on the part of Japanese elites.[1] In fact, throughout the 1990s, Japanese political elites showed ambivalence between formal apology and frequent statements that glorified their colonial rule. Even as late as 2014, Japan considered revising the Kono Statement of 1993, the clearest official acknowledgement of Japan's past wrongdoings, provoking criticism from not only its Asian neighbors but also the United States. This chapter shows that this sort of historical amnesia, or lack of political will to address historical injustices, largely stems from the ways in which colonial and wartime atrocities were handled in the postwar period, leaving virtually no one in Japan to blame.

This chapter focuses on two major postwar settlements between Japan and the Allied powers led by the United States: the International Military Tribunal for the Far East, convened in Tokyo (known as the Tokyo War Crimes Tribunal), and the San Francisco Peace Treaty of 1951. As in other chapters, we seek to explain how both settlements have contributed to the production of divided historical memories in the Asia-Pacific region by showing variations both between and within nations. The settlements were international in nature, but the United States played a leading role in both of them, and thus their nature and legacy have been subject to contention between Japan and the United States, as well as between Japan and its Asian neighbors. We discuss how this contention over postwar settlements contributed to the hindering of historical reconciliation in the region and explore how the United States as a responsible player may facilitate the process of historical reconciliation in Northeast Asia.

*Postwar Settlements in Asia*

The Allied powers, led by the United States, settled Japan's wartime aggression through court trials of war criminals and a formal treaty.

After the Japanese defeat in the Pacific War, the International Military Tribunal for the Far East (IMTFE, also known as the Tokyo War Crimes Tribunal) was convened in Tokyo on May 3, 1946, to address the question of Japan's war crimes and atrocities. The Tokyo War Crimes Tribunal featured a panel of eleven judges presiding, one from each of the victorious Allied powers (the United States, the Republic of China, the Soviet Union, the United Kingdom, the Netherlands, the Provisional Government of the French Republic, Australia, New Zealand, Canada, British India, and the Philippines). Unlike the Nuremberg trials, which were conducted in four languages, only two languages, English and Japanese, were used in the Tokyo tribunal. This later became a contentious matter, as it indicated to the Allied powers that the supreme commander and the United States government were determined to go ahead with the tribunal on American terms. The IMTFE selected twenty-eight Class A defendants, the majority of whom had occupied the highest governmental and military positions in Japan during the war, for prosecution at the Tokyo tribunal. The trials proceeded in the order of testimony, countertestimony, rebuttal, counterrebuttal, and closing statements of both the prosecutor and the defense and were concluded on April 16, 1948, until they reconvened in November of the same year, when sentences were handed down.

The Tokyo tribunal, unlike the Nuremberg trials in Europe, focused on "crimes against peace" and ignored "crimes against humanity." Charges of crimes against humanity (Class C offenses) were not brought against any suspect of war crimes, and even the Nanjing Massacre was prosecuted only as an infringement on the laws of war. As a result, the Tokyo War Crimes Tribunal has been criticized for allowing Japan the leeway to avoid greater punishments and war crime responsibilities. It also avoided possible charges against the United States for committing crimes against humanity, such as the atomic bombings of Hiroshima and Nagasaki, as discussed in chapter 9. Of the twenty-five Japanese defendants (all of whom were convicted), seven were sentenced to hang, sixteen were given life imprisonment, and two were sentenced to lesser terms. Except for those who died early of natural causes in prison, none of the imprisoned Japanese war criminals served a life sentence. Instead, by 1958, the remaining prisoners had been either pardoned or paroled.[2] War crimes charges against more junior personnel were dealt with separately, in other cities throughout Far East Asia, such as in the Nanjing War Crimes Tribunal and the Khabarovsk War Crimes Trials.

The judgments of the war crimes trials were accepted by Japan when it signed the San Francisco Peace Treaty, which formally brought the war to a close. The San Francisco Peace Treaty, signed on September 8, 1951, between Japan and forty-eight other nations, came into force on April 28, 1952, making extensive use of the UN Charter and the Universal Declaration of Human Rights to enunciate the Allies' goals. The treaty settled Japan's obligations to pay reparations for its wartime acts and formally ended World War II. Attending countries were Argentina, Australia, Belgium, Bolivia, Brazil, Cambodia, Canada, Chile, Colombia, Costa Rica, Cuba, Czechoslovakia, the Dominican Republic, Ecuador, Egypt, El Salvador, Ethiopia, France, Greece, Guatemala, Haiti, Honduras, Indonesia, Iran, Iraq, Japan, Laos, Lebanon, Liberia, Luxembourg, Mexico, the Netherlands, New Zealand, Nicaragua, Norway, Pakistan, Panama, Paraguay, Peru, the Philippines, Poland, Saudi Arabia, the Soviet Union, Sri Lanka, South Africa,

Syria, Turkey, the United Kingdom, the United States, Uruguay, Venezuela, and Vietnam. Among these fifty-two nations, Czechoslovakia, Poland, and the Soviet Union refused to sign. Both China and Korea, two primary victims of Japanese aggression in Asia, were excluded from signing the treaty.

The treaty officially renounced Japan's rights to Korea, Formosa (now known as Taiwan) and the Pescadores, Hong Kong (then a British colony), the Kuril Islands, the Spratly Islands, Antarctica, and Sakhalin Island. The negotiations over the former Japanese territories were a lengthy process. Several drafts were prepared prior to the final version of the San Francisco Peace Treaty. Earlier drafts were long and detailed, providing clear border demarcations and specifying the names of small islands near the borders of postwar Japan. But these drafts underwent various changes and were eventually simplified. In the end, there was some ambiguity with regard to which islands Japan had renounced sovereignty over, and this led to later territorial disputes over the Kuril Islands, the Senkaku/Diaoyu Islands, Dokdo/Takeshima, and others.

In addition, the San Francisco Treaty absolved Japan of any responsibility for reparations. In particular, Article 14(b) states that "except as otherwise provided in the present Treaty, the Allied Powers waive all reparations claims of the Allied Powers, other claims of the Allied Powers and their nationals arising out of any actions taken by Japan and its nationals in the course of the prosecution of the war, and claims of the Allied Powers for direct military costs of occupation." This passage became the basis for later court rulings against lawsuits by Asian victims in both Japan and the United States. Drafted at the height of the Cold War largely by the United States and without the participation of China and Korea, the article has had the consequence of stripping Asian nations and their citizens of legal means to obtain compensation from Japan.

The two pillars of the postwar settlement—the war crimes tribunal and the peace treaty—form the principal legal legacy of the war and remain a source of controversy for the issues that were unresolved. There are a number of deficiencies to the Tokyo tribunal, and its legacy has significantly shaped the ways in which Asians have remembered the wars and dealt with historical injustices. First of all, unlike the Nuremberg court, the Tokyo trial was not sufficiently represented by judges from those nations that suffered the most from Japanese aggression: only three of the eleven judges at the trial represented Asian countries, and there was no representative from Korea. As a result, it has been charged that the U.S.-led tribunal failed to appreciate the massive suffering of Chinese and Koreans at the hands of Japanese invaders and colonizers and the need to address the deep well of anger left behind. The proceedings paid only cursory attention to Japanese aggression against Asians, such as Japan's invasion of Manchuria in 1931, the Nanjing Massacre, and the use of forced Korean labor in Japanese mines and factories and "comfort women" by the Japanese military.[3] Instead, the tribunal focused on the Japanese actions that had most directly affected Western allies—the surprise attack on Pearl Harbor and the mistreatment of Allied prisoners of war. This neglect of crimes against Asians is, in one Korean scholar's view, "one of the most serious defects of the Tokyo trial . . . [since] many of the victims of these crimes were left helpless by the injuries they suffered, and they have been left without redress to this day."[4] These flaws and specific omissions, as many scholars argue, "discredited the evidence of war crimes that the trials did uncover, tainted the concept of postwar justice, and restored the legitimacy of the very leaders the trials had sought to impugn."[5]

Another important legacy of the Tokyo tribunal was the decision to preserve the Showa emperor. There still exists no consensus about the extent of the emperor's responsibility for Japanese militarism and war crimes,[6] and even in the tribunal, there were disputes over the level of the emperor's responsibility. However, U.S. leaders of the Allied forces in Japan believed that keeping the emperor as a social institution, deprived of political power, would facilitate the occupation and reconstruction of postwar Japan. The Australian judge and chair of the tribunal, Sir William Webb, opposed the idea of keeping the imperial institution intact, calling the emperor "the leader in the crime,"[7] but his was a minority view in the U.S.-dominated court.[8] Unlike in Europe, where key Axis leaders of the war and the Holocaust were punished for their atrocities and crimes, the opportunity to address the personal and institutional role of the emperor in Japanese historical injustices was clearly lost.

Consequently, the failure to confront the issue of Emperor Hirohito's war responsibility greatly influenced the ways in which the Japanese would remember the war years and approach reconciliation issues with their Asian neighbors. As Jennifer Lind asserts, "Psychological warfare officials and occupation authorities alike crafted a mythology of Japanese victimhood in which the public had been duped by a militarist clique into launching an ill-fated war." This "military clique thesis," according to Lind, pardoned the Japanese of guilt and fostered an already ubiquitous "sense of self-pity."[9] As historian Herbert Bix acutely notes, "As long as Hirohito remained on the throne, unaccountable to anyone for his official actions, most Japanese had little reason to question their support of him or feel responsibility for the war, let alone look beyond the narrow boundaries of victim consciousness."[10] A study on historical disputes in Northeast Asia by the International Crisis Group reached a similar conclusion: "The absolution of the emperor left the country without anyone to blame."[11]

From the Japanese side, however, the Tokyo tribunal was an unfair assertion of "victor's justice." As mentioned above, it focused on dealing with "crimes against peace," and actions, especially American actions, that could be perceived as "crimes against humanity" have never been officially addressed at the court. It is hardly any secret that the Japanese, many of whom were civilians, suffered from the U.S. military's actions toward the end of the war. Besides the well-known atomic bombings of Hiroshima and Nagasaki, the United States killed numerous civilians in the course of its massive firebombing of Japanese cities. Even at the time, the targeting of entire cities for destruction with conventional weapons (known as "area" or "carpet" bombing) was controversial,[12] and Japan to this day remains the only country hit by nuclear weapons. Justice Radhabinod Pal of India argued during the Tokyo tribunal that "in the war in Asia the only act comparable to Nazi atrocities was perpetrated by the leaders of the United States."[13] While never intending to offer a juridical argument for whether a sentence of not guilty would have been a correct one, Pal contended that the United States had clearly provoked the war and insisted that all defendants were not guilty. Nevertheless, no discussion of the American bombing of civilians was ever allowed at the Tokyo tribunal,[14] and the question of wartime responsibility has been put on the back burner throughout the postwar period for the sake of strengthening the Japan-U.S. alliance. In a survey of Japanese opinion conducted by the *Asahi Shimbun* in April 2000, only 17 percent said that "the [Tokyo] trials justly judged those who were responsible for the war," while 34 percent said they believed that "the trials were an unjust and unilateral judgment of the defeated nations by the victor nations."[15]

A sense of "victor's justice," as John Dower notes, "provided fertile soil for the growth of a postwar neo-nationalism" in Japan.[16] An exemplary case in point is an award-winning essay by the then chief of staff of the Japanese Air

Self-Defense Force, General Tamogami Toshio, in the fall of 2008. In what the *Economist* labels a "warmed-through hash of thrice-cooked revisionism," Tamogami claims that the war was Japan's attempt to defend its legally held territories of China and Korea against communist conspirators, Pearl Harbor was nothing but an American trap, and Japanese colonial rule was a benevolent undertaking viewed with gratitude by its East Asian neighbors (see more about his views below).[17] What is more worrisome, as Togo Kazuhiko notes, is the fact that the most eloquent criticism of U.S. responsibility for the atomic bombings comes from "the best of 'human rights advocates' who are usually seen with sympathy and respect by Anglo-Saxon and European-Japan analysts."[18] Such figures include Ienaga Saburo, who sued the Japanese government for thirty years for not allowing the description of more detailed atrocities committed by Japanese soldiers, and Yuki Tanaka, who is well known for his contributions to the comfort-women issue. Tanaka was also instrumental in organizing an international people's tribunal held in 2006, which found "15 Americans [including Presidents Roosevelt and Truman as well as Robert Oppenheimer] . . . guilty of decision-making and issuing, passing on and carrying out the orders to drop the bombs."[19]

The San Francisco Treaty is no less problematic for the participants in the war.

The treaty was an agreement between the Allied powers and Japan, but neither the Republic of Korea nor the People's Republic of China was invited to the San Francisco Peace Conference, and neither was party to the 1951 treaty. The Republic of China (Taiwan) concluded a separate Treaty of Peace with Japan in 1952. These Asian nations, though they were the primary victims of Japanese acts of aggression in colonialism and war, were not part of the formal process of settling Japan's responsibilities. By then, the People's Republic of China had become an enemy of the United States, and Korea was weak, divided, and in the midst of an international war. Japan's responsibility toward China and Korea was not settled but, rather, overlooked.

Nevertheless, the 1951 treaty became a major basis for later court rulings on wartime atrocities and crimes. For instance, in April 2007, Japan's Supreme Court foreclosed all pending and future lawsuits arising from actions taken by Japan in the course of colonialism and war. The court cited as main grounds the relevant provisions of the San Francisco Treaty, especially Article 14, which included no separate mention of Japan's reparations for its Asian victims and has been interpreted as waiving those victims' rights to claims altogether. Apparently, the Japanese Supreme Court regarded the treaty, drafted at the height of the Cold War largely by the United States and without the participation of China and Korea, as having stripped other Asian nations and their citizens of legal means to obtain compensation.

The same article has been cited in U.S. cases. In the *Hwang Geum Joo v. Japan* decision handed down by the U.S. Court of Appeals for the D.C. Circuit on June 28, 2005, for example, the presiding judge noted that Article 14 "expressly waives 'all claims of the Allied powers and their nationals arising out of any actions taken by Japan and its nationals in the course of the prosecution of the war.'" Chinese, Taiwanese, and Korean plaintiffs in this case, former comfort women, objected that their countries were not party to the 1951 treaty. They also argued that subsequent treaties between their nations and Japan should not prevent private tort suits. However, this argument was rejected on the standard and rigidly mechanical reasoning that waiver stipulations applied in these subsequent treaties as well.[20]

In addition, deficiencies of the San Francisco Treaty have hindered the resolution of current territorial disputes in Northeast Asia. For instance, early drafts of the treaty specified that Dokdo/Takeshima (referred to as "Liancourt Rocks" by the U.S. government) was initially Korean territory and changed to Japanese territory in 1949, but in the end, the treaty omitted any reference to the area. Similarly, the USSR was initially named the recipient of the Kurile Islands, but this, too, was deleted in the final stage of treaty drafting. However, the lack of specification was neither a coincidence nor an error. Instead, as Kimie Hara points out, "various issues were deliberately left unresolved due to the regional Cold War."[21] The United States was responsible for designating sovereignty over the islands but "sidestepped doing so at the time, making Washington's feigned disinterest ever since the proverbial elephant in the room."[22] As Hara explains further, "with the emergence of the Cold War, the peace treaty changed, from punitive to generous, as U.S. strategic thinking focused on securing Japan within the Western bloc and assuring a long-term U.S. military presence in Japan, particularly in Okinawa."[23]

There was an opportunity to remedy the deficiencies of the San Francisco Treaty when Japan and South Korea normalized relations, but the questions of historical injustice and territorial issues were once again put aside. In 1965, under heavy pressure from a United States anxious to solidify its Cold War security alliance system and bolster the South Korean economy, the Republic of Korea agreed to normalize relations with Japan despite intense domestic protests. In exchange, South Korea received a substantial economic assistance package from Japan, but Japan refused to term this assistance "reparations." Issues such as disputed territories and Japan's colonial rule were again swept under the rug. Unlike in Western Europe, where the United States established a multilateral security arrangement (i.e., NATO) and pushed for Franco-German reconciliation, in Northeast Asia the United States established a bilateral "hub and spoke" alliance system with Japan and the Republic of Korea and did not press for a fundamental historical reconciliation between the two U.S. allies. As a result, "normalization" occurred at the governmental level but without addressing popular demands for the redress of historical injustices. As one former U.S. senior diplomat notes, "For American policymakers, strategic considerations have consistently trumped issues of equity in historic disputes involving Japan since World War II."[24]

### *Mainstream Narratives: History Textbooks*

Whether the Tokyo War Crimes Tribunal and the San Francisco Peace Treaty were "just" or "fair" have been points of contention, and various views appear in the history textbooks of involved countries, reflecting their contested nature.

Chinese textbooks, in general, hold a critical view of U.S. and Japanese attitudes. One textbook reads, "In consideration of its own interests, the U.S. exempted some Japanese fascist war criminals who killed many Chinese from accusation. The U.S. also tried to maintain Tennoism in Japan."[25] Another reads,

> When the prime minister of Federal Germany, Brandt, visited Poland . . . [he] kneeled down before the memorial of the massacre in Warsaw, in order to confess to the crimes that the German people had committed throughout history. However, in Japan, since Prime Minister Takeo Miki visited the Yasukuni Shrine in 1975, many prime ministers have visited and prayed at the shrine at which dead spirits are recalled, where all the class A war criminals are enshrined. What do you think of the different understandings of war crimes in Germany and Japan?[26]

Japanese textbooks focus in detail on the rulings of the tribunal, listing the sentences given to criminals, and emphasize the sufferings of the Japanese after their defeat. One textbook reads, "The result of the trial was that guilty sentences were handed down in November 1948 to all of those tried (excluding three who died from natural causes), beginning with the death penalty for Tojo [Hideki] and six of his subordinates, whose executions were carried out in December of the following year. Individual national leaders were tried as war criminals at the trial, which was unprecedented."[27] Another reads, "Among the former Japanese military officers and soldiers who were in Manchuria when Japan lost the war, roughly 600,000 were detained as prisoners by the Soviet Union in Siberia and Mongolia, forced to perform hard labor, and when their internment ended in 1956, more than 60,000 had perished due to, among other things, food shortages."[28] Justice Pal's dissenting view, which was dismissed at the time of the tribunal, has also been given attention in Japanese history textbooks. One of the textbooks reads, "There were, however, conflicts of opinion among the eleven judges; other than the majority ruling that was pronounced, judges such as Pal of India and Röling of the Netherlands wrote dissenting opinions."[29] The Yasukuni Shrine and the Kyoto Ryozen Gokoku Shrine have monuments especially dedicated to Justice Pal.

Surprisingly, however, Korean textbooks include very little description of the trials; only one of the three textbooks we examined mentioned anything about the postwar trials. The *Keumsung World History* textbook devotes half a page to explaining that, for the first time in history, war of aggression was deemed a crime and that mankind had demanded political and military leaders who had initiated the war to take on legal responsibility. The textbook goes on to compare the Nuremberg and Tokyo trials and writes,

> However, [unlike the Nuremberg trials] the Tokyo trials were limited in that they were conducted while excluding the Emperor Hirohito, who was a central leader in the war. Moreover, within the increasing context of the Cold War, due to American policies designed to keep Japan within the free bloc, the Japanese war criminals of the political and financial circles reclaimed power, and, thereafter, Japan has ceaselessly created friction among neighboring nations. Japan's unrepentant attitude pales in comparison with that of Germany, where even after the Nuremberg trials, it took Nazi war criminals to trial and paid compensation to wartime victims, reflecting on its history and war of aggression.[30]

U.S. textbooks also provide limited descriptions of the war crimes trials. Giving more weight to the Nuremberg trials, Prentice Hall's *World History* reads, "Similar war crimes trials were held in Japan and Italy. The trials showed that political and military leaders could be held accountable for actions in wartime,"[31] and *The American Pageant* reads, "Following the pattern in Germany, top Japanese 'war criminals' were tried in Tokyo from 1946 to 1948. Eighteen of them were sentenced to prison terms, and seven were hanged."[32]

Although it provided for the conclusion of peace settlements and the basis of the postwar order in East Asia, the San Francisco Peace Treaty receives minimal mention in textbooks in China, Korea, and the United States. Not surprisingly, in China and Korea, only world-history textbooks make any reference to the treaty, because the treaty itself is not part of those countries' national histories, as neither was a signatory of the treaty. China's *Modern and Contemporary World History II* textbook reads, "With the intensification of the Cold War, especially the situational change in mainland China, the U.S. changed its Japan policy and started to support Japan. In 1951, the U.S. signed a peace treaty with Japan that (unjustly [偏袒]) favored Japan and concluded its occupation of Japan."[33] Likewise, Korea's *Keumsung World History* textbook speaks about the treaty only in passing, limiting its coverage of the treaty to a single sentence: "Japan, which had been controlled by the four Allied powers, regained its sovereignty based on the decision of the San Francisco Peace Treaty in 1951."[34]

Textbooks used by the two main actors of the treaty, Japan and the United States, describe the treaty in more detail; however, the textbooks' emphases differ. American textbooks, although they include a little more detail than their Chinese or Korean counterparts, nevertheless pay scant attention to the treaty. In American textbooks, the focus of San Francisco Peace Treaty is clearly on the U.S.'s termination of its occupation of Japan, not on issues of Japanese reparations or details of the settlement. The U.S. textbook *World Civilization* reads, "Occupation [of Japan] lasted until 1952, a year after Japan signed a peace treaty with most of its wartime opponents."[35] The Prentice Hall *World History* describes the treaty as follows: "As Cold War tensions heightened, the U.S. grew eager to end the occupations. In 1952, it signed a peace treaty with Japan."[36] As a final example, *The Americans* reads, "Japan was occupied by U.S. forces under the command of General Douglas MacArthur. During the seven-year American occupation, MacArthur reshaped Japan's economic recovery, and also worked to transform Japan's government."[37]

Japanese textbooks, on the other hand, allocate much more space to their treatment of the document, with explicit focuses on reparations and settlement aspects of the treaty. *Yamakawa Japanese History B* devotes an entire section to the treaty's settlement:

> In September 1951, the San Francisco Peace Treaty was signed between our country and 48 other nations at a peace conference held in San Francisco. The treaty came into effect in April of the following year and the Occupation came to an end after close to seven years, restoring Japan's sovereignty as an independent nation. The treaty greatly reduced Japan's reparation obligations to warring nations, but included strict limitations on its territory, and Japan agreed on the independence of Korea and the disclamation of Taiwan, Southern Karafutu [Sakhalin], and the Chishima Islands, and that Okinawa and Ogasawara be placed under U.S. administration.

The book adds,

> The San Francisco Peace Treaty stipulated that Japan was obliged to pay restitution to nations that had been affected by the war mainly by providing reparations, but the United States and many other warring nations renounced their right to claim compensation due to the escalating Cold War situation. Correspondingly, four Southeast Asian countries that had been occupied by the Japanese Army—the Philippines, Indonesia, Burma, and South Vietnam—signed reparation agreements with Japan, as a result of which the Japanese government paid an aggregate total of 1 billion dollars in restitution. Because payments took the form of services such as construction work and the provisioning of produced goods, they were an important foothold for the foray into Southeast Asia of Japanese commodities and business ventures. Further, the Japanese government also made payments pursuant to reparations to the nonbelligerent nations of Thailand and Korea.[38]

In addition, the textbook quotes directly from Articles 3 and 6 of the San Francisco Peace Treaty, which lay out territorial and security agreements.[39] Japan's *Shoseki Japanese History B* reads,

> The San Francisco Peace Conference was held in September 1951, and Prime Minister Yoshida attended as chief plenipotentiary from Japan and signed the San Francisco Peace Treaty with the 48 Allied nations. However, due to the conflict between the U.S., Britain, and the Soviet Union, neither the Republic of China (Taiwan) nor the People's Republic of China was invited, and three countries including the Soviet Union did not sign the treaty. According to the treaty, it was decided that when Japan was released from occupation, its sovereignty

would be restored, Korea would regain its independence, and Japan would renounce its overseas territories acquired after the first Sino-Japanese war and territorial claims to the Chishima Islands, while also guaranteeing the U.S. trusteeship of Okinawa and Ogasawara.[40]

Similar to *Yamakawa Japanese History B*, *Shoseki Japanese History B* reproduces the language of Articles 1, 3, and 6 in a textbox.[41]

As apparent above, both Chinese and Korean textbooks provide only minimal descriptions of the treaty, although the Chinese *Modern and Contemporary World History II* textbook places a little more weight on the event and adds the slight criticism (or at least some negative nuance) that the United States unjustly favored and supported Japan. The U.S. textbooks give relatively detailed descriptions of the treaty but with a focus on only one aspect of the treaty: that it ended U.S. occupation of Japan. Japanese textbooks have much to say about the treaty, as it is an event that is, on the whole, more meaningful to the Japanese than to others. Japanese textbooks devote most of their sections covering the treaty to laying out the details of the settlement and asserting that Japan's responsibilities, as articulated by the treaty, have been taken care of.

## Contending Views in Civil Society

As expected, there exist diverse and contending views of the Tokyo trials in the Asia-Pacific region. In particular, controversies have arisen over three interrelated issues: (1) whether the trials were fair or only victor's justice; (2) whether the Japanese emperor was responsible and, therefore, should have been removed from power or further punished; and (3) the extent of the United States' responsibility for historical injustices. Victims (Koreans and the Chinese) tend to endorse the view that the trials were just but that the emperor should have been held responsible. On the other hand, the Japanese tend to believe that the trials were largely victor's justice, a viewpoint with which Americans, in general, disagree. Besides such expected cross-national variation and contrary to conventional wisdom, we also find important diversity in views within each nation, even in China, from our interviews.

Most of our Chinese and Korean interviewees regard the trials as largely fair and just. Su Zhiliang, a historian at a Shanghai research center, for instance, argues that "the trials were absolutely just. Had there not been a trial, the invaders might have invaded again in the future. So they had to be punished."⁴² The Nanjing Massacre Memorial Hall director, Li Zongyuan, agrees that "the trials were just because Japan had started an unjust war. The party with justice on its side has the right to try those without it. If it were not like this, the world would not be fair. Furthermore, it was not just one country but eleven countries conducting the trials. A lot of Japanese say that this was victors' justice, but I disagree with this view."⁴³

At the same time, many feel that the trials could and should have gone further. In their views, the U.S.-led tribunal, because of ignorance, did not pay proper attention to crimes committed against Asian victims or did not go far enough for geopolitical or practical reasons. Chung Hyun Baek of Korea points out that "crimes the Japanese committed in Asia were not dealt with sufficiently because of lack of research [reliable statistics, data, or documents that could serve as evidence of such crimes]."⁴⁴ Bu Ping of China also contends that "in order to resist the USSR, the U.S. did not try many of those who should have been tried, including the emperor. Second, they did not try anyone for violating international conventions, for the use of chemical and biological weapons. Third, no one was tried for crimes against the ordinary people, forced laborers, comfort women, etcetera."⁴⁵ In novelist Shi Zhongshan's view, "the trials were of no use in giving Japan or its people any kind of warning or teaching them a lesson. Even though many years have passed since the war, Japan has never apologized to any of the countries it invaded."⁴⁶ Song Qiang goes further in criticizing the lenient nature of the trials: "Our leniency didn't get us any recompense. In fact, I know that many [Japanese] soldiers went home and established veterans' groups and all kinds of organizations which espoused the same views they had before—that the war was right."⁴⁷

However, dissenting views exist among the Chinese. Referring to the Indian Justice Pal, for instance, Li Datong observes that "the countries conducting the trials did their best to provide fair conditions, but ultimately it could only be victor's justice."⁴⁸ Wang Xiaodong, a popular blogger, goes further, saying, "The victors have never been tried. The U.S. was the victor. From a historical perspective, there is no justice or injustice, only victors and vanquished. If we want to talk about war crimes, of course the victors also committed crimes against humanity, but it's impossible to try the victors. There is no court for that. From a Chinese perspective, if we are speaking of the word 'justice,' the U.S. did not try a lot of those who, in China, had committed some of the worst crimes."⁴⁹ He laments that some of these people did very well in postwar Japan: "because [those who worked for Unit 731] gave the results of their experiments to the U.S., they not only avoided being tried but also got a lot of money from the U.S."⁵⁰

Americans largely believe that the trials were fair. John Dower, while acknowledging that the proceedings in many ways represented an instance of victor's justice, argues that they were also very idealistic in many aspects. One idealistic aspect of the trials, he contends,

> was that by the end of the trial, there were twenty-five Japanese defendants. Each one was given a defense attorney. Many of them were American defense attorneys. And they were allowed to present their defense at the trial, and the defense actually spent more time presenting its case than the prosecution. These things take enormous time because of translation problems and everything, but one of the major purposes of those trials was to establish a historical record, and another was to establish a sample of fair trial. Whether it's fair or not we can argue about, but they did give these people the opportunity to present their cases at length.⁵¹

Kirk Saduski, too, feels that it was victor's justice, but with an emphasis on "justice": "I think the crimes were so extraordinary that extraordinary legal precedent—international legal precedent—had to be set. And it takes victors. Without a victor, you can't put people like Milošević on trial. That kind of justice, I think, can only be meted out by victors, and I do consider it justice."⁵²

Many Japanese believe that the trials were not fair and were only victor's justice. Some even say that the United States also should have been tried. As General Tamogami contends, "The U.S. would be guilty in terms of international law. But in the real world, the victor obviously isn't tried by the vanquished. Victor's justice."⁵³ Ito Takashi makes a similar point: "There should have been [a] war crimes tribunal of the U.S. There were many badly flawed trials, just retribution. Go see what MacArthur said to the Senate on this subject. He said that Japan was acting in self-defense. And he's the one who did this trial. A-classes were tried for crimes of peace, not crimes against humanity. But the soldiers were all B and C, especially those who came from Korea. They were the ones, in many cases, who were most violent."⁵⁴ Author and historian Hosaka Masayasu makes his point more bluntly: "In some basic way, the war crimes tribunal was really MacArthur's trial. He gave the order, and for him the question was how he was going to go about controlling Japan, and so he thought about what would and wouldn't work, the merits and demerits of everything, and this was at the base."55 In fact, several of our Japanese interviewees shared such a view.

On the other hand, other Japanese regard the trials largely as "fair" and "just" and even say that they were necessary because Japan would never have tried its own people. The filmmaker Takahata Isao, for instance, argues, "You cannot just say it was victor's justice and ignore it. Although it was victor's justice, and clearly there was a lot that was not fair, still, there are aspects that were, and, therefore, I think that as Japanese we cannot just discard it, saying it was victor's justice, particularly because the Japanese never put their own on trial."56 Wakamiya Yoshibumi of the liberal *Asahi Shimbun* agrees that "of course it was a victor's trial, and of course not everything was fair. But in war, it always follows *that* path. What if Japan had won, after all? Within that general rubric, I think the trials were fairly rational overall; the conclusions did not stray very far from the conventional wisdom. If you look at the conclusions the *Yomiuri* came to, [they are] not really very different from the Tokyo trials themselves. Some people think Japan should have done trials of their own, but in reality that's a very difficult thing."57

Some Japanese go further, however, saying that the trials were insufficient. Watanabe Tsuneo states, "I actually think the war crimes tribunal didn't go far enough. Many more should have been penalized. Such atrocities were committed, and they were only sentenced to some tens of years, and then the occupation ended, and they were released and got out and became high politicians. . . . I think they should have been exiled and that many more should have come under scrutiny."58 Takagi Kenichi agrees, comparing the Tokyo and Nuremberg trials and suggesting that Class B and C criminals should have been tried. In his view,

> The war crimes tribunal was not at all just. The biggest difference between Nuremberg and Tokyo was that in Japan, only the leaders and military were tried. In Germany, it was scholars, it was companies, it was the private sector, too. That is because in Japan all that was really put on trial was the aggressive war [and] crimes against peace, whereas Germany tried C more than A, which is to say the crimes against humanity more than the conspiracy to wage war. Japan's trials did not do C at all. It did a little bit of B with respect to the prisoners, but they didn't deal with the crimes against humanity at all. That's a big lack in those trials. I think that's because America and England didn't even have in their line of sight the Asian victims at all. So this was not justice at all.59

Thus, with regard to the fairness of the Tokyo trials, there is no consensus. However, contrary to conventional wisdom, many Japanese believe that the trials were largely fair and even that they should have gone further. There exists a similar diversity regarding the question of whether the Japanese emperor should have been tried.

Few would argue that the Japanese emperor was entirely innocent. However, people disagree about the extent of his war involvement or responsibility and even more so with regard to the legacy of not trying him at the Tokyo trials. Some contend that the emperor should have been held responsible, while others believe that keeping the emperor system intact was the right decision from a geopolitical perspective, because his presence as a symbolic figure was needed in rebuilding Japan in the U.S.-occupied postwar era. As another legacy, others point to the development of historical amnesia among the Japanese that continues even today.

Many of our Chinese and Korean interviewees say that the emperor should have been tried and held responsible, though they remain vague about what kind of punishment he really deserved. Song Qiang of China says that while the emperor's role in governing the country was minimal, "some degree of punishment should have been imposed on him as a symbol [of the Japanese state]."[60] Yang Tianshi of the Chinese Academy of Social Sciences concurs: "What kind of punishment the emperor should have received is debatable, but he should not have been able to avoid responsibility for having started the war."[61] Park Won-soon of Korea concurs: "We cannot exactly compare him with Hitler, but it is clear that he was the most responsible person in the war."[62]

However, there is disagreement even among Korean and Chinese interviewees. Lee Hong Koo of Korea, for instance, believes that "since nearly all Japanese people did not feel that the emperor himself was responsible in making all these decisions, [the attempts to demonize him] wouldn't have worked." In his opinion, "it was [the] right decision to keep the emperor in place because every nation, particularly large countries—and Japan is a large country—has its own identity. Only when you could preserve that identity one way or another [would] the country's political system and all the acts as a nation gain sufficient legitimacy."[63] Similarly, Yi Won Bok of Korea says, "The emperor was the greatest symbol of their national identity. In Chinese history, there were seventy-three dynasties. In Japan, there has been only one. Therefore, the emperor had to be there in Japan because he was the Japanese national identity. MacArthur made the right decision. He knew the Japanese."[64]

Yet some Japanese, like Takahata Isao, are more ambivalent: "[The] Japanese never put their own [people] on trial. Not just the emperor but any of them at all, any of the people who had power. Japan never conducted trials of its own, so all that is left is the Tokyo War Crimes Tribunal. I suppose on some fundamental level the emperor should have been tried, but it's hard to give a clear answer. Because whatever his own opinions or acts were, it's so clear he was manipulated and maneuvered, and there were things he couldn't help but do. So maybe he should have stepped down, but I can't really say."[65] Likewise, Hosaka Masayasu says, "When you use the term 'war responsibility,' it's too ambiguous, and the leftists always used it that way and never tried to explore it in a concrete way. I can say the emperor felt his responsibility. He felt responsible for starting the war. He didn't feel legally or historically or politically responsible. But he felt responsible as a human and on behalf of his people."[66]

American views are somewhat divided on this issue. John Dower does not downplay the role of the emperor and argues that, from a historian's point of view, it is "correct to see the emperor as one of the major political actors of the period. That is to say, you have to understand that his role was profoundly important—[it was] a symbolic role, and he was a political actor at that time."[67] Kirk Saduski also thinks that although it was the military—and not the emperor—that had an extraordinary amount of influence on, if not control of, politics, the emperor was certainly in agreement with the decisions of the military and "did nothing to reverse what the military had in mind."[68] Many others believe that the emperor was merely a figurehead and was minimally involved in the decision to go to war. Lester Tenney argues, "It was the military and the political powerhouse that involved Tojo and his entourage, and that's strictly what it was. And I think the emperor was just a figurehead who didn't even know what was going on."[69] Mark Peattie also expresses some doubt: "I won't argue that the emperor was involved. But was he like George W. Bush when he decided to go to war? No, I don't think so."[70]

## The United States' Role and Responsibility

Few would dispute that the United States has played a most important role in postwar settlements with Japan. However, there is considerable disagreement about the extent of U.S. responsibility in the incomplete nature of postwar settlements. As noted above, some believe that the U.S. did not go far enough in bringing justice to Japanese aggression for geopolitical reasons and that the insufficiencies of the trials have led to historical amnesia among the Japanese.

Several of our interviewees feel that U.S. handling of postwar settlements, including the question of the emperor's responsibility, was right from a geopolitical perspective, as it helped to reconstruct postwar Japan and strengthen U.S.-Japan ties. Chung Hyun Baek of Korea believes that the United States' actions were not sufficient in addressing Japanese aggression but understandable given geopolitical situations at the time: "I think the U.S. policy in postwar Japan or Asia was done in a very pragmatic way. We cannot probably ask the U.S. to deal with this process more morally. Americans chose practical approaches to deal with war crimes."[71] Rhee Yong Hoon of Korea likewise says that "the emperor has war responsibilities. But he was treated in a diplomatic manner. It was politically served. If the U.S. had executed the emperor, the Japanese people would have strongly resisted."[72] Togo Kazuhiko of Japan argues that it was wise to keep the emperor in power and believes that this increased Japanese trust of the U.S. In his view, the "best aspect of the war crimes tribunal was its successful and careful avoidance of the emperor's responsibility, as the U.S. had promised, however vaguely, on August 14. The motives might have been pragmatic, but the result was that they observed their commitment. This led to the credibility and trust underlying the last sixty-five years. Had the U.S. acted differently, it would have led to deep psychological distrust."[73] Many Koreans feel that they were given short shrift by the San Francisco Peace Treaty and that many issues relevant to Koreans were not settled fairly or adequately. Yang Mi Kang, for example, suggests that because it was not resolved by the San Francisco Peace Treaty, the Dokdo/Takeshima controversy will perennially be used by political leaders as a diplomatic bargaining chip.[74] Won Yu Chol likewise expresses disappointment that the major powers thought neither to allow Korean representation nor to clarify pressing questions of territorial claims.[75]

However, when it comes to the question of historical justice and reconciliation, our interviewees tend to be more critical of the U.S. decision. While Chung acknowledges that the United States made the "practical choice" to govern postwar Japan, she laments that "because of these practical solutions, Japanese society could not develop in a more progressive or reasonable way."[76] Referring to Unit 731, the bacteriological warfare unit that conducted experiments on Chinese people, Wang Xiaodong, a Chinese writer, charges that "they were allowed to escape punishment by giving secrets to the U.S., though they committed crimes far worse than those for which others were sentenced to hang."[77] As a result, some interviewees point out, Japan was not taught a proper lesson but rather was left in a position to promote the view that the war was right.

The double nature of the United States' role and responsibility is best captured by Chinese civic activist Tong Zeng. He concurs that it was a wise decision, geopolitically, not to try the emperor when he says that "at the time, the U.S.—MacArthur—realized that if they tried the emperor as a war criminal, it might cause more trouble for them. They didn't want chaos to erupt in Japan or to lose any more of their own people. So perhaps this is why they let it go, let the emperor off the hook." At the same time, he adds, this led to the notion among Japanese that "if the emperor is not guilty, we are not guilty."[78]

Americans generally seem to believe that not trying the emperor was the right decision but that not allowing him to testify or forcing him to abdicate was the wrong decision. Lester Tenney says, "I think they did it correctly because, by doing that, they at least got the Japanese people to be willing to consent to certain things. I think had they taken the emperor to task, which would have been to try him as a war criminal, that that could have caused a complete uprising of the Japanese people. They were so involved and so indoctrinated to the emperor that it would have just been an uprising that could have taken another ten years to resolve. So in that respect, I think that [MacArthur] did the right thing. In the total picture, [he] did the right thing." But Tenney goes on to say, "Not trying him was right. Not having him testify was wrong. I think that the United States should've gotten some firsthand information from the emperor about what happened. So I think not having him testify was wrong. That wouldn't have been a disgrace at all."[79] Mark Peattie believed that the United States should have compelled the abdication of the emperor and put his son on the throne,[80] while Barton Bernstein suggests that not trying the emperor was "morally wrong but politically astute."[81]

As shown above, the United States played a highly important role in postwar settlements; therefore, it is imperative to raise the question of the

United States' responsibility and role in dealing with the unfortunate past in Northeast Asia.

There has been some debate in U.S. academic and policy-making circles about the role that the United States might play in helping to resolve historical disputes and achieve reconciliation in Northeast Asia. A predominant view has been that these issues are primarily matters for Asians or better left to historians. Some fear that if the United States were to take a specific position, it could be pulled into the Sino-Japanese rivalry or forced to take sides between its key allies in the region (namely, Japan and South Korea).[82] In this vein, the U.S. State Department has consistently taken the position that the San Francisco Peace Treaty protected Japan from demands for compensation from victim nations. The contrary view contends that the United States can hardly afford to stand outside these disputes, particularly when it was a key player in their formation. Gil Rozman, for instance, urges the United States to "explicitly challenge revived nationalist interpretations in Japan while also trying to calm historical grievances in South Korea and China." In his view, "benign neglect of Japanese nationalism threatens to unravel the spirit of reconciliation in East Asia."[83]

Yet despite its proclaimed neutrality, the record shows that the U.S. government has not acted always in a neutral manner. When former forced laborers filed claims against Japan, for example, the United States took a position that was very different from the one that it had taken in the German case. The U.S. government pressed hard to force the reluctant German government and corporations to admit their responsibility for wartime atrocities, make a public apology to the victims, and provide compensation. Toward the Japanese government, however, the U.S. position has been precisely the opposite, protecting it against claims at every step, even before the San Francisco Peace Treaty. The 1951 treaty, once again, became the legal basis for the argument that Japan has no more responsibility to fulfill toward foreign forced laborers.[84]

Despite the policy stance adopted by the U.S. executive branch, the U.S. House of Representatives has taken up Asian history issues more proactively by introducing various bills on Japan's responsibility for wartime comfort women. For instance, in April 2006, two members of the U.S. Congress, Representatives Lane Evans (D-Illinois) and Chris Smith (R-New Jersey), introduced a nonbinding resolution that called on the government of Japan to "formally acknowledge and accept responsibility for its sexual enslavement of young women" during the 1930s and 1940s. Although previous efforts had failed, as discussed in chapter 1, the House in 2007 passed a resolution, House Resolution 121, criticizing the Japanese handling of the comfort-women issue and urging the country to adequately address it.[85]

As many have observed, any reexamination of the U.S. "national myth" with respect to wartime atrocities is likely to provoke controversy and spirited rebuttals in the United States. Understandably, there are objections to any efforts that could open this Pandora's box, as it could become easily and overly politicized. Still, Washington must not overlook the issues at hand and should reconsider its hands-off posture to take a more proactive role. The United States not only has a responsibility for helping to resolve the disputes but also has a clear interest in ensuring that the peace and prosperity of a region so vital to its future is not undermined by controversies rooted in the past. In other words, resolving the history issue is not simply a matter of helping Asians achieve overdue reconciliation; it is also important, if not imperative, for U.S. alliance relations and strategic considerations in the region.

How, then, can the United States involve itself in facilitating historical reconciliation in the region? Some experts advocate an active U.S. intervention in Asian history issues that presses Japan to confront its unfortunate past. For instance, G. John Ikenberry argues that Japan's history problem is an American problem, and, therefore, "Washington should encourage Japan to pursue [a] German path, tying 'normalization' to redoubled commitments to regional security cooperation."[86] It is a noble aim but not an effective strategy. It would not be convincing in the eyes of the Japanese, whose own victim consciousness vis-à-vis the United States requires "true closure with the U.S. over World War II" first.[87] Not surprisingly, the Abe government in Japan reacted negatively to the U.S. Congress's passage of a resolution on the issue of comfort women. In addition, many in the region, especially in Korea, want the United States to take a clear position on contested historical and territorial issues. However, that does not appear to be a sensible approach either, since—as skeptics have noted—the United States would necessarily have to take sides between two vital allies. For example, U.S. Secretary of State Hillary Clinton's reported correction that the term "enforced sex slaves" should be employed instead of "comfort women" pleased Koreans but left many Japanese unhappy.[88]

Instead, we propose a *self-critical, self-reflective approach* on the part of the United States. That is, the United States needs, first and foremost, to acknowledge its own past wrongdoings in the region and any responsibility that it holds in the handling or mishandling of history issues. For instance, it could recognize the sufferings of Japanese victims of the atomic bombing and express regret for having paid scant attention to Asian issues during the tribunal. This acknowledgment would help to endow the United States with moral power and establish a solid basis for encouraging Japan to address the history question with its Asian neighbors. In doing so, however, the United States must make it clear that such an expression is not meant to vindicate Japan's victim identity or support the Japanese rightist view that assigns blame to the United States for Japanese imperialism and human suffering during the Pacific War. It also must be clear that Japan would be expected to follow suit with its Asian neighbors. The United States should not be seen as siding with Japan over China or Korea regarding historical disputes.

In addition, the United States could help efforts to reinterpret Article 14 of the San Francisco Peace Treaty in order to allow victims to file claims against the Japanese government and corporations, as was done with Germany. Generally, cases brought by individual victims of Japanese war crimes in U.S. courts have been dismissed on the grounds that they would have uncertain but predictably negative consequences for healthy bilateral and economic relations. Robert Bork, former solicitor general and defeated nominee for the U.S. Supreme Court, asserts that individual tort cases filed against governments would have a "certain potential to interfere with United States foreign policy."[89] However, the general U.S. aversion to consideration of such cases begs the question of the difference between the Japanese and German cases with regard to the American role in reparation and reconciliation. The U.S. government played a facilitating role in the negotiations between Nazi slave-labor victims and the German government and companies, which led to the creation of the German Fund for the Future.[90] In contrast, the U.S. government, in close consultation with the State Department, filed a statement of interest in the cases of litigation against the Japanese government and companies favoring the Japanese government.[91] In other words, the U.S. government took a largely *political* approach toward the German case, encouraging both parties in the litigation to make settlements, whereas it took a strictly *legalistic* approach toward the Japanese case by denying the rights for individual claims with reference to the San Francisco Peace Treaty.[92]

The U.S. government needs to consider adopting a more political approach toward the Japanese case, as in the German case. Of course, the momentum for such an initiative must come from Japan and the Japanese parliament, as the German initiative did in Germany, but the process can be encouraged and aided by the United States. Unlike in the case of Japan, the U.S. government did not actively oppose suits filed in U.S. courts against German firms seeking compensation. In fact, it was a largely political decision on the part of the U.S. government when it granted Japan a waiver of all reparations claims in the San Francisco Peace Treaty. As John Dower asserts, "We wanted Japan on our side because China was now seen as an enemy. And this meant not burdening Japan with reparations (any more than necessary), not burdening Japan with future claims. That is the treaty of 1951. . . . And it also meant the Americans set about whitewashing and sanitizing Japan's war responsibility and war crimes."[93] In this context, one can legitimately question the validity of the strictly legalistic interpretation of a treaty borne out of political considerations. Here, the United States must show political leadership in encouraging Japan to be more receptive to reparations issues; such leadership could spark a new process of reconciliation in the region.

The United States is not an outsider free of responsibility for the history problem, especially with regard to the history of the Pacific War and postwar settlements. The United States has played a crucial role in shaping the contours of this region for much of the second half of the twentieth century and still has a significant stake. It is time for Americans to take seriously the issues of historical injustice and responsibility in Northeast Asia.

PART FOUR

*Conclusion*

ELEVEN

# Toward Historical Reconciliation in the Asia-Pacific

Like many other cases around the world, reconciliation in Northeast Asia first occurred between governments. With the exception of North Korea, Japan normalized diplomatic relations with all of the countries it had once invaded or colonized and became one of the strongest allies of its former enemy the United States. Nevertheless, many issues from the unfortunate past were left unresolved, and they continue to shape the countries' relations with one another. Japan paid no reparations to its former colonies—though it gave grants and aid to South Korea for normalizing relations and provided major economic assistance to the People's Republic of China—and many Japanese feel uneasy about the lack of true closure with the United States over the Asia-Pacific War. As discussed earlier, China and Korea were not included in the San Francisco Peace Treaty that settled the Asia-Pacific War, but their legal claims for compensation are still rejected on the basis of the treaty. Historical issues such as war responsibility, disputed territories, and Japan's colonial rule and atrocities were largely overlooked during the Cold War years. Accordingly, to use David Croker's term, reconciliation in the region has been "thin."[1]

Since the early 1980s, however, the region has no longer been able to ignore the history question, and wounds inflicted in times of colonialism and war have resurfaced to become highly contentious diplomatic matters. Sino-Japanese relations have been conflict-ridden, due in no small measure to both countries' failure to reconcile their differing views of the past. Similarly, friction between Japan and South Korea about Japan's role as colonizer has constrained their bilateral relationship. China, Japan, and South Korea are constantly involved in territorial disputes in one way or another, and these disputes are closely related to history issues. South Korea and China have sparred over the status of the ancient kingdom of Koguryo, and even the United States has been subject to controversy over its involvement in events in Northeast Asian history.

Northeast Asians have recognized the weight of the burden of history in their relations. In a 2014 survey jointly conducted by *China Daily* and Japan's Genron NPO, both the Chinese and Japanese identified resolving the territorial issue as the biggest barrier to improving their bilateral relations, at 64.8 percent and 58.6 percent of respondents, respectively.[2] Similarly, a joint survey by the *Asahi Shimbun* and the *Dong-A Ilbo* from December 2011 shows that 88 percent of Korean respondents and 90 percent of Chinese respondents felt that "past issues" with Japan, such as colonialism and war, had not been resolved.[3] In a more recent survey, conducted by the same media groups in 2015, 95 percent of Korean respondents and 42 percent of Japanese respondents held the view that "past issues" between the two countries had not been resolved.[4] These results clearly show that attitudes toward history and territorial issues have not much changed over time and remain central to improving relations among Northeast Asian nations. Likewise, a joint public-opinion poll conducted by Korea's East Asia Institute (EAI) and Japan's Genron NPO in 2014 reveals that 70.9 percent of Korean respondents and 54.4 percent of Japanese respondents viewed the other country unfavorably, for reasons mostly to do with history: over 76.8 percent of South Korean respondents who held an unfavorable view of Japan cited "inadequate repentance over the history of invasion" or "continuing conflicts on the issue of Dokdo," and over 20 percent cited "unfavorable words and actions by Japanese politicians." In comparison, 73.9 percent of Japanese respondents who held an unfavorable view of Korea pointed to "criticism of Japan over historical issues" as their primary reason for this attitude.[5] Another survey conducted in 2014 by Gallup Korea suggests that 96 percent of South Koreans hold the view that Japan has not apologized sincerely, and 86 percent felt that Abe's visit to Yasukuni Shrine was unacceptable.[6]

To be sure, these nations have employed various means, from apology to common history writing to litigation, to achieve reconciliation. However, they have reached clear limitations in solving the history problem, largely because of the existence of divided, contested historical memories in the

Asia-Pacific region.[7] Questions about what happened in the past touch on the most sensitive issues of national identity, the formation of historical memories, and the national myths that play a powerful role to this day. In addition, as the previous chapters show, imbalance in focus in the formation of colonial and wartime memory creates misperceptions of the other. As a result, involved nations are simultaneously bound together and separated by distinct, often contradictory, historical accounts and perceptions, hindering historical reconciliation. These are deeply embedded in the public consciousness and transmitted to succeeding generations, both formally, by education, and informally, through the arts, popular culture, museums, and mass media.

The road to historical reconciliation is a complex process involving multiple players and a protracted, long-term journey ridden with difficulties and challenges. There are many forces affecting the process of reconciliation, sometimes complementing and other times contradicting each other. In this context, it is worth reviewing past efforts for reconciliation and accessing the major forces affecting historical reconciliation in the Asia-Pacific region.

### Apology, Joint History, Litigation, and Civil Action

*Apology* diplomacy has been a major tactic in the reconciliation process. Since 1984, Japanese government officials have issued a number of direct apologies to China and Korea. Until the 1990s, the key terms used were "regret" or "remorse," which did not necessarily signify an apology; the word "apology" finally appeared in 1992, when Miyazawa Kiichi, meeting with Roh Tae-woo, stated, "I, as prime minister, would like to once again express heartfelt remorse and offer an apology to the people of your nation."[8] Despite Japan's repeated use of the term "apology" from that point on, its neighbors have continued to respond with skepticism. As Caroline Rose points out, Japan's efforts to "apologize" have not been backed by actions to "reinforce the apologies"; instead, they are often coupled with ambiguous wording and counterproductive statements and behavior on the part of the government.[9] In fact, throughout the 1990s, Japanese political elites vacillated between formal apologies and frequent statements glorifying their colonial rule.[10] Repeated statements by right-wing officials, such as Abe, denying war crimes—"there is no evidence that comfort women were coerced through violence or coercion by military or government authorities"[11]—aroused severe criticism.

A 2013 survey conducted by *Asia Today* and *Realmeter* in Korea reveals that 66.1 percent of respondents felt that Japan had not apologized to Korea about its past wrongdoings in an appropriate manner; 30.9 percent felt that Japan had apologized but that the apologies were lacking in sincerity; and only 1.6 percent felt that Japan had apologized sufficiently.[12] Furthermore, 91.6 percent of respondents felt that Japan must reapologize—in a sincere manner—for its role in regional history; this figure reveals the high dissatisfaction with the way Japan's apologies have been delivered. In sharp contrast, a 2013 survey jointly conducted by the *Seoul Shinmun* and the *Tokyo Shimbun* shows that 63.4 percent of Japanese respondents find Korea's continued demands for apology incomprehensible and react negatively with "apology fatigue,"[13] indicating a widening perception gap between the two peoples.

Along with Abe's attempt to revisit the Kono Statement and his recent visit to the Yasukuni Shrine, the outpouring of ultranationalist Japanese books, films, and magazines raising doubts about the veracity of their past aggression has led neighbors to question the sincerity of the Japanese apology.[14] People in Korea and China have gradually realized that the formal ritual of apology is but one element in the politics of remembrance with questionable utility as a means of furthering historical reconciliation. According to Alexis Dudden, politics surrounding state-issued apologies have largely negated the putative intent of apologizing and, if anything, have set Japan back in terms of actually reconciling with its neighbors. She sees the problem as "apology failure" (apologizing for the past as a means to capitalize on it in the future), rather than failure to apologize, and asserts that the general effect has only "perpetuated a disastrous policy failure."[15] Decades of this failure has created a deadlock in the East Asian reconciliation process that will not be broken until Japan addresses its identity mythmaking.

History education plays such a powerful role in the formation of collective memory and national identity that *collaborative history writing* has been another approach toward narrowing the gap in views. Frequent clashes over history textbooks in Northeast Asia demonstrate that history is not simply about the past. Government oversight makes textbooks a natural and legitimate subject for debate, and it is no coincidence that textbooks have become a nexus for tension in the region.[16] One approach has been to form official and unofficial committees to produce jointly written accounts of history.

The first official attempt to deal jointly with history textbooks occurred in October 2001, when Koizumi Junichiro and Kim Dae-jung established the Japan-ROK Joint History Research Committee, a state-sponsored effort toward placing a reconciled view of the past in a new regional history framework. The committee, while not entirely a failure, has yet to attain the success envisioned. Although it adopted the UNESCO model of writing a "parallel history" in May 2005, the two sides failed to come to a consensus on what should be incorporated into the textbooks, disagreeing over how to interpret Japan's colonial rule, including its role (or lack thereof) in Korea's modernization.[17] Following Koizumi's visits to the Yasukuni Shrine, the work of the joint committee was put on hold until October 2006, when Abe and Roh Moo-hyun relaunched its efforts. In April 2007, a new subgroup—in addition to existing groups studying ancient, medieval, and contemporary history—formed to study history textbooks to try to reduce the differences between the textbooks of the two nations. Another report was released in 2010 but still failed to reach a consensus on Japan's 1910–1945 colonial rule, notably on the recruitment of Korean laborers and comfort women, as well as on the drafting of Koreans into the Japanese military.[18]

Japan and China launched a similar effort as part of the thaw that followed the leadership transition from Koizumi to Abe. Modeled after the Japan-ROK format, the Joint History Research Committee agreed to conduct a joint study and produce an account of two thousand years of Sino-Japanese interaction by 2008. Not surprisingly, the Japanese wanted to focus on the postwar era, while the Chinese were more interested in taking inventory of the colonial and wartime periods.[19] Each side was to separately write its own version of bilateral history texts and exchange written comments on controversial issues. They agreed on a list of major historical events to be discussed, including the Nanjing Massacre and Japan's Twenty-One Demands.[20] The final report was made public in January 2010, after a one-and-a-half year delay,[21] though at Chinese insistence, the section on modern history after the formation of the People's Republic of China was not released to the public. The two sides did narrow differences on some issues, such as the characterization of Japan as an aggressor and on the nature of the Marco Polo Bridge Incident as an unplanned trigger for the war, but they could not reach an agreement about a number of controversial modern events, including the scale and nature of the 1937 Nanjing Massacre.[22]

Writing a shared history has offered important lessons for the nations involved. It is, for instance, almost impossible to arrive at a common rendition of events, particularly regarding the most controversial aspects of history. Northeast Asian governments have considerable influence in textbook production, which make textbook a nexus of tension in the region. The experience of the past two decades underlines how profoundly historical writing—especially the writing of history textbooks—is affected by nationalist politics. Thus, a shared regional history is politically infeasible.

Compensation for the victims of Japanese aggression has been another contentious issue between Japan and its neighbors. Most Koreans and Chinese believe that Japan has yet to compensate victims, while Japan has objected to such compensation on legal grounds. In seeking a settlement between the victims and those responsible for crimes against them, *litigation* has been adopted as a major tactic in redressing historical injustice. Unlike in the West, however, litigation's efficacy has proven to be very limited. Almost all lawsuits that Asian victims have filed in Japanese courts have been either thrown out or left unresolved, though courts have recognized the fact of victims' suffering.

Some have taken their plight to the United States in hopes of finding more sympathetic ears. The legal basis by which foreigners may file outside claims in U.S. courts is the two-century-old Alien Tort Claims Act of 1789 (ATCA). This statute provides a means for noncitizens to seek recourse in the United States for violations of standing international law and has been the legal hook utilized in recent decades by a variety of non-U.S. plaintiffs. Since comfort women had anticipated little, if any, chance of success in Japanese courts, they saw the ATCA as a window of opportunity. However, the U.S. court ruled that the Japanese government did indeed enjoy sovereign immunity from such claims, as set forth in the San Francisco Peace Treaty, and that the legal interpretation of peace treaties must remain at a "government-to-government level."[23] Korean forced laborers' unsuccessful litigation struggle using California Senate Bill 1245 by Tom Hayden between 1999 and 2004 further proved the limits of the litigation tactic.

To further complicate matters, in 2012 the South Korean Supreme Court ruled in favor of eleven South Koreans who demanded that Japanese firms pay them for forced labor during Japan's colonial rule of Korea, marking the first legal victory of South Korean forced laborers. The court repealed lower court decisions that ruled against South Koreans seeking unpaid wages and financial redress from Mitsubishi Heavy Industries Ltd. and Nippon Steel Corp. for forced labor from 1941 to 1945, paving the way for South Korean forced laborers to seek compensation for their work nearly seven decades after Korea gained independence from Japan.[24] Japan's response remains to be seen, but the two involved companies have not yet taken any measures to comply with the ruling.

Finally, there have been increased *social and cultural exchanges* as part of larger efforts to redress historical injustice. The official opening of cultural exchange between Korea and Japan in 1998, their cohosting of the 2002 World Cup, and the pop-culture industry boom between them, which even resulted in the coining of the term *Hallyu* ("Korean Wave"), have all helped ease deep-seated antagonism, mistrust, and fear. High-school history teachers and students of both countries are convening at joint summer camps every year to learn more about Japanese and Korean history. More and more Koreans come to study in China and Japan, while China has been attracting an increasing number of Japanese and Korean tourists. Such multi-level social and cultural interactions across borders will be useful resources in achieving the ultimate grace of forgiveness, liberation from victim and aggressor identities, and the development of a new regional identity based on a vision of peaceful coexistence—but this, of course, will be a gradual process.

Bilateral, state-oriented approaches to the history issue have now expanded to multifaceted, transnational activism in which government, civil society, academia, and the media have all become involved. Several Asian NGOs have collaborated to address the issue of comfort women by jointly sponsoring events such as the Women's International War Crimes Tribunal of December 2000. This was preceded by the groundbreaking creation of the Asian Women's Fund—the first time Japan sought to confront its past through a public-private collaboration.[25] A sort of ripple effect took place as civil society in both Korea and Japan enlisted several NGOs to the cause of confronting the two states' divided conceptions of their shared history. In November 2004, a group of Korean and Japanese scholars formed the Hanil Yondae 21 (Korea-Japan Solidarity 21) with an aim to promote deep introspection and build regional solidarity between the two nations for future generations. Research centers in Korea, Japan, and China often hold joint workshops and conferences addressing historical and territorial issues. All these efforts reflect the hopes of a growing civil society that East Asia can confront its future as a regional collaborative entity, rather than as a region wracked by division and conflicting interpretations of history.

## What Affects Historical Reconciliation?

Historical reconciliation takes place within multiple frameworks.[26] Within the framework of domestic politics, it can be greatly affected by *democratization*. Some see hope for reconciliation in the growing forces of *regional integration* and *globalization*. But perhaps the most potent force in shaping reconciliation remains that of *nationalism*, which is persistent, if not pernicious, in its influence.

According to conventional wisdom, "thick" reconciliation is possible only in a democratic context. Authoritarian government tends to sanction a particular view of history and repress any dissenting opinions within its own society. In addition, nongovernmental dialogue—crucial for forging ties and building trust among peoples—in a country lacking any vibrant civil society can have little real, lasting impact. Democratic societies also allow for greater introspection on past internal injustices. The freedom to criticize one's government and a willingness to subject one's own past record to the same standard of moral judgment that one applies to the history of other nations are crucial elements in overcoming a historical bias against a foreign adversary.

There is no doubt that democratization has opened the door to the historical redress movement in Northeast Asia. South Koreans have brought issues of historical injustice, such as comfort women and forced labor, to the public by questioning the ways in which their authoritarian regimes handled the history question. By examining the thorny question of Korean collaboration with Japanese colonizers, South Koreans have also begun to consider to what extent they are responsible for such injustices. Through these self-critical and reflective processes, Koreans came to realize that they were not merely victims; they had also been perpetrators. Apart from internal suppression of civilians by the South Korean dictatorial governments, for instance, they acknowledged that Korean troops had committed the same kind of atrocities against innocent Vietnamese that Americans were accused of carrying out against Koreans during the Korean War. With democratization, issues of historical injustice are no longer monopolized by the government. Instead, civil society and transnational NGO groups have become increasingly involved in issues of historical injustice and reconciliation.

However, the proposition of "democratic reconciliation" may not have much relevance to relations between Japan and China, let alone Japan and North Korea, except that one must wait until these communist regimes become democratic. While there are "history activists" in China, they are largely sanctioned by the government. As Kawashima Shin notes, "So-called reconciliation is something that basically can be achieved between democratic countries. So it is more possible to engage in dialogue between Japan and South Korea and Japan and Taiwan than between Japan and China."[27]

Still, China is undergoing an important transformation in its state-societal relations, which opens up both opportunities and risks. Even if the regime has a long way to go before becoming a democracy, it has already had to deal with "voices of the people" in ways unheard of since 1949. Public opinion is becoming more important, and expressions of nationalism are becoming increasingly vocal and frequent in China. With regard to the history question, history activists have been playing a key role in leading efforts to demand compensation from Japan and mobilizing Chinese public opinion on issues related to Japan. Recently, the Internet and other social media have also begun to play a critical role in shaping people's thoughts and behaviors, and they have often challenged the official view of historical reality. In the spring of 2005, the Internet, including instant-messaging services, was used in organizing groups of demonstrators to take part in a series of anti-Japanese protests.

Democratization is no panacea, however. It is not easy in a democracy, especially one that has a dark past to settle, to push for redress without opposition. Interpretations of the past are unavoidably political, producing divided memories, and there is a strong temptation to politicize the process of reconciliation for a current ideological purpose. In South Korea, the progressive administrations of Kim Dae-jung and Roh Moo-hyun brought up the issue of collaboration with Japanese colonizers, even publishing the list of Korean collaborators, but were accused of using the "history card" for narrow partisan interests, provoking intense contention between conservative and progressive forces. This episode illustrates that democracy does not necessarily make reconciliation easier. On the contrary, the opposite can be true, making reconciliation a messier process. The advent of democracy in China, which may not be far off, is likely to complicate the situation.

Issues of historical memories and reconciliation have become a global phenomenon. In the past, realpolitik—the belief that realism or interests rather than ideology or ethics should drive politics—was the guiding principle of international relations. But beginning with the end of World War II and accelerating since the end of the Cold War, morality, justice, and human rights have gained more attention in international diplomacy. The post–Cold War era witnessed renewed global attention to historical injustice (especially in the former Soviet empire) and a massive surge of public and scholarly interest in coming to terms with the past as a more universalized topic. Today the United Nations and other transnational nongovernmental organizations are actively involved in addressing human-rights issues in many parts of the world, and we have seen a global trend toward a better appreciation of human-rights issues.[28]

Global regimes empower and embolden local social movements in order to increase pressure on target governments from below, while local activists appeal to international forums for help from international activists to influence governments from above.[29] With the intensification of domestic social movements, international pressure from neighboring countries, and global concern for human rights, arguments in favor of apologies and compensation to victims have gained traction in recent years. National discourse has been transformed into a universal discourse of human rights and reparation for past wrongdoings. Globalization thus facilitates collaboration among victims, experts, activists, and NGOs in different parts of the world.

Growing global attention to ethnic and national identity, human rights, and historical injustice has certainly contributed to the rise of the "history question" in Northeast Asia. For the Northeast Asian region, globalization has opened up more space for reckoning with the past. It has broadened and diversified views and approaches to the issue of historical injustice. In the past, for instance, Koreans looked at the issue of comfort women primarily from a nationalist standpoint. More recently, there has been a growing tendency to approach it from a more scholarly feminist or human-rights perspective.

Globalization has also facilitated collaboration among victims, experts, activists, and NGOs in the Asia-Pacific region. Chinese groups have worked with U.S.-based organizations to engage in debates on the Nanjing

Massacre, and Korean American community activists helped Korean victims' lawsuits against the Japanese government in a U.S. court. A strong advocacy network has emerged to support the efforts on the comfort-women issue in Asia and the United States, lobbying UN human-rights organizations and building an international coalition to raise the profile of the issue. As South Korean activist Yang Mi Kang notes, the relative success of the comfort-women movement can be attributed to its linkage to the global gender movement.[30]

Thus, with the rise of cross-cultural awareness, people's perspectives have broadened to recognize the arguments and perspectives of the other side. There obviously exist considerable differences in the way each side within the involved countries perceives the issue of conflict. However, with an invigorated exchange of information and opinions among the citizens of these countries, there has been a growing recognition that there need to be some changes in how each side regards the more contentious aspects of their shared history.

Regionalization is another important process that has shaped relations among nations in Northeast Asia. European integration has been attributed to the success that Western Europe has had in reconciling with its history. Though still lagging behind Europe, a similar regional dynamic, especially in the realms of economics, culture, and society, is also developing in Northeast Asia, with many implications for historical reconciliation in the region.

First, there has been tremendous growth in economic interdependence in the region. China has replaced the United States as the largest trading partner of Japan and South Korea, and there are discussions about signing free-trade agreements among the three Northeast Asian nations. Growing economic interdependence increases intersocietal interaction. Closer economic ties necessarily increase flows of people, products, and ideas—even if they are for purely business-related activities—across the border, which will no doubt increase societal interactions and enhance understandings of the society, culture, and identity of other nations.

Second, cultural interpenetration has become a growing trend within Northeast Asia. The phenomenal success of Korean pop culture is particularly noteworthy. It has produced favorable impressions of Korea among Japanese and Chinese, and there is some hope that cultural exchanges will facilitate reconciliation and cooperation in the Northeast Asian region.

Although its long-term implications for reconciliation remain to be seen, there is evidence that pop-culture genres such as TV dramas, films, and music are having a "softening" effect on once-antagonistic relations among Northeast Asian nations.

Finally, regional interactions have promoted transnational linkages among NGOs in addressing the issue of historical injustice. As noted above, Asian NGOs have worked together to address controversial historical issues. There are also educational exchanges and dialogue among youth. Japanese students have visited places like the House of Sharing (a shelter for former comfort women and a museum) and met with surviving comfort women. Korean students have, likewise, visited the Hiroshima Peace Memorial Park. As Yang Mi Kang, who has led such educational exchanges, notes, these "on-the-spot discussion meetings had an eye-opening and consciousness-raising impact on the students."[31] Even the South Korean Red Cross worked with the Japanese Diet in bringing back Koreans from Sakhalin who had been taken there during the war years.

To be sure, increased contact between societies does not in itself lead to better mutual understanding. At times, the opposite can be true. The popularity of Korean cultural products has led to the emergence of *Kenkanryu* ("Hating 'the Korean Wave'") in Japanese manga and magazines, spreading through the Internet,[32] and Chinese and Japanese tourists to Korea have sometimes become a source of tension among locals. Still, increased economic, social, and cultural interactions are expected to create a political environment conducive to achieving historical reconciliation.

Despite many encouraging signs, we should be cautious about unwarranted optimism regarding globalization and regional integration. We see the continuing power of identity politics in the nations of Northeast Asia, and recent memory transformation shows nationalistic tendencies in all three countries. Certainly, Northeast Asian nations have been democratizing and promoting globalization since the 1990s, but neither democratization nor globalization has weakened the power of nationalism in the region. If anything, globalization and regional interdependence may produce a crisis of national identity and thus strengthen nationalist sentiment in some quarters.

In Korea, nationalism has long guided its approach to the issue of historical injustice. Nationalism has produced master narratives of colonial history and offered a dominant framework for dealing with historical injustices.[33] It forces issues to be framed in binary opposition—victims versus aggressors—and allows little gray area, making it difficult to formulate a shared view of historical injustice. Ironically, the nationalism that gave rise to historical injustice in the first place continues to inform victims' approaches to reckoning with past wrongs.

In Japan, uncertainties and anxieties created by the post–Cold War security environment and a decade of economic stagnation provided fertile ground for nationalist politics. Nationalist scholars are making headway in producing textbooks to make Japanese proud of themselves, and nationalism is a prevailing theme in the military history museum attached to the Yasukuni Shrine, which Prime Ministers Koizumi and Abe visited during their tenures despite outcries from neighbor nations and the concerns of many Japanese. The restoration of such symbols as the flag and the national anthem are part of Japan's quest to become a "normal nation." If there is any difference between Korea and Japan, it is that the left in Korea—as opposed to the right in Japan—is at the forefront of nationalist politics of the history question.

In China, too, political leaders promote nationalism (or patriotism, in their words) to bolster social and political cohesion. Beijing is in need of a new unifying force to mobilize the nation in the face of the rapid (and disruptive) processes of socioeconomic modernization. Nationalism is the force behind China's territorial disputes with Japan and Southeast Asian neighbors as well in straits relations.

Thus, despite increased intra-Asian trade, cultural exchange, and talks about East Asian community, Korea, Japan, and China all still find politics of national identity appealing. After all, nationalism not only is about ideology but also thrives on narrowly defined national interests. Disputed territories serve as symbols of national sovereignty that cannot be compromised. The mutual suspicion of Japan and China over the disputed Senkaku/Diaoyu Islands and other territorial waters and the escalation of Japanese-Korean tensions over Dokdo/Takeshima are but two potent reminders.

History education reinforces nationalist sentiments in Northeast Asia. In both Japan and South Korea, the ministry of education requires that all textbooks undergo a strict screening process, and in China, the government plays an even stronger role in history textbook writings. In all three countries, nationalism is the guiding principle of official historical narratives, as they are each focused on a single historical memory that stresses their struggles with outside aggression. Because history textbooks affect national identity, the politics of nationalism invariably influence their writing, which, in turn, promotes nationalist sentiments in the new generation.

Thus, the key challenge facing Northeast Asia is how to tame the power of nationalism while continuing to promote vibrant civil society, which requires global thinking as well as regional interaction. Also, while some expect that generational change and increasing people-to-people exchanges can heal wounds from the past, the picture seems mixed. In China and Korea, surveys among the countries' youth regularly register a highly negative view of Japan because of history issues. It may be true that the passing of the war generations will end some of the vivid, bitter animosities. On the other hand, the importance that subsequent generations attach to past issues and how they perceive them reflect not only time but also the historical knowledge they acquire through education, films, and other media.

## Historical Reconciliation in Comparative Contexts

The question of historical disputes and reconciliation is not unique to Northeast Asia. Most countries that have experienced colonialism or war have been confronted with the same issue. However, as Northeast Asia is often compared with Western Europe in dealing with historical injustices, it is worth addressing the frequently asked question of why Japan has failed to emulate Germany in dealing with its past wrongdoings. Many have compared Japan unfavorably to Germany in this respect and have maintained that East Asia is lagging far behind in achieving a substantive reconciliation with the victims of its unfortunate past. One explanation for this difference is that central governments in East Asia wield greater influence in shaping discourse on history issues and hinder civil society's ability to address these issues.[34] Although some NGOs have been engaged in redressing historical injustices, in comparison to Europe, civil society has been weak (Japan), almost nonexistent (Communist China), or not much interested in historical issues (Korea). There exists no major transnational organization or culture that might play a central role in achieving historical reconciliation.[35] Besides, while Germany had to address the history issue in order to be part of a new Europe, Japan saw no such need.

Japan was unquestionably a major aggressor in the region and must unequivocally assume its responsibility. Still, it is important to consider

Japanese psychology in dealing with historical injustices, as a strong sense of victimhood exists among Japanese. Nazi war crimes were well documented and could not be denied, such that the German right-wingers lacked the political ammunition to engage in any kind of denial politics; in Asia, there have been controversies over the extent and responsibility of Japanese war crimes, including the role of the Japanese emperor, and victim consciousness has led to the rise of rightist nationalism in Japan. As a result, Japanese conservatives claim that Western nations were committing equally terrible—or worse—violations of human rights in their respective colonies, while their progressive counterparts highlight the suffering of their own citizens during the Asia-Pacific War. In both cases, they end up downplaying the severity of Japan's war crimes and ignoring Asian victims of Japanese aggression.

In addition to the Japanese sense of suffering, postwar geopolitics has had a profound impact on the ways in which Northeast Asia and Western Europe have dealt with the historical injustices of the prewar period. U.S. leaders of the Allied forces in Japan believed that keeping the emperor as a social institution, deprived of political power, would facilitate the occupation and reconstruction of postwar Japan. Unlike in Europe, where key Axis leaders of the war and the Holocaust were punished for their atrocities and crimes, the opportunity to address the personal and institutional role of the emperor in Japanese historical injustices was clearly lost. The United States did not press Japan to reconcile with its neighbors, either, as it had pressured Germany in the years following 1945. Instead, as Japan's importance as a bulwark against communism in the region increased with the intensification of the Cold War, the United States simply put aside issues of historical responsibility.

The comparison of East Asia and Western Europe brings up the question of an appropriate U.S. role and the extent of U.S. responsibility in addressing historical disputes and reconciliation. As shown in this book, the United States is undoubtedly an integral part of the history question in the Asia-Pacific region. In particular, the United States is the single most important country in the formation of Japanese war memories. The United States not only engaged in wars in Asia but also shaped the ways in which Asians, especially the Japanese, handled the question of historical injustice after 1945 through the Tokyo War Crimes Tribunal, the San Francisco Peace Treaty, and the bilateral alliance system. It is on this premise that we hope to see the United States play a facilitating role in the protracted and difficult process of achieving historical reconciliation in Northeast Asia.

## Looking Forward

In her speech to a joint session of the U.S. Congress in May 2013, South Korean President Park Geun-hye contended, "Asia suffers from what I call 'Asia's paradox,' the disconnect between growing economic interdependence on the one hand, and backward political, security cooperation on the other." This is, she noted, because "differences stemming from history are widening," and "how we manage this paradox" will determine the configuration of a new order in Asia.[36]

Other leaders of the region would agree with her assessment, though they might differ on how to manage the paradox. Pessimists worry that colonial and wartime history problems will persist and that there is not much that we can do about it. Conversely, optimists believe that history issues will inevitably fade over time as the wartime generation passes away and the countries of the region become increasingly integrated economically and culturally.

While only time can tell us which view is correct, we cannot rely on time alone to heal these wounds. When issues of the past posed a stumbling block in ameliorating relations between China and Japan in the 1970s, Chinese leader Deng Xiaoping said, "Our generation is not wise enough to find common language on this question. Our next generation will certainly be wiser. They will surely find a solution acceptable to all."[37] Contrary to his expectations, however, the two countries are stricken today with a worse situation involving history and territorial disputes, and the younger generation tends to be even more afflicted by the fever of nationalism.

This is a moment of both danger and opportunity for Northeast Asia. The current impasse in regional relations demands a commitment to confronting the corrosive nationalism fed by the unresolved issues of history. Disregarding or ignoring an unfortunate past means not only evasion of historical accountability but also a missed opportunity to learn from history. Germany's failure to learn from its defeat in World War I led to the rise of Nazism and another world war. The German experience should provide a valuable lesson for all, especially Japan.

Sustainable reconciliation is inherently a complex process that involves a multitude of actors from the state, civil society, and international organizations. Despite controversies and frustrations, there have been important changes in wartime memories over the years, and it is encouraging to see the rise of diverse views within China, Japan, and South Korea, as well as in the United States. Also, civil society in these nations has been more active in facilitating historical reconciliation through close collaboration beyond governmental efforts. One needs to be reminded that Northeast Asia only began to address these issues in earnest in the 1980s, while European efforts for reconciliation started much earlier. In addition, the regions have distinctive histories, experiences, and memories and perhaps even different cultural modes of reconciliation. Thus, one needs not only to be patient with the slow pace of reconciliation in Northeast Asia but also to continue to search for an East Asian model while learning from the European experience. As shown in this book, Northeast Asia and the United States still face a great deal of challenges in coming to terms with the past, but, even so, the current trend toward reconciliation gives some hope for the future.

APPENDIX

# Opinion Leaders Interviewed

## China

Interviews were conducted in Beijing, Nanjing, and Shanghai, China, April 19–29, 2010, with the exception of Yang Tianshi's interview, which was conducted in Palo Alto, California, at Stanford University, in May 2010.

**Bu Ping**—born in 1948; historian, director of the Institute of Modern History, Chinese Academy of Social Sciences (CASS), head of the China-Japan Joint History Research Committee

**Li Datong**—born in 1952; journalist for *China Youth Daily*

**Li Zongyuan**—born in 1970; director of the Nanjing Massacre Memorial Hall

**Lu Chuan**—born in 1971; film director

**Rose Liquo**—born in 1969; television journalist for Phoenix Television

**Shi Zhongshan**—born in 1964; novelist, television writer, nationalist author

**Song Qiang**—born in 1964; journalist, public intellectual, nationalist author

**Su Zhiliang**—born in 1956; historian, director of the Research Center for Chinese Comfort Women at Shanghai Normal University

**Tong Zeng**—born in 1956; civic activist, leader of movements on reparations for Chinese victims of the war and on territorial disputes with Japan

**Wang Hongzhi**—born in 1937; historian, textbook author for People's Education Press

**Wang Xiaodong**—born in 1955; writer, public intellectual, blogger

**Yang Tianshi**—born in 1936; historian, researcher at CASS

**Zhang Yunling**—born in 1945; academic, director of the Institute of Asia-Pacific Studies, CASS

**Zhang Zhenkun**—born in 1926; historian, researcher for the Institute of Modern History, CASS

312  Appendix

## South Korea

Interviews were conducted in Seoul and Yongin, Korea, December 15–21, 2009, and April 3, 2010, with the exception of Rhee Yong Hoon's interview, which was conducted in Palo Alto, California, at Stanford University, on January 13, 2010.

**Bok Geo il**—born in 1946; novelist, representative of the Forum for Cultural Future
**Cho Gap Je**—born in 1945; former journalist for *Chosun Daily* and *Chosun Monthly*
**Cho Jeong Rae**—born in 1943; historical novelist, attended Dongguk University
**Chung Hyun Baek**—born in 1959; historian, professor at Sungkyunkwan University
**Im Kwon Taek**—born in 1936; film director
**Kim Yeong Dok**—born in 1944; historian of Japan, professor at the Gwangju Institute of Science and Technology, former head of the Northeast Asian History Foundation
**Lee Hong Koo**—born in 1934; scholar, diplomat, politician, former prime minister
**Park Won-soon**—born in 1956; human-rights lawyer, civic activist, mayor of Seoul
**Rhee Yong Hoon**—born in 1951; economic historian, professor at Seoul National University
**Won Yu Chol**—born in 1962; politician, member of the Korean National Assembly
**Yang Mi Kang**—born in 1960; activist, ecumenical Christian minister, organizer for the Asian Peace and History Education Network
**Yi Won Bok**—born in 1946; cartoonist, author

## Japan

Interviews were conducted in Tokyo, Hiroshima, and Naha, Japan, February 27–April 11, 2010.

**Hosaka Masayasu**—born in 1939; nonfiction author, oral historian
**Ito Takashi**—born in 1932; historian, professor at Tokyo University, member of the Japanese Society for History Textbook Reform
**Kawashima Shin**—born in 1969; historian, professor at University of Tokyo
**Kitaoka Shinichi**—born in 1948; diplomatic historian, head of the Japan-China Joint History Research Committee, policy advisor to prime ministers
**Ogata Sadako**—born in 1927; diplomatic historian, former United Nations High Commissioner for Refugees; former director of a Japanese overseas aid organization
**Ota Masahide**—born in 1925; journalist, historian, former governor of Okinawa
**Sakurai Yoshiko**—born in 1945; journalist, television news anchor, public intellectual

**Takagi Kenichi**—born in 1944; human-rights lawyer
**Takahashi Akihiro** (deceased)—born in 1931; former director of the Hiroshima Peace Memorial Museum
**Takahata Isao**—born in 1935; filmmaker, collaborator with Studio Ghibli
**Tamogami Toshio**—born in 1948; conservative activist and politician, former chief of staff of Japan Air Self-Defense Forces
**Togo Kazuhiko**—born in 1945; diplomat, historian
**Wakamiya Yoshibumi**—born in 1948; journalist, former editor of the *Asahi Shimbun*
**Watanabe Tsuneo**—born in 1926; journalist, editor in chief and chairman of the board of the *Yomiuri Shimbun*
**Yagi Yasuo**—born in 1950; television film director, director of the Tokyo Broadcast System

*United States*

Interviews were conducted in La Jolla, Santa Monica, San Jose, and Palo Alto, California, and Boston, Massachusetts, July 15–August 31, 2010, and May 18, 2012.
**Michael Armacost**—born in 1937; academic, diplomat, former ambassador to Japan
**Barton Bernstein**—born in 1936; historian, professor at Stanford University
**Ying-Ying Chang and Shau-Jin Chang**—born in 1940; parents of Iris Chang, author and activist
**John Dower**—born in 1938; historian, professor emeritus at Massachusetts Institute of Technology
**Mike Honda**—born in 1941; teacher, member of U.S. Congress
**Mark Peattie** (deceased)—born in 1930; military historian, former research fellow at Hoover Institution at Stanford University
**Kirk Saduski**—born in 1954; film producer for Playtone Productions
**Lester Tenney**—born in 1920; survivor of Bataan Death March, former POW, businessman, activist for POW rights and dialogue with Japan

# Notes

*Chapter 1*

1. For further discussion of history and memory, see Sheila Jager and Rana Mitter, eds., *Ruptured Histories: War, Memory, and the Post–Cold War in Asia* (Cambridge, MA: Harvard University Press, 2007); and Kirk Denton, *Exhibiting the Past: Historical Memory and the Politics of Museums in Post-Socialist China* (Manoa: University of Hawaii Press, 2014).

2. White House, "Press Conference with President Obama and President Park of the Republic of Korea," April 25, 2014, https://www.whitehouse.gov/the-press-office/2014/04/25/press-conference-president-obama-and-president-park-republic-korea.

3. Ibid.

4. Daniel Sneider, "Behind the Comfort Women Agreement," *Tokyo Business Today*, January 10, 2016, http://toyokeizai.net/articles/-/99891.

5. See also the discussion in Ian Buruma, *The Wages of Guilt: Memories of War in Germany and Japan* (New York: Farrar, Straus and Giroux, 1994).

6. For further discussion of national identity, see Brad Glosserman and Scott Snyder, *Japan–South Korea Identity Clash: East Asian Security and the United States* (New York: Columbia University Press, 2015).

7. See Gi-Wook Shin, "Historical Reconciliation in Northeast Asia: Past Efforts, Future Steps, and the U.S. Role," in *Confronting Memories of World War II: European and Asian Legacies*, ed. Daniel Chirot, Gi-Wook Shin, and Daniel Sneider (Seattle: University of Washington Press, 2014), 157–185.

8. See Gi-Wook Shin and Daniel Sneider, eds., *History Textbooks and the Wars in Asia: Divided Memories* (London: Routledge, 2011).

9. See Michael Berry and Chiho Sawada, eds., *Divided Lenses: Screen Memories of War in East Asia* (Manoa: University of Hawaii Press, 2016).

10. See Daniel Chirot, Gi-Wook Shin, and Daniel Sneider, eds., *Confronting Memories of World War II: European and Asian Legacies* (Seattle: University of Washington Press, 2014).

11. Bu Ping, interview by the authors, Beijing, China, April 19, 2010.

12. See Hsin-Huang Michael Hsiao, "One Colonialism, Two Memories: Representing Japanese Colonialism in Taiwan and South Korea," in Shin and Sneider, *History Textbooks and the Wars in Asia*, 173–190.

13. Kiyoteru Tsutsui, "The Trajectory of Perpetrators' Trauma: Mnemonic Politics Around the Asia-Pacific War in Japan," *Social Forces* 87, no. 3 (2009): 1389–1422.

14. Hisayoshi Ina, "A Historical Thorn Between Japan and United States," *Nikkei*, April 12, 2009, p. 2.

15. Peter Duus, "War Stories," in Shin and Sneider, *History Textbooks and the Wars in Asia*, 101.

16. Caroline Rose, "Changing Views of the Anti-Japanese War in Chinese High School History Textbooks," in *Imagining Japan in Post-war East Asia: Identity Politics, Schooling and Popular Culture*, ed. Paul Morris, Naoko Shimazu, and Edward Vickers (Abingdon, UK: Routledge, 2013), 131.

17. Li Datong, interview by the authors, Beijing, China, April 24, 2010.

18. James Reilly, "China's History Activists and the War of Resistance Against Japan: History in the Making," *Asian Survey* 44, no. 2 (2004): 276–294.

19. Yi Won Bok, interview by the authors, Seoul, South Korea, December 16, 2009.

20. Xiaohua Ma, "Constructing a National Memory of War: War Museums in China, Japan, and the United States," in *The Unpredictability of the Past: Memories of the Asia-Pacific War in U.S.–East Asian Relations*, ed. Marc Gallicchio (Durham, NC: Duke University Press, 2007), 157–158.

21. Jasper Heinzen, "'Memory Wars': The Manipulation of History in the Context of Sino-Japanese Relation," *New Zealand Journal of Asian Studies* 6, no. 2 (2004): 149.

22. Ma, "Constructing a National Memory of War," 157.

23. Nagano Shigeto, interview, *Mainichi Shimbun*, May 4, 1994.

24. Lee Dong-min, "Bush Urges Asia to Forget Bitter Past," *Yonhap News*, November 9, 2005, http://newsgroups.derkeiler.com/Archive/Soc/soc.culture.china/2005-11/msg00156.html.

25. Richard McGregor and Simon Mundy, "Ill Will Between Japan and South Korea a Strategic Problem for US," *Financial Times*, November 21, 2013, http://www.ft.com/intl/cms/s/0/d40e3b00-5232-11e3-8c42-00144feabdc0.html#axzz3SAijKDZ9.

26. See Kazuko Kuramoto, *Manchurian Legacy: Memoirs of a Japanese Colonist* (Lansing: Michigan State University Press, 1999); and Kodo Yasuyama, *Collection of Memoirs of the Atomic Bombardment of Nagasaki, 1945–55* (Nagasaki, Japan: Nagasaki Association for Hibakusha's Medical Care, 2005). Even these personal memoirs carry the risk that one's select experiences have been influenced by social memory.

27. T. G. Ashplant, Graham Dawson, and Michael Roper, eds., *The Politics of War Memory and Commemoration* (London: Routledge, 2000).

28. Alison Landsberg, *Prosthetic Memory: The Transformation of American Remembrance in the Age of Mass Culture* (New York: Columbia University Press, 2004), 19.

29. Ibid., 22.

30. Shin and Sneider, *History Textbooks and the Wars in Asia*.

31. Bu, interview by the authors.

## Chapter 2

1. Mark Peattie, Edward Drea, and Hans van de Ven, eds., *The Battle for China: Essays on the Military History of the Sino-Japanese War of 1937–1945* (Stanford, CA: Stanford University Press, 2011), 46–47.

2. Zhu Cheng Shan, interview by the authors, Nanjing, China, April 26, 2010.

3. Ibid.

4. Zheng Wang, "National Humiliation, History Education, and the Politics of Historical Memory: Patriotic Education Campaign in China," *International Studies Quarterly* 52, no. 4 (2008): 783–806.

5. Zhu, interview by the authors. For a description of these events, see Daniel Sneider, "The War over Words: History Textbooks and International Relations in Northeast Asia," in *History Textbooks and the Wars in Asia: Divided Memories*, ed. Gi-Wook Shin and Daniel C. Sneider (London: Routledge, 2011), 246–268.

6. Li Datong, interview by the authors, Beijing, China, April 24, 2010.

7. Chengjun Zhang and Jianye Liu, *An Illustrated History of China's War of Resistance Against Japan* (Beijing: Foreign Languages Press, 1995), 7.

8. Li Zongyuan, interview by the authors, Beijing, China, April 22, 2010.

9. Peattie, Drea, and van de Ven, *The Battle for China*, 422.

10. Ibid.

11. Ibid.

12. The sections of those textbooks dealing with the 1931–1951 wartime era were translated in full by the Divided Memories and Reconciliation project at Stanford University, directed by the authors of this volume. The material cited here is drawn from the full translations prepared for that project.

13. Sneider, "The War over Words," 252–260.
14. Li Datong, interview by the authors.
15. Polling data are available on the Genron NPO website at http://www.genron-npo.net. For example, see Genron NPO, "The 9th Japan-China Public Opinion Poll," August 12, 2013, http://www.genron-npo.net/en/opinion_polls/archives/5260.html#2.
16. Genron NPO, "The 10th Japan-China Public Opinion Poll: Analysis Report on the Comparative Data," September 9, 2014, http://www.genron-npo.net/en/pp/archives/5153.html.
17. Lu Chuan, interview by the authors, Beijing, China, April 25, 2010.
18. Ibid.
19. Ibid.
20. Sneider, "The War over Words," 252.
21. Bu Ping, interview by the authors, Beijing, China, April 19, 2010. All quotations by Bu in this section come from this interview.
22. Li Datong, interview by the authors. All quotations by Li in this section come from this interview.
23. David Shambaugh, *China Goes Global: The Partial Power* (New York: Oxford University Press, 2013), 27.
24. Peter Hays Gries, review of *China Can Still Say No*, by Song Qiang, Zhang Zangzang, Qiao Ben, Gu Qingsheng, and Tang Zhengyu, *China Journal*, no. 37 (January 1997): 182.
25. Wang Xiaodong, interview by the authors, Beijing, China, April 20, 2010.
26. Ibid.
27. Song Qiang, interview by the authors, Beijing, China, April 21, 2010. All quotations by Song in this section come from this interview.
28. Tong Zeng, interview by the authors, Beijing, China April 21, 2010. All quotations by Tong in this section come from this interview.
29. "Petition to Chinese NPC on Claiming War Compensation from Japan," April 15, 1991, *BBC Summary of World Broadcasts*, April 19, 1991.
30. Su Zhiliang, interview by the authors, Shanghai, China, April 27, 2010.
31. Zhang Zhenkun, interview by the authors, Beijing, China April 24, 2010. All quotations by Zhang in this section come from this interview.

## Chapter 3

1. "Ryu Gwansun," *ilovekorea* (blog), October 26, 2015, http://ilovekorea.blog.rs/blog/ilovekorea/generalna/2015/10/26/ryu-gwansun-en.
2. "Address by President Park Geun-hye on the 96th March First Independence Movement Day," Cheong Wa Dae, March 1, 2015, http://english1.president

.go.kr/activity/speeches.php?srh%5Bboard_no%5D=24&srh%5Bview_mode%5D=detail&srh%5Bseq%5D=9532&srh%5Bdetail_no%5D=40#sthash.n6IsV3WN.dpuf.

3. Gi-Wook Shin and Daniel C. Sneider, eds., *History Textbooks and the Wars in Asia: Divided Memories* (New York: Routledge, 2011), 36.

4. Yoksa Munje Yon'guso Minjok Haebang Undongsa Yon'guban [A Study Group on National Liberation Movements of the Center for Historical Studies], *Minjok haebang undongsa: Chaeongjom kwa kwaje* [History of national liberation movements: Issues and tasks] (Seoul: Yoksa Pip'yongsa, 1990), 12–13.

5. Namhee Lee, "The South Korean Student Movements, 1980–1987," in *Chicago Occasional Papers on Korea*, ed. Bruce Cumings (Chicago: Center for East Asian Studies, University of Chicago, 1991), 225.

6. Mark Caprio, *Japanese Assimilation Policies in Colonial Korea, 1910–1945* (Seattle: University of Washington Press, 2009).

7. Truth and Reconciliation Commission, *Comprehensive Report*, vol. 1, pt. 1, *History and Activities of the Commission* (Republic of Korea: Truth and Reconciliation Commission, 2010), 12.

8. Ibid.

9. Cho Jeong Rae, interview by the authors, Seoul, December 17, 2009.

10. Cho Gap Je, interview by the authors, Seoul, April 3, 2010.

11. Kim Yeong Dok, interview by the authors, Seoul, December 15, 2009.

12. See Gi-Wook Shin, "Neither 'Sprouts' nor 'Offspring': The Agrarian Roots of Korean Capitalism," in *Transformations in Twentieth Century Korea*, ed. Yunsik Chang and Steven Hugh Lee (New York: Routledge, 2006), 33–63.

13. See An Pyongjik, *Kundae Choson ui kybngje kujo* [The economic structure of modern Korea] (Seoul: Pibong Press, 1989); Carter Eckert, *Offsprings of Empire* (Seattle: University of Washington Press, 1991); and Gi-Wook Shin and Michael Robinson, eds., *Colonial Modernity in Korea* (Cambridge, MA: Harvard Asia Center, 1999).

14. Soon-Won Park, "Colonial Industrial Growth and the Emergence of the Korean Working Class," in Shin and Robinson, *Colonial Modernity in Korea*, 128–160.

15. Chulwoo Lee, "Modernity, Legality, and Power in Korea Under Japanese Rule," in Shin and Robinson, *Colonial Modernity in Korea*, 21.

16. See An, *Kundae Choson ui kybngje kujo*.

17. Gi-Wook Shin and Michael Robinson, "Introduction: Rethinking Colonial Korea," in Shin and Robinson, *Colonial Modernity in Korea*, 17.

18. Cho Jeong Rae, interview by the authors. All quotations by Cho in this section come from this interview unless otherwise noted.

19. Jo Jung-rae, interview by Literature Translation Institute of Korea, *YouTube*, August 29, 2013, https://www.youtube.com/watch?v=lWkE3F7KDFk.

20. Quoted in Antti Leppänen, "Jo Jung-rae on Holocaust and the Japanese Occupation," *Antti Leppänen's Notes on Korea* (blog), July 23, 2005, http://hunjang.blogspot.com/2005/07/jo-jung-rae-on-holocaust-and-japanese.html.

21. Lee Hong Koo, interview by the authors, Seoul, December 21, 2009. All quotations by Lee in this section come from this interview.

22. Park Won-soon, interview by the authors, Seoul, December 19, 2009. All quotations by Park in this section come from this interview unless otherwise noted.

23. Etsuro Totsuka, "Commentary on a Victory for 'Comfort Women': Japan's Judicial Recognition of Military Sexual Slavery," *Pacific Rim Law and Policy Journal* 8, no. 1 (1999): 48.

24. Won Soon Park, "Japanese Reparations Policies and the 'Comfort Women' Question," *Positions* 5, no. 1 (1997): 108.

25. Ibid., 114.

26. Ibid., 127.

27. Quoted in Owen Miller, "The Idea of Stagnation in Korean Historiography," *Korean Histories* 2, no. 1 (2010): 9.

28. Ibid., 10.

29. Ibid., 11.

30. Rhee Yong Hoon, interview by the authors, Palo Alto, CA, January 13, 2010. All quotations by Rhee in this section come from this interview unless otherwise noted.

31. Japan-China-Korea Committee on Common History Teaching Materials, *A History That Opens the Future: Modern and Contemporary History of Three East Asian Countries* (Tokyo: Kôbunken, 2005), quoted and translated in "History Textbooks: Joint East Asia Supplementary History Textbook," *Memory and Reconciliation in the Asia-Pacific*, https://www.gwu.edu/~memory/issues/textbooks/jointeastasia.html.

32. Ibid.

33. Soon-Won Park, "A History That Opens the Future: The First Common China-Japan-Korean History Teaching Guide," in Shin and Sneider, *History Textbooks and the Wars in Asia*, 237.

34. Yang Mi Kang, interview by the authors, Seoul, December 21, 2009. All quotations by Yang in this section come from this interview unless otherwise noted.

35. Yang Mi-kang, "100 Years after Forced Annexation," *Korea Times*, September 29, 2010, http://www.koreatimes.co.kr/www/news/opinon/2013/08/198_73705.html.

36. Stephanie Strom, "Seoul Won't Seek Japan Funds for War's Brothel Women," *New York Times*, April 22, 1998, http://www.nytimes.com/1998/04/22/world/seoul-won-t-seek-japan-funds-for-war-s-brothel-women.html.

## Chapter 4

1. Tetsuya Takahashi, "Legacies of Empire: The Yasukuni Shrine Controversy," in *Yasukuni, the War Dead, and the Struggle for Japan's Past*, ed. John Breen (New York: Columbia University Press, 2008), 105–124.

2. "Paper: Yasukuni, State in '69 OK'd War Criminal Inclusion," *Japan Times*, March 29, 2007, http://www.japantimes.co.jp/news/2007/03/29/national/paper-yasukuni-state-in-69-okd-war-criminal-inclusion/#.Vv2o52QrLYU.

3. Tomita's memo was published by the *Nihon Keizai Shinbu* in 2006. See Takahashi, "Legacies of Empire," 108; and "Hirohito Visits to Yasukuni Stopped over War Criminals," *Japan Times*, July 21, 2006, http://www.japantimes.co.jp/news/2006/07/21/national/hirohito-visits-to-yasukuni-stopped-over-war-criminals/#.Vv21H2QrLYU.

4. Franziska Seraphim, *War Memory and Social Politics in Japan, 1945–2005* (Cambridge, MA: Harvard University Press, 2006), 235–257.

5. Justin McCurry, "Japan's Shinzo Abe Angers Neighbours and US by Visiting War Dead Shrine," *The Guardian*, December 26, 2013, http://www.theguardian.com/world/2013/dec/26/japan-shinzo-abe-tension-neighbours-shrine.

6. Takashi Yoshida, "Revising the Past, Complicating the Future: The Yushukan War Museum in Modern Japanese History," *Asia-Pacific Journal*, December 1, 2007, http://apjjf.org/-Takashi-YOSHIDA/2594/article.html.

7. Western media reports on the exhibit prompted shrine authorities to slightly rewrite the captions that implied American responsibility for the start of the war, though similarly troubling depictions of the war in Asia were not redone.

8. As cited in Yoshida, "Revisiting the Past," some of the exhibition panels were slightly rewritten recently in response to American complaints, particularly those that attributed the attack on Pearl Harbor as a justified response to the American pressures on Japan.

9. John Breen, "Yasukuni and the Loss of Historical Memory," in Breen, *Yasukuni, the War Dead, and the Struggle for Japan's Past*, 155.

10. Philip A. Seaton, *Japan's Contested War Memories: The "Memory Rifts" in Historical Consciousness of World War II* (New York: Routledge, 2007), 2–3.

11. Ota Masahide, interview by the authors, Naha, Japan, March 2, 2010.

12. Julia Yonetani, "Peace Wars: The Politics of Presenting the Past in Contemporary Okinawa," Japan Policy Research Institute Working Paper No. 65, February 2000, http://www.jpri.org/publications/workingpapers/wp65.html. On the response to the textbook changes, see "Fukuda Government Responds Quickly to Okinawa Textbook Issue Due to Huge Public Outcry in Okinawa," *Mainichi Shimbun*, October 3, 2007.

13. Takahata Isao, interview by the authors, Tokyo, March 8, 2010.

14. Ibid.

15. Phillip Seaton, "Pledge Fulfilled: Prime Minister Koizumi, Yasukuni and the Japanese Media," in Breen, *Yasukuni, the War Dead, and the Struggle for Japan's Past*, 177–179.

16. "Other Reasons for Dropping the Bomb," http://www.pcf.city.hiroshima.jp/virtual/VirtualMuseum_e/visit_e/est_e/panel/A2_2/2201c.htm (accessed February 10, 2016).

17. Benedict Giamo, "The Myth of the Vanquished: The Hiroshima Peace Memorial Museum," *American Quarterly* 55, no. 4 (2003): 704.

18. Watanabe Tsuneo, interview by the authors, Tokyo, March 4, 2010.

19. Ibid.

20. Ibid.

21. Ibid.

22. Ibid.

23. Watanabe Tsuneo, foreword to *Who Was Responsible? From Marco Polo Bridge to Pearl Harbor*, ed. James E. Auer (Tokyo: Yomiuri Shimbun, 2006), 9.

24. Sakurai Yoshiko, "Hiding Behind the Skirts of Local Prosecutors: The Cowardly Diplomacy of Kan and Sengoku," *Shukan Shincho*, October 7, 2010, http://en.yoshiko-sakurai.jp/2010/10/06/1960.

25. Sakurai Yoshiko, "The Public Hit the Roof," *Sankei Shimbun*, December 9, 2010.

26. Sakurai Yoshiko, "As North Korea Runs Amok, China Pursues World Hegemony," *Shukan Shincho*, December 9, 2010, http://en.yoshiko-sakurai.jp/2010/12/06/2222.

27. Sakurai Yoshiko, "Hu Jintao's 'Smile Diplomacy' Meant to Pave the Way for 'Usurping Japan,'" *Shukan Posuto*, January 28, 2011.

28. Sakurai Yoshiko, interview by the authors, Tokyo, March 5, 2010.

29. Committee for Historical Facts, "The Facts," *Washington Post*, June 14, 2007.

30. Sakurai, interview by the authors.

31. Tadao Takemoto and Yasuo Ohara, *The Alleged 'Nanking Massacre': Japan's Rebuttal to China's Forged Claims* (Tokyo: Meisei-sha, 2000).

32. Higashinakano Shudo, *The Nanking Massacre: Fact Versus Fiction* (Tokyo: Sekai Shuppan, 2005). This book was first published in Japanese in 1998.

33. Ibid., vii.

34. Sakurai, interview by the authors.

35. Tamogami Toshio, "Was Japan an Aggressor Nation?" 2008, http://ronbun.apa.co.jp/images/pdf/2008jyusyou_saiyuusyu_english.pdf.

36. Toshio Tamogami, interview by the authors, Tokyo, February 28, 2010.

37. Tamogami, "Was Japan an Aggressor Nation?"
38. Nagano Shigeto, interview, *Mainichi Shimbun*, May 4, 1994.
39. Daniel Sneider was part of this group of journalists who visited Sakhalin in 1989. His account of this exchange appears in "In Search of the 'Long Ruble,'" *Christian Science Monitor*, September 20, 1989, p. 6.
40. Takagi Kenichi, interview by the authors, Tokyo, March 10, 2010. All quotations by Takagi in this section come from this interview.
41. The foundation's English-language website explains its history and role in great detail. See http://www.stiftung-evz.de/eng/home.html.
42. Takahata, interview by the authors. All quotations by Takahata in this section come from this interview.
43. Togo Kazuhiko, interview by the authors, Tokyo, February 27, 2010. All quotations by Togo in this section come from this interview unless otherwise noted.
44. Togo Shigenori, *The Cause of Japan* (New York: Simon and Schuster, 1956), 21.
45. Ibid.
46. Ibid., 189.
47. Ibid., 339.
48. Quoted in "Japan Emperor Repeats Regret over WWII Fight with Netherlands," *Kyodo News Service*, May 23, 2000, http://www.thefreelibrary.com/Japan+emperor+repeats+regret+over+WWII+fight+with+Netherlands.-a062372060.
49. "Government Must Expedite New War Memorial," *Yomiuri Shimbun*, June 6, 2005.
50. Watanabe, interview by the authors. All quotations by Watanabe in this section come from this interview unless otherwise noted.
51. Watanabe, foreword to *Who Was Responsible?*, 8.

## Chapter 5

1. See "Reading 1: The Attack on Pearl Harbor," National Register of Historic Places, http://www.nps.gov/nr/twhp/curriculumkit/lessons/arizona/5facts1.htm (accessed February 11, 2016).
2. Ibid.
3. Gerald A. Danzer, J. Jorge Klor de Alva, Larry S. Krieger, Louis E. Wilson, and Nancy Woloch, *The Americans: Reconstruction to the 21st Century* (Evanston, IL: McDougal Littell, 2006), 544.
4. David M. Kennedy and Lizabeth Cohen, *The American Pageant* (Boston: Wadsworth, 2013), 794.

5. John W. Dower, *War Without Mercy: Race and Power in the Pacific War* (New York: Pantheon, 1986), 8.

6. Ibid., 11.

7. Kirk Saduski, interview by the authors, Santa Monica, CA, July 22, 2010.

8. *Anatomy of the Pacific War*, produced by HBO, http://www.hbo.com/the-pacific/about/video/anatomy-of-the-pacific-war.html.

9. Saduski, interview by the authors.

10. Ibid.

11. Ibid.

12. See John T. Correll, "Revisionism Gone Wrong," *Air Force Magazine*, April 2004, http://www.airforcemag.com/MagazineArchive/Pages/2004/April%202004/0404revision.aspx.

13. Ibid.

14. Letter from W. Burr Bennett Jr. to John T. Correll, August 6, 1993, http://digital.lib.lehigh.edu/trial/enola/files/round1/monroe_hatch.PDF.

15. Correll, "Revisionism Gone Wrong."

16. "The Smithsonian and the Enola Gay: Frequently Asked Questions," *Air Force Magazine*, http://www.airforcemag.com/SiteCollectionDocuments/Enola%20Gay%20Archive/EG_faq.pdf (accessed February 11, 2016).

17. Sheldon Drobny, "The Myth of Hiroshima," *Huffington Post*, May 25, 2011, http://www.huffingtonpost.com/sheldon-drobny/the-myth-of-hiroshima_b_56245.html.

18. Barton Bernstein, interview by the authors, Palo Alto, CA, May 18, 2012.

19. On August 6, 2015, Under Secretary of State for Arms Control and International Security Rose Gottemoeller visited Hiroshima and Nagasaki, becoming the first senior American official in office to visit and attend the Hiroshima Peace Memorial Ceremony.

20. John Dower, interview by the authors, Boston, August 12, 2010.

21. Iris Chang, *The Rape of Nanking: The Forgotten Holocaust of World War II* (New York: Penguin, 1998), 5.

22. Ibid., 216.

23. Ibid., 220.

24. Ying-Ying Chang, interview by the authors, Palo Alto, CA, August 31, 2010.

25. Ibid.

26. Ibid.

27. Ignatius Ding, interview by the authors, Palo Alto, CA, August 31, 2010.

28. Ying-Ying Chang, interview by the authors.

29. Ding, interview by the authors.

30. Ibid.

31. Ibid.

32. Joshua Fogel, "Reviewed Works: *The Rape of Nanking: The Forgotten Holocaust of World War II* by Iris Chang," *Journal of Asian Studies* 57, no. 3 (1998): 818.

33. David M. Kennedy, "The Horror," *Atlantic Monthly*, April 1998, http://www.theatlantic.com/past/issues/98apr/horror.htm.

34. Ibid.

35. Fogel, "Reviewed Works," 819.

36. Ibid.

37. Ying-Ying Chang, *The Woman Who Could Not Forget: Iris Chang Before and Beyond "The Rape of Nanking"* (New York: Pegasus Books, 2011), 409.

38. Ibid.

39. John Dower, *Cultures of War: Pearl Harbor, Hiroshima, 9-11, Iraq* (New York: Norton, 2011).

40. Dower, interview by the authors. All quotations by Dower in this section come from this interview unless otherwise noted.

41. John Dower, *War Without Mercy: Race and Power in the Pacific War* (New York: Pantheon, 1986), 78.

42. Ibid., 26.

43. Ibid., 78.

44. Ibid., 301.

45. John Dower, *Embracing Defeat: Japan in the Wake of World War II* (New York: Norton, 1999), 25.

46. Ibid.

47. Ibid., 26.

48. Ibid., 27.

49. Ibid., 28.

50. Ibid., 470.

51. Ibid., 563.

52. Ibid., 563–564.

53. John Dower, "Don't Expect Democracy This Time: Japan and Iraq," *History and Policy*, April 1, 2003, http://www.historyandpolicy.org/policy-papers/papers/dont-expect-democracy-this-time-japan-and-iraq.

54. Mike Honda, interview by the authors, San Jose, CA, August 16, 2010.

55. Ibid.

56. Ibid.

57. Commission on Wartime Relocation and Internment of Civilians, *Personal Justice Denied: Report of the Commission on Wartime Relocation and Internment of Civilians* (Seattle: University of Washington Press; Washington, DC: Civil Liberties Public Education Fund, 1997), 459.

58. Michael M. Honda, "Japan's War Crimes: Has Justice Been Served?" *East Asia* 18, no. 3 (2000): 28.

59. Ibid., 33–35.

60. Quoted in Tim Johnson, "Rift Flares Anew over Japan's Wartime 'Comfort Women,'" *McClatchy DC*, August 9, 2007, http://www.mcclatchydc.com/news/nation-world/world/article24467950.html.

61. Quoted in "'Comfort Women' Historian Alarmed," *China Daily*, March 12, 2007, http://www.chinadaily.com.cn/world/2007-03/12/content_824829.htm.

62. David Pilling, "US Congress Reignites Japan Sex Slave Row," *Financial Times*, June 28, 2007, http://www.ft.com/cms/s/0/26c62bc6-2514-11dc-bf47-000b5df10621.html#axzz45x1Eveyk.

63. Letter from Ryozo Kato to U.S. House of Representatives, June 22, 2007, http://www.jiaponline.org/documents/KatoLetter22June07.pdf.

64. Kinue Tokudome, "The Japanese Apology on the 'Comfort Women' Cannot Be Considered Official: Interview with Congressman Michael Honda," *Asia-Pacific Journal*, May 2, 2007, http://apjjf.org/-Kinue-TOKUDOME/2438/article.html.

65. "Sense of House That Japan Should Apologize for Its Imperial Armed Force's Coercion of Young Women into Sexual Slavery," *Congressional Record*, July 30, 2007, p. H8871, https://www.gpo.gov/fdsys/pkg/CREC-2007-07-30/pdf/CREC-2007-07-30-pt2-PgH8870.pdf.

66. Honda, interview by the authors.

67. Mark Peattie, interview by the authors, Palo Alto, CA, July 19, 2010. All quotations by Peattie in this section come from this interview unless otherwise noted.

68. Mark Peattie, *A Historian Looks at the Pacific War* (Stanford, CA: Hoover Institution Press, 1995), 2.

69. Mark Peattie, *Ishiwara Kanji and Japan's Confrontation with the West* (Princeton, NJ: Princeton University Press, 1975), 352–353.

70. Mark Peattie, "The Poisoned Well: Fifty Years of Sino-Japanese Animosity," in *Cross Currents: Regionalism and Nationalism in Northeast Asia*, ed. Gi-Wook Shin and Daniel C. Sneider (Stanford, CA: Walter H. Shorenstein Asia-Pacific Research Center, 2007), 171.

71. Ibid., 204.

72. Lester Tenney, interview by the authors, La Jolla, CA, July 9, 2010. All quotations by Tenney in this section come from this interview unless otherwise noted.

73. Lester Tenney, *My Hitch in Hell: The Bataan Death March* (Dulles, VA: Brassey's, 1995), 50.

74. Ibid., 171–172.

75. Ibid., xvii.

76. Lester Tenney, "War Has Ended, but Not the Memories," *San Diego Union-Tribune*, August 15, 2005, http://www.sandiegouniontribune.com/union trib/20050815/news_mz1e15tenney.html.

77. Quoted in "A Historic Apology," *Armchair Asia* (blog), February 28, 2010, http://armchairasia.blogspot.com/2010/02/historic-apology.html.

78. "Bataan Survivors Hear Apology from Japan Official," *Associated Press*, May 31, 2009, http://www.lindavdahl.com/FrontPage_Links/Japanese%20Apology .htm.

79. Associated Press, "Japan Offers 'Heartfelt Apology' to U.S. POWs," *NBC News*, September 13, 2010, http://www.nbcnews.com/id/39145098/ns/world_news -asia_pacific/t/japan-offers-heartfelt-apology-us-pows.

## Chapter 6

1. "눈물로 쌓은집, 평화를 노래하다" [A house built with tears sings a song of peace], *Chosun Daily*, May 4, 2012, http://news.chosun.com/site/data/html_dir/ 2012/05/04/2012050400216.html.

2. Josh Rogin, "Japanese Comfort-Women Deniers Force White House Response," *Foreign Policy*, June 6, 2012, http://foreignpolicy.com/2012/06/06/ japanese-comfort-women-deniers-force-white-house-response/.

3. Kirk Semple, "In New Jersey, Memorial for 'Comfort Women' Deepens Old Animosity," *New York Times*, May 18, 2012, http://www.nytimes.com/2012/05/19/ nyregion/monument-in-palisades-park-nj-irritates-japanese-officials.html.

4. Kim Il-myon, *Tenno no guntai to chosenjin ianfu* [The emperor's army and the Korean comfort women] (Tokyo: San'ichi Shobo, 1976), 79.

5. Yuki Tanaka, *Hidden Horrors: Japanese War Crimes in World War II* (Boulder, CO: Westview Press, 1996), 99.

6. "Sex Slaves Put Japan on Trial," *BBC News*, December 8, 2000, http://news .bbc.co.uk/2/hi/asia-pacific/1061599.stm; Ustinia Dolgopol and Snehal Paranjape, *Comfort Women: An Unfinished Ordeal* (Geneva, Switzerland: International Commission of Jurists, 1994), 201, http://icj.wpengine.netdna-cdn.com/wp-content/ uploads/1994/01/Japan-comfort-women-fact-finding-report-1994-eng.pdf.

7. R. J. Rummel, *Statistics of Democide: Genocide and Mass Murder Since 1990* (Charlottesville, VA: Center for National Security Law, University of Virginia Law School, 1997), http://www.hawaii.edu/powerkills/NOTE5.HTM.

8. See, for example, Naitou Hisako, "Korean Forced Labor in Japan's Wartime Empire," in *Asian Labor in the Wartime Japanese Empire: Unknown Histories*, ed. Paul H. Kratoska (Armonk, NY: M. E. Sharpe, 2005), 98.

9. Rummel, *Statistics of Democide*.

10. See Gi-Wook Shin and Paul Y. Chang, eds., *South Korean Social Movements: From Democracy to Civil Society* (London: Routledge, 2011).

11. U.S. Office of War Information, "Report No. 49: Japanese Prisoners of War Interrogation on Prostitution," October 1, 1944, http://www.exordio.com/1939 -1945/codex/Documentos/report-49-USA-orig.html.

12. Bonnie Oh, "The Japanese Imperial System and the Korean 'Comfort Women' of World War II," in *Legacies of the Comfort Women of World War II*, ed. Margaret Stetz and Bonnie Oh (Armonk, NY: M. E. Sharpe, 2001), 15.

13. "Japanese Army Abducted Comfort Women," *Asahi Shimbun*, January 11, 1992.

14. Ministry of Foreign Affairs of Japan, "Statement by the Chief Cabinet Secretary Yohei Kono on the Result of the Study on the Issue of 'Comfort Women,'" August 4, 1993, http://www.mofa.go.jp/policy/women/fund/state9308.html.

15. Dongwoo Lee Hahm, "Urgent Matters: Redress for Surviving 'Comfort Women,'" in *Legacies of the Comfort Women of World War II*, ed. Margaret Stetz and Bonnie Oh (Armonk, NY: M. E. Sharpe, 2001), 139.

16. Tomiichi Murayama, "On the Occasion of the 50th Anniversary of the War's End," August 15, 1995, http://www.mofa.go.jp/announce/press/pm/ murayama/9508.html.

17. In 2007, when he served as the prime minister, Abe stated again that "there is no evidence to prove there was coercion, nothing to support it." See Hiroko Tabuchi, "Japan's Abe: No Proof of WWII Sex Slaves," *Washington Post*, March 1, 2007, http://www.washingtonpost.com/wp-dyn/content/article/2007/03/01/ AR2007030100578.html.

18. Quoted in "Chinese to Sue Japanese Company over Forced Labor During WWII," *Xinhua News*, September 6, 2010, http://news.xinhuanet.com/english 2010/china/2010-09/06/c_13481400.htm.

19. Dolgopol and Paranjape, *Comfort Women*, 199, 202.

20. *Chinese Modern and Contemporary History*, vol. 2 (Beijing: People's Education, 2003), 35.

21. Peter N. Stearns, Michael Adas, Stuart B. Schwartz, and Marc Jason Gilbert, *World Civilization: The Global Experience* (Boston: Addison-Wesley, 2001), 916.

22. *Keumsung Contemporary Korean History* (Seoul: Keumsung), 162.

23. Ibid., 162A.

24. Ishii Susumu, Gomi Fumihiko, Sasayama Haruo, and Takano Toshihiko, *Japanese History in Detail* (Tokyo: Yamakawa Shuppansha, 2002), 332.

25. Ibid., 342.

26. Yamamoto Hirofumi et al., *Japanese History B* (Tokyo: Shoseki Shuppansah, 2003), 348.

27. *Korean National History Textbook* (Seoul: Ministry of Education and Human Resources Development), 117.

28. Ibid.

29. *Keumsung Contemporary Korean History*, 163.

30. Ibid.

31. Yang Mi Kang, interview by the authors, Seoul, December 21, 2009.

32. Daniel Chirot, "Europe's Troubled World War II Memories: Are They That Different?" in *History Textbooks and the Wars in Asia*, ed. Gi-Wook Shin and Daniel C. Sneider (London: Routledge, 2011), 269–285.

33. Chung Hyun Baek, interview by the authors, Seoul, December 18, 2009.

34. "Files: Females Forced into Sexual Servitude in Wartime Indonesia," *Japan Times*, May 12, 2007, http://www.japantimes.co.jp/news/2007/05/12/national/files-females-forced-into-sexual-servitude-in-wartime-indonesia/#.VK14POcyB14.

35. Ito Takashi, interview by the authors, Tokyo, March 10, 2010.

36. Wakamiya Yoshibumi, interview by the authors, Tokyo, March 5, 2010.

37. Takagi Kenichi, interview by the authors, Tokyo, March 11, 2010.

38. Sakurai Yoshiko, interview by the authors, Tokyo, March 5, 2010.

39. Ito, interview by the authors.

40. Sakurai, interview by the authors.

41. Takahata Isao, interview by the authors, Tokyo, March 8, 2010.

42. Togo Kazuhiko, interview by the authors, Tokyo, February 27, 2010.

43. Sakurai, interview by the authors.

44. Wakamiya, interview by the authors.

45. Kawashima Shin, interview by the authors, Tokyo, March 7, 2010.

46. Ibid.

47. Ibid.

48. Kirk Saduski, interview by the authors, Santa Monica, CA, July 22, 2010.

49. John Dower, interview by the authors, Boston, MA, August 12, 2010.

50. Mike Honda, interview by the authors, San Jose, CA, August 16, 2010.

51. Rogin, "Japanese Comfort-Women Deniers."

## Chapter 7

1. Ogata Sadako, interview by the authors, Tokyo, March 9, 2010.

2. Ito Takashi, interview by the authors, Tokyo, March 10, 2010.

3. Michael Armacost, interview by the authors, Palo Alto, CA, July 15, 2010.

4. Mark Peattie, interview by the authors, Palo Alto, CA, July 19, 2010.

5. Yang Tianshi, interview by the authors, Palo Alto, CA, May 16, 2010.

6. Bu Ping, interview by the authors, Beijing, April 19, 2010.

7. Ibid.

8. Zhang Zhenkun, interview by the authors, Beijing, April 24, 2010.
9. Kitaoka Shinichi, interview by the authors, Tokyo, March 4, 2010.
10. Ibid.
11. Mark Peattie, "The Poisoned Well: Fifty Years of Sino-Japanese Animosity," in *Cross Currents: Regionalism and Nationalism in Northeast Asia*, ed. Gi-Wook Shin and Daniel Sneider (Stanford, CA: Shorenstein Asia-Pacific Research Center, 2007), 177.
12. Ibid.
13. Ibid., 199.
14. Zhang, interview by the authors.
15. Rana Mitter, *The Forgotten Ally: China's World War II, 1937–1945* (New York: Houghton Mifflin Harcourt, 2013), 378.
16. Ibid., 379.
17. Ibid.
18. Ito, interview by the authors.
19. Tohmatsu Haruo, "The Strategic Correlation Between the Sino-Japanese and Pacific Wars," in *The Battle for China: Essays on the Military History of the Sino-Japanese War of 1937–1945*, ed. Mark Peattie, Edward Drea, and Hans van de Ven (Stanford, CA: Stanford University Press, 2011), 434.
20. Ibid., 442–443.
21. Ronald Spector, "The Sino-Japanese War in the Context of World History," in Peattie, Drea, and van de Ven, *The Battle for China*, 480.
22. Mitter, *The Forgotten Ally*, 134.
23. Yang, interview by the authors.
24. Peattie, "The Poisoned Well," 200.
25. Ibid.
26. Ito, interview by the authors.
27. Hosaka Masayasu, interview by the authors, Tokyo, March 4, 2010.
28. Ibid.
29. Ibid.
30. Ibid.

## Chapter 8

1. Herbert Feis, *The Road to Pearl Harbor: The Coming of the War Between the United States and Japan* (Princeton, NJ: Princeton University Press, 1950), 16.
2. Hosaka Masayasu, interview by the authors, Tokyo, March 2010.
3. Jeffrey Record, *A War It Was Always Going to Lose: Why Japan Attacked America in 1941* (Washington, DC: Potomac Books, 2011), viii.

4. David Kennedy and Lizabeth Cohen, *The American Pageant: A History of the American People*, 15th ed. (Boston: Wadsworth Cengage Learning, 2013), 794.

5. Ishii Susumu et al., *Japanese History in Detail* (Tokyo: Yamakawa Shuppansha, 2002), chap. 10. The excerpts cited in this chapter were translated by the Stanford Divided Memories and Reconciliation project in 2007.

6. Ibid., 335.

7. Ibid., 336.

8. Ibid., 337.

9. Ibid., 337–339.

10. Ibid., 339.

11. Record, *A War It Was Always Going to Lose*, 12.

12. Tamogami Toshio, "Was Japan an Aggressor Nation?" 2008, http://ronbun.apa.co.jp/images/pdf/2008jyusyou_saiyuusyu_english.pdf.

13. Ibid.

14. Tamogami Toshio, interview by the authors, Tokyo, March 2010.

15. Ibid.

16. Tamogami, "Was Japan an Aggressor Nation?"

17. Ito Takashi, interview by the authors, Tokyo, March 2010.

18. Tamogami, interview by the authors.

19. Record, *A War It Was Always Going to Lose*, 4.

20. Eri Hotta, *Japan 1941: Countdown to Infamy* (New York: Knopf Doubleday, 2013), 19.

21. Watanabe Tsuneo, interview by the authors, Tokyo, March 2010.

22. Mark Peattie, interview by the authors, Palo Alto, CA, July 19, 2010.

23. Michael Armacost, interview by the authors, Palo Alto, CA, July 2010.

24. Record, *A War It Was Always Going to Lose*, 12.

25. Kennedy and Cohen, *The American Pageant*, 808.

26. Ibid., 810.

27. Ibid., 818.

28. Gerald A. Danzer, J. Jorge Klor de Alva, Larry S. Krieger, Louis E. Wilson, and Nancy Woloch, *The Americans: Reconstruction to the 21st Century* (Evanston, IL: McDougal Littell, 2006), 583.

29. Susumu et al., *Japanese History in Detail*, 343.

30. Ibid.

31. Yamamoto Hirofumi et al., *Japanese History B* (Tokyo: Shoseki Shuppansah, 2003), 332. Excerpts from this book were translated by the Stanford Divided Memories and Reconciliation project.

32. Ibid.

33. Ota Masahide, interview by the authors, Naha, Japan, March 2010.

34. Ibid.

35. Masahide Ota, *The Battle of Okinawa: The Typhoon of Steel and Bombs* (Tokyo: Kume, 1984).

36. Fujioka Nobukatsu, "Do Not Repeat Folly of Political Compromise on Mass Suicide and School Screening Textbook," *Sankei Shimbun*, June 21, 2007, p. 13.

37. Norimitsu Onishi, "Japan Textbooks to Restore Reference to Wartime Suicides," New York Times, December 27, 2007, http://www.nytimes.com/2007/12/27/world/asia/27japan.html.

38. Kirk Saduski, interview by the authors, Santa Monica, CA, July 2010.

39. Wakamiya Yoshibumi, interview by the authors, Tokyo, March 5, 2010.

## Chapter 9

1. "Potsdam Declaration: Proclamation Defining Terms for Japanese Surrender," July 26, 1945, http://www.atomicarchive.com/Docs/Hiroshima/Potsdam.shtml.

2. U.S. Army Manhattan Engineer District, "Total Casualties," in *The Atomic Bombings of Hiroshima and Nagasaki*, http://avalon.law.yale.edu/20th_century/mp10.asp.

3. Harry S. Truman, *Memoirs* (Garden City, NY: Doubleday, 1955), 419.

4. Daikichi Irokawa, *The Age of Hirohito: In Search of Modern Japan* (New York: Free Press, 1995), 37, cited in Richard B. Frank, *Downfall: The End of the Imperial Japanese Empire* (New York: Random House, 1999), 351.

5. Winston Churchill, speech to the British House of Commons, August 16, 1945.

6. Gabriel Kolko, *The Politics of War: The World and United States Foreign Policy, 1943–1945* (New York: Pantheon, 1990), 539–540.

7. "United States Strategic Bombing Survey: Summary Report (Pacific War)," July 1, 1946, p. 26, http://www.anesi.com/ussbs01.htm.

8. Kyoko Selden and Mark Selden, *The Atomic Bomb: Voices from Hiroshima and Nagasaki* (Armonk, NY: M. E. Sharpe, 1989).

9. Shimoda et al. v. State, Tokyo District Court, December 7, 1963.

10. Kazuhiko Togo, "Healing the Scars of War: On the Japanese Government's Apology to American POWs," *Mainichi*, May 18, 2009, p. 4. It was not until May 10, 2009, when the Japanese ambassador to the United States, Ichiro Fujisaki, offered the Japanese government's apology to American former POWs for the Bataan Death March.

11. Sadao Asada, "Japanese Perceptions of the A-Bomb Decision, 1945–1980," in *The American Military and the Far East: Proceedings of the Ninth Military History*

*Symposium*, ed. Joe C. Dixon (Colorado Springs, CO: U.S. Air Force Academy, 1980), 201.

12. Ibid., 211.

13. Jeff Kingston, "Nanjing's Massacre Memorial: Renovating War Memory in Nanjing and Tokyo," *Asia-Pacific Journal: Japan Focus*, August 2008, http://apjjf.org/-Jeff-Kingston/2859/article.html.

14. "Other Reasons for Dropping the Bomb," http://www.pcf.city.hiroshima.jp/virtual/VirtualMuseum_e/visit_e/est_e/panel/A2_2/2201c.htm (accessed February 10, 2016).

15. Agreement Between Japan and the Republic of Korea Concerning the Settlement of Problems in Regard to Property and Claims and Economic Cooperation, Article II, June 22, 1965, *Wikisource*, May 20, 2014, https://en.wikisource.org/wiki/Agreement_Between_Japan_and_the_Republic_of_Korea_Concerning_the_Settlement_of_Problems_in_Regard_to_Property_and_Claims_and_Economic_Cooperation.

16. *Modern and Contemporary World History II* (Beijing: People's Education, 2003), 58.

17. According to Professor Han Hong Koo of Sungkonghoe University, "Those people were ignored by the Japanese and by the Korean government. Korean people were not welcoming them either. . . . There was no support from the government, so why should people admit they were atomic bomb victims? There was no reason to tell it loudly." As Han notes, the victims remained silent for many reasons. "Japan capitulated after the bombing of Hiroshima and Nagasaki. Many people believe that the nuclear bombs liberated Korea." He goes on to admit that "as a historian I did not know that so many Koreans had been killed until a year ago. . . . Our schools do not tell much about the dangers and horrors of nuclear weapons. In Hiroshima and Nagasaki, about 50,000 Koreans were killed in a day and there is nothing about it in the school books." Quoted in Andreas Hippin, "The End of Silence: Korea's A-Bomb Victims Seek Redress," *Asia-Pacific Journal* 3, no. 8 (2005): 1, 2, 4, http://apjjf.org/-Andreas-Hippin/1973/article.pdf. In recent years, however, greater attention has been paid to the Korean victims of the Hiroshima and Nagasaki atomic bombings, as some of the survivors and descendants of the victims—who had remained silent for a couple of decades—have started to seek redress. Attention to these victims has only been reinforced by media coverage. On September 8, 2015, Japan's highest court ruled for the first time in favor of South Korean atomic bombing victims and ordered full compensation for victims residing outside of Japan.

18. Gerald A. Danzer, J. Jorge Klor de Alva, Larry S. Krieger, Louis E. Wilson, and Nancy Woloch, *The Americans: Reconstruction to the 21st Century* (Evanston, IL: McDougal Littell, 2006), 585.

19. Ibid.

20. David M. Kennedy, Lizbeth Cohen, and Thomas A. Bailey, *The American Pageant: A History of the Republic* (Boston: Houghton Mifflin, 2002), 855.

21. Yamamoto Hirofumi et al., *Tokyo Shoseki Japanese History B* (Tokyo: Shoseki, 2003), 354.

22. Ibid., 354n4.

23. Sato Tsugikata, Kimura Seiji, and Kishimoto Mio, *Yamakawa World History B* (Tokyo: Yamakawa Shuppansha, 2002), 317.

24. Ibid.; Yamamoto et al., *Tokyo Shoseki Japanese History B*, 353–355; Ishii Susumu, Gomi Fumihiko, Sasayama Haruo, and Tokano Toshihiko, *Yamakawa Japanese History B* (Tokyo: Yamakawa Shuppansha, 2002), 344–345.

25. Ishii et al., *Yamakawa Japanese History B*, 345; Yamamoto et al., *Tokyo Shoseki Japanese History B*, 354n4.

26. Kawashima Shin, interview by the authors, Tokyo, March 7, 2010.

27. Togo Kazuhiko, interview by the authors, Tokyo, February 27, 2010.

28. Sakurai Yoshiko, interview by the authors, Tokyo, March 5, 2010.

29. Takahata Isao, interview by the authors, Tokyo, March 8, 2010.

30. Barton J. Bernstein, "The Atomic Bombings Reconsidered," *Foreign Affairs* 74, no. 1 (1995): 135.

31. Lester Tenney, interview by the authors, La Jolla, CA, July 9, 2010.

32. Mark Peattie, interview by the authors, Palo Alto, CA, July 9, 2010.

33. Wakamiya Yoshibumi, interview by the authors, Tokyo, March 5, 2010.

34. Barton Bernstein, interview by the authors, Palo Alto, CA, May 18, 2012.

35. Tenney, interview by the authors.

36. Takagi Kenichi, interview by the authors, Tokyo, March 11, 2010.

37. Takahashi Akihiro, interview by the authors, Hiroshima, March 1, 2010.

38. John Dower, interview by the authors, Boston, August 12, 2010.

39. Kirk Saduski, interview by the authors, Santa Monica, CA, July 22, 2010.

40. Kawashima, interview by the authors.

41. Tetsu Miyata, "Mr. Obama, Please Come to Hiroshima! Atomic Bombing Survivors See a Light of Hope from the Speech on 'Elimination of Nuclear Arms,'" *Mainichi*, June 16, 2009, p. 2.

42. Ogata Sadako, interview by the authors, Tokyo, March 9, 2010.

43. Takagi, interview by the authors.

44. Tamogami Toshio, interview by the authors, Tokyo, February 28, 2010.

45. Sakurai Yoshiko, interview by the authors, Tokyo, March 5, 2010.

46. Fumio Matsuo, "Tokyo Needs Its Dresden Moment," *Wall Street Journal*, August 16, 2005, http://www.wsj.com/articles/SB112415703044914053.

47. Ibid.

48. Takahiro Takino, "*Visit to Hiroshima by President Bush Considered* in 60th Postwar Year," *Mainichi*, January 3, 2009, p. 1.

49. David Straub, "The United States and Reconciliation in East Asia," in *East Asia's Haunted Present: Historical Memories and the Resurgence of Nationalism*, ed. Tsuyoshi Hasegawa and Kazuhiko Togo (Westport, CT: Praeger Security International, 2007), 215; Takahiro Takino of the *Mainichi* says that "the plan did not materialize because a school girl in Okinawa was raped by three U.S. marines in September that year." Takahiro, "*Visit to Hiroshima by President Bush*," 1.

50. See Warren Kozak, "LeMay and the Tragedy of War: When Basic Survival Trumps Civil Liberties," *Wall Street Journal*, May 18, 2009, http://online.wsj.com/article/SB124234559143121723.html.

## Chapter 10

1. Caroline Rose, *Sino-Japanese Relations: Facing the Past, Looking to the Future* (London: Routledge, 2005), 102.

2. It was revealed later by newly declassified Japanese diplomatic documents that Japan sought an agreement with countries involved in the war crimes tribunal to have ten Class A war criminals' sentences reduced, under advice from the United States. See "U.S. Advised Japan on Obtaining Reduced Sentences for War Criminals," *Kyodo News International*, December 22, 2010.

3. In Dower's view, the Tokyo trials focused on "crimes against peace" but ignored "crimes against humanity," including "murder, extermination, enslavement, deportation, and other inhumane acts committed before or during the war, or persecutions on political or racial grounds in execution of or in connection with any crime within the jurisdiction of the Tribunal, whether or not in violation of the domestic law of the country where perpetrated." Many war crimes against Asians such as forced labor, comfort women, and mass killings of civilians belong to the second category. John W. Dower, *Embracing Defeat: Japan in the Wake of World War II* (New York: Norton, 2000), 456, 473–474.

4. Chihiro Hosoya, Andō Nisuke, Ōnuma Yasuaki, and Richard H. Minear, eds., *The Tokyo War Crimes Trial: An International Symposium* (Tokyo: Kodansha, 1986), 54. This Korean scholar (Paik Choong-Hyun) contended that "historical evidence demonstrates that there was a larger number of cases of crimes against humanity: murder, extermination, enslavement, deportation, and other inhumane acts committed by the then existing Japanese government, or with the acquiescence of that government, against minority populations in Japan, Korea, Manchuria, China, the Philippines, and the other Asian regions under Japanese control. But the victorious Allied powers paid very little attention to crimes committed

against these colonial peoples, perhaps because the victims of these crimes were not nationals of the victorious nations." Ibid.

5. Jennifer Lind, *Sorry States: Apologies in International Politics* (Ithaca, NY: Cornell University Press, 2008), 30–31. Moreover, the United States provided immunity to those Japanese who tested biological weapons on live prisoners of war and civilians, in exchange for information obtained from the experiments, further questioning the legitimacy of the tribunal. A former judge at the Tokyo trial, B. V. A. Röling, recalled in 1983, "The prestige of the trial has also been severely damaged by the revelation of the existence in Manchuria of a Japanese laboratory for research into bacteriological weapons. These weapons were tested on prisoners of war and cost thousands of lives. This incident would have provided a case, rare at the Tokyo Trial, of centrally organized war criminality. But everything connected with it was kept from the tribunal. The American military authorities wanted to avail themselves of the results of these experiments, criminally obtained by Japan, and at the same time to prevent them from falling into the hands of the Soviet Union. The judges in Tokyo remained ignorant. The Japanese involved in these crimes were promised immunity from prosecution in exchange for divulging the information obtained from the experiments." See B. V. A. Röling, "Introduction," in Hosoya et al., *The Tokyo War Crimes Trial*, 18.

6. An April 2006 survey by the *Asahi Shimbun* showed 16 percent of respondents believing that the emperor bears "extremely heavy responsibility" for the war, while 15 percent said that he has "no responsibility." Another 22 percent responded that the emperor bears "heavy responsibility," and 42 percent said he has "some degree of responsibility." See "Tokyo Trials Poll," *Asahi Shimbun*, May 2, 2006, http://www.mansfieldfdn.org/backup/polls/2006/poll-06-3.htm. For excellent accounts of Emperor Hirohito's war responsibility, see Herbert P. Bix, *Hirohito and the Making of Modern Japan* (New York: Harper Collins, 2001); and Herbert P. Bix, "War Responsibility and Historical Memory: Hirohito's Apparition," *Asia-Pacific Journal: Japan Focus*, May 2008, http://apjjf.org/-Herbert-P.-Bix/2741/article.html.

7. Hosoya et al., *The Tokyo War Crimes Trial*, xx.

8. For example, see Arnold C. Brackman, *The Other Nuremberg: The Untold Story of the Tokyo War Crimes Trials* (New York: William Morrow, 1987), 86. Brackman, a correspondent for the United Press who covered the Tokyo War Crimes Tribunals, noted that "to his credit, [Joseph B.] Keenan (then the Allied chief prosecutor) admitted after the trial that 'we gave a good deal of thought' to indicting [the emperor] and that 'strictly legally Emperor Hirohito could have been tried and convicted because under the Constitution of Japan he did have the power to make war and stop it.' That, of course, was the Australian argument." Ibid.

9. Lind, *Sorry States*, 30–32.

10. Ibid., 17.

11. International Crisis Group, "Northeast Asia's Undercurrents of Conflict," December 15, 2005, p. 10, http://www.crisisgroup.org/~/media/Files/asia/north-east-asia/108_north_east_asia_s_undercurrents_of_conflict.pdf.

12. Mark Selden, "Japanese and American War Atrocities, Historical Memory and Reconciliation: World War II to Today," *Asia-Pacific Journal*, April 2008, http://apjjf.org/-Mark-Selden/2724/article.html.

13. Dower, *Embracing Defeat*, 473–474.

14. President Ronald Reagan signed the Civil Liberties Act of 1988, which offered apologies and reparations to survivors among the 110,000 Japanese and Japanese Americans who had been interned by the U.S. government in 1942–1945. In this case, however, as Mark Selden noted, "the victims' descendants are American citizens and apologies proved to be good politics for the incumbent." See Selden, "Japanese and American War Atrocities."

15. The remaining 48 percent answered that "the trials had problems, but were necessary to bring closure." See "Tokyo Trials Poll."

16. Dower, *Embracing Defeat*, 444.

17. "Japan and Its History: The Ghost of Wartimes Past," *The Economist*, November 6, 2008, http://www.economist.com/node/12570595.

18. Togo Kazuhiko, *National Bureau of Asian Research's Japan Forum*, June 15, 2009.

19. "The International Peoples' [*sic*] Tribunal on the Dropping of Atomic Bombs on Hiroshima and Nagasaki," July 16, 2007, http://www.k3.dion.ne.jp/~a-bomb/indexen.htm.

20. Hwang Geum Joo v. Japan, 413 F.3d 45 (D.C. Cir. 2005).

21. Kimie Hara, "Cold War Frontiers in the Asia-Pacific: The Troubling Legacy of the San Francisco Treaty," *Asia-Pacific Journal* 4, no. 9 (2006), http://apjjf.org/-Kimie-HARA/2211/article.html.

22. Alexis Dudden, "Dangerous Islands: Japan, Korea, and the United States," *Japan Focus*, August 11, 2008, p. 2.

23. Hara, "Cold War Frontiers in the Asia-Pacific." See also Kimie Hara, *Cold War Frontiers in the Asia-Pacific: Divided Territories in the San Francisco System* (London: Routledge, 2006).

24. David Straub, "The United States and Reconciliation in East Asia," in *East Asia's Haunted Present: Historical Memories and the Resurgence of Nationalism*, ed. Tsuyoshi Hasegawa and Kazuhiko Togo, (Westport, CT: Praeger, 2008), 215.

25. *Modern and Contemporary World History II* (Beijing: People's Education, 2003), 65.

26. Ibid., 80.

27. Ishii Susumu, Gomi Fumihiko, Sasayama Haruo, and Takano Toshihiko, *Yamakawa Japanese History B* (Tokyo: Yamakawa Shuppansha, 2002), 349.

28. Yamamoto Hirofumi et al., *Tokyo Shoseki Japanese History B* (Tokyo: Shoseki, 2003), 358.

29. Ishii et al., *Yamakawa Japanese History B*, 349.

30. *Keumsung World History* (Seoul: Keumsung, 2002), 288.

31. Elisabeth Gaynor Ellis and Anthony Esler, *World History: Connections to Today* (Upper Saddle River, NJ: Prentice Hall, 2005), 791–792.

32. David M. Kennedy, Lizabeth Cohen, and Thomas A. Bailey, *The American Pageant: A History of the Republic* (Boston: Houghton Mifflin, 2002), 878.

33. *Modern and Contemporary World History II*, 71–72.

34. *Keumsung World History*, 288.

35. Peter N. Stearns, Michael Adas, Stuart B. Schwartz, and Marc Jason Gilbert, *World Civilization: The Global Experience* (Boston: Addison-Wesley Educational, 2001), 919.

36. Ellis and Esler, *World History*, 859.

37. Gerald A. Danzer, J. Jorge Klor de Alva, Larry S. Krieger, Louis E. Wilson, and Nancy Woloch, *The Americans: Reconstruction to the 21st Century* (Evanston, IL: McDougal Littell, 2006), 587.

38. Ishii et al., *Yamakawa Japanese History B*, 359–360.

39. Article 3 reads, "Japan will concur in any proposal of the United States to the United Nations to place under its trusteeship system, with the United States as the sole administering authority, Nansei Shoto south of 29 deg. north latitude (including the Ryukyu Islands and the Daito Islands), Nanpo Shoto south of Sofu Gan (including the Bonin Islands, Rosario Island and the Volcano Islands) and Parece Vela and Marcus Island. Pending the making of such a proposal and affirmative action thereon, the United States will have the right to exercise all and any powers of administration, legislation and jurisdiction over the territory and inhabitants of these islands, including their territorial waters." Article 6 reads, "(a) All occupation forces of the Allied Powers shall be withdrawn from Japan as soon as possible after the coming into force of the present Treaty, and in any case not later than 90 days thereafter. Nothing in this provision shall, however, prevent the stationing or retention of foreign armed forces in Japanese territory under or in consequence of any bilateral or multilateral agreements which have been or may be made between one or more of the Allied Powers, on the one hand, and Japan on the other. (b) The provisions of Article 9 of the Potsdam Proclamation of 26 July 1945, dealing with the return of Japanese military forces to their homes, to the extent not already completed, will be carried out. (c) All Japanese property for which compensation has not already been paid, which was supplied for the use of

the occupation forces and which remains in the possession of those forces at the time of the coming into force of the present Treaty, shall be returned to the Japanese Government within the same 90 days unless other arrangements are made by mutual agreement."

40. Yamamoto et al., *Tokyo Shoseki Japanese History B*, 369.
41. Article 1 reads, "(a) The state of war between Japan and each of the Allied Powers is terminated as from the date on which the present Treaty comes into force between Japan and the Allied Power concerned as provided for in Article 23. (b) The Allied Powers recognize the full sovereignty of the Japanese people over Japan and its territorial waters."
42. Su Zhiliang, interview by the authors, Shanghai, April 27, 2010.
43. Li Zongyuan, interview by the authors, Beijing, April 22, 2010.
44. Chung Hyun Baek, interview by the authors, Seoul, December 18, 2009.
45. Bu Ping, interview by the authors, Beijing, April 19, 2010.
46. Shi Zhongshan, interview by the authors, Beijing, April 23, 2010.
47. Song Qiang, interview by the authors, Beijing, April 21, 2010.
48. Li Datong, interview by the authors, Beijing, April 24, 2010.
49. Wang Xiaodong, interview by the authors, Beijing, April 20, 2010.
50. Ibid.
51. John Dower, interview by the authors, Boston, August 12, 2010.
52. Kirk Saduski, interview by the authors, Santa Monica, CA, July 22, 2010.
53. Tamogami Toshio, interview by the authors, Tokyo, February 28, 2010.
54. Ito Takashi, interview by the authors, Tokyo, March 10, 2010.
55. Hosaka Masayasu, interview by the authors, Tokyo, March 4, 2010.
56. Takahata Isao, interview by the authors, Tokyo, March 8, 2010.
57. Wakamiya Yoshibumi, interview by the authors, Tokyo, March 5, 2010.
58. Watanabe Tsuneo, interview by the authors, Tokyo, March 4, 2010.
59. Takagi Kenichi, interview by the authors, Tokyo, March 11, 2010.
60. Song, interview by the authors.
61. Yang Tianshi, interview by the authors, Palo Alto, CA, May 16, 2010.
62. Park Won-soon, interview by the authors, Seoul, December 19, 2009.
63. Lee Hong Koo, interview by the authors, Seoul, December 21, 2009.
64. Yi Won Bok, interview by the authors, Seoul, December 16, 2009.
65. Takahata, interview by the authors.
66. Hosaka, interview by the authors.
67. Dower, interview by the authors.
68. Saduski, interview by the authors.
69. Lester Tenney, interview by the authors, La Jolla, CA, July 9, 2010.
70. Mark Peattie, interview by the authors, Palo Alto, CA, July 19, 2010.
71. Chung, interview by the authors.

72. Rhee Yong Hoon, interview by the authors, Palo Alto, CA, January 13, 2010.

73. Togo Kazuhiko, interview by the authors, Tokyo, February 27, 2010.

74. Yang Mi Kang, interview by the authors, Seoul, December 21, 2009.

75. Won Yu Chol, interview by the authors, Seoul, December 18, 2009.

76. Chung, interview by the authors.

77. Wang, interview by the authors.

78. Tong Zeng, interview by the authors, Beijing, April 21, 2010.

79. Tenney, interview by the authors.

80. Peattie, interview by the authors.

81. Barton Bernstein, interview by the authors, Palo Alto, CA, May 18, 2012.

82. See Straub, "The United States and Reconciliation in East Asia."

83. Gilbert Rozman, "Japan and Korea: Should the US Be Worried About Their New Spat in 2001?" *Pacific Review* 15, no. 1 (2002): 26.

84. David Palmer, "Korean Hibakusha, Japan's Supreme Court and the International Community: Can the U.S. and Japan Confront Forced Labor and Atomic Bombing?" *Asia-Pacific Journal*, February 2008, http://apjjf.org/-David-Palmer/2670/article.html.

85. The text of the resolution is available at https://www.govtrack.us/congress/bills/110/hres121/text.

86. G. John Ikenberry, "Japan's History Problem," *Washington Post*, August 17, 2006, http://www.washingtonpost.com/wp-dyn/content/article/2006/08/16/AR2006081601427.html. See also Gi-Wook Shin, "Beyond Apology, Moral Clarity," *Christian Science Monitor*, April 2, 2007, http://www.csmonitor.com/2007/0402/p09s02-coop.html.

87. Fumio Matsuo, "Tokyo Needs Its Dresden Moment," *Wall Street Journal*, August 16, 2005, p. A16.

88. "Clinton Says 'Comfort Women' Should Be Referred to as 'Enforced Sex Slaves,'" *Japan Today*, July 11, 2012, http://www.japantoday.com/category/politics/view/clinton-says-comfort-women-should-be-referred-to-as-enforced-sex-slaves.

89. Susan Jenkins Vanderweert, "Seeking Justice for 'Comfort' Women: Without an International Criminal Court, Suits Brought by World War II Sex Slaves of the Japanese Army May Find Their Best Hope of Success in U.S. Federal Courts," *North Carolina Journal of International Law and Commercial Regulation* 27, no. 1 (2001): 181.

90. There was no specific legal reference to Germany's responsibility for reparations, unlike with Japan through the San Francisco Peace Treaty.

91. See Kinue Tokudome, "POW Forced Labor Lawsuits Against Japanese Companies," JPRI Working Paper No. 82, November 2001, http://www.jpri.org/publications/workingpapers/wp82.html.

92. One reason for the contrasting responses on the part of the U.S. government may have to do with the apparent difference between Japanese and German war crimes. While there have been controversies over the extent and responsibility of Japanese war crimes, Nazi war crimes were better documented and could not be denied, such that the German right-wingers lacked the political ammunition to engage in any kind of denial politics. Thus, the United States was able to better accept German war crimes and deal with them accordingly. The other reason may have to do with the difference in political mobilization of respective ethnic communities. The Jewish American community has been better organized and continuously pressured the U.S. government to be proactive in dealing with this history issue. See Michael J. Bazyler, *Holocaust Justice: The Battle for Restitution in America's Courts* (New York: New York University Press, 2003); Marianne R. Sanua, *Let Us Prove Strong: The American Jewish Committee, 1945–2006* (Waltham, MA: Brandeis University Press, 2007); Shlomo Shafir, *Ambiguous Relations: The American Jewish Community and Germany Since 1945* (Detroit, MI: Wayne State University Press); and Yossi Shain, "Ethnic Diasporas and U.S. Foreign Policy," *Political Science Quarterly* (1994): 811–841. On the other hand, the Asian American community is newer to the country and further behind in addressing the history issue in its members' home countries, though Asian Americans were quite successful in demanding redress for the wartime internment of Japanese Americans. However, recently, Asian Americans have been more active, as illustrated by the case of House Resolution 121 regarding comfort women. Mike Honda, a Japanese American legislator, introduced the resolution, and the Chinese and Korean American communities mobilized in support. It is likely that the Asian American community will become more active with regard to the history issue in the coming years and that, as American citizens, Asian Americans will press the U.S. government to be more forthcoming. Asian American activism is an area that merits more careful attention with regard to the U.S. role in dealing with the history question in Northeast Asia.

93. Quoted in Tokudome, "POW Forced Labor Lawsuits."

## Chapter 11

1. David Croker, "Reckoning with Past Wrongs: A Normative Framework," *Ethics and International Affairs* 13, no. 1 (1994): 43–64.

2. Genron NPO and *China Daily*, "The 10th Japan-China Public Opinion Poll: Analysis Report on the Comparative Data," September 9, 2014, http://www.genron-npo.net/en/pp/docs/10th_Japan-China_poll.pdf.

3. *Dong-A Ilbo*, "Korea-China-Japan Public Opinion Survey," January 6, 2012, http://news.donga.com/3/all/20120106/43121061/1.

4. *Dong-A Ilbo*, "Donga-Asahi Joint Public Opinion Survey in the Light of the 50th Anniversary of Normalization of Japan-Korea Relations," June 18, 2015, http://news.donga.com/View?gid=71928976&date=20150618.

5. Genron NPO, "The 2nd Joint Japan–South Korea Public Opinion Poll (2014): Analysis Report on Comparative Data," July 16, 2014, http://www.genron-npo.net/en/pp/archives/5142.html.

6. Gallup Korea, "Public Opinion Poll on Korea-Japan Relations," March 18, 2014, http://www.gallup.co.kr/gallupdb/reportContent.asp?seqNo=536.

7. See Gi-Wook Shin, "Historical Reconciliation in Northeast Asia: Past Efforts, Future Steps, and the U.S. Role," in *Confronting Memories of World War II: European and Asian Legacies*, ed. Daniel Chirot, Gi-Wook Shin, and Daniel Sneider (Seattle: University of Washington Press, 2014), 157–185.

8. "List of War Apology Statements Issued by Japan," *Wikipedia*, January 18, 2016, http://en.wikipedia.org/wiki/List_of_war_apology_statements_issued_by_Japan (accessed February 14, 2016).

9. Caroline Rose, *Sino-Japanese Relations: Facing the Past, Looking to the Future?* (London: Routledge, 2004), 102.

10. For more on Japanese conservatives' views of Asia, see Wakamiya Yoshibumi, *Sengo hoshu no Ajia kan* [How Japan's conservatives view Asia] (Tokyo: Asahi Shimbunsha, 1997).

11. Yoshiaki Yoshimi, "Government Must Admit 'Comfort Women' System Was Sexual Slavery," *Asahi Shimbun*, September 20, 2013, http://ajw.asahi.com/article/forum/politics_and_economy/AJ201309200068.

12. "Seven of Ten Koreans Say Japan Has Not Apologized," *Asia Today*, November 21, 2013, http://www.asiatoday.co.kr/news/view.asp?seq=896846.

13. Dong-hwan Ahn, "94 Percent Koreans Say Japan Feels No Regret for Its Past Wrongdoings; 63 Percent Japanese Find Korean Demand for Japanese Apology Incomprehensible," *Seoul Shinmun*, January 4, 2013, http://www.seoul.co.kr/news/newsView.php?id=20130104001010.

14. For instance, see the Society for the Dissemination of Historical Fact, "SDHF Newsletter No.4: Top Secret Documents Reveal the Truth About Nanking Incident," June 15, 2015, http://www.sdh-fact.com/mail-magazine/432. According to this source, "An examination of those documents reveals that the provenance of accusations that Japan perpetrated a massacre in Nanking is wartime propaganda initiated by the Nationalist intelligence organization. They also expose European and American Nationalist agents who were intimately involved in the concoction of 'Nanking Massacre' propaganda."

15. Alexis Dudden, *Troubled Apologies Among Japan, Korea, and the United States* (New York: Columbia University Press, 2008), 33.

16. Daniel C. Sneider, "The War over Words: History Textbooks and International Relations in Northeast Asia," in *History Textbooks and the Wars in Asia: Divided Memories*, ed. Gi-Wook Shin and Daniel C. Sneider (New York: Routledge, 2011), 246–268.

17. International Crisis Group, "North East Asia's Undercurrents of Conflict," December 15, 2005, p. 13, http://www.crisisgroup.org/~/media/Files/asia/north-east-asia/108_north_east_asia_s_undercurrents_of_conflict.pdf.

18. "Japan, S. Korea Researchers at Odds over Forced Labor, 'Comfort Women,'" *Japan Times*, March 24, 2010, http://search.japantimes.co.jp/cgi-bin/nn20100324a3.html.

19. In his opening speech, Bu Ping proclaimed, "In Japan, speeches and activities not admitting the responsibility for the war of aggression and denying the historical facts of the war have existed until now. Those irresponsible words and actions going against the common interests of the two countries have constantly hurt the public sentiment of a war victim nation." See Mure Dickie and David Pilling, "Sino-Japanese Historians Battle to Find Consensus," *Financial Times*, February 16, 2007, http://www.ft.com/cms/s/0/7fe74b56-bd75-11db-b5bd-0000779e2340.html#axzz44cgGutj9.

20. See "No Common History View with China," *Japan Times*, March 21, 2007; and "Historians Agree on China-Japan Joint Study Topics," *Xinhua*, March 21, 2007.

21. "China-Japan Scholars' Report Completed," *People's Daily*, February 1, 2010, http://english.people.com.cn/90001/90776/90883/6884274.html.

22. "New Study Fails to Bridge Japan, China History Divide," *AFP*, January 31, 2010, http://www.akfiles.com/forums/showthread.php?t=62457.

23. Hwang Geum Joo et al. v. Japan, Civil Action 00-02233 (HHK) (D.D.C. Oct. 4, 2001), 23.

24. "Supreme Court Rules Japanese Firms Must Pay for Forced Labor," *Chosun Ilbo*, May 25, 2012, http://english.chosun.com/site/data/html_dir/2012/05/25/2012052501084.html.

25. See Andrew Horvat, "A Strong State, Weak Civil Society, and Cold War Geopolitics: Why Japan Lags Behind Europe in Confronting a Negative Past," in *Rethinking Historical Injustice and Reconciliation in Northeast Asia*, ed. Gi-Wook Shin, Soon-Won Park, and Daqing Yang (London: Routledge, 2007), 222.

26. The argument presented in this section was made previously in Gi-Wook Shin, Soon-Won Park, and Daqing Yang, eds., *Rethinking Historical Injustice and Reconciliation in Northeast Asia: Korean Experiences in Regional Perspective* (London: Routledge, 2006); it is further elaborated here.

27. Kawashima Shin, interview by the authors, Tokyo, March 7, 2010.

28. North Korea's human-rights record has been widely condemned, especially by Amnesty International, Human Rights Watch, the European Union, and the United Nations. Most recently, the UN General Assembly passed a resolution on December 18, 2014, urging that North Korea be referred to the International Criminal court for its human-rights situation.

29. Kiyoteru Tsutsui and Hwa Ji Shin, "Global Norms, Local Activism, and Social Movement Outcomes: Global Human Rights and Resident Koreans in Japan," *Social Problems* 55, no. 3 (2008): 391.

30. Yang Mi Kang, interview by the authors, Seoul, December 21, 2009.

31. Ibid.

32. Rumi Sakamoto and Matthew Allen, "'Hating "the Korean Wave"' Comic Books: A Sign of New Nationalism in Japan?" *Asia-Pacific Journal*, October 2007, http://www.japanfocus.org/-Mathew-Allen/2535#.

33. See Gi-Wook Shin and Michael Robinson, "Introduction: Rethinking Colonial Korea," in *Colonial Modernity in Korea*, ed. Gi-Wook Shin and Michael Robinson (Cambridge, MA: Harvard University Asia Center, 1999), 1–18.

34. Ibid.

35. For instance, Christian groups, imagery, and language played an important role in Franco-German reconciliation, and even the concept of reconciliation has Christian overtones (i.e., forgiveness). It is difficult to envision an entirely analogous movement toward international reconciliation in Northeast Asia, which does not have the same degree of presence of transnational Christian groups. See Elizabeth A. Cole, "Introduction: Reconciliation and History Education," in *Teaching the Violent Past: History Education and Reconciliation*, ed. Elizabeth A. Cole (Boulder, CO: Rowman and Littlefield, 2007), 1–28.

36. "Full Text of Park's Speech at U.S. Congress," *Yonhap News Agency*, May 8, 2013, http://english.yonhapnews.co.kr/national/2013/05/08/4/0301000000AEN20130508010800315F.HTML.

37. "Vice-Premier Teng at Tokyo Press Conference: New Upsurge in Friendly Relations Between China and Japan," *Peking Review* 21, no. 44 (1978): 16.

# Index

*Page numbers in italics indicate material in figures.*

"ABCD (American-British-Chinese-Dutch) encirclement," 104, 234, 238
Abe Shinzo: and comfort women issue, 176–178, 201, 287, 295–296, 328n17; and parallel history model, 297; trip to Beijing, Seoul (2006), 36; visits to Yasukuni Shrine, 5, 56, 102, 294, 296, 305
Ahn Byeong-jik, 72
Ahn Jung-geun, 4
Akiba, Tadatoshi, 262
Akihito (emperor), 140–141
Alien Tort Claims Act (ATCA; U.S., 1789), 298
Alperovitz, Gar, 257
Ambrose, Stephen, 153
American Defenders of Bataan and Corregidor Memorial Society, 190, 192
*The American Pageant* (textbook), 151, 276
*The Americans* (textbook), 151, 256–257, 276
Anti-Comintern Pact (1936), 239
APHEN (Asia Peace, History, and Education Network), 95
apology diplomacy, 295–296
"apology fatigue," 7, 296
*Arirang* (Cho), 76
Armacost, Michael, 216–217, 242
Asada, Sadao, 253

*Asahi Shimbun*, 163, 200, 207, 281; on atrocities by Japanese soldiers, 229; on irrationality of Pacific War, 248; publishing official documents on comfort women, 95; retraction of comfort women story, 212; survey on "past issues" with Japan, 294; Tokyo Trial poll (2006), 336n6
Asian American community, 341n92
Asian Women's Fund, 125, 141, 176, 200, 299
Asia-Pacific Area War Compensation Forum, 124
"Asia's paradox," 308
atomic bombings of Hiroshima and Nagasaki, 250; American versus Japanese views of, 9, 12, 110–111, 151, 244; Bu Ping on, 39; civilian targets of, 39; compared to firebombing, 45; hypothetical comparison with Germany, 254; Korean victims in, 68, 93, 123, 255–256, 333n17; Li Datong on, 45; not mentioned in Chinese textbooks, 30; not mentioned in Korean textbooks, 68, 251; opinion leaders' views of, 11, 39, 44–45, 50, 63, 75, 87, 93, 113, 145, 189, 254, 260–261; questions regarding military necessity of, 252–253; Supreme War Council

## Index

atomic bombings of Hiroshima and Nagasaki (*continued*)
  response to, 138; and treatment of U.S. prisoners of war, 188–189; as war crimes, 252
*Awakening Lion* sculpture, 24

*Band of Brothers* miniseries, 153–155
*banzai*, 210
Basilone, John, 154
Bataan Death March, 150, 187–188, 243
*The Battle for China* (Peattie, Drea, van de Ven), 185
*Battle of China* (Capra), 163
Battle of Pingxingguan Pass (1937), 43
Beard, Charles, 152, 237
Bernstein, Barton, 157, 260, 285
Bix, Herbert, 271
*Blue Swallow* (film), 72
Bork, Robert, 288
Brackman, Arnold C., 336n8
Brandt, Willy, 78
Breen, John, 104
*Bridge on the River Kwai* (Lean), 153
Britain, 61
Bu Ping, 9, 19, 34–40, *35*, 217, 219, 279, 343n19
Bush, George W., 17, 171, 177, 263

California, 175, 201, 298
Camp Amache, 171–172
Campbell, Kurt, 17
Capra, Frank, 163
Caprio, Mark, 69
Carter, Jimmy, 174
*The Cause of Japan* (Togo Shigenori), 133–135
CCP (Chinese Communist Party), 27–30, 43, 56–57, 61
Cemetery of Soviet Martyrs (Port Arthur), 4
Chang, Iris, 26, 117, *158*, 158–164
Chang, Ying-Ying, 160–161, 164
Chiang Kai-shek, 30, 45, 138, 215, 221–222, 227
China: anti-Japanese protests in (2005), 34, 301; Anti-Japanese War in textbooks of, 30–31; censoring of postwar history, 38; Communist Party (CCP), 27–30, 43, 56–57, 61; coverage of Nanjing Massacre in, 27–28, 31; as the critical theater in World War II, 29, 31; and differing views on Japanese invasion, 13; "history activists" in, 13; and lack of knowledge of Pacific War, 232; Li on demands for reparations, 45–46; Mao's "protracted war" strategy, 30; Patriotic Education Campaign, 27–28, 30–31; populist nationalists ("nativists") in, 46–47; renouncing reparation demands, 54–55; split with Soviet Union, 52
*China Can Still Say No* (Song et al.), 47
*China Daily*, 33, 294
China Federation for Defending the Diaoyu Islands, 51
"China Incident" exhibit, 103
*China Is Unhappy* (Song and Wang), 47–48
"China Quagmire," 224
*The China That Can Say No* (Song et al.), 47
*China Youth Daily*, 42–43
Chinese Association for Claiming Compensation from Japan, 52
*Chinese Modern and Contemporary History* (U.S. textbook), 202
Cho Gap Je, 71–72
Cho Jeong Rae, 71, 74, 74–78
Chulwoo Lee, 73
Chun Doo-hwan, 69, 85
Chung Hyun Baek, 206, 279, 284–285
Chung Teong Young, 121
Churchill, Winston, 91, 138, 239, 244, 252
*City of Life and Death* (Lu), 33–34
Civil Liberties Act (U.S., 1988), 174, 337n14
Class A war criminals, 101–102, 139–140
Clearing Up Past Incidents for Truth and Reconciliation, 69–70
Clinton, Bill, 263–264
Clinton, Hillary, 287
Cohen, Lizabeth, 234–235, 243
collaborative history writing, 296–298
"colonial modernization" debate, 72–74, 89–90, 98–99
comfort women: Abe's denial of coercion of, 295–296; apology for, 141, 200–201,

296; compensation/reparations issue, 6, 8, 99, 210–212; contacting Tong Zeng, 53–54; denials regarding, 95, 116–117, 200, 207–208, 212; Dutch women prisoners as, 116, 141; Glendale, California, statue of, 196; Hayden Act regarding, 201; Japanese military men aiding, 124; Japanese scholars' research on, 66, 206–207; Korean activism regarding, 94, 205–206; Korean collaboration regarding, 206–209; lower court ruling on (1998), 86; and Nazi gas chamber comparison, 76; near consensus on, 12; Obama statement on, 5–6; and rallies at Japanese Embassy in Seoul, 8, 93, 95; and role of Korean brokers, 90; Seoul statue of, 195; in Shanghai, 54; starting to speak out (1960s), 15–16; U.S. congressional resolution regarding, 175–178
Commission on Wartime Relocation and Internment of Civilians, 174
Committee for Historical Facts, 178
Committee for Restoration of National Normalcy, 71
Committee of Concerned Asian Scholars, 167
Communist Party (Japan), 145
compensation/reparation demands on Japan: versus apology demands, 211–212; Chinese government renunciation of, 45, 52–54; by Chinese NGO, 55; by Chinese war victims, 52–57, 63; in comparison to Germany, 124–126, 191, 275, 289, 306–307, 340n90; and economic assistance to South Korea, 274; and globalization, 302; Hosaka Masayasu on, 230; for individual victims, 123–125; and interned Japanese Americans, 151–152, 171–174, 181, 337n14; Iris Chang on, 159–160; Japanese corporations and, 299; in Japanese courts, 298; John Dower on, 289; Korean 1965 settlement, 82–83, 255; Mike Honda on, 175–176, 179, 262; none paid to former colonies, 293; Park Won-soon on, 86; for poison gas workers, 37; role of Internet and social media in, 301; and San Francisco Treaty, 124, 191, 266, 268–269, 272–273, 276–277, 286, 293; by Southeast Asian countries, 277; textbooks on, 203–204; Tong Zeng's petition to Japan, 53–57; U.S. reluctance to pursue, 192, 286, 289. *See also* comfort women; forced labor victims
Compton, Karl T., 251–252
Coomaraswamy, Radhika, 205
crimes against humanity, statutory limitations for, 86
Croker, David, 293
*The Crossroads* (proposed exhibit), 156
cultural interpenetration, 303
Cultural Revolution, 26, 38, 60

Daniel, Clifton Truman, 249
Day of Remembrance (California), 174
democratization and reconciliation, 300–301, 304
Deng Xiaoping, 46, 308
Diaoyu/Senkaku Islands, 47, 56, 115, 269, 305
Ding, Ignatius, 161
diplomacy, art of, 136
Divided Memories and Reconciliation project, 7
Dokdo/Takeshima islets, 16, 67, 273, 284, 294, 305
*Dong-A Ilbo* survey, 294
Dongnimmun (Independence Gate), 64
Doolittle, Jimmy, 167, 151
Dower, John, 164–171, *165*; on atomic bomb, 254, 261; on compensation issue, 211–212; on emperor's role, 283; on end of hatred, 158; on idealism in trial, 280; on racism in Pacific War, 152–153; on Tokyo trials, 335n3; on victor's justice, 271, 280; on whitewashing of Japan's war crimes, 289
Dresden, 127, 263
Dudden, Alexis, 296
Dutch comfort women, 116, 141

EAI (East Asia Institute), 294
East China Sea, 47–48, 115
Eastwood, Clint, 244

*The Economic Structure of Modern Korea* (An), 74
Einstein, Albert, 252
Eisenhower, Dwight, 257
*Embracing Defeat* (Dower), 165–166, 168–171
*Empire and Aftermath* (Dower), 165
*Empire of the Sun* (film), 153
enclave-style development, 73
*Enola Gay* (exhibit), 111, 149, 155–157
Eri Hotta, 240
Evans, Lane, 286–287

Fan Wenlan, 60–61
Father Rosslyn, 59
*Fat Man* atomic bomb, 250
Feis, Herbert, 232–233
feminist perspective, 14
"Fifteen Years War," 108, 216
firebombing, 45, 109, 113, 127, 129–131, 151, 243, 245
*Fires on the Plain* (film), 106
*Flags of Our Fathers* (film), 244
Fogel, Joshua, 162–163
forced labor victims: American POWs, 124, 150, 187–190, 192, 243; building railroads, 103; Chinese nationals, 52, 55, 106, 198–199, 201–202, 208; diverse views on, 99, 124, 187, 204–211; in Germany versus Japan, 124–125, 191–192, 286; and Hayden Act, 201–202; Japanese POWs of Soviet Union, 121–122, 125, 138, 275; Korean nationals, 66, 84, 121–124, 198, 202–203, 209, 298–299; on Sakhalin Island, 120–121. *See also* comfort women; compensation/reparation demands on Japan
*Forgotten Ally* (Mitter), 223–224
Foundation for Remembrance, Responsibility and Future, 124
France, collaborators in, 87–88
Fujioka Nobukatsu, 247
Fujisaki Ichiro, 192
Fund for the Future, 124

Geneva Convention, 190
Genron NPO, 33, 294
Germany: apologies and reparations by, 53, 55, 124; bombing of London by, 45; class-action suits against firms in, 191; compared to Japan, 87, 124–126, 191, 275, 286, 289, 306–307, 340n90; "Final Solution" in, 76; German Fund for the Future, 288; and lack of victimhood mythology, 10; Nazi war crimes documentation, 307, 341n92
Giamo, Benedict, 111
Global Alliance for Preserving the History of World War II, 161
globalization, 300, 302–304
Gomikawa Jumpei, 106
Gorbachev, Mikhail, 123
Gottemoeller, Rose, 324n19
*Grave of the Fireflies* (film), 109, 128–129, 132
Greater East Asian Co-Prosperity Sphere, 16, 216
"Greater East Asian War," 216
Guadalcanal Island, 154, 243
Gwanghwamun gate, 78

*Hallyu* ("Korean Wave"), 299
Hamburg, firebombing of, 127
Han Hong Koo, 333n17
Hanil Yondae 21 (Korea-Japan Solidarity 21), 299
Hanks, Tom, 153–154, 248
Hara, Kimie, 273
*Harp of Burma* (film), 106
Hatoyama Yukio, 262–264
Hayashi, Hirofumi, 206
Hayden, Tom, 298
*Heidi* (film), 131
*hibakusa* (victims of the atomic bombs), 255
Higashinakano Shudo, 118, 163
Hirohito (emperor): Allied decision not to prosecute, 40, 111, 113, 125, 169–170; and Communist abdication demands, 145; decision of, to surrender, 139; ending visits to Yasukuni, 102; Japanese anger toward, 106; MacArthur's reliance on, 169–170; opinion leaders on, 39–40, 45; renouncing divinity, 145; role of, in World War II, 39–40, 63, 87; surrender

radio broadcast by, 131; Watanabe on, 145–146
Hiroshima: call for U.S. presidential visit to, 11; casualty figures, 250; Chinese workers in, 53; as justification for Japanese victim theme, 8–9; Korean atomic bomb victims in, 93, 255, 256, 333n17; memorial museum in, 25–26, 109; Peace Memorial Museum, 249, 254. *See also* atomic bombings of Hiroshima and Nagasaki
*Historical Exhibits of the Nanjing Massacre Committed by Japanese Aggression*, 15
historical memories, 7, 294–295; differences in weighting of, 10; and disputes arising in 1980s, 15; greater diversity of, in democracies, 13; opinion leaders and, 17–19; perception gaps in, 11–12; and textbook writing, 12
historical reconciliation, 6, 300–306; apology diplomacy, 295–296; collaborative history writing, 296–298; German example, 306; litigation, 298–299; multiple frameworks for, 300–306; role of memory in blocking, 6–7; social and cultural exchanges, 299; sustainability of, 308–309
*The History of the Imperialist Invasion of China*, 60
*The History of the War of Resistance Against Japan*, 61
*History That Opens the Future*, 96
Holocaust Museum (Washington, DC), 25
Honda, Mike, 116, 171–179, *172*, 196, 212, 262, 341n92
Honda Katsuichi, 163, 229
Hosaka Masayasu, 229–230, 233, 280, 283
*Hotaru no haka* (film), 109, 128–129, 132
House of Sharing, 97
Hu Jintao, 32
Hull, Cordell, 119, 135–136, 236, 239, 241
human-rights-centered perspective, 14
*Hwang Geum Joo v. Japan*, 273

Ichikawa Kon, 106
identity politics, 304
Ienaga Saburo, 272
Ikenberry, G. John, 287
Im Kwon Taek, 76
IMTFE. *See* Tokyo War Crimes Tribunal (International Military Tribunal for the Far East)
Ina, Hisayoshi, 11
incendiary bombs, 127. *See also* firebombing
Independence Gate (Dongnimmun), 64
Independence Hall of Korea, 67–69
Institute for Research in Collaborationist Activities, 71
Iraq, 171
Ishiwara Kanji, 180, 182, 184–185, 218
Ito Hirobumi, 4
Ito Takashi, 207, 209, 216, 224, 228–229, 239, 280
Iwo Jima, 137, 154, 243–244

JACL (Japanese American Citizens League), 174
Jansen, Marius, 182
Japan: annexation of Korea by (1910), 98, 104, 119; apology by, for comfort women, 141, 200–201, 296; Article 9 of constitution of, 132; bid for UN Security Council permanent seat by, 32, 35; Chinese and U.S. roles in defeat of, 62; Cho Jeong Rae on apology issue, 71, 78; compared with Germany, 87, 124–126, 191, 275, 286, 289, 306–307, 340n90; concerns about rising China in, 115; decision of, to go to war, 16, 39, 62–63, 112–113, 247–248; flawed war planning of, 183–184; forced suicide of civilians in, 107–108, 246–247; historical revisionism in, 116–117; and "invasion" versus "advance" into China, 15, 60; and karma, 50; and normalization with Korea (1965), 66; official apologies by, 86, 98, 266; opinion leaders on apology for war issue, 9, 40, 45–46, 50, 55, 63, 83, 86, 93, 98–99, 133, 159, 171, 190–192, 262, 279; pacifist narrative in, 109; Park Geun-hye's call for apology from, 67; polls on apology issue, 294, 296; postwar occupation of, 168–171; quest of, to

Japan (*continued*)
  be a "normal nation," 305; and reparations issues, 124–125, 126; and stupidity versus morality of Pacific War, 247–248; surrender of, 131, 250–251; and trade war with United States (1980s), 47; on U.S. "crimes against humanity," 10; use of chemical weapons by, 37; victim identity of, 16, 253–254, 287; withdrawal of, from League of Nations, 134
Japanese American internment, 151–152, 171–174, 181
Japanese Society for History Textbook Reform (Tsukurukai), 35
Japan-ROK Joint History Research Committee, 297
"Japan's War in Asia," 217
Jewish American community, 341n92
Jews' suffering compared to Koreans', 76. *See also* Germany
Joint History Research Committee, 297–298
just and unjust war, 109, 279

Kaiten torpedo exhibit, 103
Kan Naoto, 98, 115
karma, 50
Kawashima Shin, 210–211, 259, 261, 301
Keenan, Joseph B., 336n8
Kempeitai (thought police), 144
Kenkanryu, 304
Kennedy, David, 162–163, 234–235, 243
*Keumsung Contemporary Korean History* (textbook), 202–204
*Keumsung World History* (textbook), 202–204, 276
Khabarovsk War Crimes Trials, 268
"Kill all, burn all, destroy all" tactics, 228
Kim Dae-jung, 69, 297, 301
Kim Gu, 70
Kim Hak-sun, 199
Kim Il-sung, 81
Kim Kyung-Seok, 203
Kim Yeong Dok, 72
Kingston, Jeff, 254
Kitaoka Shinichi, 38, 220–221
Kiyose Ichiro, 254

Kiyoteru Tsutsui, 11
KMT (Kuomintang), 13, 26–28, 30–32, 42–44, 59, 61, 215
Kobe, firebombing of, 127–129
Koguryo, 294
Koizumi Junichiro, 32, 35, 102, 143, 263, 297, 305
Konoe Fumimaro, 113, 236, 239, 259
Kono Yohei, 176–177, 201, 207, 213, 266, 296
Korea: atomic bomb victims from, 68, 93, 123, 255–256, 333n17; atrocities against Vietnamese by, 13; and "colonial modernization" debate, 72–74, 89–90, 98–99; effects of democratization in, 69–70; and forced laborers for Japan, 66, 84, 121–124, 198, 202–203, 209, 298–299; Japanese annexation of, 98, 104, 119; Koreans serving in Japanese army, 48, 101; and lack of knowledge of Pacific War, atomic bombings, 97, 232; nationalism in, 304–305; New Right historians in, 72, 74, 90; and normalization with Japan (1965), 66; pro-Japanese collaborators in, 69–72, 77–78, 82, 87, 92–93, 98–99, 105, 301; purging Japanese language by, 67; and repatriation of Sakhalin forced laborers, 123; as "shrimp among the whales," 66; textbooks of, 12, 251; victim mentality of, 99
Korea-Japan Solidarity 21 (Hanil Yondae 21), 299
Korean Atomic Bomb Victims Association, 255–256
Korean Council for the Women Drafted into Sexual Slavery by Japan, 94, 97–98, 199
*Korean National History* (textbook), 203–204
Korean War and subsequent division, 75–76
Kubo, Toru, 199
Kuomintang, 13, 26–28, 30–32, 42–44, 59, 61, 215
Kwak Kwi Hoon, 255
Kwantung Army (Unit 731), 15, 37, 226, 280, 285
Kyushu, 124

*Landmine Warfare* (film), 26, 52
Landsberg, Alison, 18
Lantos, Tom, 178
Lean, David, 153
Leckie, Robert, 154
Lee, Robert E., 146
Lee Hong Koo, 79, 79–83, 282
Lee Myung-bak, 71
Lee Namhee, 69
Lee Young-hoon, 72
LeMay, Curtis E., 127, 151
*Letters from Iwo Jima* (film), 244
Leyte Gulf, 243, 244
Liberal Democratic Party (Japan), 142
Li Datong, 13, 32, 40–46, *41*, 279
Lin Biao, 43–44
Lincoln, Abraham, 146
Lind, Jennifer, 270–271
litigation, 298–299
*Little Boy* atomic bomb, 250
Liu Lianren, 201
Li Zongyuan, 29, 279
Lu Chuan, 33–34
Lugou Bridge Incident, 23–24, *24*
Lushun, China, 3

MacArthur, Douglas: and decisions on whom to prosecute, 111, 139, 169–170, 280–281, 283, 285; occupation and rebuilding under, 157–158, 169, 276; and retreat from islands, 242–243; and use of atomic bomb, 251
Mahbuni museum, 107–108
Manchuria/Manchukuo, 220; bioweapons lab in, 336n5; and Chiang Kai-shek, 30; forced labor in, 198; and Ishiwara Kanji, 180, 182, 184–185, 218; Japanese conscription in, 198; Manchurian/Mukden Incident, 134, 182, 215, 217, 232, 237; museum exhibits on, 103, 108, 149; opinion leaders on, 48–49, 56, 91, 116, 134, 180–182; Park Kyung-won and, 72; revisionism and, 118–119; and Russia/USSR, 215, 233, 275
Manhattan Project, 252
Mao Zedong, 30, 45, 222
map of Asia during World War II, *xi*

Marco Polo Bridge Incident, 23–24, *24*, 30, 216–217, 219; as chance event, 62; Joint History Research Committee on, 297
Maruyama Masao, 106
mass graves, 26, 36
Matsuno Takayasu, 15
Matsuo, Fumio, 263, 265
Meiji emperor, 100
Memorial Hall of the Nanjing Massacre, 15, 25
memory formation and transformation, 14–16
military history versus history of war, 164
Milošević, Slobodan, 280
Minetta, Norman, 173
Ming (Flash Gordon character), 173
Mitsubishi Heavy Industries Ltd., 299
Mitsui Mining Company, 188, 191
Mitsuyoshi Himeta, 199
Mitter, Rana, 223–224, 227
Miyazaki Hayao, 129, 132
Miyazawa Kiichi, 200, 295
*Modern and Contemporary World History II* (textbook), 276, 278
modernization theory, 73
Morgenthau, Henry, 239
Mukden/Manchurian Incident, 134, 182, 215, 217, 232, 237. *See also* Manchuria/Manchukuo
Murayama Tomiichi, 141, 200
Museum of Evidence of War Crimes by Japanese Army Unit 731, 15
Museum of the War of Chinese People's Resistance Against Japanese Aggression, 24–25
*My Hitch in Hell* (Tenney), 190
*My Neighbor Totoro* (film), 132

Nagano Shigeto, 16, 119
Nagasaki, 25–26, 93, 250, 333n17. *See also* atomic bombings of Hiroshima and Nagasaki
Nagoya, firebombing of, 127
Nanjing Massacre (1937), 8; American soldiers' awareness of, 155; casualty figures for, 13, 39, 62; Chinese depictions of, 26, 30, 33; deniers of, 116–119; *Historical*

Nanjing Massacre (1937) (*continued*)
    *Exhibits of the Nanjing Massacre Committed by Japanese Aggression*, 15; Joint History Research Committee on, 297–298; near consensus on, 12; as part of Japanese character, 55–56; Song Qiang on, 50; and War Crimes Tribunal, 268. *See also* Rape of Nanjing
Nanjing Massacre Memorial Hall, 33, 158–159
*The Nanking Massacre: Fact Versus Fiction* (Higashinakano), 163
"national liberation movements" in Korea, 69
national memory, formation of, 14–16
National Mobilization Law (Japan), 198
National People's Congress (NPC), 53
neo-Marxism, 90
Netherlands, 116, 140–141
*New History Textbook* (Japan), 32, 207
Niksch, Larry, 212
Nimitz, Chester W., 150
Nine-Power Treaty of Washington (1922), 232
*Ningen no joken* (films), 106
Nippon Steel Corp., 299
Nitze, Paul, 252–253
Nomonhan Incident, 233
nongovernmental organizations (NGOs), 13–14
North Korea, 115
Nuremberg trials, 125

Obama, Barack, 5, 8–9, 157, 196, 262, 264
Ogata Sadako, 216, 262
Ohara Yasuo, 163
Ohka glider exhibit, 103
Okada Katsuya, 192
Okayama, firebombing of, 109, 129–131
Okinawa: American landing on, 137; Battle of Okinawa, 154, 245–246; and civilians conscripted into Japanese army, 101, 246; and civilians killed by Imperial Army, 247; Okinawa Prefectural Peace Memorial Museum, 107–108; return of, to Japanese sovereignty, 140; under U.S. administration, 277

Omura Masujiro, 100
Operation Ichigo, 225
Oppenheimer, Robert, 272
Ota Masahide, 108, 246–247

*The Pacific* (miniseries), 153–155
Pacific War, 216–217; Allied advance in, 243–244; battle for Okinawa, 244–247; Japanese early victories in, 242–243; lack of knowledge of, by Chinese, Koreans, 232. *See also* atomic bombings of Hiroshima and Nagasaki; Pearl Harbor
Paik Choong-Hyun, 335–336n4
Pal, Radhabinod, 104, 271, 275, 279
Palisades Park, New Jersey, 195, 206, 213
parallel history writing, 38, 297
Park Chung-hee, 199; assassination of, 85; as a collaborator, 69, 71, 78, 87–88, 92–93; economic modernization under, 78, 93; end of rule of, 75; military dictatorship under, 85; and normalizing relations with Japan, 15, 199; opinion leaders on, 92-93, 87–88
Park Geun-hye, 66–67, 308
Park Kyung-won, 72
Park Won-soon, 83–88, *84*, 282
Peace, Friendship, and Exchange Initiative, 253
Peace Institute for Christian Women, 97
Peace Memorial Museum (Hiroshima), 109–110
Pearl Harbor, 216–217, 231; conspiracy theories about, 119, 152, 237–240, 242, 254; and Japan's war responsibility, 240–242; and late declaration of war, 137; lead-up to attack on, 51, 113, 232–237; Song Qiang on, 51; Watanabe Tsuneo on, 112, 144
Peattie, Mark, *179*, 179–186, 283; on atomic bombs, 260; on emperor abdication issue, 283, 285; on forced labor numbers, 199; on Ishiwara Kanji, 180, 182, 184–185, 218; on Japanese policy in China, 221–222; on "Japan's War in Asia," 217; on Nanjing Massacre, 228; on Pearl Harbor, 241–242
Peleliu, 154

People's Solidarity for Participatory Democracy, 85
perception gaps, 11
Perry, Matthew, 184–185
Philippines: American loss of, 149–150, 242; American retaking of, 137, 243, 244; Bataan Death March, 150, 187–188, 243; comfort women from, 122, 124, 176, 198; Japanese apology, reparations to, 192, 277; long-range bomber deployment to, 242; war crimes trials in, 126. *See also* Tenney, Lester
Phillips, Sidney, 154
Pingxingguan, 32
political versus legalistic approach, 288
politics of memory, 18
pop culture, 303–304
Port Arthur, China, 3–4
post–Cold War era, 302
"postwar compensation," as term, 126
Potsdam Declaration, 138, 250, 258
progressives' versus conservatives' narratives, 96–97; in Japan, 12–14, 16, 105–109, 181, 206–207, 216, 245–247, 307; in Korea, 12–13, 15, 69–74, 82, 98, 301
"prosthetic memories," 18
public opinion, court of, 57, 123, 294, 301
Pyle, Ernie, 167

Rabe, John, 117, 162, 164
racism in U.S.-Japanese conflict, 152–153, 166–167, 253–254
Rape of Nanjing, 163, 227. *See also* Nanjing Massacre (1937)
*Rape of Nanking* (Chang), 26, 118, 159, 162
Reagan, Ronald, 337n14
realpolitik, 302
Record, Jeffrey, 234, 242
regional integration and regionalization, 300, 303
reparations. *See* compensation/reparation demands on Japan
Rhee Syngman, 70, 76, 81–82
Rhee Yong Hoon, *88*, 88–93, 284
*Road to the Battle of Okinawa* exhibit, 107–108
*Road to War* exhibit, 149

Roh Moo-hyun, 297, 301
Roh Tae-woo, 295
Röling, B. V. A., 275, 336n5
Roos, John, 8–9, 249
Roosevelt, Franklin D.: Chicago "quarantine" speech by (1937), 232–233; and Churchill, 239; Day of Infamy speech by, 180; international people's tribunal on, 272; and Japanese American internment, 151–152, 171–174, 181; Pearl Harbor conspiracy theories regarding, 119, 152, 237–240, 242, 254; policies toward Japan under, 135, 234–235
Rose, Caroline, 295
Rozman, Gil, 286
Ruff O'Herne, Jan, 177
Russo-Japanese War (1905), 3, 66, 219
*Ryuichi Shimoda et al. v. State*, 253
Ryu Kwansun, 64–65

Saduski, Kirk, 154, 211, 248, 261, 280, 283
Sakhalin Island forced laborers, 120–124
Sakurai Yoshiko, *114*, 114–120, 208–210, 259–260, 263
San Francisco Peace Treaty (1951), 267–269; Japan's sovereignty under, 277; Judge Walker's citing of, 202; Korean views of, 284; legalistic rather than political approach of, 288–289; not including China, Korea, 284, 293; and reparations issue, 124, 141, 175, 191; textbooks on, 276–277; U.S. views of, 286
*Saving Private Ryan* (film), 153
Selden, Mark, 337n14
self-critical, self-reflective approach, 287–288
Senkaku/Diaoyu Islands, 47, 56, 115, 269, 305
Seodaemun Prison, 64–65, *65*, 78
*Seoul Shinmun*, 296
*The 70 Year History of Japanese Aggression Against China*, 61
Shigehara, Matsumoto, 228–229
Shigemitsu, Mamoru, 140
*Shindler's List* (film), 153
Shi Zhongshan, 279
Shorenstein Asia-Pacific Research Center, 7

*Shoseki Japanese History B* (textbook), 277–278
Showa emperor, 270
Sino-Japanese War: beginning of, 214–218; casualties and refugees of, 23; Chinese museums commemorating, 24, 24–28; Chinese texts on, 61; influence of, on outcome of World War II, 222–226; Japanese blunders in, 184; Japanese goals in, 218–222; Japanese war crimes during, 226–230; under KMT leadership, 23; Korean involvement in, 66; monuments commemorating, 3–4; mutual misperceptions of, 185–186; as "war of aggression," 39. *See also* Nanjing Massacre (1937)
*Slaughterhouse-Five* (Vonnegut), 127
Sledge, Eugene B., 153–154
Smith, Chris, 286–287
Smithsonian National Air and Space Museum, 111, 149, 155–157
Snow, Edgar, 222
social and cultural exchanges, 299
Society for the Dissemination of Historical Fact, 178
Song Qiang, *46*, 46–51, 279, 282
Son Jin Doo, 255
Soon-Won Park, 73, 96
South Korea, 12–13, 123, 298–299
sovereignty of islets, 16
Soviet-Japanese Neutrality Pact, 138, 258
Soviet Union: Chinese split with, 52; entry of, into war against Japan, 30, 63, 113, 138–139; Japanese POWs in, 125; military occupation of northern Korea by, 70; recognition of South Korea by, 123
Spector, Ronald, 225
*Spirit of the Samurai* exhibit, 103
Stalin, Joseph, 63, 138, 233
statutory limitations and war crimes, 86
Stilwell, Joseph, 222
*Stilwell and the American Experience in China* (Tuchman), 222
Stimson, Henry, 257
*Student Soldiers of Okinawa* (film), 246
Summer Rain Poetry Society, 48
Sun Yat-sen, 47, 214

Su Zhiliang, 54, 278–279
Suzuki Kantaro, 137
Szilard, Leo, 252, 257

*Taebaek Mountain Range* (Cho), 75–77
Taiwan, 9, 32, 101
Takagi Kenichi, *120*, 120–126, 207–208, 261, 262, 281
Takahashi Akihiro, 261
Takahata Isao, 109, *126*, 126–133, 209, 259–260, 281, 283
Takemoto Tadao, 163
Takeshima/Dokdo islets, 16, 67, 273, 284, 294, 305
Tamogami Toshio, 118–119, 237–240, 247, 262–263, 272, 280
Tanaka, Yuki, 272
Tanaka Memorial, 166, 218
Tang Shengzhi, 227
Tansill, Charles, 152
Tenney, Lester, *186*, 186–192, 260, 283, 285
textbooks, 7, 12; on atomic bombings, 256–263; and attempt at joint China-Japan history, 38–39; *Chinese History*, 29–30; and desire to maintain younger generations' respect, 16; governments' involvement in, 305–306; *History That Opens the Future* teachers' guide, 96; Japanese, 32, 106; joint German-French, 38; Korean high-school history, 68; Korea's demand for corrections in Japanese texts, 15–16, 36; Pacific War in, 243, 244–245; removal of Japanese "invasion" language from, 28, 60; on Tokyo War Crimes Tribunal, San Francisco Peace Treaty, 274–278
*Thread of the Silkworm* (Chang), 161
Tiananmen Square protests, 43
Togo Fumihiko, 133, 135, 139, 140
Togo Kazuhiko, *133*, 133–142, 209–210, 253, 259, 272, 284
Togo Shigenori, 133–140
Tohmatsu Haruo, 224–225
Tojo Hideki, 61, 102, 113, 133, 135, 137, 139, 246, 275, 283
Tokyo, firebombing of, 45, 109, 127, 243, 245

*Tokyo Shimbun,* 296
*Tokyo Shoseki History B* (textbook), 203, 258
Tokyo War Crimes Tribunal (International Military Tribunal for the Far East), 13, 267–269; and archived materials on comfort women, 117, 206–207; and decision not to prosecute emperor, 40, 111–113, 125, 169–170; and emperor's responsibility, 278–279, 282–283, 284–285; fairness of, 278–281; judgments of, 104; on Nanjing Massacre, 227–228; not focused on crimes against Asians, 170, 279, 281; and public anger toward wartime regime, 106; textbooks on, 274–278; Togo Kazuhiko defending father before, 133–134; and U.S. historical responsibility, 278, 283–2889; *Yomiuri Shimbun* on, 143–144
Tomihisa Tanoue, 262
Tomita Tomohiko, 102
Tong Zeng, *51,* 51–57, 285
*Torture Done by Japan* display, 67–68
Totsuka Etsuro, 85–86
Tripartite Pact, 135
Truman, Harry, 138, 249, 250–251, 256–257, 272
Tsukurukai, 35
Tuchman, Barbara, 222
*Tunnel Warfare* (film), 26, 52

United Nations, 302; Commission on Human Rights, 86, 205, 212; Fourth World Conference on Women, 205; Security Council, 32, 35; UNESCO parallel history writing, 297
United States: Alien Tort Claims Act of 1789 (ATCA), 298; California Senate Bill 1245, 298; concerns about intra-Asian tensions in, 17; and *Enola Gay* exhibit, 111, 149, 155–157; excluded from Japanese reconciliation project, 253; extent of Asia-Pacific involvement by, 307; firebombing of Japanese cities by, 10, 45, 109, 113, 127, 129–131, 151, 243, 245; and framing of post-1945 regional order, 16–17; House Congressional Resolution 121 (2007), 176–178, 196, 212, 287; House Congressional Resolution 195 (2001), 176; and immunity to Kwantung personnel, 226; lingering Civil War issues in, 146; military occupation of southern Korea by, 70; and movies about effects of atomic bombing, 155; National Museum of the Pacific War, *148,* 150–151; nonbinding House resolution on Japan (2006), 286–287; as offering only victor's justice, 278–279; policy differences of, toward Japan versus Germany, 288–289; and prisoners of war in Kyushu, 124; and proclaimed neutrality in allies' disputes, 286–287; protest of Abe's visits to Yasukuni shrine by, 102; and question of presidential visit to bomb sites, 263–265; and *Road to War* exhibit, 149; and simplistic views of Pearl Harbor, 147–148; and Sino-Japanese War, 61; treatment of Japanese war crimes by, 16; use of atomic bomb by, 8–10, 109–110; wartime killing of Korean civilians by, 69
United States Strategic Bombing Survey (1946), 252
Unit 731 operation, 226, 285
Universal Declaration of Human Rights, 268
Uno, Edison, 174
UN Special Rapporteur on Violence Against Women, 205
USS *Arizona* Memorial, 147

Venona files, 239
veterans forming antiwar organizations, 37
victim identity, 16, 253–254, 287
victor's justice, 271, 278–281
Vogel, Ezra, 185
Vonnegut, Kurt, 127

Wakamiya Yoshibumi, 207, 210, 248, 260, 281
Walker, Vaughn, 202
*Wall of Calamity* (at Nanjing memorial), 26

Wang Jingwei, 221
Wang Xiaodong, 47–48, 279, 285
war crimes, 86, 279
war itself as the enemy, 109
*A War It Was Always Going to Lose* (Record), 234
War of Resistance, 44, 217
Warsaw Ghetto, 78
*War Without Mercy* (Dower), 152–153, 165–168
"Was Japan an Aggressor Nation?" (Tamogami), 118–119
Watanabe Tsuneo, 112–113, 142–146, *143*, 241, 281
Webb, William, 270
"We the People" website, 196
White, Harry Dexter, 239
Wigner, Eugene, 252
*The Woman Who Could Not Forget* (Chang), 164
Women's International War Crimes Tribunal on Japan's Military Sexual Slavery in Tokyo, 54, 205, 299
Won Yu Chol, 284
*World Civilizations* (U.S. textbook), 202, 276
World Cup, Korea-Japan joint sponsorship of (2002), 83, 97, 299
*World History* (U.S. textbook), 276

*Yamakawa Japanese History B* (textbook), 203, 235–237, 244–245, 258, 277–278

Yamamoto Isoroku, 240, 241
Yang Mi Kang, 93–99, *94*, 205–206, 284, 303
Yang Tianshi, 217, 228, 282
Yasuda Shoji, 145
Yasukuni Shrine, 10–11, 100–105; Abe's visits to, 5, 294, 296, 305; Class A war criminals enshrined in, 101–102; Junichiro's visits to, 32, 143, 263; Koizumi's visits to, 32, 35, 56, 297, 305; Li Datong's visit to, 45–46; seen as denial of war responsibility, 101, 103–104; Takeo's visit to, 274; Watanabe on, 146. *See also* Yushukan War Museum
Yeosu-Suncheon Rebellion, 76–77
Yi Won Bok, 14–15, 282–283
Yi Wu, 256
Yoksa Research Institute, 85
*Yomiuri Shimbun*, 112–113, 142–143, 145–146, 241, 281
Yoshida, Seiji, 212
Yoshida Shigeru, 165, 167
Yoshimi, Yoshiaki, 198, 206
Yoshito Sengoku, 115
Yunida (gardener for Peattie family), 181
Yushukan War Museum, 10, *101*, 102–105, 254. *See also* Yasukuni Shrine

Zero Fighter exhibit, *101*, 102, 103
Zhang Zhenkun, 57–63, *58*, 219–220, 223
Zhifen Ju, 199
Zhu Cheng Shan, 25, 27–28

ALSO PUBLISHED IN THE
SHORENSTEIN ASIA-PACIFIC RESEARCH CENTER SERIES

*Contested Embrace: Transborder Membership Politics in Twentieth-Century Korea*
Jaeeun Kim (2016)

*The Colonial Origins of Ethnic Violence in India*
Ajay Verghese (2016)

*The New Great Game: China and South and Central Asia in the Era of Reform*
Edited by Thomas Fingar (2016)

*Rebranding Islam: Piety, Prosperity, and a Self-Help Guru*
James Bourk Hoesterey (2015)

*Global Talent: Skilled Labor as Social Capital in Korea*
Gi-Wook Shin and Joon Nak Choi (2015)

*Failed Democratization in Prewar Japan: Breakdown of a Hybrid Regime*
Harukata Takenaka (2014)

*New Challenges for Maturing Democracies in Korea and Taiwan*
Edited by Larry Diamond and Gi-Wook Shin (2014)

*Spending Without Taxation: FILP and the Politics of Public Finance in Japan*
Gene Park (2011)

*The Institutional Imperative: The Politics of Equitable Development in Southeast Asia*
Erik Martinez Kuhonta (2011)

*One Alliance, Two Lenses: U.S.-Korea Relations in a New Era*
Gi-Wook Shin (2010)

*Collective Resistance in China: Why Popular Protests Succeed or Fail*
Yongshun Cai (2010)

*The Chinese Cultural Revolution as History*
Edited by Joseph W. Esherick, Paul G. Pickowicz, and Andrew G. Walder (2006)

*Ethnic Nationalism in Korea: Genealogy, Politics, and Legacy*
Gi-Wook Shin (2006)

*Prospects for Peace in South Asia*
Edited by Rafiq Dossani and Henry S. Rowen (2005)

The authorized representative in the EU for product safety and compliance is:
Mare Nostrum Group
B.V Doelen 72
4831 GR Breda
The Netherlands

www.ingramcontent.com/pod-product-compliance
Lightning Source LLC
Chambersburg PA
CBHW031752220426
43662CB00007B/375